Origins of the State and Civilization

BY THE SAME AUTHOR

Spanish-Guarani Relations in Early Colonial Paraguay

Tobati: Paraguayan Town
(By Elman R. Service and Helen S. Service)

Evolution and Culture
(Edited by Marshall D. Sahlins and Elman R. Service, with contributions by the editors and by Thomas G. Harding and David Kaplan)

The Hunters

Cultural Evolutionism: Theory in Practice

Primitive Social Organization, Second Edition

Profiles in Ethnology, Revised Edition

Origins of the State and Civilization

The Process of Cultural Evolution

Elman R. Service

UNIVERSITY OF CALIFORNIA, SANTA BARBARA

W · W · NORTON & COMPANY · INC · NEW YORK

Published simultaneously in Canada by George J. McLeod Limited, Toronto.
Printed in the United States of America.

FIRST EDITION

THIS BOOK WAS TYPESET *in Linotype Fairfield Medium and composed by New England Typographic Service. It was printed by the Murray Printing Company.*

Library of Congress Cataloging in Publication Data

Service, Elman Rogers, 1915–

Origins of the state and civilization.

Bibliography: p.

Includes index.

1. Government, Primitive. 2. Social evolution. 3. Civilization—History.
I. Title.

GN490.S44 1975 321.1'2 75–1494

ISBN 0–393–05547–7 cloth edition
ISBN 0–393–09224–0 paper edition

1 2 3 4 5 6 7 8 9 0

To Morton H. Fried

and the Fellows of the M.U.S.

Contents

Prologue

It is something of a contradiction that in writing a book the opening bit of text (the "front matter") is usually the last to be written. But this fact gives me the opportunity to make a final statement for the sake of emphasis. And here I can also acknowledge prominently the help of those who in various ways ministered to the manuscript and to me along the way.

In its successive drafts, this book changed in important ways—as though it somehow evolved. The method of research was designed to foster such a possibility, but nevertheless one of the major emphases developed so unexpectedly that it was as though the manuscript took control. When I began work, I accepted the usual formula that equates the rise of civilization with the origin of the *state,* which in turn is defined by the presence of repressive controls based on physical force. I continue to believe that this definition of "state" can be usefully applied to some modern primitive societies. But I have found that these characteristics, while they may be found sporadically in some archaic civilizations, do not typify most of them. The repressive-force concept of the state, I have come to see, is not useful in defining archaic civilization; it does not describe the origin of civilization, nor is it an identifying criterion of civilization.

Furthermore, my researches do not confirm the widely accepted epitomization of civilization as urbanism. Cities were not, I find, either essential to the development of the archaic civilizations or even closely correlated with that development.

Another long-standing notion about the statelike repressive institutions is that their origin has something to do with preserving or regulating private wealth. From Plato and Aristotle, the Stoics and the Epicureans, through social contract theorists as varied as Rousseau and Hobbes, to the prevalent modern theory, the Marxist, the prominent political thinkers buttressed their theories about the nature of human beings and of governing institutions on some notions about primitive society and the primal origin of government, and nearly always the arguments had to do with the relation of property to politics and which one was, or should be, dominant. For example, Lenin's famous *State and Revolution* was written to remind liberal socialists, those thinking of reforms of the extant government, of the "true historical role and meaning of the state." The state arose in the beginning, Lenin argued (as had Morgan, Marx, and Engels), as an organ of forceful repression of the majority of the people in order to protect the interests of the minority propertied class, and it should be opposed in all its forms by socialists, for its original purpose reveals its true nature.

The present research provides no evidence for the class-conflict theory of the origin of either the state or civilization, nor does it support any other of the many versions of conflict and conquest theory. But so prevalent have these been in our intellectual history that a complete chapter of "negative conclusions" seems necessary in order to adequately rebut them. The final chapter, however, states my findings in positive terms: The origins of government lay essentially in the institutionalization of centralized leadership, which in developing its further administrative functions grew into a hereditary aristocracy as well. Both the historically known "primitive states" and the six primary archaic civilizations were developments, however dissimilar in result, out of *chiefdom* ("hierarchical") societies that had themselves grown out of *segmental* ("egalitarian") societies. (Since it was the evolution of leadership which created in its wake the hereditary hierarchy, the label "chiefdom" seems more evocative of the actualities of the process than "hierarchical." Symmetrically, "segmental" [= no "central nervous system"] therefore is preferable to "egalitarian," although both accurately characterize aspects of that earlier stage of sociopolitical evolution.)

Of the three characteristic uses of political power—providing leadership, reinforcements, and mediation in the maintenance of a society—leadership clearly seems to have had a causal priority, with economic and sacred reinforcements developing in turn as the nascent bureaucracy increased its services and autonomy (and of course its size). Its mediative legal functions in private law seem to have come about only as a consequence of its successful development of the other two kinds of activities. ("Public law," law involving the relations between the individual and the government, was probably prior as a form of law.) Thus primal government worked to protect, not another class or stratum of the society, but *itself*—legitimizing itself in its role of maintaining the whole society. The two basic strata were the *governors* and the *governed;* and the governors created themselves, so to speak, rather than having been the creation of others, such as a "propertied," or economically favored, class.

In studying both the modern primitive states and the archaic civilizations, we are considering essentially the evolution of a bureaucracy of theocratic authority, a bureaucracy that was also the creator and administrator of the important parts of the economic system. Even in the earliest, simplest systems this political power organized the economy, rather than vice versa; and it was a redistributive, an allocative, system, not an acquisitive system that required personal wealth in order to acquire personal power.

Such seem to have been the widespread bases for the origins of modern primitive states, as well as of the primary civilizations, the splendid flowerings of those potentialities. But these original civilizations were at best only six in number in all of human history, which must mean that very rare concatenations of specific events and special environmental characteristics had conspired to enable their achievement. It is the exploration of these events and environments that constituted the great bulk of the research reported in the pages that follow.

Part I, "The Origins of Government," begins with a chapter outlining the means by which societies maintain themselves, and discussing how these means differ in primitive and civilized societies. Chapter 1 also lays the basis for an examination of the meaning of "state" and "civilization." Here too is introduced the concept of the chiefdom as an intermediate stage between primitive societies and civilizations. Finally, the difficulties and advantages of comparing archaic civilizations with modern primitive states are discussed.

A number of classical theories of the origin of the state, or law, or civil society, are discussed in chapter 2. It is not a main purpose of this book to judge Aristotle and Plato, Hobbes and Rousseau, Vico and Engels, for example, but since they are interesting for their own sake, the concluding chapters will seek to evaluate briefly their formulations in terms of the findings of this investigation.

Chapters 3 and 4, to repeat, are important for background. Long before this investigation began, I came to feel that probably—perhaps necessarily—a stage composed of chiefdoms lay between egalitarian segmental primitive society and the actual formation of primitive states. I suspected the likelihood of this for some time because I kept running into it in actual ethnological and historical descriptive writings. Chapter 4, therefore, contains important theoretical assumptions that have influenced the outcome of this book. Appendices at the end of the book direct the reader to further sources for material on chiefdoms and on segmental societies.

The chapters on the origins of particular states and civilizations can stand alone, each with its own set of meanings; each has its own tentative conclusion and implications for further research. In addition to the descriptive and historical materials, in a few of the chapters we will encounter another author's theories about the general origin of *the* state based on the data from the particular one he is reporting on. One should not attribute an unwarranted degree of empiricism to these discussions, but it will be interesting as well as appropriate to view the theories on the ground of their authors' own choice.

The chapter on the Zulu is the first of the chapters in part II, "The Modern Primitive States," because this is such a famous case of state formation and because the events were described by European eyewitnesses. The transition from chiefdoms through periods of most violent terrorism to an instituted state government is a particularly striking example of the political problems that attend attempts to make a conquest state.

The next two chapters deal with other African conquest states. Our data on the actual origins of these states are not so complete as in the case of the Zulu, but theories about the origin and nature of the state are presented as discussed by specialists in these areas. For the same reasons, the chapter on the Cherokee is presented as a vehicle for Fred Gearing's theory of state formation as well as for its historical interest.

The three salient instances of historically known state formations in Polynesia are Hawaii, Tahiti, and Tonga. They are treated together in a single chapter because our conclusions are similar for each case, although the three cases involve different degrees of external influence from European sources. It is particularly important for any study of primitive political processes to have some grasp of the significance of *tabu* and *mana* in the theocratic chiefdoms of Polynesia.

The chapters in part III, "The Archaic Civilizations," are considerably more difficult to present, particularly because of the difficulty of specifying exact stages of the societies' development in terms of archaeological data. It is hoped that some of the ideas elicited from the previous historical and ethnological chapters will be useful in pondering these problems of origins, stages, types, and above all, of cause-and-effect in the evolution of civilization.

Of all the primary civilizations, Mesoamerica has been best researched by modern archaeologists whose interpretative aims—and hence investigative methods—accord well with the aims of this book. For that reason it leads off the next section of the book. Mesopotamia would logically be next for similar reasons, but because we have to consider the possibility of cultural connections between Mesoamerica and Peru, it seemed better to treat these latter two in adjacent chapters.

The discussion of Mesopotamia is followed by a chapter on Egypt, again because of the need to discuss the possibility of cultural transmission. The Indus River Valley civilization lies between the above two and China, chronologically as well as geographically, so it is placed before the discussion of China. China, the subject of the last chapter in part III, is not only an apparently independent development of a primary civilization, but provides the setting for the creation of one of the most interesting sets of ideas about the origin of civilization, the pathfinding ecological theory of Owen Lattimore.

The problem of the origins of civilization and primitive states has been a preoccupation of mine since I simultaneously discovered anthropology and Marxism in the late 1930s. I quickly became converted to both and carefully read Morgan's *Ancient Society,* Engels's *The Origin of the Family, Private Property, and the State,* Lenin's *State and Revolution,* and finally the nineteenth-century anthropological-sociological evolutionists, supplemented later, of course, by the modern evolutionary works of L. A. White and V. G. Childe as soon as they appeared. I eventually became dissatisfied with Marxism and, I hope, with all forms of "systematic" thought. But, although I learned enough to see what was wrong with the ideas of Morgan, Marx, Engels, et al., I never gave up my strong approval of the significant questions they asked. The present work, therefore, is in no sense intended to be an *anti*-Marxist tract, however *non*-Marxist the intention.

Inasmuch as these interests have been fermenting for such a long time, it will be impossible to sort out the various personal aids and influences except for a few salient early instances and the recent readers of this manuscript.

At the University of Michigan, Professor L. A. White taught some anthropology courses that brought Morgan, Marx, and cultural evolutionism into an interesting kind of juxtaposition, and it was one of these courses that combined so well with my leftward political leaning of the time as to determine many of my subsequent interests. I do not know that he will be pleased to see such prominent mention of his place in my early history, since the present book (as well as previous ones) has departed so far from the Morganism that he taught. But so be it, and I *am* grateful.

After World War II, as a graduate student at Columbia University, I took some courses with the late Professor J. H. Steward. Among his interests at that time was a form of the comparative method (he called it "multilinear evolution") that he employed in analyzing the development of the archaic civilizations. Here again my interest was sharpened in this major evolutionary problem. The reader should be warned, however, that although I owe Steward many thanks, I cannot agree now with his causal theory.[1]

A student friend of those days, Morton H. Fried, shared these interests with me then and later when we were colleagues during my four years of teaching at Columbia. His *Evolution of Political Society* (1967) uses a conception of stages of sociocultural integration rather similar to the present work, with emphasis on the origins of inequality. The present effort diverges from Fried's book in concentrating more on the actual origins of the state, whereas he has only one chapter on this subject. My findings are distinct from his in other respects as well, but the history of our shared interests and friendship since 1946 has been an important intellectual prop for me.

Some modern archaeologists have done excellent work in particular geographical areas, and have made theoretical contributions, as well. They will be discussed in the relevant chapters. It is rather daunting, in an age of increased specialization, to try to put them all together: One is not only vulnerable to their detailed criticism, but to the suspicion of arrogance. But when I sent various chapters to be criticized by specialists, I was tremendously pleased by their helpful, sometimes even enthusiastic, responses.

Several people have read the entire rough draft and made helpful comments. I am pleased to thank Professors Donald Brown, Charles Erasmus, Thomas Harding, Elvin Hatch, M. Kay Martin, and Barbara Voorhies, all of the University of California at Santa Barbara. It is a lot to ask of anyone, but to read such a rough draft and still follow the main route and be so encouraging takes much time and attention and lies well beyond the call of

1. The paper of Steward's most influential on my own thinking about evolution—and I would guess on Fried's and several others' as well—was "Levels of Sociocultural Integration: An Operational Concept."

a colleague's duty. They have passed my most dire test of friendship.

Some of the theoretical chapters were read by colleagues Mattison Mines, Manuel Carlos, and Albert Spaulding, for which I am grateful. Professors Robert Manners of Brandeis University and Robert F. Stevenson (SUNY) read the manuscript as publishers' readers, and then as an act of friendship and interest provided me with very helpful detailed comments and impressions. Drs. Robert Carneiro and Gertrude Dole helpfully read part I.

I am very pleased to thank the specialists who reviewed the chapters on particular ethnological and archaeological areas:

Chapters 5, 6, and 7, all dealing with Africa, were read by Professors David Brokensha and Brian Fagan of the University of California at Santa Barbara.

Chapter 9, on Polynesia, was read by Professor Thomas Harding of the University of California at Santa Barbara.

Chapter 10, on Mesoamerica, was a crucial chapter because it has been the important arena (along with Mesopotamia) for the major contending theories of the origin of civilization. I owe a great debt to Professor William T. Sanders of the Pennsylvania State University for his critique of chapter 10. Professor Jeffrey Parsons of the University of Michigan helpfully reviewed the chapter and also gave me unpublished versions of his recent researches, as did Professor Richard Blanton of Hunter College.

Professor Richard Schaedel of the University of Texas was helpful with comments and by supplying unpublished materials on Peru.

Professor Robert McC. Adams carefully reviewed chapter 12, on Mesopotamia. He also gave me numerous unpublished papers that were very helpful.

Chapters 14 and 15 were helpfully reviewed by Professors Mattison Mines and Donald Brown of the University of California at Santa Barbara. Both men are Orientalists.

A book of this kind is necessarily controversial, and the people whose aid I have acknowledged above have not necessarily endorsed the whole book. One of the greatest pleasures of this long-drawn-out production was the responsiveness of readers of the manuscript.

It is also a pleasure to acknowledge the patience, skill, and encouragement of Joseph B. Janson, II, and Katherine L. Hyde of W. W. Norton & Company.

E.R.S.

Santa Barbara, California
September, 1974

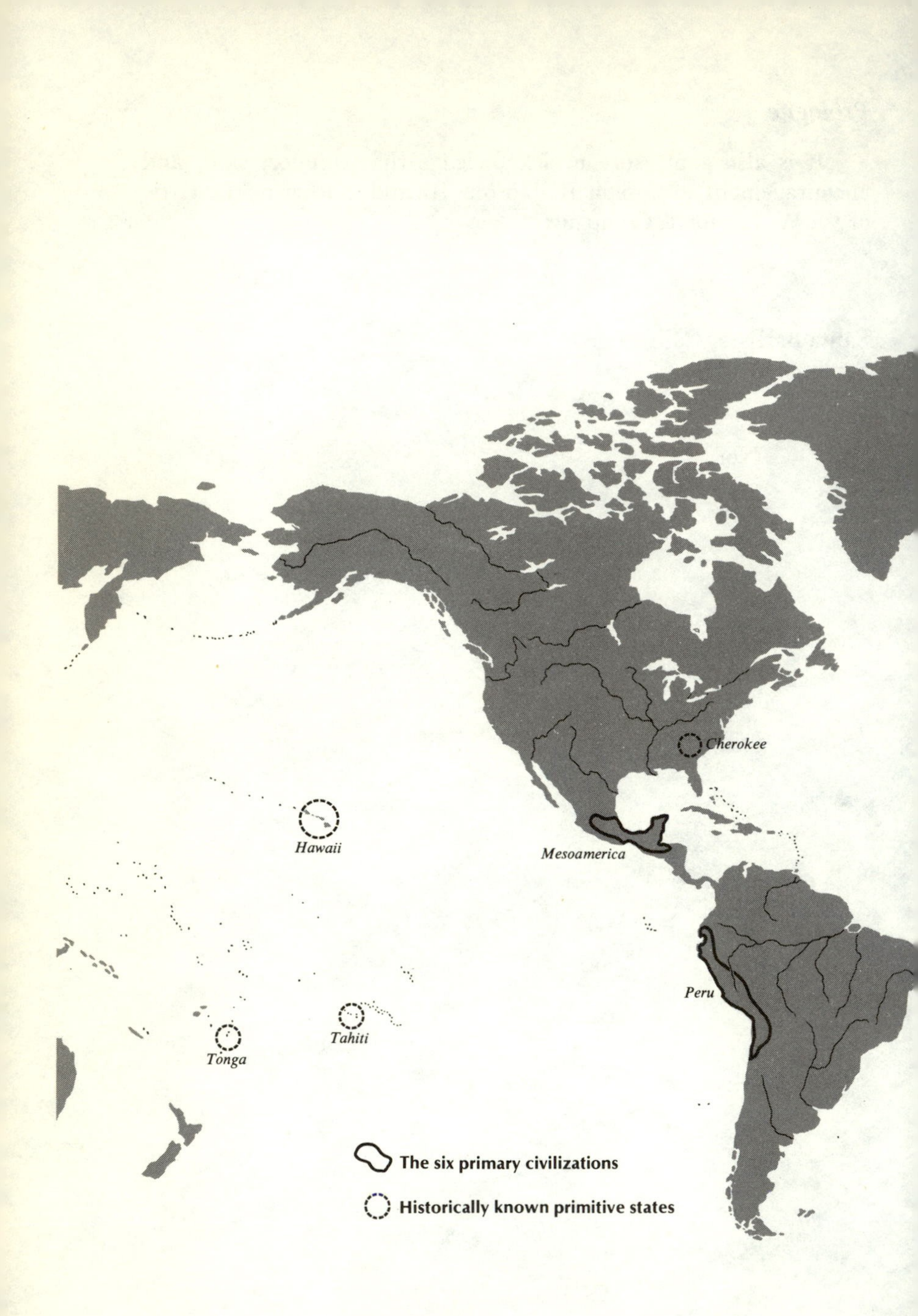
Cherokee
Hawaii
Mesoamerica
Peru
Tahiti
Tonga
The six primary civilizations
Historically known primitive states

Mesopotamia
Egypt
Indus River Valley
Shang-Chou
Nupe
shanti
Ankole
Kongo
Zulu

1

The Origins of Government

1

Introduction

THE HUMAN ACHIEVEMENT was the creation of culture, the means by which societies tame and govern their members and create and maintain their complex social organization. Culture also has technological, economic, religious, artistic, and recreational functions, among others. All of these depend on the ability of the political aspect of the culture to integrate and protect the society. The gravest problems, aside from sheer subsistence, are political, and all societies must be able to solve them in order to perpetuate themselves. But some societies have done more: they have found political-cultural solutions that not only have preserved the community but also have enabled it to grow to ever-greater size and complexity, usually at the expense of competitors of its own as well as of other species.

The Great Divide

The watershed in the evolution of human culture occurred when primitive society became civilized society. As we know from modern anthropological studies, primitive societies were segmented into kin groups that were egalitarian in their relations to each other. Eventually some of them became hierarchical, controlled and directed by a central authoritative power—a power instituted as a government. Clearly, these societies were tremendously changed by the advent of this new stage in cultural evolution. Interpretations of this achievement have been the keynotes of some of the most significant historical, philosophical, and scientific writings in Western civilization from the time of classical Greek thinkers like Plato and Aristotle to today.

The evolution of civilized society has been contemplated by the important thinkers of all civilizations, but particularly in recent centuries by Western Europeans. Evolutionary ideas pervaded the philosophy of the Enlightenment and, later, nineteenth-century sociology and anthropology, and it is from these schools of thought that we have inherited much of our interest in the origin of government. But the philosophers were too remote from the real world of primitive peoples. Even the nineteenth-century authors knew little of primitive peoples at first hand, and the sources of data were still poor. New data available to us today demand a reassessment of their theories and some of their concepts—but not at the cost of losing their valuable evolutionary perspective.

Frequently these theorists unfairly and misleadingly called the primitive peoples savages and barbarians—implying wildness and animality. On the other hand, the words "urban" and "civil," applied to the nonprimitive side of the divide, came also to suggest "urbane" and "civilized" in the sense of high personal refinement, again to the disparagement of the primitives. Let us define a few necessary terms less pejoratively and apply them consistently.

Urban and *civil* can be accurately used to mean that the society was characterized by the presence of cities or large towns and that the inhabitants were citizens of some kind of legal commonwealth. It is these meanings of urban and civil that were prior and that evoked the other meanings only metaphorically—at least at first. Conversely, the earlier, simpler stage of society was characterized by the absence of urban agglomerations and formal legal structures and their associated institutionalized governments. This is what we shall take *primitive* to mean: simple, early, original, primary; lacking developed governmental institutions. However informal may seem this way of defining the subject of this book, it has the virtue of holding to the central core of meaning in most modern statements of the problem of the differences between primitive and civilized society. These will be discussed in the next chapter.

Modern anthropologists know something that neither Plato nor Aristotle, Hobbes nor Rousseau understood. All of these and countless other commentators on human nature and the civilizational problem (but not Marx and Engels) equated government or civilization with society itself, and precivilization was not understood as anything but anarchy, with people constrained only by nature rather than by cultural institutions. But we know now that over 99 percent of past human history (and, for a part of the world's population, even history today) was spent in societies that did not govern themselves by legalistic, institutionalized systems of control. But primitive society was nevertheless not anarchical, for social behavior was strikingly constrained. How this was done will be discussed in chapters 3 and 4.

The archaic civilizations ancestral to modern civil societies evolved in different times and places: about 3500–3000 B.C. in Mesopotamia and Egypt, and about 2500 B.C. in the Indus River Valley, 1500 B.C. at the Great Bend of the Yellow River in China, and B.C./A.D. in the Valley of Mexico and in coastal Peru (see table 1). It is of course possible that some of these were related episodes, especially those in Mesopotamia and Egypt, and in the New World, in Mexico and Peru.[1] But some of these civilizations must have developed independently; most obviously, those of the New World were unrelated to those of the Old World. This is a most significant fact, for it affects our perspective. Were it one single development that spread to the other areas by conquest, diffusion, emulation, or whatever, then the problem would be "historical"—that is, our concern would be simply, what happened? When? But since it happened several times independently we immediately wonder, even if it only happened twice (in the New World and in the Old World), what *causes* or repetitive

1. V. Gordon Childe's very influential books, *Man Makes Himself* (1936) and *What Happened in History* (1942), concentrated on Mesopotamia, Egypt, and the Indus River civilizations. His last, most definitive, formulation of the "urban revolution" (1950) added to these a brief discussion of the Maya. Since then, however, most anthropologists have cited the above six. Glyn Daniel (1968) makes seven by subdividing Mesoamerica. Table 1 above omits the Indus River Valley.

TABLE 1 / *Absolute Chronology of Major Areas**

	Mesopotamia	Egypt	N. China	N. Peru	Meso-America
2000					
					Cyclical Conquests
1000					
			Cyclical Conquests	Cyclical Conquests	
A.D. B.C.				Regional Florescent	Regional Florescent
	Cyclical Conquests	Cyclical Conquests	Dark Ages		
1000			Initial Empire	Formative	Formative
		Dark Ages	Regional Florescent	Incipient Agriculture	Incipient Agriculture?
2000	Dark Ages				
			Formative		
	Initial Empire	Initial Empire	Incipient Agriculture		Hunting and Gathering
3000					
		Regional Florescent		Hunting and Gathering	
	Regional Florescent				
4000		Formative	Hunting and Gathering		
		Incipient Agriculture			
	Formative				
5000					
	Incipient Agriculture	Hunting and Gathering			
6000					
	Hunting and Gathering				
7000					
8000					
9000					

* These dates have been revised on the basis of Braidwood's estimates for the Near East (*The Near East and the Foundations for Civilization,* Eugene, Oregon, 1952) and of radiocarbon dates for the Near East and America. These new dates place the origin of agriculture about 2,000 years more recent than was formerly believed in the Near East and about 2,000 years earlier in the Andes. Period dates for India and China are revised to fit the Near East dates, but still presumably show a time lag. (New World dates are taken from *Radiocarbon Dating* (Assembled by Frederick Johnson), Memoir of the Society for American Archaeology, *American Antiquity.*

processes were at work. We want to know, by careful comparison, what were the shared factors: the antecedent conditions; the geographical, technological, economic, social, and ideological settings; the role of warfare and the nature of the surrounding political environment. If civilization had originated only once, it would not even pay to speculate as to whether or not it was an historical accident, with this causal network unanalyzable. But not only did some of the archaic civilizations probably develop independently; they also developed surprisingly similar kinds of new cultural features, some of which have been seen as indicative of civilization as an evolutionary stage.

Lewis H. Morgan and others in the last century felt that writing was the hallmark achievement of the archaic civilizations. (Peru seems like an exception, but the Peruvians did have the *quipu,* a mnemonic device of strings with knots for decimal places and colors for categories of things. If a main function of all early writing systems was record-keeping, then the Peruvians were only barely off the track.) In recent times, archaeological interest in socioeconomic factors has been greater, resulting in widespread acceptance of V. Gordon Childe's conception of the origin of the first civilizations as an "urban revolution." This rubric stands for the following set of functionally linked features (here only briefly summarized, following Childe 1950): urban centers (Childe provisionally suggested they were between 7,000 and 20,000 in population); a class of full-time specialists (craftsmen, merchants, officials, priests) residing in the cities; a "social surplus" in the food production of the peasants, which could be extracted by the government; monumental public buildings, symbolizing the concentration of the surplus; a "ruling class" of upper-level priests, civil and military leaders, and officials; numerical notation and writing; the beginnings of arithmetic, geometry, and astronomy; sophisticated art styles; long-distance trade; and, finally, an institutionalized form of political organization based on force—termed the state. The foundation of the state, as Childe expressed it, was the "glaring conflict in economic interests between the tiny ruling class, who annexed the bulk of the social surplus, and the vast majority who were left with a bare subsistance and effectively excluded from the spiritual benefits of civilization" (p. 4).

We should note at this point that the researches to be reported in this book do not support the core of this concept of an "urban revolution." We shall see that although a number of urban centers were found among some of the archaic civilizations, they seem to have been not only inessential to the development of the archaic civilizations, but also clearly dependent, most usually, on the prior development of the civilizations. In fact, Childe's ten criteria are only very generally and imperfectly coincident. There has been, consequently, a tendency to pick out one, or a very few, of the elements in Childe's scheme as the basic diagnostic feature(s) of the origin of civilization—or in some salient instances, as the causative prime mover. The most provocative feature thus selected has been the last on Childe's list, the Marxian notion of the *state,* based on repressive force, working to protect the economic interests of the ruling class.

The notion of the state as based on repressive physical force can be usefully applied, as we will see, to some *modern* primitive states. But our findings do not support the economic-class element in the definition of "state" set forth by Childe et al. And furthermore, our researches do not bear out the notion that the rise of civilization was founded on the origin of the state.

The alternative thesis to be presented here locates the origins of government in the institutionalization of centralized leadership. That leadership, in developing its administrative functions for the maintenance of the society, grew into a hereditary aristocracy. The nascent bureaucracy's economic and religious functions developed as the extent of its services, its autonomy, and its size increased. Thus the earliest government worked to protect, not another class or stratum of the society, but itself. It legitimized itself in its role of maintaining the whole society.

Political power organized the economy, not vice versa. The system was redistributive, allocative, not acquisitive: Personal wealth was not required to gain personal political power. And these first governments seem clearly to have reinforced their structure by doing their economic and religious jobs well—by providing benefits—rather than by using physical force.

In the course of this book, we will see how these hierarchical, institutionalized political structures developed out of the matrix of egalitarian primitive society.

Modern governmental creations such as legislatures, formal law codes and courts, police and militias, and so on, are all alike in that they are formal *institutions,* purposely established and specialized for carrying out major political functions, especially the maintenance of social order. But we should be reminded at this point that many behavioral restraints occur at an informal level also, within face-to-face communities like the household, especially, and in schools, neighborhoods, clubs, and so on. The most powerful socializing forces at this level are personal-social punishments and rewards that have strong psychological consequences—of which the more obvious are sanctions such as praise and blame. These are not usually visibly institutionalized and thus are not confused with our modern conceptions of *the* law and *the* state.

But if over 99 percent of human history has passed before the origin of institutionalized political systems, how did societies govern themselves? Obviously they must have done so in essentially the same way that our domestic families and modern primitive societies do, entirely by means of personal-social sanctions and by familistic allocations of authoritative status (as to elders) to praise, blame, and settle disputes.

Most anthropologists are inclined to use very broad (or loose) definitions of law and state in order to talk about primitive society in the same terms as modern nations. But those of us interested as much in contrast as in similarity—as in the present endeavor—have to use narrower definitions. An argument by Walter Goldschmidt seems helpful with respect to this kind of problem concerning the comparative method. He says (1966, p. 31), "What is consistent from culture to culture is not the institution; what is consistent are the social problems. What is recurrent from society to society is solutions to these problems." Looking at it this way, we can choose easily between comparison and contrast. An organized conscript *army* at war is an institution not found among primitives, although all societies get involved in fighting from time to time. Similarly, if a formal adjudicative *court* with a professional *judge* appears in the history of a society, we want to note it and consider its significance as a new institution even though in all cultural stages disputes have been settled by some means. Thus we may sometimes want to contrast civic problems with domestic problems, and civil or governmental juridical institutional officials with familistic statuses. This attempted solution to the problem of comparing institutions is necessary above all because we want to know what was *new* at the point of the appearance of the state and civilization, and most of the new is obviously institutional. We do want to know, as anthropologists conventionally do, what are the continuities and recurrent problems and processes that link one kind of society to another; but in the present instance we are also determined to sort out the discontinuities, which are usually the institutional forms.

Gabriel Almond squarely faced the problem of comparative politics in his interesting introduction to *The Politics of Developing Areas* (Almond and Coleman 1960). He felt that it was of "operational importance" not to dichotomize societies into state and nonstate types. He says (p. 12), ". . . We are arguing that the classic distinction between primitive societies which are states and those which are not should be reformulated as a distinction between those in which the political structure is quite differentiated and clearly visible and those in which it is less visible and intermittent. We are dealing with a continuum and not a dichotomous distinction."

In our phrasing of Goldschmidt's idea, it would seem that Almond's problem is resolved: the "continuum" is one of similar political *problems* and of political *contexts of behavior,* but there really is a "dichotomous distinction" in the *institutionality* of forms in states and nonstates. However, as we noted, the term "state" in the view of many modern anthropologists normally is understood to mean that the basis of political organization is repressive physical force. Let us retain this meaning, and when we wish to speak of an instituted polity, without committing ourselves regarding the factor of repressive force, let us use the somewhat more vague word *government:* a bureaucracy instituted to rule a populace by right of authority.

Maintenance of Society

At this point we should carefully define a few labels for some functional contexts to which political problems and related patterns of behavior can be referred for analysis. Certainly the universal problem is simply *maintenance*—maintenance of social order within the community and of the community itself in defense against outsiders. Internal and external aspects of maintenance are always so distinct (though frequently related) that we will usually treat them separately.

The most ubiquitous form of internal maintenance of order in daily social life, a form universal among societies, must be simply *etiquette.* Next comes the teaching of *morality* and its internalization as conscience. Finally, *social sanctions* are informal, personal-social ways of punishing and rewarding, usually simply by the subtraction or addition of prestige, or by social repulsion and attraction, as related to the obeying or ignoring of certain social rules. These three categories are all in the realm of custom, or more explicitly, of normative ideology. It is in the last category, the maintenance of society by *power* and *authority,* that we begin to consider rather different contexts of behavior.

Hannah Arendt (1961, pp. 92–93) has made the distinction neatly:

> Since authority always demands obedience, it is commonly mistaken for some form of power or violence. Yet authority precludes the use of external means of coercion; where force is used, authority itself has failed. Authority, on the other hand, is incompatible with persuasion, which presupposes equality and works through a process of argumentation. . . . The authoritarian relation between the one who commands and the one who obeys rests neither on common reason nor on the power of the one who commands; what they have in common is the hierarchy itself, whose rightness and legitimacy both recognize and where both have their predetermined stable place.

"Power" is a commonly used word and therefore has many meanings. Let us use it in its broadest sense, as simply the relative ability of a person or group to cause another person or group to obey, or conversely, the ability to "not have to give in." Such a conception obviously includes radically different kinds of things. A person may do another's bidding because the latter is *in* authority—as a priest obeys the bishop—or because he is *an* authority, respected for his knowledge. The power of authority ideally rests solely on an hierarchical relationship between the persons or groups, so that the obedience is not compelled by some kind of forceful bullying dominance but rather by custom, habit, ideas of propriety, benefits, or other considerations that effectively reinforce and legitimize the power and make it acceptable. The physical power to coerce we may label simply *force.* Although many political organizations exercise power both by virtue of hierarchical "rightness" and by force or threat of it, it is useful to distinguish them because in many societies there exists only one or the other form of power, ruling alone—especially in primitive society, where we often find the traditional hierarchy ruling adequately without using any force whatever.[2] The recourse to force signifies the failure of authority at the time of its use, as Arendt states. Even at this early point in our investigation it is certain that the analyses of societies to be made in subsequent chapters must feature careful use of the distinction between authority and force (Arendt's "power").

The Uses of Political Power

Political power, whether based on authority or force, or both together, seems to have three usual behavioral contexts in which it is employed. These are sometimes called the engineering of consent, decision-making, and judging. At this moment, because of the cross-cultural, comparative purposes of this book, we must be alert to choose concepts that label the usual processes and related problems, not the culture-bound institutions that operate so variably in relation to the problems.

Engineering consent, the creation of legitimacy, persuasion, reinforcement, benefits, negative sanctions, *lèse majesté* laws, and so on, all refer to means by which a political structure strives to safeguard its rule and increase its power. Frequently, of course, especially in modern times, it is a consciously wrought means by which one group maintains its ascendency over others in the society—serving itself. Sometimes, of course, its best service to itself is to serve the society—"doing well by doing good." Often the consequence of useful actions by the political structure is a sense of benefit felt by the citizenry. Sometimes the opposite is

2. Easton (in Siegel 1959, p. 217) tellingly criticizes Fortes and Evans-Pritchard's *African Political Systems* (1940) for having defined political organization in terms of the "control and regulation of physical force." He thinks *authority* is central in political organizations, some of which might not use force at all. Certainly Easton is correct, especially with respect to many African societies.

the case and the people are kept in line by fierce laws against loosely defined treason or *lèse majesté.* And, as we hear from modern behavioral psychology, positive rewarding sanctions as well as repressive ones will cause the citizens' behavior to take desirable routes even when they are not consciously aware of the reasons for their choices. Any of these conceptions may be usefully noted when we are sure we are actually encountering them in our investigation, but most are not general enough to serve the present overall purpose. Let us retain the word *reinforcement* as a general term for the effort that, under whatever institutional guise, the political or authority structure expends to integrate and preserve the society—and of course itself at the same time. In this broad sense, reinforcement carries no restriction in meaning as to whether the citizenry is aware or unaware of the forms of behavioral guidance, or whether the government consciously plans its constraining actions (as in "engineering" consent) or is strengthened by unsought accidental means (such as a favorable climatic cycle). To reinforce a structure is to strengthen it by various means—but the means are at this point unspecified.

The second context for the use of political power often has been called decision-making, and sometimes administration. The first of these is too general—everybody makes decisions, nearly all the time—and the second is too formal-sounding, too suggestive of institutions rather than problems, functions, or processes. *Leadership* is really what we need to talk about in the context of the evolution of political power. A concerted action may be agreed on by consensus, unanimity, argumentation, or whatever, or compelled by authority or force; and it may be organized in various ways and be successfully accomplished—that is, administrated. But it is when concerted action is a response to some form of leadership and is guided and accomplished *by that leadership* (not merely by "administration") that we have a kind of action, or process, which goes through the various permutations and finally institutional forms that are of major interest in any concern with the origin of political power.

The third context of the uses of power has been called judging, adjudication, arbitration, mediation, and other such terms. All refer to the more or less special powers of a third party to do something in stopping or composing disputes or feuds.

Judging and the near-synonym adjudication are too formal and restrictive to serve as labels for the general process we want to consider. They occur in societies with formal officials who can pronounce binding decrees. And arbitration is a special kind of third party settlement involving a voluntary agreement of the parties of the dispute to abide by the decision—thus far too restricted to special societies and to special situations in them. It is the actions of third-party mediation that constitute the general process which, like the leadership discussed above, can take the various institutional forms that we may be able to arrange in an evolutionary series. By *mediation,* then, we shall mean simply intervention by some unspecified form of political power into the disputes of contending persons or groups. The term can refer not only to the actions of a formal court of law but also to the use of a supernatural ordeal controlled by a priest or the intervention of "public opinion" after the harangue of a village elder.

The above are all means by which the power of either authority or force may be used to solve problems for the maintenance of the society as a whole, and as such they conform to a definition of the actions that we usually consider *political.* But we should remember that egalitarian primitive society, when it is a small, close-knit, face-to-face group primarily made up of relatives does not have the same proportion of political actions as does a modern nation, nor are they on the same scale. Problems of social order are more often met in terms of etiquette, normative ideology, and customary personal-social sanctions, and if these do not suffice in certain circumstances, then some conventional familistic authority may be called upon. But there is very little occasion for the political use of force in any primitive society—within the society. This "permissiveness" has been commented on by countless ethnologists, missionaries, and early travelers.

The State

Civil law and formal government, elements that characterize states, are distinguishable from the usual forms of political power in primitive society by the fact that they are institutionalized, enacted, official, and they employ, threaten, or imply the actual use of force. However legitimized by custom, however conventionalized, and however acceptable the hierarchical relations embodied in them, law and government are usually considered unique among all the social devices in that all their requirements can be backed by force rather than by public opinion alone or some form of independent personal action. To be sure, force may be applied in a primitive society, as when a father spanks a child at the time he says "stop that!" Is this in some sense law and government? Certainly—in some sense. But is it a useful sense? Some American anthropologists think so and find law and the state variously in primitive kinship society, differing only in degree of complexity (Robert Lowie's *The Origin of the State* [1927] is the most extreme example).

At this point it would be unwise to attempt a formally adequate definition of law, and particularly to state that *all* laws (that is, every individual law) must be backed by threat or use of force. This problem will be discussed in chapter 4, "The Institutionalization of Power." But the *state* is backed by the force pertaining to its complete legal edifice, even if every law does not say so. This is true of most definitions of the state. We must declare that the power of force in addition to the power of authority is the essential ingredient of "stateness" simply because that is the only way to identify the subject of the investigation, which may be stated informally as: How did the institutionalization of the power to govern, by force as well as by the power of authority, come about?

Chiefdoms

Many important theories and debates connected with the origin of the repressive state have been handicapped because it is so difficult to account convincingly for its appearance out of the matrix of egalitarian primitive society. Its origin would have to be quite sudden and cataclysmic, therefore, which may be one reason that conflict/conquest theories of one kind or another are so common. But modern ethnohistorical records argue powerfully for the presence around the world of varyingly developed *chiefdoms,*[3] intermediate forms that seem clearly to have gradually

3. The concept of *chiefdom* first came to my attention when Kalervo Oberg (1955) used it to designate a type of lowland South American society

grown out of egalitarian societies and to have preceded the founding of all of the best-known primitive states. At this point it seems highly probable that similar stages preceded the flowering of the archaic civilizations.

Chiefdoms have centralized direction, hereditary hierarchical status arrangements with an aristocratic ethos, but no formal, legal apparatus of forceful repression. The organization seems universally to be theocratic, and the form of submission to authority that of a religious congregation to a priest-chief. If such nonviolent organizations are granted the status of an evolutionary stage, then the origin of the state (as we defined it above) is much simplified, turning on the question of the use of force as an institutionalized sanction. Of course, one then is led to wonder about the rise of chiefdoms and their hierarchical form of governance.

Enough of this for now. Only the minimum of definitions have been made and in only their simplest form in order to get started. Complications, it is hoped, will be avoided by the procedure of bringing up new problems gradually in their ethnographic and historical context, chapter by chapter. Also, the casting up of various contrasting authoritative definitions against each other has been avoided at this point. Important modern anthropological interpretations and related definitions will appear when we need them, whenever possible in the area and context chosen by the authority.

On Perspective and Method

Because the usual models for social scientists are derived from the natural sciences, a frequent practice is to stress determinism, or the role of impersonal cause-and-effect in human

---

that lay between segmented tribes and true states. I borrowed it as the name for a full evolutionary stage in *Primitive Social Organization* (1962). I have found the conception of this intermediate stage enormously useful in several problems, and use it throughout this work.

Societies of the chiefdom stage, combining as they do some of the minimal features of states, are nevertheless usually considered "primitive." There has been, possibly due to this fact, a great deal of argument which seems at first to be merely definitional: Do primitive societies have *law? Politics? Government?* (Lucy Mair's introduction to her *Primitive Government* [1962, pp. 7–32] is a convenient summary of these arguments.)

affairs, as opposed to free-willism and human intention, especially as manifested by important political leaders, warriors, and inventors. Do humans create culture or does culture create humans? In the perspective taken in this book, the answer is yes to both statements. Culture *is* created by the human species as a whole, and through all generations. But culture also is creative in the sense that every human animal became distinct from all other animals by being cradled and constrained in a near-infinity of ways that were created by the culture it was born into.

But this effect of culture does not mean that human beings do not have intention behind their actions, for purposeful acts are the very motor of society. And there are some remarkable leaders, too. For example, Shaka Zulu, whom we will discuss in chapter 5, was undoubtedly a very innovative war leader and the creator of the first native kingdom in South Africa. Had Shaka not been born would the Zulu state have been different? This is a pointless question because there is no way to answer it: Presumably if *anything* were different the results would have been different. What we do want is to find out all we can about the antecedent events, the interrelated conditions, the interplay of forces—the historical environment of causes, effects, and adaptations within which Shaka was entangled. These things we can discover in some part at least, and they will help us to know why Shaka was able to do one thing but not another. More importantly, we may find as we go along from chapter to chapter that conditions similar to those in Shaka's Africa seem to elicit responses similar to his. But remember: This is not a "determinism versus great man" argument, for that question is not being addressed. We are simply taking an arbitrary perspective on events that eliminates speculation about the unknown personal and psychological abilities of long-dead or anonymous leaders in order to concentrate on the knowables. Science, like politics, might well be defined as "the art of the possible"—and that is the aim of the method used herein.

As for the comparative method, it should be understood now that the procedures of this investigation will seem quite informal. That is, we are not following some logical scheme of statistical or mathematical tests of concordance, procedures for selecting a representative sample, and so on. The method to be used here does not require any of those formalities, but only the scholarly care, caution, and attempt at reasonableness needed in any historical reconstruction.

There is no problem here that requires any statistical or sampling procedures simply because the instances of state formation that are documented well enough to be useful are so few—i.e., our sample is the known universe. Chapters 3 and 4, to be sure, contain some grand generalizations about primitive society as a whole, but they are not discoveries or arguments that should require proof. They are offered simply as well-established conclusions useful as background for the investigations of the origins of states. The actual cases described in these early chapters simply illustrate the general background statements.

Our Contemporary Ancestors

It should be emphasized at this point that this work departs from usual modern historical and anthropological procedure. Historically and ethnologically known cases will be used to help in the interpretation of societies that are known only archaeologically. Whether this is a good thing to do should depend on the care with which it is done—admittedly it is a tricky procedure—and on the results. Certainly it merits further description.

What is the justification of the comparative method when it moves from extant stages to extinct ages? Is it justifiable to look to the historically known formation of primitive states, as in the first part of this book, in order to better interpret or reinterpret the formation of the archaic civilizations that are known only through archaeology and distant ancient history? Most early twentieth-century anthropologists, following Boas's injunction, foreswore this procedure, though in many cases they could well have used it while making clear the possible dangers, as described below.

This method originated when philosophers began to use contemporary accounts of primitive peoples in thinking about their own past. This was the first empirical way to interpret the less-known history of simpler times. There is a long and classic history of the usefulness of the approach: Aristotle used it in his *Politics,* as did Thucydides in his *History of the Peloponnesian War.* It was the primary tool of such great philosophers of civilization during the Enlightenment period as Hobbes, Ferguson, Lafitau, Montesquieu, Rousseau, and Turgot, and finally in later times most notably by Spencer, Frazer, and Marc Bloch.

The most evident danger in the method in those early days was with respect to the validity of data. Untrained travelers' accounts, and the later reports of missionaries and traders, were often gross exaggerations or mistakes—though not always. But this is no more insurmountable in the present case than is the use of naive documents in historiography in general. In many ways they are more interesting and useful than someone's *re*interpretation. One should apply tests of reasonableness that are based on as much comparative ethnology as possible. In dealing with modern times, paradoxically, the greater dangers lie in using the "scientific" ethnographies of trained anthropologists because, even though the descriptive data may be more accurate and analytical than a traveler's account, the reports are descriptive of only highly acculturated remnants of societies that were among the few survivors of the Euro-American colonial and imperial expansions. It is particularly dangerous to use some mechanical statistical method that eschews critical judgment of the reliability of the sources (in the manner of the Human Relations Area Files, or the Ethnographic Atlas), when the sample is taken to represent aboriginal cultures—which of course it does not.

The problems in the present volume are not so great. The comparisons will not be mechanical and the data have been evaluated critically by several expert historians and ethnohistorical anthropologists. The greatest problem in going from the best known to the least known in the present instance is how to evaluate the structural and functional adaptive differences between secondary or derivative states—those that arose in response to relatively modern outside pressures and circumstances—and those primary ("pristine" or "naive") civilizations that were the original independent responses in their own areas (see Fried 1967, 1968).

The intellectual utility of comparing the primitive states of historical times and the primary civilizations will to a considerable extent turn on our ability to maintain Goldschmidt's distinction between political *problems* and processes as they apply to both, on the one hand, and the more variable kinds of *institutions* that may be only historically evanescent—and thus evolutionary discontinuities.

The "pristine" versus "secondary" dichotomy, as proposed by Fried, is very important to the thesis of this book, particularly in contrasting the states of part II with the civilizations of part III. But frequently "pristine" does not seem quite right. "Precocious" is preferable in some contexts because it is a relative term: A society might be *more* evolved, because of having *earlier* achieved an advanced evolutionary feature, than its neighbors. The term "pristine" (vs. "secondary"), being absolute, poses problems that are not always entirely to the point (a related argument is found in Sanders and Marino [1970, pp. 104–105]). In other words, I don't want to say whether Olmec or Chavin culture was the *first* government (in Mexico and Peru), with Teotihuacán or Mochica second or third on the list. All that is necessary to argue is that the first manifestation of a new development *among adjacent societies* (the potential rivals), even though it may have been, like Kaminaljuyu in Guatemala, clearly a secondary off-shoot, would be in its local precocity tremendously advantaged and thus widely influential. The Petén Maya, the Indus River culture, the Chou in North China, Tiahuanaco in the Peruvian highlands, and others as well, may have actually been secondary in Fried's sense (or even tertiary), but they were precocious in a very wide environment and dominated it easily. For our present purposes in understanding evolutionary movements of rise and fall, local relative precocity, rather than absolute "pristineness," is what is significant.

2

Theories of the Origin and Nature of Government

EVOLUTIONARY THEORIES about the nature of the state seem inevitably to involve an interest in its origin. A mature state has acquired in its later history so many special features and manifest functions that its *main* function, its "true nature," is often obscured. The feeling seems to be that the nature of the state is best revealed—and best discussed—in the context of a consideration of its origin and early, rudimentary functioning.

Allied to this interest in the evolution of government (the bureaucratic state in a broad sense) is the notion found in modern times that a perspective of determinism, of cause-and-effect, could be used in comprehending it. And if that notion is accepted, then the nature of science entails that if such materials are reducible to comprehension then perhaps even control is possible. It is axiomatic that it is in the arena of differences of opinion about government ("politics") that citizens have their best opportunities to do something for the good of themselves, their class or profession, and their society. The most free-willist of any, however, must admit that what persons take to be their choices are also in terms of what they believe to be the nature of their environment—which includes not only habitat but also other persons and other cultural institutions. It follows that free-willists as much as the most rigid of determinists ought to believe that the better they comprehend the nature of man, society, and cultural institutions, the more rational and effective will be their choices.

But it was not always thought that government or the social structure of a society emerged from something else, to develop and change in response to comprehensible chains of events. Nor was it always thought that reasonable people could do anything about government even after understanding something scientific of human ways and of the nature of the government.

"Since the social world, government especially, is the work of men, men should be able to change it." Such a creed is in total contrast to the view that prevailed in Europe and America—with a few individual exceptions—until the period of Enlightenment. It could easily be argued, in fact, that the distinguishing feature of Enlightenment thought was precisely that governments and forms of society were not immutable and God-given, and that intelligence and knowledge could be efficacious in changing the government of a society. It is for this reason that our brief excursion into the history of theories of government begins with the Enlightenment period.

The classical Greek and Roman philosophers, so various as Plato and Aristotle, the Stoics and the Epicureans, thought of the state as coterminous with society itself; all before was anarchy. During the Revival of Learning in Europe from the thirteenth to the fifteenth century, Aristotle's idea of *natural law* to be fulfilled in terms of an ideal universal state, or *cosmopolis,* was united with Stoic philosophical thought to become finally theistic, particularly as the basis for the "natural" (i.e., God-given) desirability of the state. Thus the theory was finally antievolutionary, antideterministic, and antiscientific.

Ibn Khaldun (1332–1406), of Tunis, is the best known of those few who finally escaped the religious stultification of the studies of history and social science. His *Introduction to History* (1377) is a repository of important ideas about historiography, about social-structural factors as differentiated in nomadic and sedentary cultures, and especially the dynamic relations between these two kinds of societies. It is this latter perspective on the conflict of societies that provided his idea of the motive force in the historical process, a view that has since been adopted by modern sociologists of the "conflict school." He should receive credit also, however, for his insistence on the influence of climate and geography on the kinds of society that are adapted to them.

About a century later Niccolo Machiavelli was notable for the same basic reason that Ibn Khaldun commands attention: They both regarded the state from an almost completely secular point of view. "Machiavellian" has come to suggest political cunning, or bad faith in political maneuvering, but this derives from the fact that Machiavelli, like Ibn Khaldun, had divested himself of moralistic theological and metaphysical attitudes in order to see the state in realistic perspective. Machiavelli's analysis of the state springs from the Epicurean-like premise that human self-interest amid the innumerable desires for happiness was the motivation of human activity.

Machiavelli was overwhelmed with the idea of Italian unity, and he concentrated on realistically depicting the practical means for concentrating power in the hands of a single overlord. His classic statement in *The Prince* reveals a sophisticated, objective ability to analyze the nature of kinds of states, and his treatment of government as having its own end, the strength to govern, is certainly a classic description of the ideals of the nation-states that were later to arise in Europe. As Lord Acton said, "The authentic interpreter of Machiavelli is the whole of later history."

Later in the sixteenth century, the realistic, naturalistic study of political forms was continued brilliantly by Jean Bodin. The national, dynastic states had continued their struggling evolution and Bodin, like Ibn Khaldun and Machiavelli, witnessed the turmoil that resulted from the absence of strong government, this time in France before the founding of the Bourbon dynasty by Henry IV.

Bodin's theory of the origins of government was essentially like that of Ibn Khaldun, that the state rises out of conflict. Also like Ibn Khaldun and Machiavelli, Bodin differed from the ecclesiastical dogmas of God-given stasis by recognizing that stability is practically unattainable and that good government must be able to cope with change. And finally, Bodin dwelled on the differences in temperament between city-dwellers and nomads and the effects of fertile and barren geographical regions.

The similarity of the theories of Bodin to those of Ibn Khaldun should not be allowed to diminish the former. In the first place it seems highly unlikely that Bodin was acquainted with the earlier Islamic literature. And since Bodin was the first to describe and analyze politics comparatively and inductively from the historical materials of Western Europe, he was also the most important direct influence on the great and influential thinkers of the Enlightenment. His conflict theory was at least in harmony with, if not a direct influence on, the Scottish philosophers Hume and Ferguson and others who opposed the social contract school. And obviously Bodin's influence on the French was great, especially on Montesquieu with respect to his anthropogeographical comparative studies.

The Enlightenment in Great Britain and Europe[1]

The Enlightenment in Britain produced many marvelous philosophical writings. Of these we shall briefly consider the works of Thomas Hobbes (1588–1679) and David Hume (1711–1776), and toward the end of this chapter, Adam Ferguson (1723–1790). The middle sections of the chapter belong chronologically and developmentally to continental Europe.

Hobbes claimed to be the founder of the science of politics. By using the word "science," he meant to ally himself with the newly burgeoning interest in the mechanical, cause-and-effect view of the universe as inaugurated by Bacon, Copernicus, Galileo, and Harvey. Hobbes lived amid the turmoil of civil and foreign war, and he was particularly conscious of the precarious balance of governance caused by the church-state conflict. He once said that he and fear, like twins, were born together. No wonder, then, that Hobbes's primary motivation was a desire for peace, which meant, in his unsettled experience in exile, a stable government of complete authority.

Hobbes's aim was to describe human behavior in terms of a kind of social physics. Thus the tendency of physical objects to

1. This section is especially dependent on the interpretations of Peter Gay (1969).

pursue their own trajectory—when left to themselves—could be translated into an egoistic principle for human beings, that they pursue their own interests in the line of least resistance. This, of course, is the source of social conflict, of "war, as is of every man, against every man."[2]

The life of early man, Hobbes suggests, was one of continual fear, as well as "solitary, poor, nasty, brutish, and short." But men were able, finally, to agree to a *social contract,* accepting a common power, the state, which limited some of their egoistic liberties in favor of peace. Only after this could the civilized arts and industries develop. This argument is something like that of the Stoics in that it urges the desirability of individual submission to society and the state.

The writings of David Hume marked the beginning of the eighteenth-century attack on this kind of rationalism. Hume argued essentially from an empirical position rather than reasoning deductively from self-evident principles. He argued against Newton's mechanical universe with a relativistic, anthropological theory that "principles" of cause-and-effect, for example, are mental habits that are different in different times and places and not self-evident at all. "Custom is the great guide of human life" was his classic phrase (following John Locke's important argument).

In political theory he continued his emphasis on varying institutions and habits, including the belief that community life is based on conventions, not natural law. And as for "right" and "wrong" in society and in ethical systems, Hume felt that conventions could vary and thus could be more or less beneficial in their contributions to a stable and just society.

2. It may be well to emphasize that Hobbes, who has often been misunderstood, was talking about threatened or potential war as much as actual fighting. "Out of civil states, there is always war of every one against every one. Hereby it is manifest, that during the time men live without a common power to keep them all in awe, they are in that condition which is called war; and such a war, as is of every man, against every man. For WAR, consisteth not in battle only, or the act of fighting; but in a tract of time, wherein the will to contend by battle is sufficiently known: and therefore the notion of *time,* is to be considered in the nature of war; as it is in the nature of weather. For as the nature of foul weather, lieth not in a shower or two of rain; but in an inclination thereto of many days together; so the nature of war, consisteth not in actual fighting; but in the known disposition thereto, during all the time there is no assurance to the contrary. All other time is PEACE" (Hobbes 1651, p. 82).

Giovanni Battista Vico (1668–1744), Italian jurist and philosopher, laid out a more modern-sounding set of assumptions and prescriptions for a social science. In *The New Science* (1725) he skillfully criticized the logicomathematical form of deduction that Descartes and his numerous followers had given as a model for all knowledge and all of the sciences. Philosophically, he is like Locke and Hume in arguing that rationality was not a constant, but a variable historical and social acquisition. *The New Science* offered a new inductive approach to the study of history, conceived in nearly modern terms of cultural evolution. A comparative study of the history of cultures at different times and places, he felt, would show that nations passed through the same cycle from primitivism to civilization. Of special significance in this scheme is the consistently held anti-Cartesianism, that "the order of ideas must follow the order of institutions." All other writers of the time were concerned with the "mind" of an age or of a nation, as though it were the entity that had created the institutions.

Vico was not influential in the eighteenth century, nor was he known outside Italy until the French historian Jules Michelet came upon a reference to *The New Science* that so interested him that he set out to translate the book. Edmund Wilson considers Michelet's popularization of Vico in the early nineteenth century such an important intellectual event that he begins his study of modern revolutionary theory (*To the Finland Station* [1940]) with a description of Michelet's discovery of *The New Science.* Two related elements in Vico's book were responsible for the excitement: one was the organismic analogy of functional deterministic connections between institutions in a society; the other was that scientific knowledge of nations' histories could enable mankind to erect rational governments and cultures. As we know, these are the basic assumptions of most modern reforming movements, especially of Marxism. But Vico was ahead of his time and out of place.

In France the writings of Charles Louis Secondat de la Brede, Baron de Montesquieu, were the most influential in creating the wave of political critiques that characterized so much of the work of the *philosophes.* Although he was an aristocrat, and essentially conservative in many respects, he was, like much of the French aristocracy of the time, critical of the absolutism of the Bourbons.

In his major work, *The Spirit of Laws* (1748), he pays the more or less automatic obeisance to Cartesian systemization and rationalism typical of his time, but his full emphasis is more like Hume's relativistic empiricism. The "spirit" of law and government was therefore no universal natural law, but variable in time and place as the laws adapt to the geographic conditions of a region and the related temperament of the people. Montesquieu's argument was born out of his desire to replace monarchical absolutism with a constitution like that of the English that would reflect, with a built-in system of checks and balances, the varying desires and motives of different groups in the society.

In contrast, most of the French *philosophes* did not argue for a different *structure* of government, but rather tried to uncover and promulgate the true laws of nature so that the enlightened monarch might rule more rationally. It was not until the publication of *The Social Contract* in 1762 by Jean-Jacques Rousseau that a new kind of argument appeared that was to have great significance in the history of modern political philosophy. His use of the popular phrase "social contract" has made for confusion, for his view of governments and how to evaluate them (in his terms, how to evaluate their "legitimacy") and his notions of "liberty" were at great variance with those of Hobbes and other social contract theorists.

Liberty for Rousseau is not "natural freedom" but "civic freedom," for which it is exchanged. The civil entity is a moral entity that men are required to obey. But ideally the requirement is not made by force, but instead by the social contract, by which one surrenders one's egoistic demands to the *general will.* In a sense, Rousseau is saying that man surrenders his natural ego to society rather than to a state, as Hobbes would have it. That is, a *legitimate* government is an agent of society, not its master, and it rises out of a society that is governed by the general will. Whereas most liberal people of the Enlightenment thought of the political problem as consisting of the antagonism between personal freedom and civil authority, Rousseau tried to unite the two. If the state were truly legitimate, Rousseau believed, it would serve the general will, and as a consequence the individual, who would have also agreed to serve the general will, feels free—unrepressed by any outside force.

Such a conception obviously depends heavily on certain social conditions, the most important of which is political and economic equality. In conditions of near equality, according to Rousseau, a properly educated public is likely to manifest a civic spirit that will result in a tendency toward unanimity of opinion on important policy questions rather than simply "majority rule." But of course all this depends, in the end, not only on education in the formal sense, but on a sound *moral* training. Rousseau was above all a moralist trying to establish a theory of obligation—not submission to governmental force, but an intelligent adjustment to society. It should be noted that despite his use of the often-quoted term "the noble savage" he did not advocate a return to the primitive or a destruction of the arts and sciences. He felt simply that it was time to ascend to a better, more moral, adjustment of individuals to a better society than was present in his time. Rousseau belongs, really, in the company of the utopians.

It might be relevant to an understanding of all of the various social contract theorists that they must have been heavily influenced by Europe's feudal past. The disorder in Europe during the so-called Dark Ages was succeeded by local systems featuring hierarchies of personal relationships that apparently were somewhat voluntaristic, with the bonds symbolized by pledges of fealty by the inferior and by obligations to render military aid and various prestations (rents, taxes, or dues) in return for protection (Bloch 1961). This system was in fact a "social contract" of a sort (and also reminiscent of a primitive charismatic "followership" called the big-man system [see below, chapter 4]).

A few evolutionary schemes of the late Enlightenment were simply teleological and hence not very instructive to us in these days. As described by the two most prominent examples, Condorcet and Turgot, evolutionary progress, stage by stage, consists of inevitable improvements in rationality. Civilized man had simply reasoned his way out of primitivity. Turgot's famous Sorbonne discourse on this subject in 1750 was significantly titled, "On the Successive Advances of the Human Mind." Cultural progress, in this view, is thus immanent in the human mind—through variable in outcome due to differences in geography, historical fortunes, and so on.

Outside France, especially where different forms of government, including colonial governments, were to be found, these latter *philosophes* did not have an impact equal to some of the earlier ones. And it is evident that within France some of the important groundwork of a truly comparative inductive science was ignored.

Montesquieu, however, was exceptionally influential abroad. His influence on the Scottish "moral philosophers" was especially great and the basis of his perspective and method was enthusiastically promulgated and elaborated by Adam Ferguson in particular. In 1767 Ferguson published *An Essay on the History of Civil Society,* which he based on Montesquieu while extending the latter's method by drawing more upon the observations of primitive peoples made by contemporaneous missionaries and travelers such as Charlevoix, Lafitau, Dampier, and others, as well as the classical sources. His attempt to describe human nature, or "men in a state of nature," was in terms of a careful evaluation of the evidences from primitive life. He had at once more data to work with than Montesquieu and also a more severely questioning attitude toward its validity—although it should be remarked that evaluation of data had a much more central place in Montesquieu's work than in that of the other *philosophes* such as Rousseau.

Ferguson more than agreed with Montesquieu about the falseness of the common idea that "man in a state of nature" was free to be his natural self. Man is governed by society, and never was outside it—he has always wandered or settled "in troops and companies." Man's nature as seen in a study of man in society is highly composite, in the primitive world as well as in civilization—which is but a continuation and accumulation of devices from earlier times.

Ferguson saw human nature as being composed of many opposite propensities—sociability and egoism, love and hostility, cooperation and conflict—an amalgam that is necessary to allow for the different kinds of characteristics demanded by society in different times and places. Ferguson felt—contrary to Rousseau's belief—that conflict had a positive function in cultural evolution, and for that matter even in individual psychology: the stronger the hostility to outsiders, the closer the internal bonds of the collectivity; the very meaning of friendship is acquired from a knowledge of enmity.

Ferguson was notable for another extension of one of Montesquieu's interests. He went far beyond the *philosophes'* usual formal analysis of legal rights and constitutional forms to deal more directly with social and economic realities. His concern over the specialization of labor was particularly striking for his day. He saw that while increased division of labor brings greater skill and thus greater prosperity to a community, the community becomes fragmented and mechanized, with wealth increasingly unequally distributed—specialization can be a curse as well as a blessing.

It should be of interest that Adam Smith published his pathfinding *Wealth of Nations* in 1776, nine years after Ferguson's *History of Civil Society*. The two men were close friends, radical for their times, and they undoubtedly influenced each other importantly. (That Ferguson's work was published first is balanced by the fact that Smith had been lecturing on his antimercantilist economics in the 1750s). Both men were critical of the contemporaneous civilization—like *philosophes* elsewhere they tended to move from analysis to prescription—but for the first time important emphasis was laid on socioeconomic factors, rather than on "mind" and ideologies and their presumed related legal and governmental consequences. This may be one of the most important as well as the first of the truly modern reformist confrontations of "materialist" versus "idealist" perspectives.

It is interesting that a kind of test of the different political theories of the European Enlightenment occurred in North America in the 1770s and early 1780s, when some of the *philosophes* were still alive. (Most of them had died before the French Revolution: Hume died in 1776, Rousseau and Voltaire in 1778, Turgot and Lessing in 1781, d'Alembert in 1783, and Diderot in 1784.) According to the historian Peter Gay, American thinkers like Benjamin Franklin, John Adams, Thomas Jefferson, James Madison, and George Washington were all enthusiastic followers of the Enlightenment thought of Britain and France, and eventually there was an important feedback. As Gay puts it (1969, p. 555): 'The splendid conduct of the colonists, their brilliant victory, and their triumphant founding of a republic were convincing evidence, to the *philosophes* at least, that men had some capacity for self-improvement and self-government, that progress might be a reality instead of a fantasy, and that reason and humanity might become governing rather than merely critical principles." There is no doubt that the American Revolution was a tremendous catalyst for the subsequent French Revolution. Gay says, ". . . When tough-minded men looked to the young republic in America, saw there with delight the program of the *philosophes* in practice, [they] found themselves convinced that the Enlightenment had been a success."

It seems evident that of all the varying arguments of the *philosophes,* those of Montesquieu, directly and indirectly, had the most influence in America (Gay 1969, p. 325) and are those most validated by what actually happened in America.

Revolutionists Look at the State: 1789–1848

In discussing the European epoch of 1789–1848, E. J. Hobsbawm takes political and economic change, exemplified respectively by France and Great Britain, to constitute what he calls the Dual Revolution. This concept is useful in that it enables us to discuss the two aspects separately. Further, the concept does not prematurely limit our understanding of the age in the way that more restricted labels—the Triumph of the Bourgeoisie, the Age of Empire, of Capitalism, of Liberalism, of Industrialization, of World Conquest, and so on—may do. In revolutionary ideology, theories of politics and government were still dominant at the beginning of the Age of Revolution, but economic theory, with particular attention to the new technology of industrialism, was rapidly gaining ground, until finally in the theory of Karl Marx, it became the prime mover. The minds of thoughtful men must have been tremendously influenced by the Dual Revolution. The economic "take-off," especially in the 1780s in Britain (Hobsbawm 1964, p. 46) and somewhat later elsewhere, was an astonishing evidence of progressive evolution, and of the capacity of men to acquire wealth and to enhance their social station and political power. On the other hand, the more purely political events in France marked the beginnings of a growing social revolutionary tradition that forever after has dominated social and political science, the writing of history, and the rise of ideologies attached to powerful political parties.

There had been foreshadowings in the Enlightenment period of the intellectual trends toward secularism, materialism, and determinism that were much later to be combined in the philosophy of Marx and Engels. For example, Denis Diderot (1713–1784), the powerful editor of the *Encyclopedia,* and his friends Holbach and Helvetius made the most ardent philosophical arguments in favor of a materialistic determinism.[3] But these examples were only portents; they did not significantly influence the following generation.

Out of the disorder of the French Revolution and the successive reactions of the civil and Napoleonic wars and, in England, the horrors of industrialization, were born the various attempts at utopian communities, such as those established by Robert Owen. These need not detain us, since no new theory of the state or society or human nature was proposed; they simply based their proposals on the pervasive Rousseauian ideas of the time that mankind is naturally good and that that goodness can be fulfilled by isolating social communities from the perverting institutions of the surrounding society. The revolutionary significance of the utopians is the spur they put to the work of Karl Marx (1818–1883) and his friend and collaborator, Friedrich Engels (1820–1895).

Marx and Engels combated the utopians directly with works such as *The Communist Manifesto* and *Socialism: Utopian and Scientific,* and also indirectly—though more effectively from a long-term point of view—by gradually achieving a complete and integrated body of theory about the nature of society and the state that would enable revolutionaries to expend their efforts rationally in terms of a "correct" appraisal of reality.

The conflict of social classes in the political arena was familiar to all onlookers and participants of the Age of Revolution. The power differential between such visible classes as aristocracy,

3. Interestingly enough, the theory that population pressure is the basic cause of inequality of wealth, which in turn leads to "servitude," was proposed by some Enlightenment figures, most prominently Voltaire in his essay, "Equality" (see the discussion by Cocks [1974]).

peasantry, and burghers was understood by all. Marx and Engels were the first scholars, however, to root the class struggle so firmly in economic inequalities, and to describe what we may call the class subculture of societies, especially their varying ideologies, as being fundamentally a consequence of their different relations to the means of production. All "history" is the history of class struggle, said Marx and Engels. But the different kinds of class struggles and their outcome were due to laws of economic development, not to social-class struggle in and of itself. (Marx said, in the author's preface to *Capital* [1906, p. 13], "Intrinsically, it is not a question of the higher or lower degree of development of the social antagonisms that result from the natural laws of capitalist production. It is a question of these laws themselves, of these tendencies working with iron necessity toward inevitable results.")

The above is a good example of the "materialism" of Marxism. In the famous *Socialism: Utopian and Scientific* (in Mendel 1961, p. 64), Engels puts it more specifically:

> The materialist conception of history starts from the proposition that the production of the means to support human life and, next to production, the exchange of things produced, is the basis of all social structure; that in every society that has appeared in history, the manner in which wealth is distributed and society divided into classes or orders is dependent upon what is produced, how it is produced, and how the products are exchanged. From this point of view the final causes of all social changes and political revolutions are to be sought, not in men's brains, not in man's better insight into eternal truth and justice, but in changes in the modes of production and exchange.

In later years, the publication of anthropologist Lewis H. Morgan's *Ancient Society* (1877) stimulated Marx and Engels's thoughts about the actual origin of the state and its true nature as an oppressive structure. Morgan's book was an attempt to clear up the mystery of the varying contemporary forms of primitive social organization by positing the probable stages of social evolution. Primitive society, Morgan had discovered, was basically communistic, lacking important commerce, private property, economic classes, or despotic rulers. Toward the end of his book Morgan ventured that increased productivity in some primitive societies had led to increased trade, and consequently to private property and classes of rich and poor.

After Marx's death Engels published the products of their joint appreciation of Morgan's materials in his *The Origin of the Family, Private Property, and the State* (1891). Some of their earlier pronouncements about *all* history, *all* social structures, *every* society, being formed of classes based on relations to the means of production now were modified to refer only to civil societies and only to "written history." But this modification must have been gladly made, for Morgan's finding that the widespread and ancient forms of primitive society were communistic strongly supported the argument that capitalism is transitory, that it is *not* based on human nature or some universal natural law.

The materialist conception of history now was to Engels's mind also greatly justified inasmuch as it could be applied to an explanation of the transition from primitive society to civil (state) society. Essentially, the book was a more focused and expanded version of the basic ideas germinated by Morgan: Certain primitive societies had improved the technological means of production, the surplus product of which was traded; as this process was expanded, society perforce changed from a production-for-use economy to a production of commodities, and with commodity production unearned increments arose due to differences in efficiency, in supply and demand, and in the activities of middlemen; thus, with the rise of private differences in wealth, economic classes appear. Here is the economic genesis of the state: From their *material* (economic) beginnings, classes become gradually social, and finally political as well when the rich erect a structure of permanent force to protect their class interests. The political state is thus a special means of repression by the propertied class. As for the propertied basis of the nation-state, the *Communist Manifesto* put it succinctly: "The proletariate has no fatherland."

This posited origin of the state is also the exposing of its true nature. Lenin's *State and Revolution* (in Mendel 1961) was written precisely to emphasize this judgment on the "historical role and meaning of the state," in order to argue against socialist idealists and reformers who felt that the state stands above society and could be reformed in order to "reconcile" class antagonisms. According to Lenin, true Marxism reveals the necessity of the destruction of both the class system *and* the state, for the state represents and protects only the propertied class.

There was a complication in Marx's thought that we have not yet discussed. This has to do with intermediate stages in the transition from classless, production-for-use society to a class, commodity-production state. As indicated in chapter 1, some of my previous researches have suggested strongly that the communal, segmental society was succeeded by a hierarchical, chiefdom stage before the true states were formed. There is the suggestion in some of Marx's works that he too did not think there was an abrupt movement from communal to capitalistic stages of evolution. He also conceived of some intermediate routes to the capitalist state.

In the classic *Critique of Political Economy,* Marx designated the stages ("epochs") of economic progress as the Asiatic, the ancient, the feudal, and the bourgeois. E. J. Hobsbawm considers these stages, discussed further in Marx's *Grundrisse,*[4] to be "analytical, though not chronological. . . ." (Marx 1965, p. 37). The first stage is that of direct communal property and it underlies all the others, everywhere. It is best seen in historical times in the Orient and in Slavonic communes. The second stage consists in the continuation of communal property as a substratum in societies that have acquired a class system, as in "ancient" (classical Greco-Roman) and Germanic forms. The next stage is feudalism, during which *crafts* manufacture arose with greater individual control over both production and consumption. Bourgeois society is the fourth stage, in which capital and labor (in the form of a proletariat rather than as slaves or serfs) create a new kind of class system. These are obviously not four stages of unilineal evolution; rather, the Oriental and Slavic are modified, arrested, residues of the first, or communal, stage, and lie outside the historical continuum that resulted in European capitalism.

But these are stages of *economic* development, with political forms only implied, at best. Feudalism, for example, is not defined

4. Marx had the habit of making voluminous notes of data and outlines and drafts of his thoughts before attempting final versions. One huge collection of his outlines or sketches (usually referred to as the *Grundrisse*), made during his last years in London, was published in its entirety in Berlin in 1953. Hobsbawm has edited an English translation and added his own long interpretative introduction of the sections of the *Grundrisse* pertaining to *Pre-Capitalist Economic Formations* (as the book is now titled [Marx 1965]). The discussion of Marx's stages in this chapter largely follows Hobsbawm's analysis. For a modern Soviet view, see Vasilev and Stucheoskii (1967).

as a political organization but in terms of its forms of production-for-use. Its "contradictions" arose with the growth of trade and of trading-handicraft towns, with both reciprocity and conflict existing between the towns and the countryside. This agrees with most prevailing interpretations of the economics of the breakup of feudalism. But what of the political systems of feudalism? Did not petty states and kingdoms arise from time to time out of the wreckage of the Roman Empire?

Part of the trouble in interpreting the Marxian scheme arises from the theoretical confusion of trying to make universal stages out of particular historical sequences. Marx and Engels eventually set the "Oriental epoch" aside as being historically isolated from European developments, but in their view of Western civilization the succession of stages remained ancient, feudal, bourgeois. A particular historical sequence in Europe—the Roman Empire and the political decentralization, power vacuum, and local economic self-sufficiency that prevailed after its fall—was elevated to a sequence of universal stages.[5] This had caused insuperable difficulties in attempts to adapt Marxist thought to the cultural evolution of the world. And in terms of European history in particular, the evolutionary significance of the primary archaic civilizations is needlessly downgraded and feudalism elevated to a stage that it never was.

The Modern Social Sciences

Auguste Comte (1798–1857) is frequently regarded as the father of academic scientific sociology. He is also known for his insistence on the organismic analogy for human society. Social order is closely related to the distribution of functions (division of labor) and the combination of efforts (government), Comte thought. But he also thought of government, of the state, as coterminous with organized society—simply as synonymous with it.

It remained for the great French sociologist Emile Durkheim (1858–1917) to finally develop Comte's notions on the "division

5. Note that the Enlightenment thinkers also made feudalism into a universal stage when they took the voluntarism that existed in the political relations of the feudal aristocracy as a basis for their theory of the social contract.

of functions" into a coherent and logical theory of the organismic and solidary nature of society. Durkheim, it seems evident, wanted to get behind, or underneath, the legal and contractual institutional structures that Comte (and, as we will see, Spencer) had described. Not denying the presence and significance of these institutions, Durkheim felt that a more important system of less visible but more omnipresent factors had created organic solidarity. These were the systems of beliefs and sentiments held in common by the members of the society. These he called the *conscience collective.* (The French word *conscience* means in English both "conscience" and "consciousness," but it seems apparent from Durkheim's normative emphasis that he intended the first meaning. In fact, many of the "sentiments" he described are vague and probably unconsciously held, which again suggests that the English meaning of *conscience* was intended.)

Durkheim's greatest contribution to the history of evolutionary thought was his characterization of primitive society as a system of uniform, undifferentiated, *segmental* entities, held together by what he labeled mechanical solidarity, as opposed to later, structurally differentiated societies having organic solidarity. As more complicated societies came about in later evolutionary stages, the *conscience collective* itself may become more differentiated (less "collective") and be implemented by the more institutionalized aspects of law and government (see especially his *Division of Labor in Society* [1933]).

Durkheim's efforts strongly trended toward modern anthropological theory. He lacked the useful concept of *culture,* but now it seems clear that his cumbersome verbal constructions were attempts to arrive at the modern conception of it. He also argued for the scientific reality of "social facts" (culture traits), and that society (culture) exists *sui generis.* But it is in Durkheim's emphasis on arguing the significance of the *conscience collective* that he seems to diminish the role of the state or government: certainly he paid little attention to the historical or evolutionary rise of the state as such.

Herbert Spencer (1820–1903) has often been equated with Lewis H. Morgan and E. B. Tylor as a cultural evolutionist and scientist, but a reconsideration of the main influence of each one makes such close parallelism seem untenable. True, all were evolutionistic—but in varying ways, and with very different interests and effects. Morgan had almost no effect on the development of the academic social sciences (except in a negative sense, particularly stimulating the critiques of Robert Lowie). Tylor was an important influence in early British academic anthropology, but his interest was mainly in what today is often called culture-history, a concern with the origin, distribution, development, and diffusion of discrete culture traits. *Sociology,* on the contrary, was in Spencer's terms a scientific study of whole sociocultural systems, and this consuming interest is what sets him apart from the others of his time and what justifies giving him the sociological, rather than anthropological, label.

Aside from evolutionism, two aspects of Spencer's thought serve best to characterize him. One is his view of particular societies as *systems,* analogous to the structure, functioning, and specializations of parts of a living organism. He was, then, the most important, though not literally the first, proponent of the *organismic* perspective that was to characterize so much of academic sociology in the United States and France, and social anthropology in Britain. The other important aspect of Spencer was his "social Darwinism."

Social Darwinism took three forms that were not necessarily related. Those dealing with competition among businessmen and corporations need not detain us here. But Spencer's third theory about competition, however, rested on a firm scientific foundation and is well worth considering with care. This dealt with the role of conflict among whole societies. Spencer attributed the rise of the state itself to warfare, and also with important developments in legal, economic, and religious organization.

Warfare may select the stronger, more efficient societies, of course, and eliminate the weaker or cause it to be subsumed by the stronger. But it is the *prevalence* of successful warfare in a state that leads to the prevalence of military institutions, which carry their influence over to peacetime. At the same time, war unites otherwise disparate parts against a common enemy. If the warfare is prevalent, or if the threat is continuing, the subordination of the social divisions to the military governing center becomes relatively more stabilized. This is the important factor that leads a loosely compounded social aggregate toward a more consolidated society with a general governing center, with the originally independent local centers of regulation becoming dependent deputies of the general center.

The "regulating organization" has two aspects: the organization for offense and defense and the sustaining organization (Spencer sometimes calls them the "militant" and the "industrial"). These aspects vary in the ratios they bear to one another as we pass from society to society. But the militant organization creates centralized coordination, for that is in the nature of successful warfare. The sustaining organization does not necessarily create centralized government, and tends to acquire it only from the extension of militant government to the other aspects of life (including even the hierarchy of the gods and the ecclesiastical organization).

Spencer does not make a clear-cut distinction between state and nonstate, and hence his comparative data do not give the best support for his assertions. He classifies societies as simple, compound, and doubly compound, but with each category containing examples of varying degrees of "headship." Headship and the related centralization do not, in his scheme, ascend in the evolutionary order as prescribed by the stages of complexity (or "compoundings"). These latter are "social types," but each may or may not have "stable headship." A militant organization, however, with its strong centralization and subordination of parts, might characterize any of the above stages, as could the societies in which the sustaining organization is the more prominent. The Spartan and Athenian confederacies, for example, are alike in being in the doubly compound stage, but very unlike in that Sparta's militant organization was dominant while in Athens the uncoercive sustaining organization prevailed.

As far as the question of the origin of the state is concerned, Spencer seems to feel that there are two kinds of states: One is basically militant, in which the individual is subordinated to the collectivity, whereas in the other the industrial organization is a cooperative venture "which directly seeks and subserves the welfare of individuals" (1967, p. 65). Spencer thus combines, as it were, a conflict theory and a social contract theory in accounting for the origins of his broadly conceived "regulative" and "political" organizations. But Spencer's repeated emphases give the overall impression that he sees successful warfare as the major variable in political evolution. Indeed, sometimes he states this outright (in partial contradiction to other statements). We may take the following passage, in which Spencer summarizes a chapter on political heads (1967, p. 126), as his considered conclusion:

> Headship of the conquering chief has been a normal accompaniment of that political integration without which any high degree of social evolution would probably have been impossible. Only by imperative need for combination in war were primitive men led into cooperation. Only by subjection to imperative command was such cooperation made efficient. And only by the cooperation thus initiated were made possible those other forms of cooperation characterizing civilized life.

The problem of depersonalizing headship and continuing it as a developing structure was considered most brilliantly by Marx Weber (1864–1920), like Durkheim one of the truly seminal formulators of modern sociology. Weber believed that there were three types of authoritarian leadership: charismatic, traditional, and legal. Charismatic leadership is founded on the faith of the people in the ruler's extraordinary spiritual qualities or greatness. Traditional leadership is founded on the sanction of immemorial custom. Legal domination means that authority's decisions are subject to, justified and rationalized by general rules (Weber 1947, pp. 310–406).

Weber presents these types of legitimate authority as "ideal types," not usually found in such pure form in historical cases. They are useful for sharp conceptualization in systematic analysis, and a given empirical case may actually contain all three types, or be in transition from one to another. But it is important to note that he does not present these as evolutionary stages—Weber is a (somewhat unique) kind of historian-functionalist, not an evolutionist. We may be therefore doing some violence to Weber's thought, but it does seem, at least provisionally at this point, that the three kinds of authority serve to epitomize very well the leadership in turn of egalitarian-segmental societies, chiefdoms, and the government of archaic civilizations.

A few lines should be devoted to Walter Bagehot (1826–1877), an influential contemporary of Spencer's and the first avowed social Darwinist. He did not say a great deal about the origin of government, but a few paragraphs in his brief *Physics and Politics* (1872) are interesting. He felt that warlike competition among societies in early times would select for those with the best leadership and most obedient populace ("the tamest are the strongest"). A major problem in the evolution of a politically directed society is that of perpetuating the headship, making an "official" out of a hero, which in early times involved inheritance of the position.

Bagehot, like Spencer, was of great significance in developing the so-called "conflict theory" of the origin of government. As we have seen in the discussion of Spencer, this means *external* conflict, the conflict between whole societies, rather than the personal, anarchic conflict that played a part in the ideas of Hobbes. As we also have seen, Ibn Khaldun argued powerfully for the conflict origin, but he restricted the argument to the conflict between nomadic herdsmen and sedentary horticulturalists, of whom the former were the more favored. The nomads, it should be remembered, had neither class stratification nor private property, but the settled communities typically were stratified, and this factor must be regarded as a prerequisite for an important aspect of successful conquest: the preservation by force of a privileged social position as it becomes occupied by the incoming conquerors.

The conflict theorists in more modern academic times were led by sociologists Ludwig Gumplowicz, Franz Oppenheimer, Albion Small, and Lester Ward. All were heavily impressed by "Darwinian" conflict and survival theory, which they combined with an emphasis on the permanent subjugation of losers by winners—that is, they considered the state a product of *conquest* as well as of conflict-inspired selection-and-survival.[6]

An alternative to extrasocietal conflict as a reason for the rise of the state has been proposed in the present century. That the classical origins of the pristine states in Mesopotamia, the Indus River region, the Yellow River region in China, the New

6. Oppenheimer states the importance of conquest succinctly as follows (1914, p. 68): "The moment when first the conqueror spared his victim in order permanently to exploit him in productive work, was of incomparable historical importance. It gave birth to nation and state; to right and the higher economics, with all the developments and ramifications which have grown and which will hereafter grow out of them."

World Valley of Mexico, and coastal Peru all seem to have involved irrigation systems has suggested that the factors of great bureaucratic power, high population density, intensive and high agricultural production, sedentary urbanism, or various combinations of these are responsible for the rise of the state, or at least the "Oriental" version of it.

The roots of the theory lay in Marx's suggestion that the course of the evolution of civilization in the Orient was different from and independent of that of the West. A latter-day Marxist scholar, Karl Wittfogel, used this idea to buttress his own full-scale interpretation of the rise of the ancient states in the Near East and Asia. Since the extension and maintenance of an extensive "hydraulic" system (of irrigation and flood control) presupposes a central authority, Wittfogel (1957) proposed this factor as the cause of the rise of the Oriental state, and of its "despotic" character as well. Wittfogel theorized that the ancient Oriental state was centralized because its mode of production required it, but importantly also, this control over production *enabled* the centralized state to exercise total power in other spheres as well. A presumption here is that if despotism is possible, the state will exercise it. (A stray thought: a state is seen as "despotic" when it represses its citizens; but if it *needs* to forcefully repress, is not this a sign of its weakness? Wittfogel's argument ought to mean that a large intricate hydraulic system would help a state to be *centralized* and *strong*—which is not the same thing as "repressive despotism.")

As we noted in chapter 1, several modern archaeologists working with data from the areas of the archaic civilizations have made some (necessarily limited) comparisons with the aim of discovering the essential features that regularly define civilization. Their findings imply that these features attend the origin, or "birth," of civilization. The most famous of these scholars, V. Gordon Childe, summarized his thoughts in a comparison of Egypt, the Indus River valley, and Mesopotamia (1950). He felt that the "urban revolution" is the hallmark of civilization, and that it develops other salient characteristics in its wake; the main "mover" toward urbanism, he believed, was the development of intensive food production that could support not only a dense population but also provide a sufficient "concentrated social surplus" to support an elite hierarchy and a repressive state to maintain its dominance.

Others have agreed with Childe's emphasis on intensive food production, but all the cases reviewed,[7] whether agreeing with Childe or not on specifics (such as the question of the significance of "urbanism"), share one common fault. This fault lies in supposing that the presence of a certain necessary condition for the development of urbanization is a sufficient explanation of it (cf. Webb, 1968). Sufficient food for a dense population and to feed nonproducers is of course necessary, as an enabler, but as Carneiro (1961) has shown so cogently, such an enabler is not a cause: many, many societies can produce enough food to support a denser population, but do not actually "grow" or "develop" as a consequence; they just do not work hard—a perfectly natural state of rest, wholly to be expected.

Many of the aforementioned modern anthropologists, including Childe, often mention warfare, or conquest, as a contributing factor to the rise of a ruling group. This is of course an inadequate statement of causality since warfare is so general, especially among tribal societies. Perhaps warfare under some *special* ecological conditions might be specific enough to be cited as causal, or partially so. Robert Carneiro (1961, 1970) noted in numerous well-documented examples that when areas of unusually good land were surrounded by areas of very poor productivity, population pressure caused increased warfare. In tribal areas the defeated or weaker groups, being rather nomadic, simply moved away. But in areas where retreat was impossible it is likely that strong and weak groups existed in proximity, finally arriving at consistent rather than sporadic dominant-submissive and/or warlike relations. Carneiro goes on to speculate that if the situation were exaggerated, as presumably it was in the areas of the archaic civilizations (where *very* rich land was *very* circumscribed), so that defeated groups were absolutely tied down by the combination of environment and constant application of, or threat of, military dominance, this structure would easily turn into the primitive state. Malcolm Webb (1968), an archaeologist, has defended the ethnologist Carneiro's thesis with suggestive data

7. Steward (1959), White (1959), Braidwood and Willey (1962), Adams (1966), Armillas (1968).

from both the classical archaeological areas and from ethnologically known secondary states. In subsequent chapters we shall note some exceptions, however, and suggest a broader hypothesis that will not depend so heavily on geography.

In the same sense that Carneiro's circumscription theory can be amended to include more of our cases, so can Ester Boserup's (1965) closely related argument that land will not be used intensively as long as cultivators can expand to virgin areas. Geographic circumscription can thus cause a rise of population density that would stimulate a more intensive agriculture. This theory makes perfectly good sense, but, as in the case of Carneiro's, I think the circumscription is more often nongeographical, usually military (though often, of course, combined with important geographic considerations). In any and all cases, however, it is important to note that circumscription by whatever factors—geographic, social-demographic, military, or combinations of these—does not do anything by itself. It is a great circumstantial help, however, to a governing bureaucracy, which is the active agent in planning or carrying out defensive and urban arrangements, ways to intensify agriculture, and means of governing the population better. And all these factors make higher densities possible. (Boserup's theory has mostly to do with the decisions of individuals; forced by population pressure on scarce land, farmers intensify their own efforts. But here we are referring to the decisions of governments.)

Morton Fried (1967) has rather more elaborately divided the problem of the rise of states into component parts to be dealt with separately, somewhat as suggested in chapter 1 above, pp. 15–16. Fried delineates the stages of the evolution of political structures into *egalitarian* societies ("band and tribal" society in the terms I have used [Service 1962]), *ranked* societies ("chiefdoms" [Service 1962]), *stratified* societies, and *states*. These are stages in the progressive emergence of the basic elements of governmental structure, those elements being permanent centralized leadership and legalized monopoly of power to back it up.

"A rank society is one in which positions of valued status are somehow limited so that not all those of sufficient talent to occupy such statuses actually achieve them" (Fried 1967, p. 109). Rank societies may also be stratified at the same time, although Fried sees stratification as a later development. Stratification is, in Fried's view, almost synonymous with the state: "Once stratification exists, the cause of stateship is implicit and the actual formation of the state is begun" (p. 185). Fried is careful to point out that states can arise under many circumstances, "but each pristine state certainly had to traverse this stage or level [stratified society]" (p. 185n).

Fried defines a stratified society as "one in which members of the same sex and equivalent age status do not have equal access to the basic resources that sustain life" (p. 186). A stratified society is thus a *class* society in a Marxist sense, but with the refinement that the classes are defined in terms of access to capital goods (not possession of consumer goods), and not in terms of relationship to the "means of production." But this is similar to Marxism in that a basic difference in economic power is what defines the difference in the classes, and these are different kinds of *property;* or put another way, distributive systems determine political systems.

How did these different kinds of property rights originate? First, and most important in Fried's scheme, is the factor of population pressure on resources (normally land, or irrigation water for the land, which amounts to the same thing). The pressure may be from internal growth or by accretion. Whatever the means, a ranked society has powerful kinship sanctions regarding equal distribution (or redistribution) of resources, but unequal kinship statuses. In dire times of overpopulation and stress on resources, the central kin groups of higher status will exert a stronger claim to the resources than the more "distant" relatives of the chief's lineage. As the situation becomes more exacerbated so will the magnitude of the internal disputes, pressures, and conflicts (p. 225). "Nonkinship mechanisms" of political and economic power then come into play. And "in the final analysis" these manifestations of power (army, militia, police) defend the general social order, the heart of which is the central order of stratification (p. 230). As in Marxism, again, the state thus originates as a repressive structure to maintain class ("strata") inequality.

In well-reasoned and well-documented arguments, Fried explicitly denies that either warfare or slavery had a role in the origins of the pristine states (pp. 213–23). Once in existence, however, the state had the power both to make war more effectively than before, and to control captives as slaves. It should be noted also that despite his theory's basic resemblance to Marxism, Fried is not talking about the origin of the class system in Morgan and Engels's terms—commerce, the production of commodities, and "capitalistic" private property. Fried's description of strata with "differential access to basic resources" has to do with property, in the sense of differential economic control and power; but the differential may have been, and likely was, among hereditary *kin* groups rather than groups of capitalist owners and nonowners. This modification, alone should make his theory much more palatable to modern ethnology than the original Morgan-Engels theory because it conforms better to some of the facts of primitive life as we know them today.[8] But, as we shall see subsequently, mounting evidence discounts the differential access and the internal conflict theories, as it does the Marxian "class struggle" theory.

There are other modern anthropological theories of the origin of the state, but the above are the most important of the general, more philosophical sort. The most interesting of the others were developed in the course of their authors' work in their particular areas of specialization. It will be more convenient, therefore, to discuss them in the chapters dealing with those areas. For example, the theories of Oberg, Rattray, and Nadel will be described in terms of their own ethnological work in Africa; those of Childe, Braidwood, and Adams in the context of their archaeological work in the Near East; and those of Coe and Sanders and Price in the chapter on Mesoamerica, Steward in the chapter on Peru,[9] and Lattimore in the treatment of China. Others will be touched on more briefly as they come up in context. Most of these are variants of the conflict school, in the vein of either the Marxian class-conflict scheme or the conquest theory. Lattimore's is by far the most complex, however, another reason for describing it quite fully in terms of the specific data that spawned it.

8. Robert McC. Adams (1966) has reasoned similarly. His work will be discussed in the chapter on Mesopotamia.

9. Julian Steward, to be sure, had published a general theoretical article on the causes of state development (1949), but he later modified it so much (1955) that it is better to take a still later (1959) conception as developed in his discussions of Peru.

3

Man in a State of Nature: The Egalitarian Society

THE VARIOUS KINDS OF societies in the world have been classified in many ways: technologically, as in the hunting, herding, farming trichotomy; geographically, by continents or smaller "culture-areas"; racially, as red Indians, white Europeans, black Africans, yellow Asians; linguistically, as Aryans, Malayo-Polynesians, Souians; and perhaps earliest and most pervasively of all, as to their sociopolitical institutions. This latter classification distinguished mainly between peoples with some sort of formal government and those without it.

This dichotomy was, as noted earlier, of central importance in the political theories of the eighteenth century, when arguments as to the purposes of government, the evolution of civilized institutions, the future of civilization, and so on, hung importantly on conceptions of the nature of human nature and, of course, its significance in social life. The important philosophers of that period all felt that the life of primitive peoples in precivil society was life in a "state of nature," untrammeled by our form of artificial (i.e., governmental) constraint.

But as we have noted, the philosophers lacked accurate information about primitive peoples. For that reason, their versions of human nature could range from Hobbes's idea that primitive life was a "war of every one against every one" to Rousseau's conception of idyllic and peaceful freedom. Common to all, however, was the idea that primitive society was anarchical, and hence that the nature of that social life would reveal the essentials of man's inherent social qualities.

It is interesting that the actual nature of primitive prestate society as we now know it ethnologically can support both Hobbes and Rousseau, each in part. *War,* as Hobbes meant it—as threat or imminence as much as action—certainly is an omnipresent feature of primitive life, as is, in part, an appearance of the Rousseauian peace and generosity. As we shall see, these two aspects of social life coexist; the threats of violence caused by the ego-demands of individuals are countered by social demands of generosity, kindness, and courtesy. What the philosophers did not consider was that a society without governmental forms was still not truly in a state of freedom. There are numerous informal social ways of constraining people besides the explicitly governmental, and in the absence of statelike institutions these may even be correspondingly stronger than those domestic-cultural constraints that we are ourselves accustomed to.

Any society, no matter how small and primitive, is organized, with social behavior structured in important ways—otherwise it would not be a society. Even an informal part-time group like a neighborhood gang has a structure, as modern sociological research has (perhaps unnecessarily) taught us. All societies control the social relations of their members by means of rules of etiquette and normative sanctions defining right and wrong behavior. So fundamental are these that they begin in infancy—as "socialization" (in sociology-talk) and as "enculturation" (in anthropology-talk). Also universal, and very similar to the above rules and sanctions, is the subdivision of society into statuses and related behavioral roles.

In a small primitive society, much of social life is smoothly regulated by these codes, rules, expectations, habits, and customs that are related to etiquette, ethic, and role. And because these are normally not explicit, nor revealed by frequent breaches, the society might give the impression of freedom and lack of conflict, as Rousseau would have it.

But people are not all alike and an individual person varies in his lifetime so that not all persons fit their statuses and the normal role expectations smoothly. More important, probably no society is able to perfectly socialize all of its members or present unambiguous rules that fit all occasions. And of course sometimes a person is "crazy." (A perfectly good definition of a crazy person is that he behaves unpredictably, failing to do what the society expects of him.) Any society is therefore certain to have faced the problem of individual deviancy at some time or other and will have some means of dealing with it.

A greater problem is the synchronization of the relations of groups to one another. And when the groups are wholly autonomous societies the problem is of course acute. All societies must face the facts of diversity, deviancy, and group conflict at times, even if rarely. At this point we can see Hobbes's view as correct, particularly in his emphasis on the threat, the potentiality as well as the actuality, of conflict. But as in the case of Rousseau, Hobbes did not conceive of nongovernmental social devices that could so successfully function to control the conflict. Each relied on his own version of human nature to explain what went on in primitive society.

Equality and Influence

Most of the enculturation of rules of etiquette is, in small societies particularly, accomplished within the domestic family. Similarly, the most usual hierarchical statuses are also to be found in the domestic establishment. These are the various sets of parent-child, older-younger, male-female statuses—and they are, of course, profoundly inegalitarian because they are basically systems of authority.

But they are not *political* systems of authority and hierarchy; they are *domestic.* All societies have such hierarchical age-sex statuses, although of course they vary somewhat from society to society. But political problems are not domestic problems. Loosely defined, political problems concern deviant behavior that injures someone *outside* the deviant's own family, and difficulties of various kinds in the relations *among* different groups such as families and larger kin groups, rather than within them. Political problems often may be like domestic problems in certain respects —two men fighting are two men fighting—but two brothers fighting may be pulled apart and their quarrel settled by their father, whereas two men fighting who are from unrelated families present an entirely different kind of problem of mediation, one that can have very serious consequences for the whole society.

This latter case, like all cases of difficulty among families rather than within one family, are very difficult to compose in the earliest forms of primitive society simply because there is no true hierarchy of authority outside that of the kinship statuses. The greatly distinguishing attribute of these societies is that outside of the familistic age-sex hierarchy the society is so profoundly egalitarian. So striking is this, and so equally striking and profound is the *in*egalitarianism of later chiefdoms and states, that it will prove convenient as well as appropriately indicative of this great difference to label the two kinds of societies respectively as *egalitarian* and *hierarchical.* The absence of nonfamilistic authority positions in the former and their presence in the latter, of course, render their respective solutions to political problems entirely distinct.

Charles Darwin saw this problem with the first primitive people he ever encountered. He observed that the "equality" characteristic of the Indians of Tierra del Fuego "must for a long time retard their civilization." Equality, it may be remarked, retards many things of practical, day-to-day importance also. Consider, in hunting societies particularly, how frequently some sort of ascendent person, a leader, must be necessary for the success of a coordinated action, yet how difficult for him to lead when the ideal personality is self-effacing.

A leader necessarily has peculiar characteristics in egalitarian society. Since he is an authority without formal status, the position must be based entirely on personal qualities. This in turn, would mean that different activities or different contexts would probably bring different persons to the fore. A person directing a ceremony is usually an old man, well-versed in tribal mythology and ceremonial customs because of his age; the leader of a war party, on the other hand, might be distinguished by his youthful vigor and courage.

Adam Ferguson long ago recognized this characteristic of egalitarian societies (1767, pp. 83–84):

. . . They have in fact no degree of subordination different from the distribution of function, which follows the differences of age, talents, and dispositions. Personal qualities give an ascendant in the midst of occasions which require their exertion; but in times of relaxation, leave no vestige of power or prerogative.

A superior person seems to be essentially an advisor, not an executive. For example, Father Le Jeune, in 1634, spoke of the Canadian Cree Indians thus (in Thwaites 1896–1901, vol. 6, p. 243):[1]

All the authority of their chief is in his tongue's end; for he is powerful insofar as he is eloquent and he will not be obeyed unless he pleased the Savages.

Father Le Jeune said of another Indian group, the Montagnais-Naskapi of Labrador, that the individual Indian will not "endure in the least those who seem desirous of assuming superiority over others" (ibid., p. 165).

M. J. Meggitt has said, with reference to the Australian elders (1962, p. 250): "Whatever *de facto* control they had over the actions of others simply derived from their ability to make suggestions based on first-hand knowledge of commonly-occurring situations. . . ." This is reminiscent of the Eskimo, who call a person of importance by a title, *Isumatag,* which means, "he who thinks."

R. L. Sharp points out with respect to the Yir Yoront of Australia that whereas kinship statuses are unequal by their nature, this confers no absolute high or low status (1958, p. 5):

1. The illustrations that follow are quite unbalanced, for they represent a larger sample from hunting-gathering bands than from the more numerous tribal societies. This imbalance was caused by the fact that such very primitive peoples as the Eskimos, African Bushmen, and Australians, for example, particularly have, because of their relative isolation in marginal habitats, preserved a more purely aboriginal culture into modern times than have most horticultural tribes. For a wider sampling, consult the studies listed in appendix 1.

The nature of the [kinship] roles which are played by every Yir Yoront means that every individual relationship between males involves a definite and accepted inferiority or superiority. A man has no dealing with another man (or with women, either) on exactly equal terms. And where each is at the same time in relatively weak positions and in an equal number of relatively strong positions, no one can be either absolutely strong or absolutely weak. A hierarchy of a pyramidal or inverted-Y type to include all the men in the system is an impossibility. Without a radical change in the entire kinship structure, the Yir Yoront cannot even tolerate mild chiefs or headmen, while a leader with absolute authority over the whole group would be unthinkable.

Sometimes a person combines high degrees of skill, courage, good judgment, and experience so that his very versatility in a variety of contexts might give the appearance of authority of full chiefship. But even in such a case, this is not an *office,* a permanent position in the society. Rather, it depends entirely on his personal qualities, real and ascribed—power of the sort usually called *charismatic.* But just because this position is personal rather than a post, he cannot truly command. He can only hold the position so long as people respect him and listen to him; it is a kind of moral influence that he wields. Radcliffe-Brown (1948, p. 45), writing of the Negritos of the Andaman Islands, mentioned how certain personal qualities such as skill in hunting and in warfare may be combined with generosity, kindness, and freedom from bad temper, such that the person becomes highly respected and his opinions carry more weight than other still older men. But Radcliffe-Brown is careful to point out that this is entirely personal *influence* and not a position of authority.

The self-effacement of men of influence is well illustrated by the South African Bushmen. Elizabeth Thomas, in describing the case of a man who had won high status over two other men who had expected to hold it, says (1959, p. 183):

But neither ever contested Toma's position as leader for it was not a position which Toma held with force or pressure but simply by his wisdom and ability, and people prospered under him. No Bushman wants prominence, but Toma went further than most in avoiding prominence, he had almost no possessions and gave away everything that came into his hands. He was diplomatic, for in exchange for his self-imposed poverty, he won the respect and following of all the people there. He enjoyed his position, and, being strangely free from the normal strains and jealousies of Bushmen, he saw justice clearly and hence he led his people well.

An important characteristic of an influential person is (among others) the ability to sense public opinion. This is described as particularly important among the Athabascan Indians of Canada (MacNeish 1956, p. 151):

In sum, the leader characteristically has a very tenuous position in Northeastern Athabascan society. He might serve as advisor, co-ordinator, director and perhaps initiator of specific military actions and/or occasional and particular economic activities beyond the day-to-day hunting and snaring routine. Also, by virtue of his prestige, gained from his superior abilities and his awe-inspiring powers, he might act as the prime opinion-giver in social matters within the band. His "authority" lay in putting his stamp of approval upon decisions or viewpoints arrived at by the group as a whole or, more specifically, his male peers. The wise chief or leader had his finger upon the pulse of individual and group opinions. He had to woo others to his way of thinking or, that failing, to alter his course accordingly. His position might be buttressed by the attribution of powerful medicine and by the Europeans' evalution and use as "trading chief" of his already dominant role. But the power of a strong or "great" leader lay in his influence rather than his "legal" authority. Ordinarily he had neither the moral nor physical resources to impose his will. Birket-Smith's characterization of the Chipewyan chief as *primus inter pares* keynotes the position of the Northern Dené leader.

Authority and equality must be incompatible, since true authority rests on hierarchy. Yet some of the purposes of authority found in civil society are somehow accomplished in these egalitarian societies; and certainly the same kinds of political problems exist that persons of authority normally cope with in other societies, however different in degree. As outlined in chapter 1, the activities or roles that authority normally assumes with respect to political problems are three: reinforcement, leadership, and mediation. It may be useful to discuss the peculiarities of egalitarian society in these terms.

Reinforcement

Much if not most of the reinforcing of a social order is psychological, habitual, and customary, a constraint of social behavior accomplished through systems of rewards and punishments within the domestic family. But individuals differ, families differ, and cultural systems of social behavior are not always plain to everyone, so that some of the time some person or other is likely to violate the generally accepted familistic norms of behavior. This means that all societies must have some form of sanctioned deterrence of delinquency that is political—that is, superimposed upon the domestic family's role. The term *reinforcement* will hereafter be used to include both domestic enculturation and unconscious internalization, as well as explicit, consciously applied positive and negative sanctions.

All systems of authority, in the end, seem to rest on some accepted definitions of delinquency accompanied by appropriate punishments. To civilized man, these are normally explicit as formal law. But egalitarian primitive society lacks formal authoritative offices and formal law. We find there only persons of influence and only general public customary sanctions rather than laws. Thus the negative sanctions in such a society are often not administered by any particular person at all. This is simply because most of the rules of proper social behavior in primitive society are in the realm of etiquette. Egalitarian society is normally small and the social relations are therefore mostly face-to-face. And the usual punishment in any society for a breach of etiquette is some amount of general disapproval or withdrawal from the culprit, depriving him of reciprocal courtesy and attentiveness. The extreme of such punishment is of course ostracism, in primitive society a fate practically equivalent to death. Any breach of etiquette is observable, so that no one can ever escape some consequences of it (whereas crimes can be concealed). But the sanctions against a breach of etiquette are not invoked by any designated person, but by the community itself.

It is only the rare true delinquent, the "crazy one," who can repeatedly withstand the normal sanctions of the community code. These sanctions—gossip, ridicule, withdrawal, and so on—may not stop him, and sometimes the longer they are applied the more he is committed to withstand them. But a person who so consistently misbehaves is likely to harm families and groups other than his own, and this endangers his own family because of the likelihood of retaliation—which often results in feud. It is very common in primitive society that a delinquent's own group will plot to do away with him if all other means fail to control him.

In the few contexts in which reinforcement is a function of

particular persons, it is very informal and largely a matter of social status rather than true authority. The most usual case of this is simply that of an elder admonishing a younger person. This of course is standard behavior within families—the older sibling guides and rules the younger, the parent punishes the children—and it is therefore domestic rather than political action. But in small primitive societies, the status "elder" accords some considerable measure of influence outside the elder's immediate family also, and therefore may function in the context of the reinforcement of any younger persons toward conformity. Similarly, the male status normally confers more influence than female status, and we do find in primitive societies that normally it is men who are occupied in nondomestic, political-like situations, rather than women. So, in summary, we may say that the sex and age status differentiations of domestic families may function in vague, but wider, contexts of reinforcement so that they approach true political actions. But it should be remembered that this is so only in relatively small, face-to-face societies that are themselves familistic, however attenuated the actual kinship ties.

Leadership

The role of authority on occasions of concerted group action is normally the most visible of the activities summed up by the term leadership. But as already indicated, there is no permanent position of leader in egalitarian society, no true "chief." Further, egalitarian society does not even tolerate a suggestion of it. "Bossiness" would not do, and humility is of the highest value.

It was this self-effacement of leadership and this apparent orderliness of society without visible authority positions that led such well-known writers as Walter Bagehot and Sidney Hartland to speak of the "cake of custom," the power of cultural norms over the individuality of persons. Herbert Spencer, on the other hand, was led to assume that this very egalitarianism allowed greater scope for individuals than did the later authoritarian state. Emile Durkheim, however, disagreed with Spencer in an interesting passage (1933, p. 94):

Rather than dating the effacement of the individual from the institution of a despotic authority, we must, on the contrary, see in this institution the first step towards individualism. Chiefs are, in fact, the first personalities who emerge from the social mass. Their exceptional situation, putting them beyond the level of others, gives them a distinct physiognomy and accordingly confers individuality upon them. In dominating society, they are no longer forced to follow all of its movements. Of course, it is from the group that they derive their power, but once power is organized it becomes autonomous and makes them capable of personal activity. A source of initiative is thus opened which had not existed before then. There is, hereafter, someone who can produce new things and even, in certain measure, deny collective usages. Equilibrium has been broken.

What a confusion! Opposite conclusions are drawn from the salient characteristics of small primitive societies: their egalitarianism and their social docility despite the lack of authoritarian leaders. This may mean that such societies have no formal authority positions because they do not need them, as Rousseau would have it. But why do they not need them? Because the cake of custom is so thick upon them that they can think and act only in terms of collective norms, say some.

At any rate, egalitarian society does seem to have leadership when it is needed. What it lacks is permanent and pervasive leadership positions, with the ego-satisfying embellishments that go with and mark hierarchical authority positions. This should not be interpreted as necessarily meaning that persons are leveled out in all respects, that conformity is necessarily greater than in any other kind of society. It simply means that superiority of some sort or another is intermittent and personal rather than permanent and ascribed to an office. Durkheim was as far wrong in denying individuality to the persons of egalitarian society as he was in ascribing it to a chief in other, more politically advanced societies. But more of this latter point in the next chapter.

Mediation

In the egalitarian society the right to use physical force is not monopolized by a public power or any other authority that suppresses internal conflict by legal means. Is this again a case of not needing force because the cake of custom is a sufficient deterrent? Or is it that there are enough informal means of preserving order in a small society that formal government is unnecessary? Perhaps it is some of both.

Usually, because the societies are so small, conflicts are between kinsmen. In such cases, it is often possible for an aged and respected relative whom the contenders have in common to intervene and arrange a satisfactory conclusion. Ideally, the arbitration should be by a relative who is equidistant from both so that there would be no expectation of favoritism.

In many disputes one person may be clearly in the right and the other in the wrong, so much so that public opinion is nearly unanimous. In such cases it may be said that, in a sense, the public is itself the mediator. When the issue is not clear, however, difficulties arise, since one of the salient characteristics of egalitarian society is that unanimity of opinion seems to be sought in political decisions, unlike our familiar majority-rule. One of the most usual recourses is for the disputants to engage in a public duel or contest of some sort.

Among the Eskimo, for example, wrestling and head-butting contests are typical forms of public dueling. More common, and certainly more interesting, are the famous Eskimo song duels (Hoebel 1954, p. 93):

> Song duels are used to work off grudges and disputes of all orders, save murder. An East Greenlander, however, may seek his satisfaction for the murder of a relative through a song contest if he is physically too weak to gain his end, or if he is so skilled in singing as to feel certain of victory. Inasmuch as East Greenlanders get so engrossed in the mere artistry of singing as to forget the cause of the grudge, this is understandable. Singing skill among these Eskimos equals or out-ranks gross physical prowess.
>
> The singing style is highly conventionalized. The successful singer uses the traditional patterns of composition which he attempts to deliver with such finesse as to delight the audience to enthusiastic applause. He who is most heartily applauded is "winner." To win a song contest brings no restitution in its train. The sole advantage is in prestige.

The song duel is usually carried on at some length, giving the public time to form a consensus. Most people probably have an initial idea of which side they are on, but they want to reserve expression of this opinion until they find whether it accords with that of the majority. Gradually more people are more overtly laughing at one duelist's song than at the other's, hinting at their own preference but not overtly committing them to it. But this can then turn very quickly into unanimity.

Among the Australian aborigines disputes are typically settled by means of a spear-throwing duel. From a prescribed distance the accuser is allowed to hurl a number of spears, while the defendant is allowed only to dodge them. The public can applaud the throwing ability of the accuser and the adroitness and agility of the defendant. As in the case of the Eskimo song duel, the public gradually realizes a majority opinion, which then quickly turns to unanimity. When this is in favor of the defendant, the accuser simply stops throwing. But if the defendant loses, he is supposed to allow one of the spears to wound him.

These are some of the ways disputes are settled between members of the same community. But these means will not suffice when the dispute is between members of different communities. The more distant the two groups, or the less known they are to each other, the more difficult it is to mediate a quarrel. A primitive kinship group such as a lineage or clan reacts as a whole to an injury to one of its members. Conversely, it assumes that a counter-injury to any members of the culprit band will serve the law of retribution.

Obviously there is great danger that the above injury/retribution cycle could develop into a full-scale feud. Retribution or retaliation in the "eye for an eye, a tooth for a tooth" vein does not ordinarily result in a return to the original state of equilibrium, simply because the contenders are not likely to view the original injury in the same light, which makes it unlikely that they would agree on what constituted an equivalent retaliation. People in these primitive societies seem to realize this as a danger and sometimes even to anticipate ways to prevent it. The most common attempt to prevent feuds between communities are what have been called "expiatory encounters." For example, sometimes in cases of homicide in aboriginal Australia the guilty person is required by his own kinsmen to submit to a shower of spears thrown at him by close relatives of the slain person. Once he is wounded an end to the conflict is possible, even though payment has not been made in full. Sometimes, too, the kinsmen of the culprit may punish him before the other side has a chance to retaliate—again in recognition of the danger of feud.

But sometimes, of course, feuds do occur, and they can fester and erupt into larger-scale true warfare between tribes. Warfare among egalitarian societies, however, is seldom a pitched and bloody affair. This kind of society cannot sustain very many men in the field, and hence the battles are neither large nor protracted. But more important in limiting the scale of war is the egalitarian nature of the society. Leadership is ephemeral, for one thing, and the leader has no strong organization or authority to conscript or otherwise force people to serve his bidding. And he cannot force people to be brave by threats of legal punishment for dereliction of duty. Warriors left on their own usually will not run grave risks to their lives, and hence pitched battles are rare—ambush and surprise raids are the normal form of warfare. When a real battle does take place it is more noisy than bloody, as in the following example from northern Australia (Hart and Pilling 1960, pp. 86–87):

Thus Tiwi battles had to be the confused, disorderly, inconclusive things they always were. They usually lasted all day, during which about two-thirds of the elapsed time was consumed in violent talk and mutual abuse between constantly changing central characters and satellites. The remaining third of the time was divided between duels involving a pair of men who threw spears at each other until one was wounded, and brief flurries of more general weapon throwing involving perhaps a dozen men at a time, which ended whenever somebody, even a spectator, was hit. As a result of this full day of violence, perhaps a few of the cases would be settled that night—by a father handing over his delayed daughter, or a man with a disputed wife relinquishing her to her rightful husband—but when the war party left the next day to return home, the number of cases settled was likely to be less than the number of new feuds, grievances and injuries that had originated during the day of battle. For not only did the participants carry away from the battle field a vivid memory of all the physical wounds, intended or accidental, inflicted by whom on whom, but they also brooded long and suspiciously upon who had supported whom and why, either verbally or with spear in hand.

Finally, through all these disputes and hostile actions between senior men ran their united suspicion of bachelors. The only "battle" in two years between large groups drawn from distinct bands that had a clear-cut and definite final act was one fought at Rongu in late 1928. On that occasion, after disputing and fighting among themselves from early morning until late afternoon, all the old men present from both war parties gradually channeled all their anger toward one unfortunate young Mandiimbula bachelor whom they finally accused of going around from band to band creating misunderstandings between various elders. Several elders on both sides testified publicly that their mistrust of each other had started shortly after the bachelor in question had begun hanging around their households; whereupon the senior warriors of the two opposing armies had no difficulty in deciding that most of their suspicions of each other "were all his fault," and with great unanimity ganged up on the bachelor and quickly clubbed him into unconsciousness for being a troublemaker and a suspicion spreader. In the midst of battle the gerontocracy had reasserted its solidarity by finding a bachelor scapegoat upon whom to unload all their mutual suspicions and aggressions.

External Relations

In the examples so far we have dealt largely with intrasocietal political problems. But when we turned above to questions of feuds and battles we touched on the essence of foreign political governmental problems, the ability to make war or peace. If government is mainly an organization formed to wield legal force, then it has not only the internal contexts for its use of or threat of force, but also the foreign. The two contexts should be separated, of course, for they are very different: Domestic constraints and sanctions (and law as well in civil society) are an omnipresent aspect of the problems of keeping the internal social order, but external affairs are essentially lawless, and unordered by mutual customs or public sanctions. Egalitarian society cannot wage war or make peace effectively via alliances and treaties because a responsible body, a governmental authority, is lacking. The external political problems are there, however, although the means of dealing with them are, as in the case of intrasocietal political problems, simply an extension of certain personal and domestic capabilities into the wider field.

It seems apparent, as in the previously mentioned case of feud, that primitive people recognize the danger of warfare and take measures to reduce its likelihood. These measures are various, of course, but they are all reducible to one generic mode of alliance-making, the reciprocal exchange.

Reciprocal exchanges are the ways in which all kinship organizations extend or intensify the normal interpersonal bonds of kinship statuses. Any two relationships of kinship imply standardized obligations and rights that are symbolized by exchanges of goods and favors (as well as by prescribed forms of etiquette). Such exchanges are normally both utilitarian and symbolic. This means that a valuable present given freely to a person obligates that person to respond appropriately—*as though* personal ties actually existed as symbolized by the exchange. Something like this is actually pan-human and can be observed even in the obligations of alliance that young children lay on each other in the playgrounds of the modern world. But in primitive society reciprocal exchanges are taken with great seriousness simply because the society is egalitarian and anarchical. The rules and expectations that govern reciprocal exchanges are the very essence of domestic life, of course, but they are also the sole means available to primitive people in their struggles to cope with the political problems of war and peace. Failure and success in alliance-making is failure and success at peace-making. This sounds Hobbesian—to suggest that strife tends to occur, more or less normally so to speak, unless positive actions are taken to avoid it, that the deterioration of peace-making actions tends to result in warfare. I believe this is true: It is usually idle to talk of the "causes of war"; it is the evolution of various *causes of peace* that can be studied in the human record; and a large and essential part of the evolution of political organization is simply an extension and intensification of peace-making means. More: It can be claimed that not only the evolution of government, but the very evolution of society and culture itself, depends on the evolution of the means of "waging" peace in ever-widening social spheres—by continually adding new political ingredients to the social organization.

Reciprocal exchanges in primitive society are of many kinds and have multifarious implications. Here we want to discuss only the important ones used in alliance-making among sovereign groups. These are mainly of two kinds (although each can have many variations and permutations): marriages and exchanges of goods. The latter is not exactly "trade" as we know it in modern times, for although modern trade for profit may in some senses help keep international peace, alliance-making exchanges of goods in primitive society are giftlike personal exchanges showing generosity and friendliness, rather than impersonal extractions of what the traffic will bear, "buying cheap and selling dear." The other form of reciprocity, marriage, also needs to be distinguished from its modern counterpart. Modern marriages are so often freely contracted as a product of romantic love that we often think that the purpose, or function, of marriage is to legitimize love, sexual relations, and offspring. Marriage does these things in primitive society also, but solely as a by-product of the basic, obvious, planned-for, politically schemed creation of alliances by reciprocal exchanges of marriage partners. Marriage, of course, is the way in which affinal relatives, and by the next generation, new consanguineal relatives, are created.

This obviously is the earliest, most basic, and also the surest form of alliance-making, for it extends the domestic realm outward. A marriage rule (i.e., a rule stating what sort of group must be married into, or conversely, which groups cannot be married into) regulates the reciprocal relations in the society at large. Because it is a "rule," and thus made up by the people themselves, its consequences can be anticipated; and it can be changed, as well, in order to accomplish political expedients.[2]

The rules of marriage can be remarkably complicated—complicated, that is, from our point of view. The Northern Arunta of central Australia, for example, have a marriage rule that ethnologists have called "second cross-cousin marriage." Another way of stating it, probably more indicative of the actual scheme, is that first-cousin marriage is tabu. Essentially, it means that a boy cannot marry into either his father's or mother's own local kin group (in many primitive societies, on the contrary, the mother's brother's daughter would be a favored marriage), but must marry farther out—among the mother's first-cousin group. Of this kind of marriage, it has been stated by the participants themselves: "Why marry into my mother's band? They are our allies already." This rule, then, has the effect of widening the bonds of kinship

2. E. B. Tylor (1888, p. 267) made this point long ago. "Among tribes of low culture there is but one means known of keeping up permanent alliance, and that means is intermarriage. . . . Again and again in the world's history, savage tribes must have had plainly before their minds the simple practical alternative between marrying-out and being killed-out. Even far on in culture, the political value of intermarriage remains. . . . 'Then we will give our daughters unto you, and we will take your daughters to us, and we will dwell with you, and we will become one people,' is a well-known passage of Israelite history."

far beyond those of the more usual first cross-cousin marriage.[3] At least twice as many relatives are harvested by this expedient.

In the above example, the reciprocity of the marriage can be delayed and made very general, when reciprocity refers to the actual exchange of women between two groups in successive marriages. But sometimes in egalitarian society, alliance-marriages may be so delayed in reciprocity, or so uncertain because of long distances, that immediate gifts of goods substitute for the delayed reciprocal marriage. This is, so to speak, reciprocity-on-the-spot. Its best-known manifestation is the miscalled "bride-price" or "bride-purchase," wherein the exchanges are symbolically cancelled out at the actual marriage ceremony. At some later time a return marriage is in fact likely, and a similar return of goods for the new bride.

The very common levirate and sororate marriages of primitive society demonstrate fully the fact that primitive marriage is a form of alliance, a political-like agreement, between *groups* rather than simply between the two persons who marry. The levirate marriage (after Latin *levir,* "husband's brother") follows the custom, or rule, that if a husband dies his brother—usually a younger brother—takes custody of the wife and children. The sororate marriage (Latin *soror,* "sister") maintains the alliance if it is the wife who dies, for then her sister must take her place. In both cases it is revealed how seriously the groups take the agreement. The "bargain" struck must be maintained and "not even death will us (the groups) do part."

The Limits of the Political Organization

If in egalitarian society the political extension of peace is by such personal, nongovernmental means as reciprocal exchanges of goods and marriages, then it must be that the scope of the

3. A person's cross cousin is a child of a parent's sibling of opposite sex; thus, one's maternal uncle's or paternal aunt's child. Parallel cousins are children of siblings of the same sex. This distinction occurs because of the very common primitive practice of local exogamy: one cannot marry into one's own local group, hence one's father and one's mother are from different local groups. Cross cousins, as a consequence are residents of different local groups (and thus are normally marriageable), while parallel cousins grow up in the same local group and cannot marry each other.

political organization is not particularly plain, nor its boundaries consistently visible. Most primitive societies have overlapping and interlocking sets of social (hence potentially political) relations with other apparently autonomous societies.

This rather indeterminant character of primitive political bodies is largely created by the ephemeral nature of leadership and by the fact that different political problems are solved directly and expediently, if they are solved at all, after which the system relapses into anarchy. And added to this is the fact that different kinds of problems and activities will muster different numbers of people. Assemblages called together for feasts or dances will normally attract more people than, say, a funeral. But any such assembly, because it forms a social group, however temporary, can undertake some political functions. Radcliffe-Brown put it this way, speaking of Australian aborigines (1940, p. xix):

> The point to be noted is that such assemblies for religious or ceremonial purposes consist on different occasions of different collections of hordes [local kin groups]. Each assembly constitutes for the time being a political society. If there is a feud between two of the constituent hordes, it must either be settled and peace made or it must be kept in abeyance during the meeting, to break out again later on. Thus on different occasions a horde belongs temporarily to different larger temporary political groups. But there is no definite permanent group of this kind of which a horde can be said to be a part. Conditions similar to this are found in some parts of Africa—for example among the Tallensi.

The Tallensi mentioned above are sedentary agriculturalists, a much larger society than the simple, nomadic, hunting-gathering hordes of the Australian desert. Yet they and many others, as distinct in various ways as Iroquois and North American Plains Indians, are all stateless egalitarian societies, making it difficult for an outsider to discern the limits of the society. Political events emerge from social events, the size of any gathering depends on its function, and attenuated kinship ties radiate in all directions so that the kindred—the true and constant society of relatives from the point of view of an individual—is not the same group of persons from family to family. And of course no kindred corresponds to any territorial demarkation, nor to any other distinction such as linguistic or cultural traits. The larger tribal societies, still within the category of egalitarian societies, have kinship groupings that are named and sometimes territorially demarked so that they are objectified and made corporate, so to speak, transcending the personal kindred and outlasting changes in membership from generation to generation. These are normally local lineages of patrilineally or matrilineally related persons, and clans (associations of related lineages). But even here, one cannot demark *the* society. Several clans may unite for some common purpose—ritual, festival, or war—and fall the next day into their constituent separate parts. This quality of structural subdivision and reconstitution depending on events is so formally equilibrated in some societies that they have been labeled a structural-functional type: *segmentary* societies.[4]

Evans-Pritchard epitomized this in concluding his essay on the Nuer (Fortes and Evans-Pritchard 1940, p. 296):

> . . . The consistency we perceive in Nuer political structure is one of process rather than of morphology. The process consists of complementary tendencies towards fission and fusion which, operating alike in all political groups by a series of inclusions and exclusions that are controlled by the changing social situation, enable us to speak of a system and to say that this system is characteristically defined by the relativity and opposition of its segments.

Emphasizing that egalitarian society is essentially without fixed political boundaries implies that the societies with formal political organization *are* bounded, and that this is an important function of, and aspect of, true political organization. Sir Henry Maine knew this and made it part of his famous distinction between primitive, stateless society and civilization. Political states become based on the principle of local contiguity as they grow beyond the feasibility of uniting new members by means of exten-

4. The classic examples may be found in M. Fortes, "The Political System of the Tallensi of the Northern Territories of the Gold Coast," and E. E. Evans-Pritchard, "The Nuer of the Southern Sudan," both in their *African Political Systems* (1940).

A more recent volume is devoted entirely to segmentary societies in Africa. This is John Middleton and David Tait's *Tribes without Rulers: Studies in African Segmentary Systems* (1958).

sions of kinship (Maine, 1861, p. 109). Many anthropologists have disagreed with Maine on the grounds that many primitive societies are made up of families, bands, and lineages that *are* firmly based on bounded territories. But this is beside the point: Maine clearly did not mean that primitive peoples had no conceptions of territorial boundaries at all, but that these constituent units, territorial or not, were not consistently united to each other within a boundary that enclosed the permanent political entity, whereas one of the important aspects of a state or government is the strong sense of the area within which its laws are enforced and which it defends. The pliability of egalitarian society, the great variations in its scope depending on the nature of the political problem, is dramatically illustrated in the variety of the responses of these societies to the shocking arrival of European colonists in the Americas, Africa, and Oceania.

Primitive states and chiefdoms are bounded, governed, and permanently established to a much greater degree than the egalitarian societies, and thus they offer possibilities for invaders to preserve such populations for exploitation. They may do this by replacing the governing body with their own, or more usually and more successfully, leaving the ruling group in power, as little modified as possible. This form of "indirect rule" was practiced by the Spaniards in Mexico and Peru,[5] by the English most notably in West Africa, Kenya, and Rhodesia, and by missionaries in Hawaii, Tonga, and Tahiti.

But egalitarian societies offered no such possibilities and their adaptations to the invaders are striking illustrations of their alternative capacities for "fission and fusion." Two polar responses actually happened repeatedly: In some situations, large confederations were made of a size that were never achieved under purely

5. Inasmuch as the Spaniards were able to exploit the native Mexicans and Peruvians, whereas the English were not able to exploit the native North Americans, the English promulgated the famous "black legend," that the Spaniards were cruel and exploitative and the English correspondingly benevolent. I have argued elsewhere that this exploitation in Latin America and its relative absence in Anglo America were due to the nature of the native societies: The Mexican and Peruvian Indians had well-developed states, but the North American Indians had egalitarian societies except for some weakly developed chiefdoms in the southeastern United States and the northwest coast (Service 1971, ch. 6).

aboriginal conditions; in other situations, when confederations could not withstand the kind of pressure being applied, the tribes separated instead into small units, the better to escape defeat. One thinks immediately of the Abnaki, Mohigan, Creek, and especially the Iroquoian confederacies in eastern North America and of the more ephemeral confederations of the Great Plains (such as the great multitribal army that massacred General Custer's army) as examples of the former response. The Ojibwa of the Upper Great Lakes, however, unable to cope with either the whites or the confederated Indians, fell apart so early in the colonial epoch that they have since become well-known ethnological cases of an "individualized" and "fragmented" culture.[6]

There are excellent examples of the two processes in the American West, especially in the Great Basin of Nevada and adjacent parts of Utah and Idaho. The historical disturbance came later than in the lands further to the east and therefore descriptions have come down to us describing a more purely aboriginal situation. (It was detailed by Lewis and Clark in 1805 in the northern part of the basin, by Alexander Ross in 1824–25, and later by others.) The Indians of the basin spoke the same Shoshonean language, and their aboriginal culture and social organization was generically similar. But we have known them ethnologically as very different kinds of societies, because of the very different responses to the coming of the white man to the area.

Some of the Basin Shoshone acquired horses from New Mexico (and later firearms by trade from the north) and expanded their hunting ranges so greatly and their subsistence base so markedly that they came to resemble the mobile, warlike buffalo hunters of the Great Plains. These were the tribes known to us later as Utes. With their new way of subsistence, as well as the larger societies thus made possible, they were able to defend themselves and their ranges effectively for a long time against the whites and other Indians as well. So strong did they become, finally, that they became near-professional predators, raiding whites for guns, horses, knives, and so on, but also raiding other Indians. One of the most striking of their enterprises was to go into the central

6. See Harold Hickerson's (1960, 1962) documentary accounts of this early process.

basin of Nevada, a near-desert where refugee, unmounted Shoshone had retreated, and to round up these Indians to transport them to Santa Fe for sale as slaves.[7]

These latter, the unmounted Indians, are known today as Paiutes and Western Shoshone. Because of an advantageous location, the Shoshone now known as Utes acquired horses and firearms earlier than the others. This put the horseless Indians to flight. They could not get enough men and horses together into a viable organization that could compete with the Utes because the Utes were able to prevent it. (When the Shoshone did find a horse, they ate it.) The organization that resulted was the fragmented, isolated-family form described in the famous monograph by Julian H. Steward.[8]

An interesting instance of the fission-fusion responses occurred in the northern part of the Basin-Plateau area, interesting because an Indian volunteered the same functional explanation of the changes that we here are proposing. A "Ban-at-tee" (Northern Paiute), quoted by Alexander Ross in 1824, said: "We can never venture into the open plains for fear of the Blackfoot and Piegans, and for that reason never keep horses." In 1825, a Ban-at-tee explained to Ross that his people lived in hiding because "were we to live in large bands, we should easily be discovered" (Ross 1956, pp. 176, 277–78).

In South America, egalitarian tribes of horticulturalists inhabited the lowland jungles, and nomadic hunting-gathering bands the savannahs and southern pampas. As in North America, responses tended to become polarized at the extremes of a fusion-fission continuum. Araucanians in Chile and western Argentina and the Puelche and Tehuelche of central Argentina are well-known examples of durable large-scale federations that made strong, hence aggressive (and therefore later epitomized in ethnology as "warlike"), predatory tribes.

On the other hand, some of the more remote areas became refuges for fragmented tribes. These are most notably the upper Xingu region, the Matto Grosso, the Montaña, and the Gran

7. Farnum as quoted by Steward (1938, p. 9).

8. *Basin-Plateau Socio-Political Groups* (1938). The above explanation differs from Steward's; he believed the social fragmentation was caused by the scarcity of food.

Chaco. More clearly even than in the Great Basin instances, the fragmentation of these peoples was not a consequence of the nature of the food supply, as Steward would have it, but defensive fissioning.[9]

In Africa the situation was quite different because of the greater numbers of kingdoms and chiefdoms (which often confederated to become kingdoms, most notably in coastal West Africa and in Southeast Africa). Refuge areas for the weaker societies were in Southwest Africa, the Congo jungles, and mountainous parts of East Africa. Again it seems clear that fragmentation was a form of adaptation to a political-military dominance of others, not due to the nature of the food supply.[10]

In order that the fission-fusion principle not be taken too simply as the only characteristic response of primitive peoples to invading Europeans, we should insist, rather parenthetically, that one of the most ordinary causes of fragmentation was simple decimation due to European diseases. But when this happened we still find, frequently, that the alternative adaptive responses of confederation versus fragmentation were still possible. Confederations of unrelated people, the remnants of former kinship societies, sometimes took place, although more usually the toll of diseases resulted in a society so demographically weakened that the offense-defense polity was weighted toward defensive retreat, and hence toward continued or further fragmentation. But in any case, our emphasis here is on the more purely political practices, particularly so as to widen the ethnological relevance of the very useful fusion-fission political principle whose application heretofore has been confined to the societies termed "segmentary."

But beware of this difference: Evans-Pritchard and Fortes were talking about societies that characteristically altered their composition frequently as part of an ongoing equilibrium system with respect to different political events—their label "segmentary" thus characterizes a *type of society.* But in this chapter we are talking about the political *process as such,* and it matters not that in many of the societies mentioned fusion or fission happened importantly only once in their histories, so that they cannot in the

9. Carneiro (1961).

10. Evidences are spelled out in greater detail in Service (1971, ch. 10).

previous sense be regarded as segmentary *types* of societies. We will therefore reserve the term *segmental,* in the Durkheimian (1933) sense, for the kinds of societies composed of equal and similar component groups (normally kin groups like clans or lineages). Because they are segmental in *type* they may exhibit the segmentary *process* more frequently than other kinds of societies.

Note that I have not tried to be exhaustive about the varieties of political processes in egalitarian segmental society. The present chapter is intended only to describe very generally the salient characteristics of these societies as they are relevant to the major point to be pursued in subsequent chapters—the origin of, and nature of, formal political inventions as related to the origin of, and nature of, civilization. This chapter therefore has endeavored to present some features of *not*-civilization, hoping they will be useful in thinking about *pre*-civilization, which in turn would be useful in thinking about what political habits the early states had to work with.

4

The Institutionalization of Power

RELATIONSHIPS based on differential power exist actually or potentially in all human groups. All families, of course, have internal dominant-subordinate relationships, based primarily on age and sex differences. In interfamily relationships on the band and tribal (segmental) level, the prevailing ideology and etiquette presses toward equality in social interactions, so there is no formal hierarchy of authority or other power above the level of individual families. Leaders, as discussed in the previous chapter, are ephemeral, in action only sporadically and then usually in the context only of their special spheres of competence. The power inherent in their persons renders Max Weber's original concept of charisma an appropriate designation. The society's assumption that their leaders' abilities are in fact superior accords them power. But this kind of power is so limited and so personal in most primitive societies that it is best termed *influence.*

How does an influential person come to occupy an *office,* so that as his charisma wanes the office can be filled by someone else? In other words, how does personal power become depersonalized power, corporate and institutionalized? How does a high achieved status become an ascribed status? In more societal terms, the question is: How does an egalitarian, segmental society become an hierarchical society with permanently ascribed differential ranks of high and low statuses? Still in social terms: How can we account for the "origin of the inequality of the social classes," as Gunnar Landtman entitles his work on this problem (1938). All of these questions refer to aspects of the same bureaucratic characteristic: As a form of personal power is finally established and institutionalized there will appear, in time, various subsidiary offices, forming an hierarchy. This hierarchy of offices, in all chiefdoms, was hereditary in terms of succession, and thus permanent social strata came into being.

This is a conception of bureaucracy that is rather more loose than Weber had it; especially in not citing such modern criteria as full regularization, salary, appointments, and so on (Weber 1946, pp. 196–204). The emphasis here is on a graded hierarchy and the related jurisdictions that are "offices"; that is, posts *instituted* to insure their continuity beyond the period of the competencies of the individual incumbents. This is only a part, though an important one, of Weber's conception.

Hierarchy and Authority

We find tendencies in some segmental societies that in certain circumstances might logically become aggrandized to create at least the beginnings of an hierarchical society. Above all, it seems likely that an individual who had acquired a personal following would like to have his own descendants bask in the same glory. A New Guinea tribe, as described by Kenneth Read, exemplifies this point particularly well.

Among the Gahuku-Gama of the Eastern Highlands, the normal authority system is that of standard egalitarian society, seniority among males—a familistic conception based on age-sex statuses. Read says (1959, p. 427):

> But beyond this level of segmentation authority is achieved. The most important men are "big men" or "men with a name," individuals who attract followers and wield influence because, in the first instance,

they possess qualities which their fellows admire. There is so[illegible] pectation that a son will succeed his father. People believe th[illegible] character of the parent is transmitted to his offspring, and a m[illegible] eminence may be likely to seek and to encourage in his son the q[illegible]ties which inspire confidence and dependence. Indeed, the son of a "big man" may have a slight advantage over others—access to greater wealth, for example—and various pressures may induce him to emulate his father.

Read's point, however, is that charisma still wins, normally, because in a society that is "tradition-directed," in Riesman's familiar terminology, it is the "autonomous" individuals, superior as leaders, who usually win out. The "strength" of a man may be manifested or proved in various contexts, of which at one time warfare was probably the most important. Dancing ability and gift-giving have continued to be important institutionalized occasions for demonstrating superiority. Gift-giving "places the recipient under an obligation to the donor, who, for the time being, has a measure of advantage over the other person. This applies equally—perhaps more clearly—to gift-giving between groups" (ibid., p. 428). Read elaborates interestingly about the strains and tensions that occur in a type of society that is essentially still egalitarian ("equivalence" governs the relations of age-mates and intergroup contacts) but that grants more prestige to leadership than more egalitarian societies.

In some New Guinea tribes the "big-man" is called a "center-man," focusing more attention on the circumstance, gift-giving, that is so closely associated with the nearly achieved institutionalization of this form of personal power. He is a center-man in the sense that he attracts a cluster of followers. His bigness is manifested in various ways, but the most notable are the giveaway feasts that demonstrate his ability to attract goods, especially pigs, from his followers in order to give a lavish feast to some other group. In this, the competitive aspect, and the fact that he or his group will receive goods in turn at some other time for him to redistribute, the feasts resemble the well-known *potlatch* of the American Indians of the North Pacific Coast.[1]

1. The exaggerated status rivalry manifested in the North American Northwest Coast potlatches seems to have been caused by a breakdown in the social structure (involving primogeniture, ranking by birth order, and

At any given time, a big-man and his followers may resemble an embryonic *chiefdom,* as defined in chapter 2: leadership is centralized, statuses are arranged hierarchically, and there is to some degree a hereditary aristocratic ethos. The big-man's group is much smaller, usually hundreds rather than a thousand or so, but a more important distinction is that since it rests on a purely personal form of power it is short-lived and unstable as a structure. Above all, since the power of the big-man is his charismatic magnetism, he has no formal means to enforce his authority and his command elicits only a voluntary response from his followers.[2]

How could a big-man turn an apparent embryonic chiefdom into a real one? The answer, as suggested by Read above, seems to lie in the tendency for people to believe that the character of a man is transmitted to his sons, particularly to his first-born. A review of the well-known chiefdoms of Polynesia and Micronesia, the southeastern United States, the islands and coasts of the Caribbean, many African societies, and Central Asian pastoralists reveals that inheritance of status by primogeniture must be a nearly universal feature of chiefdoms.[3] It is entirely reasonable to suppose that as this natural tendency toward primogeniture becomes stabilized as a custom or rule, just by that much has the group increased the stability and power of its leadership over time—and probably its size as well—as it has institutionalized the power of its leadership.

---

the chiefdom form of organization), which left many hereditary statuses open for occupancy. Population loss due to European diseases was a large factor in this breakdown.

In addition, the amount of European trade goods coming into the society in exchange for sea otter pelts created opportunities for ambitious potlatchers to achieve prestige. It is entirely possible that the areas in New Guinea where big-man status rivalry was strong were also areas of a certain amount of structural breakdown.

A good discussion of the big-man system of the Tiv of Nigeria is found in Bohannan (1958).

2. A classic report on big-man activities in the Solomon Islands is recommended reading: see "A Leader in Action" by Douglas Oliver (1955, pp. 422–439).

For accounts of the functions of potlatches on the Northwest Coast see Suttles (1960, 1968), Piddocke (1965), and Vayda (1967).

3. There are a few matrilineal chiefdoms with inheritance and succession moving to sister's son, but it seems to be normally the sister's *eldest* son. The line doesn't matter greatly, since the ranking by relative age is what gives the lineage its basic distinctiveness.

Redistribution also seems to be closely allied to the rise of and perpetuation of leadership. And to the extent that redistribution is extended and formalized, so may be the power of the leader, as his position as redistributor becomes more useful or necessary. Conversely, the better the leadership, and the more stable, the more it may be instrumental in extending and formalizing the exchange system. And of course once the society comes to depend heavily on the system, it depends on the continuity of the leadership.

Sedentary chiefdoms normally inhabit areas of variegated natural resources, with numerous ecological niches requiring local and regional symbiosis.[4] Some are located in mountain valleys with variations in altitude, in northerly or southerly exposure, in access to streams or lakes, and so on. Others are found in coastal regions with highly variegated land and sea resources, requiring overall coordination and redistribution in order to effectively hunt whales, net schools of halibut, or trap, smoke, and box salmon (the latter, for instance, during the tremendous spawning runs on the northwest coast of North America). The strong suggestion where this kind of distribution occurs is that certain geographic circumstances will favor the development of redistribution, and when combined with embryonic leadership like the big-man system, will tend to promote leadership toward a status hierarchy with an institutionalized system of central power. It may have typically happened, details aside, just so.[5]

Figure 1 shows a mountain valley with a rapid stream gradually slowing and meandering over a rich alluvial bottom and finally forming a swamp at the lower end of the valley. At the

4. The lowland Maya may seem exceptional, but their case will be "explained away" in chapter 10. "Sedentary" was specified because some chiefdoms are nomadic herders. It would seem that such herder-predator groups require not only good permanent leadership for their military adventures, but also for the important and frequent redistribution of booty and herds.

5. There are so many ethnological examples of chiefdoms in this kind of ecological setting, a setting which so stimulates a regional symbiosis, that I chose this model for the illustrative discussion to follow (cf. Sahlins 1963; cf. also Patterson's discussion of the Peruvian valleys [1973, pp. 95–100]). But it should be noted that diversification and specialization of local skills in a geographically homogeneous environment could provide the same redistributional impetus. This would be so especially when combined with the necessity for highly organized long-distance trade in necessities (see Rathje 1972).

upper end of the valley is a flint outcrop, and four miles away at the lower end of the valley the swamp hosts an array of fine reeds for arrowshafts, as well as food and cover for migratory waterfowl.

A horticultural hamlet has long occupied the bottomlands, growing an assortment of maize, beans, squash, peanuts, tobacco, and a few spices and herbs. This hamlet, A, eventually grew to the point that a daughter hamlet, B, was founded farther downstream where the land was not quite so good for maize, being boggier, but with the compensation of better tobacco, good fishing, more waterfowl, and good reeds. Next, a related group comes over the mountains and are peacefully allowed to settle in the northern end. This group, C, finds that maize, beans, and squash do only fairly well in the rocky soil, and tobacco not at all. The proximity to good forest hunting, especially for deer, is a compensation, as is the presence of the flint outcrop for stone tools and projectile points.

This simple sketch will do. Assuming that peaceful relations prevail, presents will be exchanged reciprocally among families of the three hamlets. A is not so dependent on the exchanges as the others, however, having a better all-around agricultural production, and being equidistant between the localized hunting and flint areas of the upper valley and the ducks, reeds, and tobacco of the lower. These desirable items would be exchanged in balanced reciprocity among the villages, but village A is in a particularly advantageous position. Not only is its status highest, because it is the original site, and its production higher, because it is in the best all-around location, but for these reasons it may also be larger. In addition, being centrally located it can more easily receive B's specialties than can C, and receive C's specialities better than can B. Other things equal, the reciprocities are likely to go from A to B and back, and A to C and back. A, then, by simply storing the goods acquired from B and later giving a part of them to C (along with some of its own production), gradually becomes in part at least the "magazine" of the valley, and A's reciprocities at that time turn into true redistribution. If A village has an adequate big-man, the situation turns very much to his advantage, raising his status and helping perpetuate his position. Meanwhile, the local specialization is so advantageous that it

FIGURE 1 / *Sketch of Villages in Area of Diversified Resources*

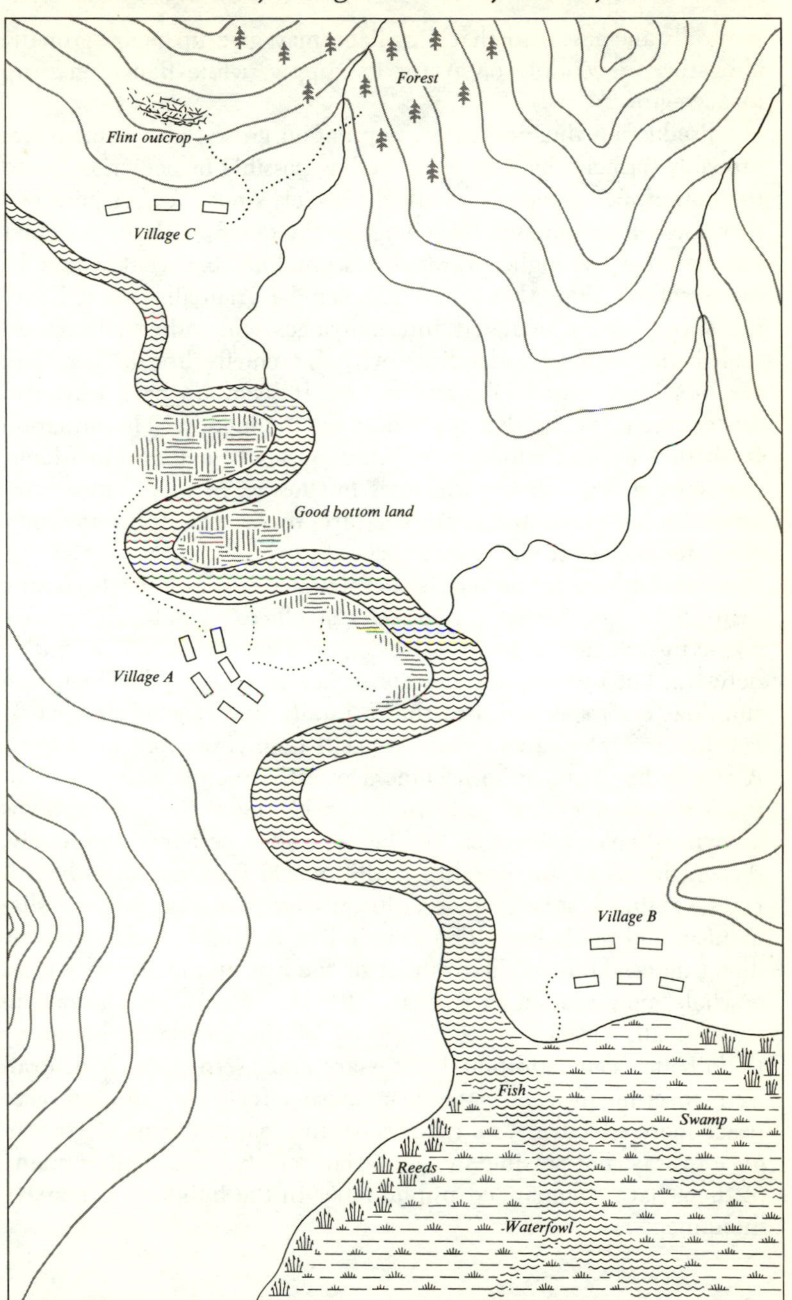

naturally increases, so that C village may give up maize-growing altogether, depending on A for its supply, while B may give up tobacco-growing.

Production thus increases, population grows, new hamlets are probably formed (by fission, as well as possibly by accretion), and the power of A—and above all, the society's *need* for A's power—increases proportionately. A village is the *chiefly* village. A's chief has founded the highest-ranked descent line, for what would be more natural than that A's oldest son be gradually trained into the succession? Calculated intermarriages with other villages establish high-ranked cadet lines with B's chiefly line higher than C's, C's higher than D's, and so on. It seems to be a universal aristocratic principle that the oldest are the highest. This situation is abetted by a circumstance found normally among chiefdoms, that sons of high aristocratic lines but lowest in inheritance prospects (a last-born, for example) are those who form the new daughter villages or marry into them.

As charismatic power is perpetuated in a line, becoming instituted as an inherited hierarchy of offices, it not only can increase the effectiveness of the local specialization and redistributive network, but increasingly take on other tasks as well. Chiefs can subsidize craft specialties so that a family line of good flint workers, for example, can increase its skill by giving more time to it. A chiefly line is likely to become a priestly line, as well, interceding with its ancestral gods in favor of the society. Chiefdoms known ethnologically seem to be typically, perhaps universally, theocracies. Ancestor worship is the typical form the priestly cult takes, adding it as a sort of cultural overlay to the original shamanism and mythology. The chiefly line is usually considered the direct descendants of the founder of the line and of the society as a whole, now exalted in status as the major deity. Such conceptions greatly strengthen the capacity of the governing hierarchy to do better some additional necessary and useful jobs. A centralized government can make war more effectively, can preserve peace more effectively, and can solve internal problems of governance in ways not possible in egalitarian society. Most visibly, many of them have commanded public labor in the building of massive monuments.

A chiefdom in good working order seems to be held together because it can accomplish the above functions well, especially redistribution—here, in fact, is the organismic model of society so beloved of the classical sociologists. The chiefdom was a very widespread form of organization, possibly because, being so successful in comparison to egalitarian tribes, it transformed its neighbors, or neighbors transformed themselves in emulation. It is also possible that a successful new chiefdom might go on expanding by accretion as well as internal growth to the point where it could not rule successfully. If such growth and dissolution were in fact usual, it would help account for the spread of chiefdoms: An expanding chiefdom transforms its new parts, if they were egalitarian societies, into small-scale replicas of the original central chiefdom simply by adopting their leaders into the prevailing hierarchy. If the whole splits into parts, for whatever reasons, the parts will all be chiefdoms, however small. It is probably the cycle of expansion and contraction that caused chiefdoms to appear rather suddenly and to diffuse so rapidly in the archaeological record.

Redistributional leadership and status, stabilized through time by primogeniture, transforms the kinship structure of the society. Thus the lineages or clans of egalitarian society become, in Paul Kirchhoff's words (1959), "conical clans," wherein all collateral lines of descent as well as individuals in the families are ranked in terms of the birth order of the founders and of the order of each successive generation of perpetuators of the line and its proliferating cadet lines. This genealogical ranking is familiar in history among the ancient Celtic peoples of Great Britain, in the European aristocratic class, and apparently among the Semitic "tribes" of the Old Testament. The use of the term "clan" by Kirchhoff presents semantic difficulties because it is normally used for the egalitarian kinship order of "common" (equal or generalized) descent from a founder. Raymond Firth (1936) called the conical group a *ramage,* from an Old French word meaning "branch." His term seems preferable because its etymology calls attention to the "branching and rebranching" of the genealogy, ranked according to distance from the "parent stem" (see figure 2). But Kirchhoff was quite correct in his argument that the "conical clan" (ramage) can evolve to a higher order, the state and archaic civilization. (He was wrong, however, in his assumption that the egalitarian clan was a "dead end." The solution must be, simply, that a chiefdom stage of development was interposed between egalitarian society and the state.)

FIGURE 2 / *Scheme of Ranking of Chiefly Ramage, Reflecting in Genealogy the Rank and Precedence of the Villages*

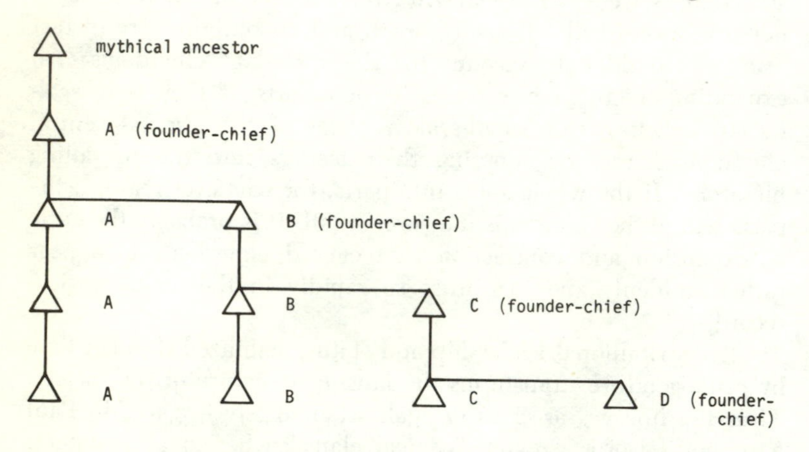

Evidently the chiefdom and its ramage kinship structures are governments in some senses, differing from peoples in a "state of nature." Obviously some new political inventions were created. We have already mentioned hereditary inequality, primogeniture, permanent leadership, and hierarchical authority. In these respects, and in some others, chiefdoms would seem to resemble societies of the historical feudal epoch in Europe. Inasmuch as Marx, notably, and others as well, had invested this feudal epoch with the characteristics of an evolutionary stage preceding the capitalist nation-state, it may be well to discuss briefly the differences and similarities between chiefdoms and feudal societies. There are, in fact, some interesting parallels, although the discontinuity remains significant—mainly because European feudalism was a particular historical variety of a political type, but not a stage itself.

Primitive Chiefdoms and Feudalism

European feudalism, of which eleventh-century France is often taken as the classical form, combined three distinct characteristics, any one of which, and sometimes two in combination, can be found in abundance in the world of primitive and peasant communities. These are: (1) the building of an hierarchy of personal relationships of a peculiarly voluntary type, usually called *vassalage;* (2) a landholding regime of *fiefs,* featuring the relationship of agricultural workers to it as serfs; and (3) an economic system of local, near-sufficiency—usually called the *manorial system*—which (like the political system) remained decentralized after the breakup of the Roman Empire.

The first feature of feudalism, vassalage, was the one emphasized by the great French authority, Marc Bloch, who said (1932, p. 204):

> In the absence then of a strong state, of blood ties capable of dominating the whole life and of an economic system founded upon money payments, there grew up in Carolingian and post-Carolingian society relations of man to man of a peculiar type. The superior individual granted his protection and divers material advantages that assured a subsistence to the dependent directly or indirectly; the inferior pledged various prestations or various services and was under a general obligation to render aid. These relations were not always freely assumed nor did they imply a universally satisfactory equilibrium between the two parties. Built upon authority, the feudal regime never ceased to contain a great number of constraints, violences and abuses. However, this idea of the personal bond, hierarchic and synallagmatic [bilateral] in character, dominated European feudalism.

The second, the tenure system of fiefs, was, as implied in Bloch's definition above, closely related to the purely personal bond of vassalage. To some writers (especially Marxists), however, the land tenure system is more the essence of feudalism, however importantly related to vassalage, because it refers to *relations of production.* Such an authority as Maurice Dobb (1946), for instance, uses serfdom, the involuntary form of dependence in land tenure, as fully synonymous with feudalism.

But the relationship of vassalage to the fief and serfdom in

European feudalism is not a necessary one in the rest of the world. The big-man system of New Guinea and the patron-client relationship in many areas of Africa, for example, are very reminiscent of the voluntary "followership" of feudalistic vassalage. But they have nothing, or very little, to do with any kind of dependent land tenure system. On the other hand, we are familiar with many modern cases of fieflike land tenure systems featuring wealthy privileged owners and debt-bound serflike peasants (*latifundia* and *hacienda* systems in colonial Latin America come to mind), but which may have no vassalage whatsoever in the system.

The third characteristic of feudalism is the relative self-sufficiency of the great manors, left high and dry after the breakup of the political and economic structure of the empire. This kind of local reconstitution after the dissolution of some greater polity has happened again and again in history, with subsequent partial reconstitution always a likelihood. If that were all that defined feudalism, then we must conclude that it is always a very probable historical phase of any empire, but certainly not a stage in the *development* of a polity—it may be best construed, in fact, as a (possibly temporary) devolution rather than evolution.

The historical peculiarity of Europe's feudal devolution, as compared with other more plain devolutions, such as that of twelfth-century Japan, was that it involved a former imperial union of societies of two disparate kinds, the Northern European (especially the Germanic) chiefdoms and the more southerly parts of the classical Greco-Roman civilization.

European feudalism, then, was historically of a very complex, and perhaps unique, sort. For this reason it cannot be considered a stage in evolution, or even a usual case of devolution. Only one of its elements, voluntaristic vassalage, has widespread counterparts in the rest of the world. Vassalage seems typically—perhaps universally—a feature of those societies variously denominated as big-man or patron-client systems. And when these systems become institutionalized as the power bureaucracies of hereditary chiefdoms, they resemble in certain important respects the hereditary aristocracies of late or postfeudal times in Europe. But none of these chiefdoms combine those features with the complicated land tenure systems and the devotion in political unity of European feudalism closely enough to be classed with it. This is not to say that the parallels are without interest.

Law

As we saw in the previous chapter, "man in a state of nature" is not an unfettered, natural man. Very powerful forces of social control inhere in small face-to-face societies; this is especially so in primitive societies where the individual normally spends his whole life among his kinsmen. Since escape is impossible he cannot recover by moving to some new group the esteem he might have lost by a social mistake in his own group. Cooperation, alliance, love, reciprocities of all kinds are totally important to the survival of any individual in primitive society. This must be why such people seem so extraordinarily sensitive to the reactions of the group to any social action. Praise and blame, affection and withdrawal, and other such socio-psychological sanctions are extremely powerful reinforcers in small societies of stable membership, and it has been noted over and over by many observers of egalitarian societies how carefully social customs, especially in etiquette, are observed—"custom is king."

Sidney Hartland's *Primitive Law* (1924) is perhaps the strongest exponent of the idea that uncoercive custom is the primitives' law. In a typical statement (p. 138), he says that the primitive "is hemmed in on every side by the customs of his people, he is bound in the chains of immemorial tradition . . . these fetters are accepted by him as a matter of course; he never seeks to break forth."

Another ethnologist, W. H. R. Rivers, in his *Social Organization,* says (1924, p. 169): "Among such peoples as the Melanesians there is a group sentiment which makes unnecessary any definite social machinery for the exertion of authority, in just the same manner as it makes possible the harmonious working of a communal ownership and insures the peaceful character of a communistic system of sexual relations."

Statements like these were a great annoyance to Bronislaw Malinowski (1934), who argued against the idea that primitive peoples were so enthralled by custom. He also argued tellingly that powerful negative, though not physical, sanctions do exist in "savage society."[6] I think he is correct that there are powerful negative sanctions, such as, importantly, the withdrawal of normal reciprocities.[7] But since these are not instituted and administered by official authority with privileged force, there are many critics of Malinowski who would deny that law in found in primitive, prestate societies.

A modern specialist, E. A. Hoebel, sees law as composed of three necessary elements: privileged force; official authority; and regularity (1954, p. 28). Robert Redfield, like Hoebel trained in law but practicing ethnology, states that "law is . . . recognizable in form: in formal statement of the rules, and in forms for securing compliance with the rules or satisfaction or punishment for their breach" (1967, p. 5). These definitions do not argue explicitly, however, that the coercion of "privileged force" and "punishment" come about necessarily with the advent of the state. They are not conceived in such evolutionary terms.

It may be that only evolutionists are convinced of the connection between legal punitive force and the state. Walter Goldschmidt says (1959, p. 99): "A true state involves the legitimate monopoly of power in the hands of its rulers." Stanley Diamond would definitely separate custom from law, with this distinction defining rigorously the difference between primitive and civilized societies: "Custom—spontaneous, traditional, personal, commonly known, corporate, relatively unchanging—is the modality of primitive society; law is the instrument of civilization, of political

6. He should have said, in the savage society he studied (the Trobriand Islanders); Malinowski too frequently generalizes about the primitive world using evidence from this single society—which, it may be relevant to note, was a low-level chiefdom.

7. It may be useful to quote one of Malinowski's statements on this point (1934, p. xxxvi):

"This positive aspect of compliance to primitive custom, the fact that obedience to rules is baited with premiums, that it is rewarded by counterservices, is as important, in my opinion, as the study of punitive sanctions; and these latter consist not in a punishment inflicted deliberately *ad hoc,* but rather in the natural retaliation of non-compliance in counter-services, of criticism and dissatisfaction within the relationship and within the institution. Any *mala fide* failure to discharge the duties fully and adequately meets with a whole series of rebukes, reprisals and disservices which must needs end in a complete disorganisation of the cooperative group, whether this be the family, the guild or the tribe."

society sanctioned by organized force, presumably above society at large, and buttressing a new set of social interests. Law and custom both involve the regulation of behavior but their characters are entirely distinct; no evolutionary balance has been struck between developing law and custom, whether traditional or emergent" (1971, p. 47).

Many others have argued in this vein at length. And it would seem that the pre-Malinowski view of the significance of custom may be making a comeback. Simpson and Stone, historians of law, state (1948, p. 3): "Despite the recent challenge of Malinowski, the orthodox explanation of the effectiveness of social control in a kin-organized society still seems the most satisfactory. The pressure of a body of custom sanctified by a belief in its supernatural origin points to social opinion and the fear of the gods as the two major weapons in the armory of rudimentary social control."

Certain problems related to the custom versus law argument are semantic, so it may be well to get them out of the way before confronting the ethnological evidence, which will require some new kind of adjudication of the argument. First of all, what does *custom* mean? We do not want to bother now with an individual's habits ("It is my custom to take a walk before breakfast"); we are concerned with the conventions of the collectivity. But these may be of two distinct kinds. Morris Ginsberg was conscious of this problem when he decided that the term *usage* would refer to "those actions habitual to members of a community, which do not possess normative character or lack the sanction of moral constraint," and that *custom* would mean "not merely a prevailing habit of action or behavior, but . . . a judgment upon action or behavior. . . . Custom, in other words, is *sanctioned* usage" (1921, pp. 106ff.).

This dichotomy is suggestive of some real differences but seems unnecessarily strict, for it could be argued that *any* deviation from conventional usage may be sanctioned to some extent in some society by some kind of disapproval from somebody. It would be hard to predict, cross-culturally, just which deviations from normal behavior would elicit strong public negative sanctions: singing a traditional song incorrectly; not wearing the "proper" hair style; a mistake in greeting style; belching; killing your clan's totem. A breach of any of these, and any of a thousand more, could be severely punished by the collectivity in some society or other. But then some of those thousand customs might also be ignored in the breach. I shall try to avoid this problem by always using the modifier *sanctioned* when indeed sanctions are attached to a custom.

Sanctioned customs are forms of social control that are reinforced positively or negatively. The positive sanctions are normally some kind of approval by the public, or some part of it. Negative sanctions are disapproval of a breach of custom, normally withdrawals of friendship and the expected reciprocities that Malinowski emphasized above. Again, as in the case of positive sanctions, the disapproval is a social punishment—by the public, or some part of it. That is, the sanctions are not applied by an official authority who stands as a "third party"; the only third party in segmental society is a person or group who has a familistic sort of authority, such as a wise, aged relative who might work as conciliator or arbitrator.

Law, on the other hand, implies a centralized, permanent authority standing above the familistic statuses.[8] It is in making the clear distinction between the rule of custom in segmental societies and the addition of law to custom in hierarchical societies that the emphasis on forceful coercion applied by the state was created. As the famous historian of law Paul Vinogradoff put it (1920–22, vol. 1, p. 95): "The state monopolizes the making and enforcing of laws by coercion, and did not exist in ancient times." Force and a political structure, the state, that monopolizes its use are usually, therefore, important elements in definitions of law that make the distinction between sanctioned custom and law.

But none of those who make this distinction have recognized the problem posed by the chiefdoms that apparently precede the state. A chiefdom stage lies between the segmental, egalitarian society and the coercive state. In a chiefdom we find one essential of true law, the authority structure that can act as a third party above the familistic level. But chiefdoms lack the coercive physical sanctions related to the monopoly of force practiced by states.

8. Apparently this is what the historian of law, William Seagle (1946), had in mind when he insisted on the significance of a *court* as the central element in law.

Note that this assumption about chiefdoms and states, and the question of the universality of the chiefdom stage in evolution, is a "given" at this point in our discussion. Its factual basis will be more fully explored in succeeding chapters.

It seems useful to divide law into its two kinds, public law and private law. Public law will refer here to the legal problems that persons (individuals or groups) have with the authority structure. Its context of greatest significance for our present purposes is that of reinforcement, as in cases of treason or *lèse majesté.* Private law will refer to legal contentions between persons (individuals or groups) themselves, which are mediated by the authority structure. (The functions of public and private law in chiefdoms, with examples, will be discussed more fully in the sections of this chapter titled "Reinforcement" and "Mediation.")

Inasmuch as we are at present interested in chiefdoms, it seems evident that we need a definition of law that will apply to them, but which will still enable us to talk about the differences between chiefdoms and states. Leopold Pospisil's experiences in the ethnology of law (1972) are useful here, particularly since his major work on the Kapauku Papuans (1958) faces the problem of the present chapter, since it is devoted to a chiefdomlike society (but rather a low-level one). He describes cases of conflict resolution as *legal* when the decisions possess four attributes: authority, intention of universal application, *obligatio,* and sanction (1972 and elsewhere).

Legal authority requires an individual (or group, like a council) powerful enough to enforce the verdict by persuasion or threat of force. (In a chiefdom, it should be added, a legal authority is likely to combine with this function still others of a political, military, economic, or priestly nature, and these are likely to give him various enforcive powers.) Disputes are frequently mediated by an authority who uses his powers of persuasion to induce compliance with his attempted arbitration. Such interference seems more informal and "primitive," or familistic, than if he were to render a *decision* that the litigants are forced to accept. This latter seems more legal to us, involving as it does the familiar uses of an authority working as a judge. But Pospisil points out (1972, p. 16) that in either case the producer of the solution was not the disputants but the "third party," a legal authority. It would seem, however, that the ability of the legal authority to enforce decisions rather than to function by suasion, as a kind of wise man, is a measure of the power of the hierarchy, of its ability to command.

But there is an important qualification to be made. A decision made by an authority is not for that reason necessarily legal; it may be political and thus expediently variable from one context to another. The decision partakes of greater legality if it incorporates the "intention of universal application." Whenever a previous case can be found that is similar to the case being considered, and which was satisfactorily solved, there is a normal tendency to use the earlier case as a precedent. Frequently, trouble cases may be quickly composed by an authority who simply calls attention to the earlier case. In other words, the third party in the case seems to find the solution informally, rather than by making an arbitrary decision. Even if the case "goes to court" and an authority has to render a decision more formally, it is still easier for him to get compliance, to strain his power less, when he has even a partial precedent. But the first case, the precedent-setting one, had to be a true *decision,* and if legal, always incorporates the intention of further application in like cases. (Of course it may have been a bad decision, not followed subsequently at all, but the *intention* of precedent-setting must have been there if it were to be a legal decision.) A difficulty with this criterion is that of discovering its presence (Lundsgaarde 1970).

Obligatio, the third attribute of law (ibid., pp. 22–23), "refers to that part of the legal decision that defines the rights of the entitled and the duties of the obligated parties." This is not yet sanction, but rather a statement as to the nature of the unbalanced relationship of the litigants. Sanction, while closely related, refers to the resolution of the conflict by restoring an equitable relationship. (In familiar modern courtroom terms, when a court comes to a factual verdict of "guilty" it is a statement of the disturbed *obligatio* relationship between the litigants; the actual sentencing is the imposition of the sanction.)

The attribute *obligatio* is particularly useful in discussing law in a theocracy. Much of such a society's reinforcement of its rules and social arrangements is religious, having to do with morals, conscience, and especially tabus. Violations of these are, so to speak, "crimes without victims"; the punishment of these crimes, if any, is imaginary and supernatural; and the litigious relationship is not between living persons. This is not to say that such things as religious tabus are not important: They may be so successful as a society's punishment-reward system that forceful sanctions may be only very rarely imposed. *Obligatio,* in other words, stands well apart from sanction in theocracies, in contrast to modern society, which often confounds the two.

Punitive sanction involving force is regarded by some anthropologists as the exclusive criterion of law, as we have seen, but it seems clear that while such sanction may be one of the usual ingredients of modern law, not all uses of sanction are in a legal context. Most prominently, a great many *ad hoc* political decisions carry sanctions, yet they are not law. As discussed above, political decisions are expediently variable and thus do not carry the intention of universal application, although they may impose sanctions.

Sanctions need not be always, or even often, of a physical nature. They may be economic (like fines and damages), and especially in a theocratic society, they may be psychological punishments (a public reprimand by a high priest, for example), or socially negative (as in excommunication, withdrawal of rewards, services, and normal reciprocities). Nor are the legal cases themselves in primitive society, in chiefdom theocracies especially, necessarily or even mostly concerned with physical violence. Private crimes are frequently "breaches of faith" concerning reciprocities, and public crimes, instances of *lèse majesté.* These latter crimes may be viewed in two separate ways in a theocracy: (1) a crime (as in a violation of a tabu) against the person of the paramount chief, or to a lesser extent, against someone in authority but lower in the hierarchy; and (2) an attack against any traditional custom or belief that somehow injures the authority of the ruler. (Such a thing as the breaking of a tabu is a legal offense only when there is *obligatio*—an offender and a person, like the chief, who is somehow "injured" by the act.) Such breaches of the law are usually something like expressions of contempt, or a curse, and if unpunished somehow weaken the authority system, which is largely based on ideological, supernatural, cultural grounds.

As we have seen in some of our quoted examples, emphasizing such coercive sanctions as violence in states has led these writers to identify law with force and both with states. We shall consider this in later chapters by analyzing some actual cases, but at this point we need to consider an argument of Pospisil's that has theoretical relevance. If a law is desirable to most members of a group and if they consider it binding, it may in time seem to an observer to be like a custom, in contrast to laws that may have to be enforced by the state, at least sometimes, against the will of many of the people. A customary law, according to Pospisil (1972, p. 30), is "internalized" so that not only do the people feel it desirable, but when it is broken the malefactor feels guilt or shame. If a law is too new, or for some other reason not sufficiently accepted and internalized, a forceful repression may be called for; but later, or in some other society, the same law may be upheld by conscience or public opinion alone. In times of social or demographic breakdown, for example, crimes without victims (such as public drunkenness) that had been prevented in stable times by psychological states of shame might have to be repressed by physical punishment or fines.

Thus the difference between the two kinds of laws is not qualitative and cannot be taken as exact or specific characterizations of the difference between state and primitive non-state. But we do want to bear in mind for later reference that the origin of the state may be accompanied by a sudden increase in the number of repressive laws, by more severe repression, and perhaps by new kinds of laws. And it is very likely that the new state will have a more visible, more formal, and more explicit judicial and punitive machinery. To the extent that the laws are new, they will not yet be internalized or even widely accepted, which might create further need for repression. We may at this point continue to accept this monopoly of force and the presence of a judicial apparatus as indicative of "stateness," but not necessarily of law. Both states *and* chiefdoms have the most necessary ingredient of law, a central authority that can create rules of behavior, enforce them, and judge the breaches of them.[9]

9. Morton Fried (1967, pp. 90–94) states his basic approval of Pospisil's definition of law, but disagrees with some of his applications of it to simple egalitarian societies. I agree with Fried, but think the problem is easily remedied if we make explicit now what was stated in the previous chapter: That *familistic* authority mediating *domestic* quarrels are found in all societies and are not *law*. Let us therefore add the simple proviso

Nonlegal Reinforcement

The same personal-social familistic sanctions that characterized egalitarian society remain within the component face-to-face residential groups of a chiefdom. But in addition, there are new political norms, rules, and sanctions that will reflect (in these groups) the new features of the social system, particularly those relating to the maintenance of the new hierarchy of status and authority. Also, since chiefdoms are larger and more complex than egalitarian tribes, there are new problems regarding the interrelation of groups.

One important form of punishment/reward that remains as a carry-over from the previous stage is the familistic admonishment/praise form by which an elder person guides and educates the younger toward conformity. But at one point the status of elders over youths is confused by the higher status of one person over another if he comes from an elder *descent* line but is in fact a younger person than another. It would seem that a youth simply avoids the confusion of confronting an older person (higher than he in age-status) when the elder is lower in descent-line status. It is difficult to confirm this judgment from enough examples in the ethnographic literature, but the very absence of examples may bespeak such avoidance. On the other hand, in some chiefdoms—those of Polynesia come to mind—young aristocrats could be deliberately cruel to elderly commoners, which suggests that perhaps the latter do the avoiding. But above all, the tabu system of extreme social distance between ranks is the best example (to be discussed in chapter 9).

The development of a permanent redistributional system not only seems to have been closely associated with the origin of chiefdoms, but also contributes powerfully to the ongoing maintenance and reinforcement of the sociopolitical authority hierarchy,

---

that legal authority is *supra*-familistic. Another possible amendment is implied in our present chapter: that the authority and sanctions need not be *secular* alone (as Pospisil and others believe); in chiefdoms, and undoubtedly in the archaic civilizations, the authority is typically sacerdotal and the sanctions supernatural. Our more evolutionary perspective thus excludes from formal-legal types of societies certain segmental examples and admits more hierarchical societies than Pospisil's.

as was emphasized earlier. It reinforces the structure mainly in two important ways: (1) the authority structure is also the structure of main and lesser redistributors—it is the basic supply system—and hence it is obviously necessary to the whole society; (2) allied to this aspect of the supply system is the fact that a redistributor could punish by withholding goods from any dissident subchief or group. All this is obvious enough.

Along with redistribution, one of the most powerful of the new politically integrative ingredients is ideological: the hierarchy of the authority system has become supernaturally sanctioned in mythology. The original founder becomes an ancestor-god, other ancestors are lesser gods, the living chief is nearly divine, lesser chiefs less divine, and the supernatural world and the living world are reflections of each other ("on earth as it is in heaven"). The Polynesians are the most striking examples of this arrangement. They even posited a kind of supernatural force, *mana,* which flowed from the ancestors in varying amounts of power, greater in first-borns and diminishing with each successive birth. Thus the paramount chief is the "holiest" (fullest of mana), and each lower step in the authority hierarchy is manned by a person having the appropriately lesser amount of mana.[10] Such beliefs, it may be imagined, give enormous stability to the social structure, making every status absolutely hereditary in theory, as well as mostly in fact.

Inasmuch as supernatural beings support the extant structure, additional stability is undoubtedly created by fear, by supernatural terrorism. The ancestors must be placated with sacrifices (sometimes human) and great ceremonies in their name must be held. These are evidences of the belief that the gods can punish by withholding rain or migrations of game, or by sending pests and diseases. Alternatively, the gods can also send benefits: They can bestow good luck in war, assure fertility, cure diseases, send rain, and so on. All of these and still other supernatural rewards and

10. *Mana*-like conceptions are widespread among theocracies. A particularly close analogy in Africa is found among the Tiv (see Bohannan 1958), who believe in *tsav,* an innate spiritual power held in varying amounts by individuals.

punishments are mediated by the priest-chiefs, and thus they are themselves greatly enhanced in importance.[11]

Ceremonialism in and of itself has a great socially integrating effect, especially when rituals and ceremonies involve the attendance of large numbers of people and are for the purposes of the whole society. This latter aspect is in a sense a technological function of the authority system; the priest-chief is "getting something done" toward a good harvest, for example, by assuring a rainfall after the ceremony. That is good. But he needs the presence of his people and perhaps the actual participation of large numbers of them, dancing, chanting, clapping, or praying. All this is a common effort for the common good, but *led by authority.* This kind of ceremony is thus organismic in its nature, like the redistributional system. But it also has an important social-psychological dimension as the people collaborate in large groups with little likelihood of friction under such circumstances. And apparently the larger the group the greater the social intoxication of the melting of the individual into the collectivity.

The paramount chiefs and the highest priests were frequently, though not always, the same person. But always the priesthood sanctified the chief, celebrated his life crisis rites, and in general supported the hierarchy by ritual and ceremonial means. Sometimes, as in Polynesia, priests were of special orders who resided in, and were custodians of, certain temples and images of gods on a full-time basis, but always these temples and gods were in the service of the authoritative bureaucracy, supporting it at every turn. This is not to say that there was no other religion in chiefdoms. The curing shaman of egalitarian society probably continued this "oldest profession," as did magicians, soothsayers, witches, and other practitioners of primitive supernaturalism. But these remained largely unorganized, whereas the hierarchy of priests was an important facet of the organized hierarchical society of chiefdoms.

In the classic chiefdoms the negative sanctions reinforcing the integrity of the society—the public laws—were typically

11. Netting (1972) has written a particularly good analysis of the primacy of religion in the institutionalization of power in stateless societies in Africa.

supernatural punishments such as curses or denunciations by a sacerdotal authority. The crime, something like treason in our society, was interpreted as *lèse majesté,* an offense against the person—hence the rule—of the high chief or of members of the hierarchy. In most chiefdoms, any failure to obey orders could be interpreted as an offense against the chief, and therefore against the gods. *Sacrilege* or *sin* may be an accurate conception of this kind of breach. It may well be that the hierarchy of the first chiefdoms, having the perpetuation of their regime much before their minds, soon promoted the *lèse majesté* sort of law. Hence the origin of an inchoate code of laws probably coincided with the maintenance problems of the new chiefdoms. What could be more natural, as the chiefdom expanded and secured itself, than for the leadership to expand the range of actions to be considered as "offenses against the hierarchy and the gods"? (The tabu systems of the ancient Polynesians, again, are the most complex example of this process.)[12]

Leadership

Leadership in action, normally with respect to concerted group projects, may be only sporadic in chiefdoms. But as already indicated in another context, the most significant group activity in chiefdoms is redistribution, which not only enables a leader to become a permanent fixture but also requires that he do his job well. This means that he must be able to command labor in agricultural and craft production, and then he must equitably and wisely decide how the goods are to be allocated. Among the important uses of the goods is to store certain of them, not only to later subsidize public labor and craftsmen, but as capital for uses in contingencies like war or a great feast for important visitors.

Such powers are economically and socially useful, having, as mentioned, a politically integrative effect. But the storehouse of a chief has still another political effect. David Malo, a native Hawaiian historian, describes it this way (1903, pp. 257–58):

12. A. M. Hocart said (1936, p. 139), "The Fijian chief has only to extend his precincts and interpret widely the traditional rules of ceremonial behavior in order to acquire a criminal jurisdiction, and increase his interference with the life of his subjects."

It was the practice for kings [i.e., paramount chiefs of individual islands] to build store-houses in which to collect food, fish, *tapas* [bark cloth], malos [men's loin cloths], *pa-us* [women's loin skirts], and all sorts of goods. These store-houses were designed by the Kalaimoku [the chief's principal executive] as a means of keeping the people contented, so they would not desert the king. They were like the baskets that were used to entrap the *hinalea* fish. The *hinalea* thought there was something good within the basket, and he hung round the outside of it. In the same way the people thought there was food in the store-houses, and they kept their eyes on the king. As the rat will not desert the pantry . . . where he thinks food is, so the people will not desert the king while they think there is food in his store-house.

It is evident that a well-managed redistributional system, by its very nature, contributes to solidarity. Most obvious, and most often remarked upon, is its organismic quality: The specialized parts depend on the functioning of the whole. But Malo's point is important, too. A head of a household growing an abundant surplus of yams, for example, probably does not mind too much giving up some of the surplus to the chief, since he knows he will later acquire things that he needs but does not produce. The exchange seems necessary and beneficial to the yam-grower, and his perception of the benefit to him is not in terms of his own dependence on a system or organism, but to the chief himself. Hence, "organismic solidarity" in truly political terms also results in personal loyalties to the administration.

Of course the most dramatic administrative uses of leadership—and for which the redistributional surplus is very useful—is in warfare. But we leave matters of foreign war-making and peace-making for another section of this chapter, "External Relations"; at this point we need only to refer to the role of leadership in preventing rebellions—i.e., internal, or "civil," war.

It has been mentioned that chiefdoms seem to have a propensity for growing to the point of imbalance or too much organizational stress. Perhaps they simply get too large to be governed by the still relatively primitive means of governance and communication. But this seems too vague; one wonders how, more specifically, a chiefdom breaks up. In any society, there are always some dissatisfied, dissident elements—centrifugal forces are always at work. In a large chiefdom, constituent elements are made up of little chiefdoms, replicas of the paramount chiefdom, and hence capable of their own hierarchical self-government. Some may be led by arrogant, ambitious, and able chiefs who want independence merely to fulfill themselves in successful competition; some may be genuinely oppressed or exploited, and resentful of this circumstance. Sahlins (1968, pp. 92–93) emphasizes this factor, thinking of Polynesia at about the contact period. He visions a sort of primitive class-struggle:

> Advanced Polynesian political systems were overtaxed. In Hawaii and other islands cycles of centralization-decentralization appear in the traditional histories: periodic violent dissolution of larger into smaller chiefdoms and, by the same means, periodic reconstitution of the great society. Sydney Parkinson accompanied Captain Cook to Polynesia and left an important account, but Northcote Parkinson would also have understood it. The expansion of a chiefdom seems to have entailed a more-than-proportionate expansion of the administrative apparatus and its conspicuous consumption. The ensuing drain on the people's wealth and expectations was eventually expressed in an unrest that destroyed both chief and chiefdom.

There is no way to tell how much the above kind of unrest characterized chiefdoms outside the large Polynesian Islands, nor whether even in those islands it was always the primary cause of administrative breakdown. But certainly sometimes large chiefdoms break up simply because of the desire of secondary chiefs to become paramount chiefs in an independent area of this own, for whatever reasons. As we shall see in later chapters, chiefdoms that preceded the native states in parts of Africa were given to that kind of movement. If, however, all potentially dissident groups were involved in society-wide efforts, solidarity of the whole is benefited.

One of the most visible results of the capacity of the theocratic chiefdoms to administrate is the use of labor in building public works. The most imposing and usual of these are the monuments of the theocratic order, pyramids or burial mounds and temples. The leadership apparently can as easily require a certain amount of man-days per community for a public project as it can a certain proportion of a crop—perhaps more easily, since the primitive work schedule allows for long seasons of inactivity between plantings and harvests.[13]

13. See Erasmus (1965) for interesting experiments on the building of monuments.

The levy on the public for labor must be very like the raising of an army—it is a conscription of men in either case. With respect to military affairs, it is probably unnecessary to argue that the centralized administration of chiefdoms makes for much more powerful armies—in size and in tactical coordination—than are possible in egalitarian societies, which depend on a kind of voluntarism. Chiefdoms, or at least some of them, are able to conscript a rather large proportion of able-bodies men, sometimes as age-grades, and among herding chiefdoms it would seem that nearly all grown men could be made available at certain seasons for military forays, since the herds could be watched over by women and children when in a safe place.

Mediation

It may be taken as axiomatic that because chiefdoms have a larger population and more centralization than egalitarian tribes and bands they will not only have more occasions for mediation but also a greater ability to do so. This does not mean that they create bodies of formal laws (or codes), nor that a formal court meeting and procedure is worked out, but only that we do find authority at work in the context of ending quarrels that threaten the integrity of the society. It makes a significant difference between hierarchical society and egalitarian society that the authority of the former is capable of intervention, rather than simply generalized public opinion aroused by an occasion such as a song duel or athletic contest.

As stated earlier, this discussion is essentially descriptive rather than an attempt to settle the semantic debates among anthropologists as to whether law is everywhere or is found only in states. Let us merely agree now that when a true state administers a codified set of laws with formal procedures and backed by force, an institutional structure has appeared that is visibly very distinct from a group of old men in Australian society giving some advice or help in settling an argument. Our problem is that chiefdoms lie somewhere between institutionalized modern law courts and primitive familistic customs with their informal public sanctions. All have the same mediating functions, but the means are distinct. Chiefdoms seem to have the beginnings of lawlike institutions, so that even the strictest definition of law would allow such characterizations as "inchoate law" or "law-stuff." However, we do want to talk about the system of mediation as it really is. As anthropologists repeatedly point out, there is danger of ethnocentrism if we stick too closely to modern legalistic terms when talking about primitive societies.

First of all, we should not expect to find in chiefdoms such extreme formality and explicitness in the law and legal procedures that enable us in modern society to so easily distinguish between "going to court" and "I'll tell your father on you." We must be watchful not to let sheer formalism be our only criterion of an adjudicative legal process. As an example of a relatively informal procedure that still conforms to Pospisil's criteria of adjudicative law-making, let us take an example from a New Guinea Papuan society investigated by Pospisil himself (1968, pp. 49–50):

> The Kapauku "process of law" starts usually as a quarrel. The "plaintiff" accuses the "defendant" of having performed an act which causes harm to the plaintiff's interests. The defendant denies this or brings forward justification for his action. The arguments are usually accompanied by loud shouting which attracts other people, who gather around. The close relatives and friends of the parties to the dispute take sides and present their opinions and testimony by emotional speeches or by shouting. If this sort of arguing, called by natives *mana koto,* goes on unchecked, it usually results in a stick fight . . . or in war. . . . However, in most instances, the important men from the village, and from allied communities, appear on the scene. First, they squat among the onlookers and listen to the arguments. As soon as the exchange of opinions reaches a point too close to an outbreak of violence, the rich headman steps in and starts his argumentation. He admonishes both parties to have patience and begins questioning the defendant and the witnesses. He looks for evidence that would incriminate the defendant, at the scene of the crime or in the defendant's house. . . . This activity of the authority is called *boko petai,* which can be loosely translated as "finding the evidence." Having secured the evidence and made up his mind about the factual background of the dispute, the authority starts the activity called by the natives *boko duwai,* the process of making a decision and inducing the parties to the dispute to follow it. The native authority makes a long speech in which he sums up the evidence, appeals to a rule, and then tells the parties what should be done to terminate the dispute. If the principals are not willing to comply, the authority becomes emotional and starts to shout reproaches; he makes long speeches in which evidence, rules, decisions, and threats form inducements. Indeed, the

authority may go as far as to start *wainai* (the mad dance), or change his tactics suddenly and weep bitterly about the misconduct of the defendant and the fact that he refuses to obey. Some native authorities are so skilled in the art of persuasion that they can produce genuine tears which almost always break the resistance of the unwilling party. A superficial Western observer confronted with such a situation may very likely regard the weeping headman as a culprit on trial. Thus, from the formalistic point of view, there is little resemblance between the Western court's sentence and the *boko duwai* activity of the headman. However, the effect of the headman's persuasion is the same as that of a verdict passed in our courts. There were only five cases in my material wherein the parties openly resisted and disobeyed the authority's decision.

A noticeable feature of this instance is that the authority did not himself truly *adjudicate* the matter so much as use his good influence to compose the differences of the two parties, and even involve public opinion to some extent. Having no police to back him, he exercised his power, which was that of authority alone, with considerable caution—not at all as an "authoritarian" leader. Like a good arbitrator, he tried to involve both sides in an acceptable solution by his powers of persuasion. This may be taken as a sign that the power inherent in his particular office was not really very great. For other reasons, as well, the Kapauku society seems to me to qualify as a chiefdom, but at a rather low level. But it is for this reason an interesting case, revealing the embryonic essence of chieftainship.

More-developed chiefdoms, like those of some of the Indians of the southeastern United States, the circum-Caribbean Indians, and the Africans and Polynesians, were much more thoroughgoing theocracies than the Kapauku; the authority positions were seen much more as buttressed by supernatural power. The evidence seems to show that the chiefs had more confidence, even arrogance, in rendering decisions as to guilt, restitution, or punishments.

External Relations

All of the foregoing instances of reinforcement, leadership, and mediation have as a main function the preservation of the society. To the extent that they are successful—especially in preventing feuds and other tendencies toward fission—the society can grow, by natural increase and by accretion. And of course, the larger and better governed, the better the society can wage war and peace in its external relations.

Such a society can wage war more effectively, obviously, because military achievements depend so heavily on leadership and discipline; but less obvious is the significance of the authority in making and preserving peace in the society's foreign affairs. If, for example, an alliance is made between two neighboring chiefdoms, it would normally mean that peaceful relations obtain between individuals of the two groups, and that they come to aid each other in case of an attack by a third group. But these relations have to be guaranteed; the authority might make the treaty, but it is no good if he cannot command the obedience of his people in maintaining it as individuals. Also, prominently, intersocietal relations are typically maintained by reciprocal exchanges of presents, people (in marriage), and hospitality. And if the two groups can exchange local specialities that the other lacks, amiable relations are better assured. All of the above depend upon the chief's ability to command labor and goods from his society.

If a society with a central authority can wage both war and peace better than an egalitarian society, which will predominate in its history? Is there more war or more peace in the chiefdom stage? Logically, when there is war it will be on a larger scale than among egalitarian groups, and more conclusive because more organized. This itself might tend to limit the number of wars. In addition, chiefdoms have a better capacity than egalitarian societies to subjugate (Otterbein 1964), rather than merely intimidate. In other words, war might be infrequent because considerably more total; but the question of the number of wars in chiefdoms simply cannot be resolved conclusively.

An important way of waging peace is by means of trade, and sometimes rather unusual institutions arise out of the necessary coincidence of peace and trade. Among the Kalinga of the Philippine Islands, for example, an exchange of specialized goods between independent regions was a powerful deterrent to war. Traders (or better, carriers) of the goods elaborated a widespread network of trade partners, that they might enjoy hospitality and safety in their visits. They made themselves ceremonial brothers, with ritual obligations and even the incest prohibitions of true brothers (i.e., their children could not marry). This institution became the basis for peace pacts between the regions, negotiated by the trade partners, who thus became ambassadors of a sort, spokesmen for their own regions in relation to others. These *pangats,* as they were called, became prominent internally as well, as mediators of disputes.

Since important trade relations between two societies are a deterrent to war between them, we may also reasonably suppose that chiefs are much inclined to foster such relations, since the subsequent chapters, the rise of civilizations out of chiefdoms be an important buttress to their authority. As we shall see in subsequent chapters, the rise of civilizations out of chiefdoms depended heavily on the organismic solidarity achieved by regional symbiosis and more distant trade as manipulated by the political authority.

The Limits of the Political Organization

It should be remembered that a segmental primitive society tends to muster different-sized groups from one time to another, particularly when the occasion or functions of the gatherings are different. The boundaries of the society are indistinct for this reason. There are of course numerous exceptions to this generalization, particularly when the society is a relatively sedentary horticultural village of the self-contained (endogamous) type. These are found frequently in the South American tropical forest and elsewhere and are probably caused by the tremendous depopulation and deculturation to which these societies have been subjected for many generations (Wagley 1940).

One of the most important reasons for the indeterminacy of political boundaries in the usual segmental society is the ephemeral nature of the leadership. It follows that to the extent a chiefdom comes to have a permanent office of paramount chief, then to that extent his following will be known and discernible "on the ground." This does not mean that territorial boundaries will be always fixed, for this would vary by type of economy—herders differing from intensive agriculturalists, as an obvious example. But the society itself is named, its membership known, and it occupies a specific space at any given time. Sometimes a sedentary chiefdom's name is also the name of its territory.

One of the main functions of an authority system is to integrate the society. To the extent that it does so the people are integrated on a relatively permanent basis, and thus the society is more distinct. Territoriality need not be the sole criterion of membership in the society, but it is a frequent one, and if not, membership is still known by some means. One of the consequences of this factor is that fissionable tendencies are overcome, as is the considerable voluntariness that characterizes egalitarian societies with respect to what associations or sodalities individuals belong to.

It must be remembered that although a well-organized chiefdom has its known membership, this is only at a given time, for they do have increasingly fissionable tendencies as they grow in size. The waxing and waning of chiefdoms over a long period of population growth should cause a wide dispersal of a common pattern of culture, although finally manifested by numerous politically distinct societies. Here we are addressing one of the most serious problems in the cross-cultural, statistical method in anthropology: What is the *unit* to be counted? It is hard enough to decide what a sociopolitical unit is, especially in egalitarian segmental society. Such units grow in distinctness and permanence, as well as in size and complexity, during their evolution, but are they also unit cultures? It seems clearly evident that a distinct society will manifest a culture, but that the culture will not necessarily be a distinctive one in most respects, peculiar to that society alone among its neighbors.

But there are ways in which certain new cultural traits might arise as characteristics of a particular chiefdom. In matters of religious ideology and ritual, items can be added and subtracted almost at will by theocratic leadership. A new chiefdom, for example, might want to distinguish itself, and especially its chiefly lineage, from the parent society and lineage by elevating new gods and diminishing or abolishing old ones, along with the rituals associated with them. A society can change elements of its culture in some respects, and even its social structure, for political reasons (Leach 1954). Changes in the tabu system in Hawaii may be taken as a prime example of this power, which is so much more inherent in chiefdoms and states than in egalitarian societies. But of course such changes are limited mostly to theocratic aspects of the culture.

II

The Modern Primitive States

5

The Rise of the Zulu State

SOUTHEAST AFRICA, and particularly the area now called Zululand and Natal, was not dominated importantly by Europeans until early in the nineteenth century. The history of the Zulu state was somewhat influenced by Europeans, but most of what happened was aboriginally "functional," a complex and interlocking series of changes from simple and numerous chiefdoms to a single full state, rather than something directly imposed by outsiders. We are extremely fortunate that this important and interesting phenomenon was so recent that elderly Zulus who had actually participated in different phases of the dramatic train of events were able to recount their adventures to modern writers.[1] Furthermore, two Englishmen were at different times resident at Shaka's court during the early phases of his regime.[2] Finally, modern ethnological field work as well as scholarly reappraisals of the historical documents, personal testimony, and folklore from natives of the region who had fled elsewhere, have all been united in the publications of a professional anthropologist, Max Gluckman of Manchester University. The rise of the Zulu state is for

1. The best of these are Bryant (1919) and Gibson (1911).
2. The eyewitness accounts are by Isaacs (1836) and Fynn (1845).

these reasons the best documented and best analyzed of all the cases of state formation recorded, and therefore we appropriately begin our study of empirical cases with it.

Nguni Chiefdoms

The early Zulu polity can be separated into three well-defined historical phases. First, during the period of about three hundred years prior to 1775, the Nguni-speaking branch of the widespread Bantu stock occupied the area as small, sometimes warring, chiefdoms. Around 1775 the character of warfare changed—for various reasons to be discussed later—and larger military chiefdoms were formed, until finally most of them were defeated and absorbed into a military regime between 1798 and 1828. During the early 1800s, the Zulus experienced a military rule by terror under the famous Zulu warrior, Shaka. The more peaceful and stable regime of King Mpande under more developed and effective governmental institutions lasted from 1840 to 1872.

According to Gluckman's (1960) reconstruction of the first political phase, the sociopolitical units were small. Chiefs were guarded by only about fifty warriors, and never more than three hundred were mustered in an attack. It is said that "dynastic disputes" occurred on the death of a chief because there was no strict and unambiguous rule of succession, and that this was the cause of the frequent fissioning of the groups that kept them so small and scattered (Otterbein 1964). But Gluckman (1960, p. 161) adds that the societies may have been small because the political means of integration available to a chief at that time were simply not sufficient to rule a population over a certain size. The splitting-up of such a society would normally occur, of course, at times when political integration was at its weakest, that is, on the death of the chief.

The occupants of the region, about 100,000 people within 80,000 square miles,[3] practiced a shifting cultivation and cattle pastoralism. There were as yet no wars of conquest; cattle were

3. Gluckman, in citing these figures given by Bryant, remarks that he thinks the population figure is too low (1940, p. 26). Stevenson concurs and states that the pre-Shaka density must have been at least 10 per square mile (1968, p. 49).

the most frequent form of booty. Tactics were simple; the warring groups approached each other until barely within throwing range of the light javelins that were the basic weapon. Casualties were low and wounds seldom fatal because the javelins could not penetrate the heavy, five-foot-long, rawhide shields. Probably another reason for the relative inconclusiveness of warfare was the lack of a political organization that could continue to dominate a defeated enemy.

During the early phase of development the Zulu were standard chiefdoms as defined in the previous chapters. A patrilineally extended family formed the basic local residential unit, called the *kraal.* Within the kraal, primogeniture was the ruling principle of hierarchy, and in the frequent cases of polygamy, the senior wives ruled over the juniors. According to all authorities, the largest permanent political unit was the clan. Bryant says (1919, p. 72): "In passing now from the kraal to the clan, we shall find that the structure and governance of the latter ran on the same lines as the former, save that here the separate huts, senior and junior, have become separate kraals, of major or minor status; and the common kraal-head, the common clan-head or chieftain, the clan, indeed, being nothing other than a magnified kraal or family."

The clans, like the kraals, were exogamous. Thus, although the clan was the largest firm political unit, that wives came from outside the clan meant that alliances of a sort were set up among different clans. In case of war, feud, or political disturbances of some kind, there was therefore a tendency for in-law relatives of different clans to side with each other. These kinds of extra-clan alliances were, of course, varyingly vague and diffuse depending on how often marriages had taken place between any two clans. This was typical "segmentary" alliance behavior, whereby the apparent political body varies in size depending on who is the opposition and what is the political context. The clan remained, then, as the only governed entity of permanent leadership. The larger entity of loosely allied clans has usually been called a *tribe* by Africanists, and that usage will be retained here, although the reader should be aware of the ambiguous use of this term in anthropological literature.

The political units were therefore of three orders of ascendency. First was the household itself; next was the kraal, which was, of course, a product of the growth of the family through time—normally within two or perhaps three adult generations (three in the case of a surviving aged patriarch and his wife or wives, a married son or two, and their grown children). But if the families were normally fecund, by the time three or four generations had come to adulthood the original kraal had split into two or more separate kraals. In this way, presumably, after only a few more generations appeared, a large-scale clan resulted. Of course, some kraals stayed the same size and others waned, and additions to a clan may have come about through adoption, or unfortunate in-laws might have sought refuge in it, and so on, but in ideology, if not always in fact, all clan members were considered to be patrilineal descendants of a founding patriarch. The clan name was used like the European "family name" and was usually the personal name of the founder, or of his place of birth. The living chieftain was his most direct descendant by primogeniture (Bryant 1919, p. 15). The larger entity, the tribe, was only a quasi-political unit—united almost by voluntarism alone—somewhat like the egalitarian segmental society described in chapter 3. Another way of putting it: true authority, that based on hierarchy, ended with the clan—the clans within the tribe were not yet firmly arranged hierarchically with respect to each other, and hence their relations were not governed. The Zulu chiefdoms, then were small but numerous—but with potentiality for a wider unity based on the hierarchical model, particularly under the stimulus of war.

The Epoch of Military Expansion

Between 1775 and 1800 warfare gradually became more intense and frequent as the population of Southeast Africa increased. Gluckman (1958, p. 31) says of this situation:

> As far as one can understand the process from the almost contemporary records, under the distribution of population then prevailing it became more difficult for tribes to divide and dissident sections to escape to independence; as the Nguni cultural stress on seniority of descent and the relatively great inheritance of the main heir caused strong tensions in the tribes, chiefs began to press their dominion not only on their subordinate tribal sections, but also on their neighbors.

The development of this trend was possibly facilitated by the unequal strength of the tribes.

The stronger tribes would be those that could muster the most warriors and organize and discipline them effectively. These are all political problems and they were apparently solved best by a leader within the Mtetwa tribe named Dingiswayo. He organized regiments of warriors on the basis of their social age-grades, and thereby increased organizational efficiency and morale. And, importantly, he preserved his dominion over defeated chiefdoms by treating them humanely and by a policy of indirect rule. Gluckman says (1960, p. 162): "After subduing a tribe with as little slaughter as possible, he left it under its own chiefly family, perhaps choosing from it a favorite of his own to rule, though the young men of the tribe had to serve in his army."

Dingiswayo had as a young man lived in exile from his tribe, and had traveled as far as Delagoa Bay, where the Portuguese had established a trading settlement. It is thought possible that he acquired some of his innovative ideas during this exposure to these foreigners. In any event, the indirect-rule policy and the age-graded regiments brought the Mtetwa to a position of dominance over a wide area. By appointing his favorite from the chiefly family to rule a conquered group, but disposing the defeated chief himself, Dingiswayo made the new ruler and the latter's family dependent on power of the Mtetwa; it was, therefore, not only a policy of indirect rule but also one of the oldest political devices of all, divide-and-rule. The age-graded regiments were a similar device: The men forming a regiment were grouped solely by a nonlocal criterion, age, and thus were separated from many other warriors from their own clan and tribe. Moreover, and perhaps more important, the warrior-chiefs who became "generals" over regiments did not command their fellow kinsmen and tribal members exclusively. This was a unique kind of divide-and-rule in African society at that time.

Dingiswayo expanded another function of chieftainship over a wider area, which helped him consolidate his hold on the people: this was his political adjudication of quarrels. Even his warring expeditions were explained as due essentially to peace-making intentions. Fynn (1845, p. 64) has said that Dingiswayo fought because "he wished to do away with the incessant quarrels that occurred amongst the tribes, because no supreme head was over them to say who was right or who was wrong. . . ." This is an example of rule by benefit rather than by coercion alone.[4]

Dingiswayo conquered and united some thirty different tribes in the early 1800s. His victories were aided by the spectacular exploits of one of his young officers, Shaka Zulu. Shaka was the illegitimate (and exiled) son of the chief of the Zulu clan. When the Zulu chief died, Dingiswayo established Shaka as their head, although he also retained Shaka as an important officer in the Mtetwa military system.

Dingiswayo was eventually killed by a rival military chieftain and Shaka was able to take over the army and also to establish his Zulus as the dominant clan in Dingiswayo's regime. By 1882 Shaka had defeated every rival in sight and was master of all of present-day Zululand and Natal. As had been Dingiswayo's practice, he "adopted" the conquered tribes, through their leaders, and in time the whole area was a sort of superchiefdom. Fortunately, the inhabitants of this region all spoke the same language, Nguni, and were similar in culture and sociopolitical organization.

Shaka was able to conquer this huge area because he adroitly used Dingiswayo's political innovations, while adding some important battle tactics and weapons. He changed the rather sporting character of war drastically, so that it became more like total war, by discarding the throwing javelin, which had been rendered so ineffective by the heavy shields, and substituting a short, heavy stabbing spear. His tactics were to encircle the enemy, close with them, and fight *à outrance,* as though bent on extermination. This terrorized most of the enemy armies, and many of the adjoining parts of Africa became burdened with refugees fleeing from the dreaded Shaka.

To conquer, however, was one thing and to consolidate quite another. Shaka kept his army of about thirty thousand men continually under arms, either on a campaign or readying for one. He found, as have others before and since, that sometimes warfare is useful as a political device in the attempt to mold a nation and keep it integrated. But about his only political-like innovation was

4. Another benefit could have been long-distance trade with the Portuguese trading post at Delagoa Bay. Fynn's report of this was accepted by Gibson (1911, p. 14), but the report is widely disputed today.

the creation of barracks in different parts of the country so that the soldiers were on duty full-time and thus detached from their home areas so that they could not be used in tribal revolts against Shaka. This device was apparently unique at that time.

Shaka continued the indirect rule of Dingiswayo, and in time had undermined the rule of succession by primogeniture so that he could keep the tribal chiefs dependent on his support. Chiefs normally had several wives, as well as concubines, but the first-born son of the first real wife, called the "Great Wife," was by tradition the one to succeed to the chieftaincy. In practice, however, it proved to be rather simple to delay designating the Great Wife or to change the designation, for the rules fixing her status as wife, as opposed to early concubine, were conflicting.

If unclear rules of succession are dangerous to the continued integration of a society, they may also be politically advantageous. Most obviously, they were useful to Shaka because he could make or unmake chieftains without doing too much violence to the peoples' regard for their hereditary "royal family." It is also possible that a conqueror, like Shaka, or any chief trying to govern too unwieldy an amalgam of peoples, can find it useful to create or change the Great Wife at will. Since the various wives normally represent political alliances of the ruler with the paramount families of the various districts, the wife likely to be designated "Great" could be the daughter of the chief of some powerful dissident tribe or faction that needed most to be placated.

Nevertheless, it must be recorded that these several political innovations and the uninterrupted military successes were not sufficient to keep the newborn "nation" integrated. Shaka soon found himself ruling tyrannically by terror. He had so many people tortured and killed—undoubtedly often unjustly—that his own brother, Dingane, assassinated him in 1828, to the apparent relief of the people.

Despite the fact that Dingane was ostensibly in revolt against Shaka's rule by terror, he eventually found himself using the same tactics. And similarly, too, people began to turn from him in favor of a younger brother, Mpande. After a civil war in which Mpande was victorious, the Zulu entered a period of relative peace and internal political order, from 1840 until Mpande died in 1872. After Mpande's death civil war broke out again when two of his sons fought for the throne. The British fought the Zulu in 1880 and from then on governed them in various ways until in 1910 they became part of the Union of South Africa. Mpande's long reign of 32 years was thus the third and final stage of the evolution of the independent Zulu state.

Mpande's Zulu State

It seems likely that Shaka's rule by terror seemed to him a political necessity, inasmuch as his successor Dingane, who came to power precisely to end the terror, soon found himself using the same devices. If this is so, then Mpande's long, peaceful, and just rule may be explained as due to some political innovations and to a changed environment rather than a different ruling personality. These innovations may be suggestive of the distinction between rule by force and by authority and regulation.

The environment had indeed changed remarkably by Mpande's time. The Zulu were now completely impounded in their territory by the strong states of the Swazi and Thonga to the north, the Boers to the west, the Basuto to the southwest, the British to the immediate south, and of course, the sea to the east. All these can make a felt threat, but by far the most significant was the presence of the Boers and the British. These groups not only posed a strong threat, but provided a tremendous contrast in race, language, and culture to the native Africans. This undoubtedly was catalytic in creating a greater sense of unity, under Zulu control, among what had been different tribes. And as mentioned earlier, all the tribes were originally similar to each other in race, language, and culture, and after conquest by the Zulus they were not arranged into castes or classes of conquerors and conquered. They all became prideful Zulus, finally, and we may presume that nation and nationalism became powerful integrating factors, given the external circumstances during Mpande's time.

Another consequence of the presence of Europeans was the greatly increased trade, especially with the British at Port Natal (now Durban). This trade continued to be largely redistributive, and thus increasing the dependence of the districts on the central organization.

Probably next in significance was the fact that with the passage of time clans and the less distinct tribes had continued to change their size—some to grow, others to diminish—so that what had originally been local, bounded kinship entities with strong in-group loyalties were now often too large, vague, and dispersed, or too small, to be of much political consequence. The political wards (districts), which at first had tended to correspond to clan and tribal borders, in the years after 1840 no longer did so, since the boundaries remained fixed while the clans fluctuated. As a consequence, the administrative districts had even before British rule become increasingly nonkinship, more purely political territorial wards, and thus easier to govern—particularly because a district head-man would not be simultaneously the chief of the local clan or other kin group. Thus we find divide-and-rule again, and in the usual form of dividing up and destroying the power of kin-groups. Nothing points up so well as this the wisdom of Sir Henry Maine's dichotomy between kin ties and territorial (in the administrative sense) ties as the essential difference between primitive and civil polities.

Some of the important innovations begun by Dingiswayo and Shaka remained in effect, and simply because of the passage of time became more effective and more functionally established in the pattern of living. The standing army, or militia, continued to be divided into age-graded units rather than units representing localities, and the soldiers lived in barracks detached from home areas. The adjucative function of the king continued, mostly as a court of capital crimes and of highest appeal. This was begun by Shaka (Isaacs 1836, p. 298), if not Dingiswayo, but again the simple passage of time probably refined the process as well as made the appeals court increasingly an obvious benefit of the government to the people. Fines assessed were retained by the king, increasing his ability to give relief to areas where crops had failed, for instance. A good deal of the normal policing against ordinary crimes, however, was taken care of in the districts themselves, for the king customarily invoked the principle of collective responsibility when crimes came to his attention.

The kinds of integrative devices that, more than any others, become fully established only after the passage of time would seem to be ideological innovations, especially religious ceremonies. The most important of the new beliefs and ceremonies were introduced in Shaka's time, but any imposed idea cannot become truly an effective belief within a single generation. For example, the idea that the king symbolizes the nation in the first fruits ceremony, and that he, as custodian of the sacred fetishes of the ancestors, can by ritual means cause or dispel rain, is something that to be effective must not have begun within the people's recent memory. The Zulu religion, in general, was based on ancestor worship—which itself implies time.

The practice of making the local chiefs of clans and tribes dependent on the governmental center for support was elaborated by Mpande in several ways. Since King Mpande was polygamous, he had many sons (whereas Shaka and Dingane did not), and he placed them in important administrative positions. His daughters were naturally married to important persons in the realm, and it was understood that the sons of these daughters would be princes and heirs to the family wealth (Gluckman 1940, p. 35).

Kinship ties, as above, can be used expediently, as in extending them by alliance marriages. But we have also seen how often an important politcial innovation consists simply of a device that cross-cuts or perhaps dilutes the power of local kinship loyalties that so often conflict with loyalties to the state. It remains to mention one or more characteristic of kinship that seems to always exist separately from stateship and often to conflict with it: the use of kinship principles, as opposed to political ones, as criteria of status. This distinction is, of course, especially important when the statuses are high, as in the case of the creation of an aristocracy.

The kinship principle of rank has largely to do with inheritance, and in the case of the Zulu this was by primogeniture. One of the most important political troubles that Shaka must have had was simply that he claimed higher rank because of his conquests than he was entitled to by the strict principle of inheritance. Thus other more properly aristocratic heads of clans themselves felt, and their people also felt, that they belonged *higher* in a political hierarchy than Shaka, not lower. This kind of problem—that of hereditary aristocracy versus the upstart self-made man—can be found in some form or another in most of the world, but in the ideology of (former) chiefdoms like the Zulu, the system of inheritance or succession in rank by primogeniture is extraordinarily strong.

An interesting case involves the Zulu origin myth. Zulu, the mythical founder of the clan, was the younger brother of Qwabe, who founded the Qwabe clan. To this day the chief of the Qwabe clan will not recognize the superiority of the Zulu king, since his clan, and thus himself as well, are superior by original seniority. Gluckman says (1940, p. 36): "People to whom I have put [the Qwabe chief's] claim consider that it is invalid: Shaka founded the Zulu nation and therefore his heirs are entitled to rule it. Nevertheless, they say, the king should 'respect' the kinship seniority of the Qwabe chief." This report is contemporary; even though Shaka had "founded the nation" over one hundred years earlier so that passage of time has endowed him with greater legitimacy and an ancestral aura of aristocracy, the feeling of ambivalence remains. But consider the strains that must have existed in his own day between Shaka and the hereditary aristocracy, involving Shaka's own relatives, friends, and self-made warrior chiefs!

In the ideology of the ruling group—the true Zulus of the clan, relatives of Shaka, and lineal descendents of Mpande—all of the original chiefs of the constituent tribes of the Zulu nation were "raised up" to their positions by Shaka or one of the later kings. As related earlier, Shaka and his successors either appointed a chief from the chiefly family of a clan or tribe or allowed the legitimate chief to continue in office under official Zulu sanction. This is, of course, weakens any contention that the aristocracy have a "natural right" to rule their clans and tribes; they must believe that they hold their power, in the end, subject to the Zulu king. Nevertheless, the original appointed political officers, even if not of royal birth, have always been succeeded by their senior sons. And if the son is incompetent, or if there is no son, a regent is chosen to serve only until the office can be returned to the main line of descent (Gluckman 1940, p. 37).

The Great Man versus the Evolutionary Process

If the rise of the Zulu state were due uniquely and entirely to Shaka's individual gifts, then it would have little meaning as an example that could teach us something about the political process of state formation. It would be of no more use than any other kind of historical accident. But it seems plain that Shaka's genius, if indeed he was so endowed, lay in his military innovations rather than in politics. Gluckman says (1960, p. 158), ". . . His rise to power was probably also the result of tides that had been running in the life of the African peoples for two centuries: the rising population in the interior of Africa, the emigration from the interior that was crowding the pasture lands of Natal, and the increasing contacts with European settlers and traders." The "state" under Shaka was not well ordered in the political sense.[5] It was primarily a terroristic military order, held together first in large part by the success of the frequent wars, and later by the threat of the Boers and the English.

Shaka's regime seems the more spectacular to us, and the more due to an idiosyncratic genius, if we are ignorant of the fact that roughly similar events happened elsewhere in Africa when the circumstances were roughly similar. The most important of the Nguni-speaking branch of the Bantu were adjacent to the Zulu and clearly affected by them. The Swazi state was formed by Zulu conquerors out of Nguni and Sotho elements in the late eighteenth century. The neighboring Ndebele also borrowed the Zulu political system, notably their reliance on conquest and tribute, territorial organization, and age-graded regiments (Murdock 1959, p. 384).

In the interior of the Republic of South Africa (principally Basutoland) were numerous kingdoms known collectively as Sotho. These include some described ethnographically in modern times, the best known of whom are the Sotho proper, and the Tswana, Basuto, Bapedi, Bavenda, and Balemba groups. All had a moderately complex state apparatus, and divine kingship. The southern and western Sotho groups (for example, the Sotho proper and several Tswana groups) were originally conquest states apparently modeled on the Zulu and neighboring Nguni states (Murdock 1959, p. 390). All had a hereditary class system, territorial wards, a pattern of tribute flowing through the territorial hierarchy to the capital with subsequent redistribution, and so on.

It would appear that the origin of the state among the Zulu was typical of the general processes of state formation elsewhere

5. In his study of African political systems, Stevenson says (1968, p. 52) that this regime was "inherently transitory and evanescent," too dubious a case to use in a comparative study of political development.

in southern Africa. Just how much the Zulu *caused* the formation of the other states cannot be stated with confidence. But whether the others were borrowed from or modeled on the Zulu, or were at least in part the result of similar cultures adapting to similar circumstances, we find nothing that contradicts the lessons of the Zulu example. To be sure, the military successes of Shaka were extraordinary, but, as we saw, the actual formation of the true state did not occur during the epoch of military successes, nor as a consequence of Shaka's use of terror.[6]

But, in any case, it was the set of important, slower, more gradual changes in the theocratic, legal, and military facets of the bureaucracy, internally, and the impounding of the whole Zulu people by external threatening foreign groups years after Shaka's time, that finally enabled Mpande to rule peacefully—with statecraft. This is a salient example of a kind of *circumscription* of the politico-military sort which, it seems evident, must have had a very important unifying effect, countering the normal centrifugal effect of dissident former chiefdoms.

6. For an interesting analysis of the relation of Shaka's terrorism to the absence of "constitutional" governmental institutions, see Walter's *Terror and Resistance* (1969). He shows that the public slaughter of innocent commoners by Shaka was not in order to punish or coerce *them,* for they were "non-persons," completely unimportant. This terror was aimed rather at impressing the chiefs, the potential rivals or dissidents.

6

The Origin of the Ankole State, Uganda

IN A FEW INSTANCES, a general theory of the origin of the state has been proposed in the context of an ethnographic and historical investigation of a particular primitive state. A theory thus propounded is difficult to assess simply because it seems so plausible—as though it had *emerged* from the data. But of course the theory may have been held by the investigator prior to the investigation, and the data winnowed or otherwise selected (however unconsciously) to illustrate the theory. In the following two chapters, the investigators' arguments will be presented as accurately as possible, with my comments only as asides. Final assessment will be reserved until they can be viewed in terms of other relevant comparative data.

History and Legend

Kalervo Oberg (1940) has interpreted the legends, ethnographic distribution of languages, and tribal customs in Uganda in terms of the classical theory of the conquest of settled horticulturalists by warlike cattle herders. His type case is the kingdom of Ankole, one of a series of small primitive states aligned from north to south in a corridor of grasslands along the western borders of Uganda. Everywhere in the corridor the pastoralists were rulers and the agriculturalists were serfs.

The heroic legends and songs of the pastoralists all tell the same story. Essentially, they describe Ankole as originally in peace, occupied by agricultural *Bairu* and a few pastoral *Bahima.* They lived apart and neither group had a developed political organization. New Bahima arrivals led to struggles between the Bahima and Bairu, with the Bahima the victors. The society became organized as a kingdom, and these legends remain to provide the traditions of the society. ("Kingdom" is not used here in any special or technical sense. Oberg evidently means personal, hereditary rule.)

But, says Oberg, "we do not need to go to native legends to account for the origin of the Banyankole kingdom. Evidence lies before the student on every hand. Even today we can observe the environmental and social forces which gave rise to the particular complexion of Banyankole society and its political institution."[1]

According to Oberg, the nature of the environment—the closed corridor described above—brought the Bairu and the Bahima into close juxtaposition, and there was no easy escape for the conquered. The Hamitic Bahima invaders numbered only one-tenth as many as the local population, which meant that the rather primitive agriculture of the Bairu was still able to provide enough surplus to make the permanent subjugation worthwhile to the Bahima, who, while basically supported by their own cattle, exacted tribute in beer, millet, and labor.

Despite being outnumbered so heavily by the agriculturalists, the Bahima were able to subjugate them because, like pastoralists elsewhere, their constant raiding had developed a superior military discipline. And like other pastoralists, they had natural logistical advantages: they carried their food along with them. For these reasons, and because the Bahima were also accustomed to cooperating among themselves, they were able to control the agri-

1. Oberg (1940, p. 125). In the Bantu languages the prefix "Ba-" is used for the names of *peoples,* as in the above "Banyankole," and the root alone for the *place*—e.g., Ankole.

culturalists on a permanent basis. Furthermore, the perpetuation of the military dominance required that the society be protected against neighboring cattle raiders. The Ankole Bahima, their subjects now settled, strove to subjugate these neighbors and exact tribute from them.

Action that should be defined as *political,* according to Oberg (p. 128), is the creation of new forms of social organization and the destruction of old ones by means of organized power. Once the two ethnically distinct groups became permanently associated the relationships between the two groups and within each group changed. The Bahima in particular had to set up political bonds among themselves simply in order to further their interests as Bahima, now in an antagonistic relationship to the Bairu. Among the most important new elements of this bond were greater cooperation, and creation of leadership over all the Bahima, arranging the formerly independent chiefs in a hierarchy. In Oberg's view, these are the bases of kingship and the dynastic principle, rising out of beginnings associated with military organization and chieftainship.

Clientship

Oberg believes that the most important institution resulting from the new political necessities was clientship, a form of voluntary fealty reminiscent of the European feudal contract. A cattle owner would go to the chief (eventually king) and swear to follow him in war and to give him a periodic tribute of a small proportion of his herd. In return the client was protected against cattle raiders and other disasters. At the same time peace was maintained among clients and any transgressors were tried before the king.

The large population of Bairu agriculturalists were not allowed to own productive herds. This may have been because ownership of cattle was a mark of high status, and confining it to the Bahima was a sort of sumptuary law, visibly defining the separation of the upper and lower groups. This castelike distinction was also maintained by the prohibition of intermarriage. Social and sexual relations between the two groups were typically those of caste societies in that Bahima men could take Bairu women as servants and concubines, but Bairu men could have no contact with Bahima women.

As in European feudalism, the Bahima were an aristocracy with a monopoly on force; the Bairu peasantry were prohibited from serving in the armed forces. Important official positions were also monopolized by the aristocracy. The Bairu had no rights to retaliate by means of blood revenge for a wrong done to them by Bahima; the wrong could only be redressed by compensation judged by an agency of the king. Bahima could exact blood revenge among themselves and from the Bairu, but the Bairu revenge was restricted to their own groups. Under no circumstances could Bairu kill or injure the Bahima.

All this is to say that the Bairu had no political mobility, no way to alter or redress the inferior status imposed by their birth as Bairu. Included in this status was the fact of economic exploitation by the Bahima herdsmen; a great deal of beer and millet was distributed among all of the Bahima. But the exacting of tribute was restricted to the chiefs and was regulated and authorized by the king; and the Bairu could go to him with complaints about bad treatment. Thus the state system, though it exploited the Bairu, also protected them in numerous ways.

The Ankole state was not a strong or complicated edifice. The king and his chiefs were important in alleviating disputes by giving judgments, but they did not punish. There was no true police organization standing apart from the society itself. A chief's judgments normally consisted of a decision as to the nature of the crime and an identification of the malefactor, followed by the granting of the right of retaliatory revenge to the aggrieved. As for offenses within the extended family, these were settled by the headman of that group.

The king was protected by a band of several hundred specially selected warriors who lived near the royal kraal. Since they were bound to do his bidding it could be said that they were, incipiently at least, a sort of internal militia that, by threat or implication, defended the state structure as well as the person of the king. The king was also surrounded by a great number of people who formed the effective government. The king's mother and sister were the most important of his relatives. A favorite chief lived in the king's kraal and acted as chief advisor. A group called the "king's relatives" had duties in the kraal, and another group, the executive chiefs, were war leaders and tribute collectors. Probably the important executives of all of these groups were blood or in-law relatives of the king.

Theocracy

According to Oberg's reconstruction, religion played such an important part in the governing of Ankole that the state could be justly called a theocracy. The most politically significant aspect of religion was the shrine and cult of *Bagyendanwa.* This shrine was simply an old, mud-walled, thatched hut that enclosed a raised altar on which stood a number of drums, some milk pots, and a carefully tended fire that was not permitted to go out except on the death of the king.

Bagyendanwa was not simply a group of drum fetishes abstractly symbolyzing national unity, but was perceived as a concrete power that could actually help the people. It was the true kingdom of which the king was only the servant. Further, the king had the interests of his own caste of Bahima at heart, whereas Bagyendanwa was impartially at the service of the Bairu as well. This was an important political aspect of the ideology regarding the drums, for the god-fetish could be appealed to not only for impartial help but also to avenge wrongs—most commonly theft, adultery, sorcery, and slander.

The drum shrine served also as a sort of redistribution headquarters. Offerings of beer, millet, and cattle were frequently made, to be cared for by the custodians of the shrine, and to be given later as wedding presents, and more importantly, to those families who had suffered from a raid or crop failure. This kind of use of surplus wealth was an important function of the king's court as well.

An important unifying feature of the Bagyendanwa was that it was peculiar to Ankole. All the Banyankole were represented by the drums, but the neighboring kingdoms and tribes had entirely different cults. Thus local and sectional cults and social differences in Ankole were overridden by the very fact that the drum cult differentiated the Ankole people as a body from all their neighbors. It may be surmised that a very important function of religious cults anywhere may reside in their ideological capacity to unify social bodies by emphasizing their uniqueness, their separateness from others.

Although the cult of the royal drums mirrored many of the functions of the king, there was one very important difference. This was the permanence of the drums as contrasted with the temporary nature of the king's rule. In all simple political societies the problem of the succession to office is formidable. Because of the tendency to regard a king charismatically, the weakness or death of the king creates political instability. In Ankole the purely physical virtues of the king, as a person, were allied with his supposed magical powers. This excessively charismatic view of the office (a very common feature of African kingdoms) required that as soon as the king's wives and close followers detected signs of his aging or weakness he had to be killed by poisoning.

The highly personalistic view of the king was also reflected in the means of succession. The new king had to be of the royal patriline and must have demonstrated his physical superiority over his brothers in a civil war over the succession. During the struggle, which could last for months, the country was in a state of near-anarchy, which had the effect of dramatizing the need for a strong king. The winner (who normally was the one with the strongest supporters) killed or drove into exile all of his brothers, so that he was finally and completely without competition. An entirely new group of retainers and chiefs were appointed to office with one exception, the important advisory status held by the king's mother. (It should be remembered that because of the mode of succession a king would have no living brothers or father's brothers to advise him.)

Oberg's general conclusions about the Ankole state can be summarized as follows. The state originated in the conquest of one ethnic group by another, resulting in a stratified society that required a mechanism of maintenance. Kinship, which was the fundamental social force in both groups, now was insufficient to hold the whole society together.

The new political relationships were serfdom, slavery, and clientship. Serfdom and slavery were compulsory, unbalanced, and exploitative relationships. Clientship, on the other hand, was a contractual, balanced relationship of political cooperation that was necessary to help maintain the exploitative relationships of Bahima over Bairu.

The royal mythology, the cult of the royal drums, the succession rites, and so on, are all comprehensible as political aspects of the state, as preserving the kingship, which in turn preserves the general position of the Bahima aristocrats over the more numerous Bairu peasantry.

The East African Lake Region

All of the native states of Uganda and some nearby regions have origin-myths of the founding of their state dynasties similar to the myths of the Banyankole. In these traditions a miraculous people called Bachwezi conquered widely in the region and in western Uganda formed a powerful empire, after which they vanished around A.D. 1500 (Davidson 1961, p. 177).

As we have seen, Oberg believes that Ankole and other neighboring states resulted from the actual history of conquest of the numerous Bantu agriculturalists by a minority of Hamitic herders.

G. P. Murdock (1959, p. 350) grants that the herders infiltrated the Bantu and became a specialized part of a unified economy, permitted to graze their cattle on land unsuited to agriculture. "Because of their usefulness to the ruling class they enjoy a respected status, but the assumption that the political systems of Uganda are conquest states founded through the subjugation of agricultural Bantu by invading pastoral nomads lacks any real basis in fact."

"On the other hand," Murdock continues, "something very much like this may well have happened in the Ruanda region." Here the endogamous castes of Nilotes [Hamitic herders] and Bantu are clearly distinct, racially and culturally, and the Nilotes are the ruling aristocracy.[2] The Ruanda states are strongly centralized, despotic, and complex, with hereditary classes of royalty, nobility, commoners, and slaves. And, as Murdock says, it is entirely possible that they were conquest states—though this cannot be proven by historical fact.

2. See Maquet (1960) for an interesting discussion of clientship in Ruanda. A useful overall source is Richards (1960).

John Beattie (1960, p. 3; 1971, ch. 3) finds that Nyoro, a a kingdom near Ankole, is similar to it, but with a complication. The Nilotic pastoralists appear to have assumed their position as lords over the Bantu agriculturalists in Nyoro by historical conquest, but this situation was compounded by the later arrival of still another group of Nilotic invaders, the Bito. This not only complicated the composition of the upper classes, but also resulted in a looser arrangement, unlike the rigid, castelike discriminations of Ankole (Roscoe 1923).

The biggest puzzle, involving perhaps the most prominent kingdom in Uganda, is that of the Baganda (Fallers 1964; Roscoe 1911). According to Gluckman (1965, p. 147), the Baganda kingdom, like others in the general region of Lake Victoria, were created—"probably in fact as well as in tradition"—by the conquest of agriculturalists by invading pastoralists. But the castelike distinction found in Ankole and Ruanda had been lost. The social distinction was, rather, that of a cleavage between king's court and bureaucracy and the commoners. At the time of the coming of the British, the Baganda had made many successful military conquests, from which much wealth had been gained. Of great importance also was the fact that the king's court played a middleman's role between incoming Arab traders and the interior hinterland as well as serving as the center of a redistribution complex (Kottack 1972). The capital, with its huge bureaucracy, became very rich relative to the rest of the country (Southwold 1961; Gluckman 1965, p. 149). Thus, the horizontal ethnic castes of Ankole and Ruanda did not characterize the Baganda, and the pational specialization of no great social or political status differ-
The ethnic separation of herders continued, but only as an occupational specialization of no great social or political status differentiation.

Again we note that warfare, conquest, and reactions to these frequently involve another variable, commerce, which, however closely related to successful warfare, can also vary independently, with highly visible consequences. Gluckman believes, in fact, that in the long run important commerce is necessary to hold a large primitive state together. His argument (1965, pp. 143–44) is worth emphasizing here, since we have already touched on the possible significance of trade and redistribution in helping unify the Zulu. He believes that whenever a state in Africa has had permanence "it will be found that this is based on some special kind of external trade, or on the internal differentiation within the nation." The "internal differentiation" made it possible for the king to redistribute the tribute from the different regions as a kind of "wide-spread and mutually satisfactory exchange of goods."

The Uganda Region in Perspective

At this point, we must be cautious enough to hold Oberg's conquest thesis in abeyance. When we compare the case of the Banyankole with others in the region, and consider that herding and agricultural groups existed in a symbiosis of some kind, at some time, in all of them, we are left with a feeling of the complexity of the historical scene. Certainly it would not be good sense to think that a conclusive case has been made that a simple conquest resulted, with a few cultural manipulations, in a true state.

There remains also, of course, the very important hypothesis that none of these were *primary* states, that is, self-generated. Military and commercial-political hegemonies extended from the East African highlands (beginning perhaps as early as the thirteenth century) all the way across the savannah to the Atlantic coast and down to the Congo River and beyond, at least by the fifteenth century. Simple conquest may have been involved in all of these developments, of course, but we know too little about the statelike and legalistic appurtenances that must accompany victory in battle in order to achieve a peace based on subordination of a conquered group.

It seems, at this point, that in the Uganda material two important variables have come to light, variables that we may find useful to consider in subsequent chapters involving different contexts. One is Oberg's *clientship,* which, because of its resemblance (perhaps superficial) to European—and for that matter Tokugawa Japanese and other—feudalistic concepts of fealty, suggests at once that we may have here a political process which at a certain stage in political evolution, or in certain adaptive contexts, may be of more general significance. The second is the widespread symbiotic *trade* that Gluckman emphasizes. This trade, again possibly only at certain stages or in certain adaptive contexts, may involve more general peace-making agreements and simultaneously productive economic relations with foreign regions, and (in its redistributive aspects) powerful integrative forces within the kingdom.

Inasmuch as more extensive and important trade characterized the African west coast and savannah, the subject of the next chapter, we should defer a fuller discussion of its significance for that context. Similarly, the problem of the feudal analogy and further discussion of the conquest theory may be appropriately postponed until later. And, perhaps above all, we shall have to face then the major question of the possibly early and widespread influence of true states that may have originated long before our more conventional histories began to describe native African polities.

7

West African Kingdoms

West Africa is a huge region of great diversity in habitats, kinds of native societies, and stages of aboriginal political evolution. It would be impossible to do justice to it without carefully delimiting our sphere of interest to the most pertinent examples and representative regions. As in the previous chapter, we also face the problem of assessing theories of the origin of the state within the context of the author's descriptions of the history and ethnography of particular examples. Of these the most prominent cases are the Nupe, the Ashanti, and the Kongo.

The Guinea coast and the adjacent lower Congo River basin is mainly a tropical forest with numerous large rivers emptying into the ocean. This coastal and riverine environment typically contains swamp forests at the coast itself, rain forests more inland, next savannahs, and then steppe-grasslands bordering the Sahara. The Congo basin itself is more exclusively dense forest, becoming savannahlike to the south.

In addition to these diverse habitats, the history of the various societies was enormously affected by their position in relation to the slave trade; some were victims of slavers, others middlemen, some specialized as slavers themselves. And these outside influences were highly variable, as in Nigeria, for example, where Moslem conquerors founded several northern states, or at least modified them profoundly. The English and French influenced coastal areas, and the Portuguese virtually monopolized the trade in the southern part of West Africa from about 1500. The complexity is so bewildering to the nonspecialist that only the extremes will be considered here, with emphasis on the interpretations of specialized Africanists when they appear relevant to our problems.

The Nupe

We begin with the inland grasslands and savannahs of the northern part of West Africa. North of the forests and south of the Sahara we encounter the complication of the influence of Islamic traders. Many black African tribes near the desert fringe converted to Islam and, like the Soninke or the Hausa, established far-flung trade routes. By 1500 these networks had become established throughout West Africa all the way to the Gulf of Guinea (Bohannan and Curtin 1971, p. 248).

Of the northern states, the Kede and the Nupe are somewhat typical. Both were studied by S. F. Nadel, whose book on the Nupe (*A Black Byzantium*) is a classic. In his studies, Nadel finds support for the conquest theory of the origin of the state. He is one of the few modern social anthropologists who uses a temporal dimension as well as functional analysis, and also one of the few who links his treatment of the *origin* and *development* of the state with a discussion of the *basic nature* of the state. He outlines his conclusions thus (1942, p. 69):

> (1) The state is a political unit based on territorial sovereignty. Membership of the state, i.e., citizenship or nationality, is determined by residence or birth-right in a territory. The state is thus intertribal or inter-racial, and distinguishes nationality from tribal or racial extraction. (2) A centralized machinery of government assumes the maintenance of law and order, to the exclusion of all independent action. (3) The state involves the existence of a specialized privileged ruling group or class separated in training, status, and organization from the main body of the population.

In discussing this third point, Nadel goes on to say that "historically, an inter-tribal sovereignty of this nature can only have arisen from the ascendancy of one ethnic group over others" (p. 69). In other words, the Nupe case supports the theory that the state is not only multi-tribal, but that it becomes so by conquest and is maintained so by force. "We cannot pass without comment the fact that the structure of the Nupe state as it exists today, with its ruling class of Fulani conquerors, and also its growth so far as we can with any claim to accuracy trace it back in history, indeed support this [conquest] theory of the origin of the state" (p. 70).

There seems to be little doubt on the face of it that the Nupe and others of the western Sudan, like Ankole and Ruanda, were themselves products of the conquest of militarily superior ethnic groups over other weaker groups. And the details of these groups' solutions to problems of governance are instructive, for a conquest state surely must be a difficult state to maintain, particularly in the earlier stages. But these solutions to political problems were clearly not original—these were secondary, not pristine (or primary) states. The true origins of statecraft in North and Central Africa—first in the Northeast, last in the Northwest—undoubtedly go back to Egypt and Mesopotamia. Later refinements and permutations were contingent on the spread of later empires.

Beginning as early as 800 A.D., a succession of large commercial city-states rose to dominate the western Sudan.[1] Ghana was powerful as the earliest manufacturer and user of iron weapons and implements, which of course increased its mastery not only over the natural environment but also over more primitive neighbors of the savannah, aiding the spreading dominion of the growing centralized and urbanized government. But even more important was the increasing development of long-distance trade, especially of gold transported from its source in the southern forest belt to caravan intermediaries of the Sahara, from whence it appeared in the Mediterranean world and finally Europe. Until the discovery of America, with its fantastic yields of precious metals, the western Sudan, particularly through the enterprise of

1. The discussion here of the city-states follows Davidson (1959, pp. 79–107).

Ghana, was one of the principal providers of gold to the Mediterranean world.

The longest-lived of all the states in the Sudan was Kanem, with its successor Bornu. Eastward of the Niger River, in the grasslands stretching toward the Nilotic Sudan, this region witnessed layer after layer of migratory incursions. Important among these were elaborating influences from Kush, the ancient outlier of the Egyptian imperial expansion. Kanem was involved in iron-smelting and international trade, had control over caravan routes, and undertook administrative centralization. The empire of Kanem, beginning around the eighth century and continuing as Bornu, maintained a powerful civilizing identity until the sixteenth or seventeenth centuries. It was the civilizing force of the central Sudan just as Mali, succeeding Ghana, was the major focus of civilization in the western Sudan.

After the empire of Mali had passed its crest of influence in the western Sudan, the Songhay people of the grasslands bordering the middle reaches of the grand Niger River accepted Islam and expanded the domination of the city of Gao into a true empire of many ethnic groups. By 1464 the Songhay people ruled the most powerful state in the Sudan, with the possible exception of Bornu to the east. As Davidson says, Islam and commerce were the allies of a powerful centralizing administrative system (1959, pp. 98–103).

The opening of seagoing commerce with the New World in the sixteenth century began a process of reorientation of commercial wealth and power that eclipsed the Mediterranean Moslem trans-Saharan trade with the Sudan—especially since gold was more plentiful and easier to transport from the Americas to Europe. Eventually, too, improvements in navigation and shipbuilding led to much greater and easier commercial contact with West African coastal peoples. The gold of the coast became much more readily accessible, as did cola nuts, palm oil, and finally, of tremendous importance, slaves for the great plantations of the New World. The western Sudan did not collapse, but it was effectively bypassed, and the commercial powers of the city-states, and as a consequence their political effects, were much reduced. The states, with their economically, politically, and religiously sophisticated bureaucracies, did not disappear. As Davidson points out at length, the European world tends to think of African history as beginning with Europe's late knowledge of it, whereas the internal developments in relation to much earlier overland commerce with the Mediterranean world are severely underestimated.

A final blow was dealt to many of the remnants of the indigenous empires when the fanatical Moslem Fulani, some of them nomadic herders, others sedentary horticulturalists, rose to military dominance after 1810. This rise of the Fulani reversed, in important respects, the Uganda and Ruanda patterns of dominance, widespread patterns apparently involving either symbiosis or the conquest of herders over horticulturalists. A few paragraphs here on the Fulani conquests may be useful, for this episode suggests possible modifications or qualifications of Oberg's generalizations discussed in the previous chapter.

The Fulani-speakers consisted of two cultures that were in considerable contrast to each other, which we may call Fulani A and Fulani B (after Murdock 1959, pp. 413–21). The As were pastoralists, rather "non-negroid" in physical type, pagan or only indifferent Moslems, peaceful and "accommodating to their neighbors," and "lacking any indigenous political organization above the level of the autonomous band and its headman." The B Fulani were strongly negroid in physical appearance, inhabited sedentary agricultural villages, and were "fanatic Moslems," given to aggressive holy wars against pagans, and building conquest states following their forays.

The conquest of the Nupe nation in 1820 was one of the last of a long series of Fulani acquisitions that established Moslem-inspired sultanates and emirates among the several Hausa states and their neighbors. Contrary to the impression given by Nadel, the conquest state that the Fulani established over the Nupe was not in any sense a case of "the origin of the state," but only a late instance in a widespread wave of related episodes. Furthermore, the Fulani-Nupe state was not even independent after it was established, for it was only one of numerous emirates tributary to a much grander sultanate. But even these conquest states were only remnants of much more powerful indigenous Sudanese empires of great power that long antedated them.

As Murdock says (1959, p. 73): "The civilization of the western Sudan, as of Egypt, lies deep in the past. Contemporary ethnography . . . can give little conception of the complexity of culture and the richness of life under the ancient empires of either region. This must await the spade of the archaeologist, which has thus far lifted perhaps an ounce of earth on the Niger for every ton carefully sifted on the Nile."

The Ashanti

In contrast to Oberg's and Nadel's analyses of Ankole and Nupe as conquest states, Robert S. Rattray (1923, 1929), while acknowledging the role of external pressures, describes the development of the Ashanti state in terms of *internal* growth and development. Much as Maine contrasted primitive or tribal-like social tendencies with more impersonal governmental institutions (the "kin tie" versus the "territorial tie"), Rattray saw the rise of the Ashanti state as a gradual growth of more and more clans and lineages that became confederated finally as territorial entities.[2]

All this began toward the end of the seventeenth century when the usual Ashanti community was a "tribe" under a chief and his sister or mother (the Ashanti had matrilineal descent). The heads of lesser kin groups (lineages or extended families), known as the elders, assisted the chief. The chief did not interfere importantly in internal family affairs and his authority in most matters was slight. There were many such communities of chiefdoms, each independent of the others, with their own land and hunting and fishing territories.

Presumably, population growth and the movement of powerful new groups, including the arrival of Europeans, created new imbalances of power, and for a time the Ashanti groups paid tribute to a state called Denkyira. The increased use of guns also

2. Jack Goody has suggested still another modification of the generalization that states have a conquest origin. He says (1971, p. 18): "Recent studies of African states make it clear that while increased centralization in the political system almost always results from conquest, it is not only in this way that states arise. The Alur, for example, extend their domination when neighboring peoples invite their chiefs to come and rule over them; we find, in effect, an upward delegation of authority rather than the assumption of power by a militarily dominant group."

made for new imbalances of power, and it is possible that direct contact with Europeans on the coast had an effect. The Denkyira king developed a splendid court, which the famous Ashanti priest Anotche visited.

The fact of their subjugation made it easier for the otherwise independent Ashanti chiefdoms to unite in a common cause—the overthrow of the Denkyira state. At any rate, the priest-leader Anotche, and the chief of the Kumasi tribe, Osai Tutu, united the Ashanti, and they defeated their enemies at the famous battle of Feyiase. They were able to preserve the military confederation on a peacetime basis to form the vigorous new Ashanti state. The confederation was simply an elaboration, on a larger scale, of the earlier primitive hierarchy. The family grew to become a lineage, lineages grew to subdivide and from the clan, clans grew to become "tribes" (chiefdoms), and now the independent tribes were united under a paramount tribe (the Kumasi). Rattray (again like Maine) sees their form of organization as a normal development out of primitive society, closely paralleling the European feudal experience whereby the barbarians consolidated themselves hierarchically and territorially.

The resemblance to feudalism was paralleled by a change in the conceptions of land tenure. A kind of "multiple proprietorship" was founded: the king claimed ownership of all the land in the kingdom, but the territorial chiefs became kinds of secondary owners of their lands, and so on down to the actual family head, proprietor of his own land.[3]

An important political innovation was made by Anotche. This was the golden stool, which Anotche was believed to have brought down from the sky. This stool represented the whole nation and the divine right that Osai Tutu and his descendants were to have over all of the Ashanti chiefdoms. The heads of the territorial subdivisions also had their stools (though not golden). As such this symbolism is reminiscent of the royal drums of Ankole.

In other respects, also, the Ashanti state used the usual theocratic devices of ancestor worship. Crimes against the political body, for example, were considered primarily as sins or sacrilegious offenses against the ancestors. The important ceremonies

3. See Goody (1963) for an excellent overview of the ascription of "feudalism" to African polities.

were chiefly worshipful of ancestors and of the Supreme One, the creator of everything, including the people and the state.

Import-export trade was in the hands of the state, which may have been a very important factor in the continuing survival of the state structure, and in its very nature, particularly since guns were acquired this way. Guns, cloth, and other items of European manufacture were redistributed to the district chiefs, who in turn passed on portions to subchiefs, and so on. Slaves, the currency that bought these goods from the Europeans, were acquired from the interior by means of the Ashanti state's dominance of those regions. The important slaving states of Dahomey and Ashanti did not allow guns and powder to pass through their territories to the inland states. This not only preserved the coastal states' dominance, but also preserved an important difference between those states and the savannah types of government.

According to Goody (1971, p. 55–56) the main difference between the forest and the savannah states was that the coastal states of the forest used guns but had no horses (partly because of difficulty in the military use of cavalry in dense forests, and partly because of the tsetse fly), whereas the savannah states had horses but no guns. The differences correspond to important contrasts in the societies. Goody explains:

> In the grasslands, the ruling estates tended to be mass dynasties, within segments of which high office often circulated. In the forest, office tended to be more autocratic and to be retained within a narrower dynasty. In the former, power was more widely diffused and the rulers relied on the dynasty as fighting cavalry; in the latter, the important fighting arm was the regiments of gun-men stationed around the capital and often recruited from prisoners and slaves.
>
> Other differences were connected in a less direct way. Since guns and gunpowder came from the sea-borne trade, it was easier for the state to control the local dealers in arms. Not only were the kingdoms more centralized as a result but a large sector of the external trade was state operated. In contrast, the markets and entrepôts of the interior were dominated by the free enterprise activities of Muslin merchants. Indeed the distinction between the Islamic traders of the interior and the Christian traders of the coast was another important aspect of the contrast and one which had significant socio-cultural implications. This situation was part of the world-wide confrontation brought about by the development of firearms. Within both Western and Muslim states the internal changes brought about by this inven-

tion were far-reaching. But as Ayalon pointed out, they had a profound influence on the course of the struggle between these two worlds. "By and large . . . the introduction of these new weapons spelt disaster to Islam"; the outstanding exception was the success with which Ottoman Turks used firearms against both their Christian and Muslim neighbors.

In sum, the evident differences between Nadel's conquest theory of the state and Rattray's developmental theory are based on their experiences with two entirely different kinds of cultures, environments, and histories. The outside ideological influences were distinct: land-based Islam versus seagoing European slavers. And the contrasts in environment—savannah versus forest and coast (favoring horse versus gun)—and in history—the long ebb and flow of powerful empires in the Sudan versus the late surge to entrepôt power of slave-dealing principalities like Ashanti or Dahomey in the coastal forests—to mention but a few varying factors, should cause clear differentiation in the two modes of statecraft. However, the history of these groups, while exhibiting significant details of how primitive cultures may become states in interaction with advanced cultures, does not tell us about the origin of *primary* states.

The Kongo and Neighbors

In the area from the mouth of the Congo River south through the open savannah lands to the Zambezi River, the major societies were the Kongo, Luba, Lunda, Kazembe, and Lozi, of which the Kongo are the best documented and most thoroughly researched. It appears that the probability that these native states and empires predated the coming of European trade and slaving is the same as with the groups we discussed earlier in the chapter. Jan Vansina, an eminent historian of the Congo region, is convinced that these kingdoms were aboriginal. In response to claims that Kongo was "a creation of the Portuguese" and that the Portuguese "organized the whole structure," he says (1966, p. 41):

> On the one hand, the organization of Kongo as it appears in documents of the late sixteenth century is similar to like organizations in other African states. On the other, there is absolutely no support for the contention that the Portuguese organized the whole structure, since

the earliest stress the territorial extent and the strength of the kingdom. Indeed, it can be said with much more justice that the Portuguese in Angola copied the territorial structure of the African states. I feel justified, therefore, in using the late sixteenth century sources to describe the state of the kingdom as it must have been in the late fifteenth century.

It may be granted that the claim that Kongo was "a creation of the Portuguese" and so forth is extreme. Nevertheless, as we have seen elsewhere in Africa, the consequences of trade monopolies, warfare, slaving, new weapons, and so on certainly must have precipitated new militaristic regimes and conquest states. The influence of the Portuguese on the political structures, in short, may have been indirect rather than direct, but no less powerful in altering the aboriginal society. Vansina at one point characterizes all of the peoples of the savannah as "kingdoms or chiefdoms—that is, they have developed political systems which have a centralized political structure and which are ruled by a single person" (p. 4). Vansina cannot be faulted for not separating states ("kingdoms"?) from chiefdoms, since many writers, especially in early sources, fail to make the distinction. But it seems evident from Vansina's own work that the coming of the slave trade and new wars and new weapons made vast changes in the political structures—just as elsewhere.

The slave trade began around 1500. Guns were bought with the proceeds, and the interior rulers (in the Congo region) had a monopoly of the weapons. Then, Vansina explains, "the Lunda used them to found the Puapula and Yaka kingdoms" (p. 247). As time went on and the slave trade grew in importance, new states arose in the interior, like the several Ovimbundu states, and became wealthy as suppliers of slaves from routes far interior, even from Katanga (Bohannan and Curtin 1971, p. 268). Others, seaports like the Ijo settlements of the Niger delta, became commercial city-states with a political organization designed for the slave trade (ibid., p. 267). Some became almost purely military machines, reorganized to specialize in the capture of slaves from the interior as did Dahomey in the late eighteenth century. It seems evident that we have in Vansina's material no better data relating to the primary origin of the state than we found in studies of Ashanti and its neighbors.

Trade and Conquest in West Africa

Strictly speaking, the various instances of state-making in West Africa that we have noted have no direct or focal bearing on the problem of the origin of primary states, although there are several important characteristics of primitive government that deserve thoughtful mention for future consideration in a more general sense, as will be noted below. States and empires in the western Sudan had long antedated these examples. What concerned Nadel (and, for that matter, Oberg in the previous chapter) were nothing more than re-creations of power relationships in polities and economies whose structural and ideological origins were far away and long before. As for coastal West Africa (especially Ashanti and Kongo), the influence of the slave trade and guns was uniquely catalytic.

There is no doubt that certain organizations did in fact conquer and dominate others by force, as Oberg and Nadel emphasize. But the use of force is nothing new or surprising, and certainly it often fails to achieve political consolidation; hence, it is not of itself a sufficient cause of the origin of the state. As we have seen, Goody emphasizes the significance of the slave trade and commerce for the rise of centralized organizations, the point being that even the secondary state is born not *simply* as a matter of warfare and conquest (1971, p. 18).

It is difficult to epitomize many of the native African polities that preceded the developments caused by European trade. They seem to have been frequently "federalized," somewhat like the early Ashanti state, but not so centralized. Apparently the powers of theocracy were in the ascendancy (especially evidenced in the widespread rule of "divine kings"), though they experienced relatively little of the later highly centralized despotism. For want of a better epithet, many European writers (including Rattray and Nadel) call such polities *feudal.* Davidson (1961, p. 29) calls it " 'tribal feudalism,' a system of centralized government that was almost always qualified by the precedents of 'tribal equality.' "

Clientship, as a form of person-to-person political amalgamation (recall Oberg's description in the preceding chapter), is one of the noteworthy parallels between European feudalism, with its vassalage and fealty, and the African "patron-client" relationship. Goody (1971) also sees this kind of equivalence in the two systems but cogently points out some important differences. The fact that land was plentiful in Africa, and agriculture was shifting and *extensive* (rather than *intensive,* as in Europe), caused a striking difference in land tenure. Land in Africa was impermanently held, and hence the rulers (and patrons for that matter) held *political* power over their subjects and clients, rather than the economic power implicit in rights to land. As Goody says (ibid., p. 74), "The chief himself was rich not in land, but in goods and services, which were not all for his own benefit." And therefore, he points out (ibid., p. 30), African chiefs "had to try to attract as well as restrain" the subjects of their rule.

One is drawn by such descriptions as these, and as well by Davidson's epithet "tribal feudalism," to see strong parallels in these African systems to primitive, though rather elaborate, *chiefdoms.* For that matter, many of the early, or outlying, societies of the earlier phases of European feudalism—for example, the Celtic (or "highland") "clans" in Britain, the Germanic "tribes" of Tacitus' account—sound like chiefdoms. And for what it may be worth, it has been long felt by many that classic feudalism in Europe was a decentralized Romanesque set of ideological remnants set over native "Germanic" chiefdom societies.

But what, then, were the large, permanently urbanized, centralized *empires* such as Ghana, Mali, Songhay, and Bornu, which preceded the epoch of European slaving? It seems evident that highly organized trade over very long distances was the basis of power (in tax and middleman profits), rather than ownership of land. (It may be of interest at this point to note that the breakup of the self-sufficient manorial system in Europe is usually accounted for by the revival of long-distance trade with the Mediterranean states.)

It is obvious that concepts like *chiefdom, feudalism, state,* and *empire* can be misapplied or misdefined. At this point in our investigation, it is too early to confidently explore the treacherous ground that these terms seem (now) to overlap. But certainly we are warranted, in terms of the evidence noted so far, in keeping track in future chapters of the great politically integrative significance of long-distance trade (which is perforce politically protected, organized, and ultimately redistributional), and of new kinds of weapons. That the latter are so frequently contingent upon long-distance trade leads to an ever-greater need for monopolistic control of that trade; securing the weapons makes a polity more able to exert such control.

8

The Cherokee Indians

The transformation of the several independent villages of the Cherokee "nation" into a state during the eighteenth century was one of the most surprising responses of American Indians to the pressures of the European colonies. The main source of data in this chapter is Fred Gearing's *Priests and Warriors* (1962). We will present not only his analysis, but also his general theory of state formation as it grew out of this particular case.

The Cherokee as Chiefdom

The Cherokee inhabited the larger river valleys of both sides of the Great Smoky Mountains. In the early 1700s they numbered between ten and twenty thousand, divided into thirty to forty villages, averaging about four hundred people each (Gearing 1962, p. 3). The mountain barriers between major stream valleys tended to isolate four major segments of Cherokees from each other, so that regional cultural differences and dialects were formed.

The villages were intensely theocratic, led by "priest-chiefs" who functioned most importantly as masters of religious ceremony, and also presided at village meetings. The war organization was separate from this; as we shall see later, this nascent separation of powers became an important basis for the formation of the new state. Internal regulation and adjudication of quarrels and crimes was mainly accomplished by the clans through "self-help," that is, outside the priestly authority system.

In the early 1700s there was no formal system that regulated the conduct of the villages to each other, coordinated joint actions, or made decisions for the whole. There was some intermarriage among members of different villages (although the villages were not strictly exogamous), which fostered amicable relations between adjacent villages. Within the villages, as among the neighboring villages, crimes were dealt with by the corporate clans: Murder was punished by blood revenge; lesser crimes by settlements arranged by the clans. In all, the adjudicative function of the chief was negligible, as in chiefdoms generally.

Administrative decisions mostly had to do with relations with alien tribes and the colonies of Europeans, although there were internal decisions to be made as, for example, when and where to move the village in quest of better land, or build a new public building. The hierarchy that was activated by the need for administrative decisions was headed by the priest-chief, aided by three other priests and one secular officer. Additionally, an important elder from each of the seven clans formed an inner council for the priest-chief. These men represented the interests of their respective clans, but also helped unite the clans in the interest of the village as a whole. All other elders constituted a third order of councilors, important in public (though not "inner") councils. All of the above elders constituted a superior prestige class called "beloved men."

Religious and secular affairs were regulated by the same hierarchy. In the town house both of these kinds of councils used the same seating arrangement. When a white standard was raised, announcing a council or ceremonial, all the people assembled. Women and children were ranged around the sides of the house as seven clans (in some villages the houses had seven sides). In front of them were young men, with elders still farther forward. The priest-chief and his officials sat on special benches in the center, with the seven-man inner council near them.

The prevailing ethos venerated the older generation in all matters: "old equals good equals honor." Only in warfare could the young men act in an untrammeled, egotistical manner. But this youthful freedom from restraint was dramatically curtailed on the warriors' return to the village when they were required to pass through a ceremony of purification to dramatize the necessary transition to the demands of deference in village life. This ceremony probably had the same function as such *rites de passage* as puberty or marriage ceremonies, symbolizing as strikingly as possible an abrupt transition from one form of freedom to a much more constrained social behavior. (Interestingly, the violent ballgames that youths engaged in during periods of peace were also followed by rites of purification.)

High status as a warrior was, of course, of the achieved kind. Gearing found, in comparing the careers of leaders, that relatively few war leaders later became leaders among the elders: 19 out of 51 (ibid., p. 64). To be a leader in the council of elders was also an achieved status, but Gearing argues reasonably that a rather different kind of basic personality type is required in the two statuses, and that age differences and ceremonies do not have the power to alter personal characteristics sufficiently to guarantee success in both. In addition to the obvious differences in the contexts, the Cherokee dramatized them further in using a red-colored standard as symbolic of war, reserving the white flag for council deliberations. These were carried over into ordinary behavior as two "structural poses," two categories of contrasting behavior, and two kinds of political personages: "A man, acting in the person of 'red' war chief, was out of turn in the context of 'white' council debates (unless, as when a decision for war was pending, exception was explicitly made)" (ibid., p. 74).

Before 1730, the Cherokee villages were chiefdoms in the sense that there was some consistent leadership, offices existed, and power was institutionalized. In other words, the society did not have only the simple charismatic leadership of warriors; there were structured means by which political reinforcement, leadership, and mediation were accomplished. The society differed from other chiefdoms in those years in that it lacked permanent authority offices inherited by primogeniture.[1]

1. Apparently good evidence pro or con for the aboriginal presence of

Gearing calls the Cherokee society as a whole a "jural community" (ibid., p. 79). That is, the villages, though independent from any higher authority, did not normally fight one another. There was, instead, a sentiment of obligation to settle disputes by mediation, and there were officials to help make this possible. It is probable, of course, that peaceable sentiments among Cherokee villages were greatly fostered by their perception of greater danger from outside Cherokee society.

The Cherokee State

The relations of European settlers to these Indians was sporadic and infrequent until after 1699, when France and England began their struggle over the control of the Southeast. The Carolina settlements in general and the Cherokee villages in particular became allies against France and against the tribes allied to the French settlers. Within a few years official Carolinian governmental trading posts were established in some of the larger Cherokee villages, but direct relations with Europeans were not as significant at that time as the pressures from the surrounding Indians, now increasingly in ferment. Hostile contact was especially frequent with the Creek Indians to the south. Enemies on the southwestern side were Chicasaw and Choctaw. The Shawnee, to the northeast, were allied to the French and consistently hostile to the Cherokee.

Each Cherokee village was independent in its decisions about its relations with outsiders. But since all the villages shared a common language and culture and practiced some intermarriage, there was a normal tendency for neighboring villages to coordinate their actions. From time to time a few villages would be more influential than others in making decisions. A village's influence depended on the prestige of its priest-chief and perhaps on its size or prestige resulting from a recent success, and above all on its location (exposed or protected; more or less accessible to a trading post). But there was no form of governmental structure to treat for the tribe as a whole. There was only the sporadically achieved prestige of a few villages and their leaders.

---

inherited ranks is lacking. Other similar Southeastern groups did have such ranks, however (Swanton 1946, pp. 661–62).

The seven clans that had representatives in each village were an important means of affecting or achieving peaceful sentiments among villages, but they were never political action groups. But the perception of Cherokee villagers was that as a whole they constituted a body as opposed to the surrounding outsiders—this whole is what Gearing calls the jural community.

Meanwhile, South Carolinians tended to act as though the tribe were a political entity. This was especially evident when the criminal actions of an individual Cherokee brought reprisal against any Cherokee. As incidents, such as stealing, or molesting a colonial trader increased, it became evident that the first political problem for the whole tribe was to create means of preventing unauthorized violence by any of their warriors. The achievement of a solution was to take more than thirty years.

The villages' "red" council structure for warfare became the first model for a tribal structure to negotiate with outsiders, mainly with the colony of South Carolina. An important function of the negotiation was to prevent reprisals for Cherokee acts by means of coercive punishments. As a first step toward tribal government this was an important move; but it did not entirely succeed in preventing unauthorized raids.

In 1730, a Scotsman named Sir Alexander Cuming traveled in the Cherokee area and urged the larger villages to choose an "emperor" for the tribe. They chose Moytoy, a war chief of the village of Tellics. Not many of the villages accepted this, but an idea had been planted and after about twenty years the institution of tribal leader seemed well established, though not really powerful.

Moytoy died in 1741 and was succeeded by his son Amouskositte, who still represented the war organization. The most important tasks were preventing unruly youths from harming traders and settlers. Whenever this happened, trade was cut off and all the Cherokee villages suffered from the misdeeds of a few. The typical war chief's task was to deal with the government at Charles Towne (Charleston). But internal governance, such as punishing miscreants, was felt to belong to the "white" council. Gradually, in the 1750s, the war-chief was supplanted, for most tasks, by Old Hop, an aged "beloved man" who was widely respected as a priest-chief. By 1758, a true tribal structure based on the traditional model for village councils was in regular operation.

Old Hop died in 1761, to be replaced by an old man named Standing Turkey as "great beloved wiseman of the Nation." This may be taken as evidence that tribal politics now had a true structure and were not simply molded by the personality of Old Hop. A tribal council took place at least once a year, at the capital village (Echota). At the apex of the council was the body of elders of the capital: the village priest-chief (Old Hop, and then Standing Turkey); his three major assistants; the speaker; and the village council of the seven clansmen. The other villages of the tribe were represented by their own priest-chiefs and assistants and perhaps some members of the councils of clansmen. The major meeting of each year was held at the New Year religious ceremonies.

From Priests to Warriors

For two and a half years, beginning in 1760, the Cherokees and the South Carolinians were at open war. After peace was established there continued a steady pressure of encroachment by settlers on Cherokee land, and a correspondingly increase in reprisals against them. The first evidence of truly coercive sanctions against uncontrolled actions by individual warriors is contained in a letter by Standing Turkey, who said, "We are now Building a Strong House, and the very first of our People, that does any dammage to the English, shall be put in there, until the English fetch them. . . ."

By 1768, a notable shift in public sentiment was evident when Great Warrior, a tribal war chief, took over the political functions of the tribal priest-chief. By this time, warriors were also accepted in the deliberations of the tribal councils, and old warriors became a recognized group.

In 1774, Daniel Boone explored the part of the Cherokee domain that is now in Kentucky, and initiated a plan for the colonial settlement of Kentucky. In 1775 real estate interests held a meeting with Cherokee chiefs and proposed to buy Kentucky. The old chiefs—Great Warrior, Little Carpenter, and others—accepted the offer, but young men led by Little Carpenter's son,

Dragging Canoe, opposed it. When the American Revolution began, loyalists initiated a policy of arming Dragging Canoe and his followers to attack rebels along the frontier. The American revolutionaries, of course, blamed the whole Cherokee nation for this and attacked them heavily, burning houses and destroying crops. The young warriors took their families south and established new settlements (later to be called the Chicamaugas), while the rest of the tribe remained.

The division of the tribe along age lines was also a division largely between the "white," priestly administration and the "red," or war-making, administration. Their present physical separation in space revealed the one-sidedness and the inadequacies of each regime. In the original villages amiable old men watched their theocratic governmental councils crumble, with no means to hold the tribe together; in the Chicamaugas the structure was thrown away, the violent young men were unrestrained and unwise, and the strong and fearless governed the weaker in a kind of lawless nightmare.

Authority versus Force

Gearing believes that the main processes of state formation in Cherokee history were shared by early Mesopotamians. He also argues that these processes were a recurrent phenomenon in the world—not the only route to statehood, but nevertheless a frequent one because it is functionally connected to a particular kind of village political system that is itself frequently found in the primitive world. This village system can become the basis for a state because the basic ingredients for statehood are already present, to become formalized as necessary under conditions of external stress.

What we have seen in previous chapters, and will continue to note subsequently, is the usual—perhaps even universal—presence of a chiefdom stage anticipating the rise of a historically known state. The Cherokee villages quite closely resemble what I have been calling chiefdoms; and obviously the most important characteristic is centralized theocratic leadership. Gearing has made a very important theoretical point in recognizing the significance of this village structure as underlying the later state.

A second important contribution is his distinction between the "structural poses" that characterize, on the one hand, the theocratic political leadership (priest-chiefs and councils of elders), and on the other, the secular military leadership. His emphasis is on the social psychological aspects of the personnel of the two structures—that is, on the personality types and codes of behavior that the two political structure select for their contexts of action. This is interesting, to be sure, but for our comparative purposes we want to emphasize the more institutional aspects. As we shall see in subsequent chapters, the rise of new or greater external political problems of war- and peace-making tends to bring about a kind of "separation of powers," usually spurring the creation of bureaucratic posts for the military that are distinct from the purely theocratic.

Another way of putting this, useful for our very broad purposes, is to say that the organization based on the power of authority alone (the "white" council and the priest-chiefs), may find itself unable to solve certain new problems of political maintenance and allows the creation of another organization (the "red" council and the military leaders) to utilize a political power based on force. The problem of the relation of these two is, as stated in chapter 1, the major question of this book. I think it is fascinating to find that in a real sense the Cherokee themselves seem to have realized the fundamental discordance between authority and force, and created cultural means of isolating the latter from the former as though to prevent contamination. The organization of authority, the theocracy, was to them the ideal form of governance; the use of force was not only a makeshift expedient, but somehow untoward, so that rites of purification were needed after repugnant kinds of expedient duties were performed.

Of considerable interest also is the fact that, although external conflicts had become very frequent and intense, the Cherokee development was clearly not a conquest state, nor a case of the war organization or its leaders taking over the society, as Herbert Spencer might have argued. On the contrary, the state was formed by Old Hop and Standing Turkey, who were village priest-chiefs. And later, in the Chicamaugas, the young men's war organization, working alone, was unable to govern. It was warfare, providing the "external stress," that was the environmental stimulus causing the theocratic leadership to purposely strengthen the positions of the war leaders. But the true origin of the state—of punitive law embodied in the "strong house"—was clearly from within the theocratic leadership, as a sort of bureaucratic expedient.

9

The Origin of States in Polynesia

POLYNESIA was the last extensive area of the world to be populated. Migrations in great seagoing double canoes were apparently made gradually from Malaysia ever eastward across the Pacific, beginning some two thousand years ago. The relative homogeneity in both language and culture over the enormous area supports the archaeological inferences about the recency of the migrations.

The most important cultural differences in Polynesia were caused by adaptive responses to the varying island habitats, particularly as they affected population size and density. There were two major kinds of islands. The large so-called *high islands* were usually remnants of huge volcanic mountains, with fertile agricultural lands and abundant fresh water. The *low islands* were small crescent-shaped coral atolls, mostly infertile except for the domesticated coconut, so that the basic economic endeavor had to be fishing. The present discussion is confined to the high islands in the Hawaiian group, Tahiti (Society group), and Tonga, for the rise of state organizations for which we have adequate historical records occurred only in these cases.

The typical high-island form of organization in Polynesia at the time of early European contact was a classical chiefdom, with a pyramidal genealogical lineage of internal ranking by primogeniture, a theocratic chieftainship, redistribution, and sumptuary classes. All of these characteristics were exaggerated in the chiefdom structure to the point of great rigidity and elaboration. Of particular importance, as we noted earlier, were the associated etiquette, beliefs, and rituals expressed in terms of *mana,* supernatural power, and as *tabu,* sets of religious prohibitions connected with mana. The following brief discussion of these topics is designed to set the stage for an understanding of the traumatic events caused by the coming of the Europeans.[1]

The usual high-island form of social structure was the kinship group based on a conception of genealogical descent from a common ancestral pair. In addition to genealogy, however, every individual was ranked within his individual family by birth order, and every family was ranked in terms of the birth order of the parents relative to their siblings. The ranks of whole families and lineages were also inherited by primogeniture, which means in theory that the highest-ranked person, the chief, was a first-born descendant of a line of first-borns that reached back to the founding ancestral god. The second son of the founding family founded his own line, and the first-born of that line held a status next in rank to the line of first-borns. As we saw in chapter 4, continuing this ordering to include all of the family lines creates a pyramidal or conical structure that has been appropriately called a ramage, calling attention to the branching and rebranching feature of this scheme of descent.[2] As in all such societies of inherited rank, it was among the more aristocratic families that the interest in pedigree was highest.

The chief and his close relatives were not only aristocratic in hereditary rank, but were also more sacred, possessing more mana —the spiritual power that is inherited from the most powerful ancestral gods. People with little mana were endangered if they

1. Standard works that deal with the material in this section are: Buck (1938), Ellis (1853), Goldman (1970), Oliver (1951), Sahlins (1958), and Williamson (1924).

2. "Ranked lineage" or "status lineage" (Goldman 1970, p. 421) are appropriate concepts also, calling attention to the hierarchical feature of the organization.

came into contact with those of much mana, hence the concept of tabu, which restricted the interpersonal contact of aristocracy and commoners. Such restrictions have a very important political consequence, for they create "social distance," which in turn preserves awe and mystery, a significant attribute of the hierarchy of authority in theocracies.

The social differentiation of ranked statuses also had an economic aspect. The commoners produced goods for their own sustenance and a surplus of strategic goods that were passed on to their chiefs. The chiefs not only were supported by these goods, but also accumulated food and craft products that they periodically redistributed to the population. The chiefs thus regulated not only sociopolitical and religious affairs but also an important aspect of the economy as well. A chief, being central to this system, could have an effect on production as well as distribution. That is, he could plan for the future, for war expeditions, for expansion of this and reduction of that, and he could, within limits, persuade people to do more work than they might otherwise be impelled to do. To the extent that he could spur production, he ended up with more goods to redistribute—and thus was his political power increasingly secured.

Within this economic fund a chief subsidized craft production, provided entertainment for important visitors, built temples, sponsored ceremonies and military campaigns, and provided the upkeep of his own elaborate establishment. This latter function of the tribute-tax is one of the sumptuary aspects of political rule. By emphasizing the differences between rulers and ruled in terms of consumption, an effect like the etiquette of tabu was achieved: Social distance can be created by distinctions in the manner of consumption as well as the etiquette of rules of tabu.

It may be that Polynesian chiefdoms sometimes grew top-heavy in their courtly apparatus and thus taxed their people too heavily. The traditional histories of Hawaii and other large islands recount the cycles of centralization-decentralization: a falling-apart, perhaps accompanied by armed revolt, and then later reconstitution of the larger chiefdom (Sahlins 1968, pp. 92–93). In this respect we should call attention to an important characteristic of chiefdoms: They do not claim, as do all states, a monopoly of force. A chief, because of his commanding position, can normally expect to command a majority of the armed force in the population (Sahlins, op. cit.), and if he cannot he probably falls. But he is sustained in his office more because it *is* an office, buttressed by so many economic, social, and ideological trappings that he may come to be regarded as immune. At any rate, the idea of rebellion was not to overthrow the system but to replace a bad chief with a good one. The true change of system came later, after the advent of Europeans, and is the subject of the rest of this chapter.

The Hawaiian Islands

This group included eight inhabited islands in precolonial times. Hawaii itself was the largest and most populated. The other main islands were Maui, Oahu, Kauai, and Molokai. The estimate of the Cook expedition was that the total population of the island group ranged from 300,000 to 400,000. The islands are very fertile in the cultivable valleys and the irrigation system was extensive and well organized. Taro, breadfruit, coconut, yams, and sweet potatoes were the basic crops, while seafood was the most important protein source, supplemented by pigs and dogs.

In aboriginal Hawaii the genealogical ranking of individuals was overlaid by a political system based on three strata. The highest in status, called the *ali'i,* were chiefs of islands and important districts and their close relatives who served as advisors and occupied important bureaucratic posts. The second level, the *konohiki,* consisted of lesser chiefs and their close relatives, administrators, and distant relatives of *ali'i.* The great majority of the population were the commoners, *maka'ainana.* These hereditary strata were largely endogamous, hence the relations among them were actually castelike.

Paramount chiefs (*ali'i nui*) of independent districts, the true chiefdoms, were believed to be direct descendants of gods. For this reason, a chief had priestly ritual functions with respect to these gods—that is, the Hawaiian political system was not only a caste system but also a theocracy. Another theocratic device, widespread among chiefdoms, is the aforementioned conception of deference and social distance between strata, in Hawaii known as tabu. For example, the ground a chief walked on became charged with mana and had to be avoided by lesser persons. When a chief appeared, all those present had to prostrate themselves in extreme humility. Numerous other elaborations on the tabu conception involved severe punishment or death for violations of the sanctified chiefly personage and his belongings.[3]

Much of the productive land was under irrigation, and the chiefs and their stewards controlled the allocation of the water, as, in theory, they controlled the land. In practice communal labor was also controlled, since effective use of irrigation involves coordinated effort in cleaning, maintaining, and extending a system. Other activities, especially those of craftsmen, were controlled and subsidized by chiefs and their local stewards out of the store collected for redistribution.

The most important activity that involved the ability of a chief to master and control manpower was warfare. Judging from the recurring theme in myths and legends, a good chief was supposed to expand his chiefdom. The chiefdoms were particularly unstable during the period of succession to the chiefly position, and thus ripe for conquest by neighbors. The largest island, Hawaii itself, was the most unstable, in part probably because it was too large for a single chief to control (Davenport 1969, p. 3).

An important internal aspect of any political system is its ability to settle disputes. In Polynesia most private disputes such as assault or theft were punished by collective action, although a chief would normally have the power to intervene when retaliations lead to counter-retaliations, threatening feud. But evidence is not clear as to the presence of a legal mediative process. It was reported by Ellis (in Sahlins 1958, p. 19) that the administrative hierarchy served as a series of courts of appeal in adjudication.

Another critical aspect of internal polity has to do with peaceful succession to office. The problem in Hawaii could not be said to have been solved, exactly, but a considerable step in that direction was achieved by ideological means. It was accepted by the populace that chiefs were of a line of first-borns going back to important gods. Both males and females of the aristocracy were ranked this way. For this reason the question of the chief's marriage was crucial in order to create a high-ranking son to succeed

3. In Polynesia it could be said that *chief's* law became *public* law and *lèse majesté* (crimes against the chief's person) were crimes against the society itself (Hogbin 1934, pp. 224–31, 273).

to the chiefly office. The very highest ranking son would be born from the marriage of the paramount chief with his own first-born sister, and this was a sometime occurrence, as reported. Such incestuous unions occurred in Egypt and Peru as well, apparently for the same reasons. This form of marriage is, in effect, the extreme case of the more usual endogamy that prevails within aristocratic lineages.

In summary, the aboriginal Hawaiian political system embodied the appurtenances of typical chiefdoms. The system was a theocracy, held together by an ideology that justified and sanctified the rule of the hereditary aristocracy, buttressed by age-old custom and etiquette. Such a system is in some contrast to a primitive state, which, although it attempts to rule ideologically and customarily, has had to erect the additional support of a monopoly of force with a legal structure that administers the force.

The Rise of the Hawaiian State • The rise of a repressive state, it is apparent from a quick perusal of history, may often be simply a recourse taken by a failed chiefdom, stricken by war and anarchy, but when it does make permanent and legal (regularized) its rule of force, it usually achieves greater integrative power, for a state then has variable means to be as repressive as situations require. Such remarks seem justified, certainly, as we review the dramatic case of the rise of the post-contact Hawaiian state.

Captain James Cook's last discovery was the island of Hawaii (he was killed there by the Hawaiians in 1778). His previous voyages, which began ten years earlier, had brought to fulfillment the scattered cartographical knowledge of other earlier navigations, and suddenly the Western world was ready to invade the Pacific in considerable numbers. The Hawaiian group was in a particularly favorable position for provisioning the increasing numbers of American whalers and of ships in the Euro-American trade with the Orient.

At the time of discovery by Cook, the paramount chief of the island of Hawaii was engaged in a campaign on the island of Maui, which continued inconclusively until 1782, when the Hawaiians were defeated. The victorious chief of Maui had by then also incorporated the former independent chiefdoms of Oahu and Molokai. This may well have been the largest consolidation ever in the island group up to that time.

Kamehameha, a principal nephew of the Hawaiian chief, had made a big reputation as a fearless warrior in the Maui campaigns. When the chief of Hawaii died, Kamehameha campaigned openly against the chief's son. (For reasons not germane here, the succession to the title was not clear.) Another district of the island declared its independence, and the island split into three rival chiefdoms.

Kamehameha's district had good anchorages and he therefore had an advantage over his rivals in trading with the European ships. After 1789 he had acquired guns and light cannon and in 1790 he employed two European ships' officers as gunners and advisors and was able to conquer Maui. By trickery, in 1792 his rival on Hawaii was killed, and Kamehameha assumed political control of both Maui and Hawaii. Later, with the aid of British ships and weapons, Kamehameha was able to conquer every island but Kauai. The port of Honolulu in Oahu became increasingly important and Kamehameha acquired a virtual monopoly over the importation of arms. In 1810 the paramount chief of Kauai capitulated without a battle and the Hawaiian Islands became a monolithic military kingdom.

Kamehameha designated his son, Liholiho (later to be known as Kamehameha II), to succeed to the kingship, and his brother's eldest son to be custodian and high priest of the state god. Since this latter post was the one held by Kamehameha in the earlier problem of succession, there was again a built-in problem that could lead to a factional struggle after Kamehameha's death.

Kamehameha died suddenly in 1819, and after the period of retreat and meditation, Liholiho was officially installed as paramount chief. The danger of civil war was not yet averted, however, and the growing factionalism was abetted by another kind of factor, the growing influence of European culture. This influence was significant militarily, of course, particularly because of European firearms and advice, but there was also a pervasive acculturation, an erosion of native habits and customs. In this respect the most dramatic effects were observed in religion, for the Europeans ignored and derided the native tabus with impunity. The whole issue of acceptance of or reaction against acculturative change became symbolically focused on the question of tabu. Just as in other colonialized areas of the world, the indigenous people were polarized in terms of "progressive" versus "conservative" attitudes toward modernism and acculturative change. This situation culminated in one of the most dramatic—and for some interpreters, the most puzzling—incidents in colonial history.

In 1819, Liholiho, the new ruler of the Hawaiian Islands, and several of his high officials deliberately flouted the most sacred tabus of their ancient religion. This was not because they had become converted to Christianity, since the first missionaries were not to arrive for several months. This startling act of irreverence for one of the basic features of Hawaiian culture was followed soon after by a series of social and cultural reforms so farreaching and fundamental that the episode is now known in anthropological history as the "Hawaiian cultural revolution."

The eminent anthropologist, Alfred L. Kroeber, used this remarkable episode to illustrate one of his basic theoretical postulates: that the choices people seem to make and the plans made by leaders do not "explain" or even describe very well the fundamentals of culture change. He saw behind the dramatic political events in Hawaii an unconscious motivation explainable in terms of group psychology—which he felt was the most important avenue of explanation an anthropologist could explore. As he wrote (1948, p. 404), ". . . The main factor seems to have been a kind of social staleness; the Hawaiians had become disillusioned and tired of their religion. To this extent the incident is illustrative of what may be called cultural fatigue." Kroeber went on to say that for important cultural changes to be legislated (like the New Deal in the Depression years of the United States, or the Japanese Emperor's sudden renunciation of divinity in 1945) there must be a general weariness of the old patterns, in order that such breakthroughs will be welcomed.

For William Davenport, on the other hand, the critical features of the violation of tabu are that it was an *intentional* political act, and that it was set off by the legitimate government. Intentionality is, of course, a frequent characteristic of political behavior, and one worth nothing, for it is a different sort of explanation of the behavior from "cultural fatigue" or "acculturation influences."

On the face of it, it seems paradoxical that the very religious tabus that were the most important buttresses to the legitimate rule of the paramount chief and the position of the aristocracy were first broken by the ruler and his advisors. This is as though a medieval ruler in Europe were to publicly deny the divine right of kings. Whatever the intention, the immediate effect was to provoke and rally the conservatives under the custodian of the state god (who in ancient theocratic belief actually had a claim to the office of paramount chief). Liholiho, apparently expecting this, quickly armed his forces and defeated the conservatives. Another rising elsewhere was also crushed. Davenport says, "If those battles were considered the critical test of strength between the powers of the gods against the power of firearms, the Hawaiians had no doubt as to which was superior. . . ." (1969, p. 16). The explanation is that Liholiho's advisors (especially his mother) felt that to force the issue quickly to a showdown before the other faction was fully prepared would insure victory. And it did just this.

Davenport stresses the intentionality and political foresight of these incidents, for other earlier interpretations of the Hawaiian cultural revolution had ignored this factor, since it appeared as though the rulers were acting against their own interests. I think Davenport is correct in this point, but now it is time, for the purposes of this book, to see what structural and evolutionary features emerge.

Malcolm Webb (1965) has made an interesting argument that the Hawaiian cultural revolution was essentially a change from the chiefdom stage of cultural evolution, with its pervasive religiosity, to a true state, which is normally more secular in its operations. Webb is not a specialist on Polynesia, and he is able to see the revolution as structurally and evolutionarily analogous to the transitions elsewhere.[4] (Davenport cites this argument with approval, for it is not, of course, in disagreement with his.) From the point of view of political expediency, again, it may be worth remember-

4. The changes from the classic Petén Maya theocracies to the Yucatán "New Empire" state are a good case in point, but discussion of this must be delayed to a later chapter.

ing that as a theocratic chiefdom becomes a state, it is normally in a state of convulsion, if not of full civil war. It is possible that frequently, as rule of force wins over the old conservative forces of theocracy, the new rulers are apt to see the old priesthood as a check against absolutism. "To remove the priesthoods was to strengthen the power of the chieftainship, even though the concept of divine rank was discredited by the removal" (Davenport 1969, p. 17). The "power of the chieftainship" we may be sure, was the power of force by this time, and the subsequent years in Hawaii were bloody.

It is too early to do more than present these ideas as possibilities. But immediately we might guess that events in Tahiti and Tonga might provide some interesting structural parallels.

Tahiti

In comparing Tahiti to Hawaii, it is of interest that the direct influence of missionaries on the rise of the Tahitian kingdom was crucial, whereas it had not been in Hawaii. Otherwise, there were many similarities. Most of the Society group are high islands. Tahiti is the largest, about thirty-five miles long and half as wide. The land is mountainous, but the valleys and coastal flats are very fertile and in aboriginal times the island supported about a hundred thousand people.

The ramage form of kinship structure in Tahiti, based on primogeniture and genealogical reckoning, was similar to Hawaii's. The class system was identical: the *ari'i* were the chiefs and their close relatives, constituting an aristocracy; the *ra'atira* were the subchiefs; and the bulk of the population, commoners or *manahune.* A system of tabus based on the conception of mana buttressed the chief's authority.

The chief was a redistributing agent and maintained his household, retainers, and craftsmen by witholding some of the people's surplus production. It is said that this was not truly exploitative, however, for the passage of goods from the chief's household was so regularized "that more than was barely sufficient for his own use seldom remained in his possession" (Ellis 1853, vol. 3, p. 128).

According to Ellis (ibid., pp. 93–94), the power of paramount chiefs in Tahiti was considerable and comparable to those of Hawaii, but this power was limited by the local power of subchiefs. As in Hawaii, chiefs did not ordinarily mediate or otherwise interfere in ordinary disputes between their subjects. Offenses against the chief, as elsewhere, were swiftly and severely punished. Great social distance between *ari'i* and others was maintained by elaborate tabus protecting the person, clothing, habitation, and other possessions of the chiefs, and by great ceremonialism whenever the chiefs appeared in public. Everything a chief touched became charged with mana and would be defiled if a commoner came into contact with it. The chief had to be carried on the shoulders of special retainers so that he did not touch the ground where ordinary people might pass. The ceremonial distinctions between ranks maintained the position of the chief, "surrounded by the priests and invested with the insignia of royalty, and divinity itself. . . ." (Ellis 1853, p. 114).

The aboriginal Tahitian political system was thus, like that of Hawaii, thoroughly theocratic, with the authority of the chiefs reinforced by their religious sanctity. There was no structure of legal monopoly of force and no system of police. Again, as in Hawaii, such a theocracy could not govern a large population very long and the size of a paramount chiefdom waxed and waned as tributary minor chiefdoms moved from dependence to independence over time. There was not, in other words, any secular state apparatus that could forcibly hold a large political system together. The integrative means were largely customs, etiquette, and religious idealogy.

Possibly the Portuguese navigator Quirós was the first European to touch the Society Islands, but no lasting effect or even memory of him remained. It was not until 1767 that Wallis arrived and claimed possession of Tahiti in the name of Great Britain. He stayed only five weeks; the French explorer, Bougainville, arrived the following year but stayed only thirteen days. The most famous of the early explorers was Captain James Cook, who arrived in 1769 to set up an observatory to chart the passage of the planet Venus across the face of the sun.

Captain Cook stayed on Tahiti for three months this time, and he was to return three more times. He explored all of the islands in the group, making scientific observations of their customs which he recorded meticulously for the British Royal Society. Cook's voyages and his thorough accounts and charts fostered the use of many Polynesian Islands as outfitting stops for whalers and merchantmen.[5]

But for the rest of the century, the contacts of Europeans with Tahitians were much more sporadic and limited than had occurred in Hawaii, which had become a major provisioning stop. However, the hospitable Tahitians did not escape the ravages of carousing sailors. Eventually it came to the attention of some fervent English evangelists that the idyllic "savages" of the south seas needed their help—help to overcome their own godless immorality and help to prevent their debauchery by contact with the very worst elements of European society, sailors and beachcombers. In 1797 the ship *Duff* arrived in Tahiti, with a band of London Missionary Society members, numbering thirty-nine, including six wives. They and their baggage and equipment were set on the beach and the *Duff* sailed away.

The political situation in Tahiti at that time was confused. A young chief named Tu had made friends with Captain Cook a few years earlier, finding that his prestige became elevated by this association. He was astute as well as practical, and always made himself useful when Europeans came. He had acquired a few muskets from the *Bounty* mutineers, and renaming himself King Pomare, he set up a ramshackle kingdom that was less a political organization than a sort of bully-boy operation based on violence. He was friendly to the missionaries and allowed them to set up housekeeping and to build a church at Matavai Bay.

The native Tahitian way of life was already in a state of decay. Debauched by alcohol, suffering from syphilis and other diseases, the population in decline, the native idols untended, and with a final loss of confidence in themselves, many natives were ripe for conversion. When Pomare (Tu) died in 1803, his son Pomare II saw the political advantages of taking on a new state religion. He was baptized in 1812 and set about making Tahiti a Christian state. He was defeated by his rivals and went into exile to the near-

5. One of the most famous of these was the stopover in 1778 of H.M.S. *Bounty*, commanded by Lt. Bligh, who had been one of Cook's men. The five months spent there were so idyllic that the men mutinied rather than resume the voyage.

by island of Moorea. He gathered more adherents, however, and won the final battle in 1815.

Pomare II followed his military success with forced conversions to Christianity. The marae temples and the ancient idols were destroyed and unbelievers put to death. Pomare built a cathedral seven hundred feet long, and the population was forced to attend services there. Pomare was firmly in the saddle, but at what a cost! Captain Cook had estimated the population of Tahiti as one hundred thousand, but by 1815 it had fallen to ten thousand (Goldman 1970, p. 172). Aboriginal culture, in addition to religion, was all but abolished.

All authorities agree that the unification of Tahiti was caused by the power of the Europeans, and contrasts with Hawaii in that the religious impetus to statehood was provided by missionaries, whereas the state in Hawaii preceded the arrival of missionaries. It is believed that since Pomare was not of the highest of hereditary chiefs he could not possibly have kept control of Tahiti without a full monopoly of naked force, and for this reason he simply destroyed his rivals (Goldman 1970, p. 176).

Tonga

Aboriginal Tongan social organization was essentially like that of Hawaii and Tahiti. There were the same three strata: chiefs and their immediate relatives (*eike*); an intermediate level of chief's attendants (*matapule*); the bulk of society, the commoners (*tua*). According to legend, the Tongan island group had a single paramount chief, the *tui tonga,* whose lineage was founded by the sky-god Tangaroa. It is possible that a single lineage of paramount chiefs could have ruled the islands as a unified chiefdom, for the total population was only twenty to twenty-five thousand (Oliver 1951, p. 130).

It is supposed that the tui tonga lineage began to rule about one thousand years ago. In the fifteenth century the head of a collatoral branch of the lineage was given charge of the secular administration, while the tui tonga retained for himself the purely spiritual function. In time, a third branch was given the secular power and this one became a dynasty more powerful in statecraft than the other two. It has already been noted in Hawaii the readiness of Polynesian theocratic chiefdoms to divide power into secular and sacred branches. It is interesting that the Tongan tradition that relates this story also specifies the motive for it, that the tui tonga reorganized the political power in order to isolate his position from any possibility of overthrow by secular violence (Thomson 1894). (Compare this with the political motives of the Hawaiian "cultural revolution.")

The degree of stratification, the power of the chief, and the centralization and administration of power in Tonga was comparable to that of a paramount chief on a major Hawaiian island. Redistribution and craft production were bureaucratically controlled, as in Hawaii, and with the same great ceremonial occasions (especially the first-fruits) for the collection and relocation of goods. (Irrigation was controlled bureaucratically in Hawaii, but not in Tonga. However, since political organizations in Tonga were otherwise similar to those in Hawaii [Sahlins 1958, p. 23], the supposition arises that perhaps the political significance of the control of water has been exaggerated in most anthropology textbooks.)

Tabus and sumptuary rules that protected the tui tonga were similar to those of Hawaii. Evidence of the chief's power to mediate disputes is contradictory or confusing, perhaps because, just as in Hawaii and Tahiti, a chief could intervene in any dispute that concerned him, but the normal disputes were settled by the kinsmen of the disputants—as in primitive society generally.

The tui tonga was surrounded by a great many tabus respecting his great sanctity, such as in Hawaii and Tahiti. He was the most "divine," the highest priest by heredity, and had no rival in status. In this sense Tonga seems to have been united and stabilized for a long time. The question, however, is whether this is indicative of a true primitive *state:* The tui tonga did not really administrate or adjudicate, nor did he seem to have war-making or peace-making prerogatives, and even the collecting and redistributing of goods was in the hands of the secular authorities. Furthermore, the Tongan population was so small compared to Hawaii and Tahiti that the problem of political unification was much lessened. Perhaps the tui tonga could be said to be the sacred high priest of an unusually large theocratic chiefdom rather than head of an unusually small state.

The islands had been visited briefly by a few early explorers, but the first important experience of Tongans with Europeans was with Captain Cook, who came first briefly in 1773, and then four years later. The islands were in political turmoil by then, but Cook was unaware of it and he named the group the Friendly Islands (Goldman 1970, p. 281). Members of the London Missionary Society arrived in 1797 and tried to reduce the turmoil. Eventually, with the coming of even more Europeans, a true monarchy in the European style was established in 1845.

The "Invisible Hand"

It would seem that of the three island groups considered in this chapter, the Hawaiian Islands had reached a somewhat higher political development toward statehood. And although the actual arrival of the state probably depended somehow on the presence of Europeans, nevertheless, as Goldman says (1970, p. 200), "Europeans have been given far too much credit for their part in bringing about a new social order in Hawaii; they were only the midwives." In a study of the origin of the primary state, the Hawaiian case is therefore much more instructive than that of Tahiti or Tonga.

But actually all three must be considered together, and their similarities noted, so that the Hawaiian instance can be seen as a good case history of a general political process rather than as a unique, unpredictable, historical aberration. One of the most interesting aspects of the Hawaiian cultural revolution, which finally established the overall hegemony of the state, is the philosophical and methodological problem of our interpretation of these political acts. Was it a unique historical manifestation of the political skill of a great man (or his great mother), or can it be seen as an inevitable consequence of the "invisible hand" of cultural or structural cause-and-effect? Most writers have seen it as a unique personal drama, inexplicable. Kroeber was the first to interpret the events on a more impersonal, less individually motivated basis—the notion of "cultural fatigue." But this is too tautological. Davenport was more specific and sophisticated in his interpretation of the events, and his interpretation is convincing. His stress is on the rational and skillful grasp of the winning politician.

This brings up another aspect of the "great man versus the invisible hand" debate. Intentionality or teleology is a frequent factor in history, especially when the events are political. If the Hawaiian cultural revolution is usefully interpreted this way, does it invalidate a cause-and-effect solution; is this paradox like the everlasting free will versus determinism arguments? Davenport does not think so, as implied by his approval of Webb's interpretation that the revolution can be seen as a manifestation of a general and normal secularizing process involved in the evolution of a chiefdom. We should agree, and welcome Davenport's special sophisticated knowledge of what actually happened (including what probably went on in the protagonists' minds), but we may also welcome, for the more general purposes of this book, a sophisticated grasp of the structural leverages and constraints that plot the actors' actions in general ways.

Chiefdoms are like any other hierarchical societies, especially vulnerable at times of transfer of power. The devices with which the Polynesians attempted to control the disruption attendant on succession were primogeniture and close endogamous marriages. The problem of the succession to chief was to insure that a person believed to be the equal of the old chief in mana, in charisma, was the normal candidate—the incumbent chief's eldest son by the highest-ranking mother possible.

Nevertheless, there were in fact serious difficulties in succession. These were caused, not by any failure of the principle of primogeniture, but rather by a tendency in theocracies to subdivide because of the dual nature of the hierarchy, to separate into two kinds of rule, sacred and secular, or better, priestly and administrative. In a chiefdom growing to large and complex dimensions, as in Hawaii, the military-administrative aspect came to have increased political power—as was demonstrated so dramatically in the great cultural revolution. This is not to discredit the skill of Liholiho in fomenting it, nor even to deny the possible presence of "cultural fatigue." But these factors must be seen in the context of processes—especially the stresses and strains—that seem to beset growing chiefdoms anywhere.

III

The Archaic Civilizations

10

The Origins of Civilization in Mesoamerica

MESOAMERICA is the term used by modern anthropologists to refer to the complex geographic region in which there have been found several examples of American Indian societies that participated in the development of a native civilization. The region includes the highlands and lowlands of central and southern Mexico and Guatemala and the lowlands of Salvador, British Honduras, and part of western Honduras. The geographical differences are enormous and the consequent variations in cultural adaptation correspondingly great. On the one hand, in the arid highlands, dense populations were agglomerated by virtue of intensive agriculture (irrigation, drainage, and terracing); on the other hand were lowlands of greater rainfall and more extensive agriculture, with more-scattered populations. The best-known examples of these two-types are the highland city-states of the Valley of Mexico (where Mexico City is found today) and the lowland Maya-speakers of Yucatán and the neighboring region of the Petén, in Guatemala.

The archaeological record reveals that in Mexico there existed for a very long period a hunting-gathering economy, with social groups consisting of small nomadic bands scattered widely over the landscape. The beginnings of cultivation in Mexico were small in scale, and the shift from primary dependence on hunting-gathering to agriculture very slow. According to MacNeish's work (1964) in the Tehuacán Valley, agriculture began in about 7200 B.C., and took until about 2500 B.C. (the "Purrón" phase) before agricultural products constituted about 70 percent of the people's diet. Pottery appeared in the valley about this time, implying somewhat sedentary villages, which in turn suggests an important dependence on agriculture. By this time many of the important Mexican crops were in cultivation: maize, beans, squash and pumpkin, avocado, chile, cotton, tobacco, tomato, and cactus (principally nopal and maguey).

Sanders and Price (1968, pp. 24–25) use this Purrón phase (2500 B.C.) to mark the beginning of the Formative period, an epoch during which most of the important cultural inventions occurred that were related to the continued development and spread of settled agricultural villages. They see the Formative stage as ending with the emergence of the various climactic local developments called Classic: Teotihuacán (in the central Plateau), Monte Albán (Classic Zapotec in Oaxaca), and the lowland areas typified by Tajín in Veracruz and Tikal and others in the Petén of Guatemala. The probable dates range from B.C./A.D. for Teotihuacán to 600 A.D. for Tajín. The most important developments of the Formative period were the gradual intensification of agriculture, continuous population growth (manifested by greater numbers of archaeological sites and their larger size), and the transformation of small simple villages into stratified societies and states (ibid., p. 29). Other experts differ in certain respects of nomenclature and dating (especially Coe 1962), but the basic notion of evolutionary growth in complexity is common to all, and the order of precedence by which the Formative became the Classic period in these regions seems to be agreed upon (table 1). They will be discussed below in that order.

Teotihuacán (ca. B.C./A.D.–800 A.D.)

The Valley of Teotihuacán is a side-valley of the huge Valley of Mexico, lying on the northeast side about twenty-five miles from Mexico City. The archaeological site of Teotihuacán in its Classic

Table 1 / *Stages and Periods in Mesoamerica*

Mesoamerica as a Whole			Central Gulf Coast	South Gulf Coast	Central Plateau	Oaxaca	Highland-Coastal Guatemala	Lowland Maya	
	Late	1500 A.D.							
Post-classic			Cempoalla	Soncuautla	Aztec	V (Monte Alban)	Chinautla	Mayapan	
	Early	1200 A.D.							
			Tajin III	Upper Cerro de las Mesas	Toltec (Mazapan)	IV	Tohil	Chichen Toltec	
		900 A.D.							
	Late				Coyotlatelco	III b	Pamplona Amatle	Tepeu	
Classic			Tajin II		Metepec (Teotihuacan)				
		600 A.D.		Upper Tres	Xolalpan	III a	Esperanza	Tzakol	Ch za
	Early		Upper Remojadas II	Zapotes	Tlamimilolpa		Aurora		
		300 A.D.			Miccaotli	II	Santa Clara	Chicanel	
	Terminal (Protoclassic)			Middle Tres	Tzacualli		Arenal		
		B.C./A.D.	Upper Remojadas I	Zapotes	Patlachique				Ch d
					Chimalhuacan	I	Miraflores		
	Late		Lower Remojadas				Providencia	Mamom	
		600 B.C.		La Venta	Ticoman		Majadas		
Form-ative					Tlatilco Amacusac	?	Las Charcas		T
			Trapiche						
	Middle			La Venta Pre-Complex A	Early Zacatenco		Arevalo Ocos		
			?						
		1500 B.C.		San Lorenzo					
				?					
	Early				Coatepec				
		2500 B.C.			Purron				
					Abejas				
Archaic					Coxcatlan				
					El Riego				
		7200 B.C.							
Early Hunters-Gatherers					Tepexpan—Ixtapan				

phase was undoubtedly the largest and most important urban center in Mesoamerica. Sanders believes that the Teotihuacán Valley population reached 150,000.[1] The urban center itself grew to cover about two thousand acres. The most striking evidence of large populations and of some kind of political control are the enormous Pyramids of the Sun and Moon, the Temple of the Feathered Serpent, and many other large civil and religious buildings. There is little doubt that Teotihuacán grew faster than its neighbors during the Formative period and was able to dominate them. In short, Teotihuacán was undoubtedly the first true urban civilization in Mesoamerica, unless Monte Albán in Oaxaca also qualifies (Sanders and Price 1968, p. 140). At any rate, the development of Teotihuacán was clearly primary, uninfluenced by the example of neighbors.

On the basis of the relationship of urban density and political development that we have seen in previous chapters, we might expect that the dominating power of Teotihuacán approached that of a true empire. In a summary of the evidence, Bernal (1967, p. 98) points out that all of the localities occupied in the classic period in the Valley of Mexico other than Teotihuacán are small towns and villages. This suggests a complete domination by the urban center. But how far outside the Valley of Mexico this power extended is of course difficult to know for certain. Some evidences and professional opinions, to be cited later, bear on the question of empire.

The huge basin that is the Valley of Mexico probably was the dominant cultural power in Mesoamerica since the origin of the first urban center there. The dominance of this area in Mexico was retained throughout the colonial and modern eras. It is natural, therefore, that a great deal of archaeological effort has been expended there. From early in this century until midcentury archaeologists were mainly interested in pottery analysis, chronology, and site description. In the 1950s and intensifying in the 1960s, broader analytical interests have become predominant, involving regional surveys and test excavations that are problem-oriented within an evolutionary-ecological theoretical framework.[2]

1. Personal communication, 1973.

2. Interpretive syntheses by Armillas (1951) and Sanders (1956) were probably the first catalysts for these broader studies. Since 1960 a

Since the region is decidedly arid, the growth in population was related to the development of water-controlled agriculture (i.e., irrigation of dry lands and drainage of swampy lands, and eventually, reclamation of lake beds), and of extensive transportation of products by water. This latter feature assumes considerable importance because the Mesoamericans lacked animal transport. In terms of population density, therefore, the geographical features of the basin—especially the lakes and rivers—meant that a large amount of coordinated labor had to be used to expand the agricultural base. But once that labor was expended, the fertility of the soil and the control over the water were tremendous compared to the earlier period of dependence on rainfall and flood alone.

Prior to the rise of the city, the Teotihuacán Valley was occupied for about one thousand years by sedentary agriculturalists practicing a form of agriculture dependent on rainfall and involving the cultivation of swiddens.[3] The settlement pattern of that period suggests a tribal form of organization. By 300 B.C. the population had grown considerably and a series of tiny chiefdoms were formed. According to Sanders and Price,[4]

> Between 300 B.C. and B.C./A.D. several striking changes in the ecosystem occurred: The population probably doubled every generation, settlements shifted to the alluvial plain, and toward the end of this period, at least half of the population was concentrated into a single, huge, sprawling, nucleated center at the site of the Classic city. Millon (1964) feels that at this time Teotihuacán was already a city and that there was extensive architectural activity. By the time of Christ, there was at least valley-wide political integration, comprising an area of approximately 500 km^2. The subsequent history of Teotihuacán is one of expansion of the size of this nucleated center, increase in density

---

large number of coordinated researches have been made: Sanders's regional surveys and excavations in the Teotihuacán Valley, Millon's intensive surveys at the Teotihuacán urban center (Drewitt 1966; Millon 1964, 1966, 1967; Spence 1968), Parsons's surveys in the Texcoco and Chalco regions (1968*b*, 1969, 1970, 1971), and Lorenzo's interdisciplinary work (1968) are some of the more important.

3. Swiddens are nonpermanent agricultural plots produced by cutting back and burning off the plant cover.

4. (1968, pp. 140–41). Sanders was for several years the head of the Teotihuacán Valley Project, and has amassed plentiful data on settlement patterns. Price (1971) has provided an excellent overview of irrigation systems.

and socioeconomic differention of the population of the center, and expansion of the orbit of its political influence. By the Miccaotli phase Teotihuacán had certainly reached the status of a city and the Teotihuacán culture the status of a civilization. The subsequent history of Central Mexico was one of cyclical rise and decline of urban civilizations with changing centers of political and economic power.

It is probable that the subsistence and demographic base for the founding of the huge city was the installation of an irrigation system. Sanders' Teotihuacán Valley Project found indirect evidence that in the Early Classic period the Lower Valley (an alluvial plain) was irrigated by springs; floodwater apparently was controlled in the Middle Valley. The slopes were probably also terraced and irrigated with floodwater (Sanders and Price 1968, p. 149.)

Water control is, of course, of tremendous significance for agriculture, so obviously so that there is no need to go into the particulars here. The result of such control, an increased and consistent food supply, must be regarded as "permissive," as an enabler, so to speak, without which a dense population, above all a city, could not be sustained. But does it *cause* a city? And does it *create* a controlling bureaucracy? Because so much controversy and speculation have surrounded this possible relationship, it seems preferable to defer discussion of its role in Mesoamerica's rise to civilization to near the end of this chapter, after other Mesoamerican regions have been discussed. At this point it is sufficient to note that the rise to urban status of Teotihuacán seems to have been accompanied by the development of systematic water control.

It has often been said that in the development of civilization urbanism is a necessary component—that city and civilization imply each other. We need not try to settle this point now, but since Childe (1950), Adams (1966), and many others do believe this, it is well to discuss the factors involved in the rise to urbanism as well as the origins of the civilization itself.[5]

Sanders (1956) has emphasized that the highlands of Central Mexico have numerous environmental areas and smaller niches

5. The population of the urbanized Valley of Teotihuacán rose to 85,000 by about 400–500 A.D. (Parsons 1968*b*, p. 875) or to 100,000, according to Sanders and Price (1968, p. 149).

that vary greatly in type of soil, amount of rainfall, kinds of irrigation possibilities (springwater, terracing for flood control, bottomland canals, drainage, and so on), altitude, forests (for wood and game), lakes (for salt and fish), and scattered mineral deposits (for obsidian, basalt, and lime). Such "symbiotic regions" normally are involved in exchanges of the varying kinds of produce; and as the exchanges become customary, regional specialization is increased. One important result of the specialization is greater efficiency in production, which in turn helps provide for an enlarged and denser population.

Specialization is also likely to have a significant social or political result. As Flannery and Coe (1966) have pointed out, in such complicated environments reciprocal exchanges between villages are not nearly so effective as a coordinated system of redistribution. Redistribution is necessarily by plan and acquiescence of the producers since the reciprocity is delayed. That is, a village producing maize and needing obsidian does not have to find an obsidian-producing group that needs maize in order to effect an immediate balanced reciprocity. Instead, it can at harvest send the regular surplus of maize to the redistribution center and acquire other things as it needs them. But for redistribution to work, it needs a coordinating center, a redistributor—an "authority" who can plan and who can make equitable-seeming allocations. The redistributive system, as we have seen in the preceding materials on the ethnology of chiefdoms, is the economic exchange aspect of this kind of power structure. And the positive feedback is apparent: The more centralized and organized the authority center, the better the redistribution and related specialization works; the better the redistribution works, the more necessary and beneficial will be the authority center. They ascend together the path toward civilization, in a pattern of mutual reinforcement.

As the system improves, the role of the authority is strengthened, which in turn makes it able to widen its scope. This seems evident particularly in the increased ability of the center to subsidize specialized craftsmen and public labor, as evidenced so strikingly in the art work and massive monuments so characteristic of the rise of early civilizations.

Redistribution, we see ethnologically, is closely associated with a ramage form of residential organization, and according to evidence analyzed by Sanders and Price (1968, pp. 155–157) this pattern must have been characteristic of the whole Mexican basin. Once this form of centralized authority exists in local organization, the possibilities of expansion and inclusion while retaining the centralization are increased.

Redistribution and its associated power center can also have a pacifying effect over a wide area. When a population concentrated through the redistributive system finally occupied all of the adjacent agricultural niches, there were two normal alternative results: competition and cooperation. Competition frequently resulted in warfare, which *may* have resulted in a special form of cooperation, wherein the defeated submitted to collaboration with others under the direction of the erstwhile alien authority. Such a consequence seems actually rare in the primitive world, and possibly is feasible only in the context of chiefdoms evolving into a state.

Jeffrey Parsons's (1971) regional surveys in the Valley of Mexico have suggested that the rise of the Teotihuacán center involved such local hostilities. In his words:

> . . . We have the impression of a highly competitive situation in Terminal Formative times throughout the Valley of Mexico. This era saw two primary centers of roughly equivalent size and power (Tezoyuca-Patlichique Teotihuacán and Cuicuilco [ca. 200 B.C.–B.C./A.D.]), together with numerous secondary centers, struggling amongst themselves, on various levels, for access to strategic productive resources and trade routes [pp. 197–98].

There should be mentioned now another rather different and special kind of competition, the disturbance caused by migrations of predator peoples. In highland Mexico such invaders were known in myth as Chichimec, nomadic warriors from the arid northern frontier called the Great Chichimeca. Teotihuacán was in fact destroyed in the eighth century A.D., and perhaps this was a consequence of invasion. Tula, a city-state at the center of the Toltec empire, had developed on the northern outskirts of the Teotihuacán civilization, and may have been itself dominated by the warrior invaders. Following a period of military and political dominance over much of Mexico (as far south as Yucatán), Tula was destroyed in the twelfth century A.D., after a series of invasions from the north (Sanders and Price 1968, p. 33). (Among the later "Chichimec" invaders were the Aztec, who grew to dominate most of highland Mexico by the time of the Spanish conquest.) It is difficult to assess the historical accuracy of these legends of Chichimec invaders, but even if the times and places are inaccurate, it does seem likely that there were such invasions, since the legends were so widely known. It seems impossible otherwise to account for them. At any rate, they were less-developed borderland peoples who made use of the existing state structure. We shall see more of this phenomenon in subsequent chapters.

If Sanders and Price are correct in their data and analysis, then all of the above features were involved in the origin of civilization at Teotihuacán.[6] It remains now to discuss more briefly the few other major civilizational centers in Mesoamerica.

The Oaxaca Valley (ca. B.C./A.D.–900 A.D.)

The archaeological record in the Oaxaca Valley shows a long span of development through the Formative and Classic periods, lasting until the Spanish conquest. Although the Oaxaca Valley's development was fairly typical of highland Mexico, and although it shared the Teotihuacán calendar, hieroglyphs, and many of the widespread art styles, the circumstances and form of adaptation differed from Teotihuacán in some important respects. The most important and most fully excavated site in the Oaxaca Valley is Monte Albán, an elite ceremonial center.

The valley lies in the southern highlands of Mexico and is the site of the present-day city of Oaxaca. The average elevation of the valley floor is about five thousand feet, a semiarid climate with rainfall mostly confined to the summer season. The valley floor is a rather flat alluvial plain, with little erosion. The farming system of the valley was intensive, with some small-scale water control by villages, but without an integrated canal system.[7]

Canal irrigation on a large scale is nowhere practical in the Valley of Oaxaca, where springs are small and surface flows are not sufficient

6. There has been no criticism of this thesis to date.

7. We are fortunate that an intensive interdisciplinary field investigation, begun in Oaxaca in 1966, has yielded important data on irrigation systems, demography, and political growth. Most of the data in the following pages are from Kent Flannery et al. (1971). Blanton (1973) supplies additional new data on settlement patterns.

for irrigating more than a small area. However, because of the unusually high water table, shallow-well irrigation is widely practiced, and this technique, which requires relatively little effort and can be performed on an individual family basis, can be traced back to at least 700 B.C. and probably earlier [Flannery et al. 1971, p. 169].

This "pot irrigation" involves digging a series of shallow wells in the fields and hand-dipping for water with large pots, which are then poured over the individual plants. It is, of course, laborious, but highly productive. Outside this area of intensive gardening, small-scale irrigation canals were formed in the upper areas of the piedmont, but this was a relatively small area. Other areas were dry-farmed, with periodic fallowing. Since the valley was surrounded by mountains, there were also zones of differential rainfall. Eventually most of the various physiographic niches were in production. The agricultural zones were probably "symbiotic," and thus participated in a redistributional system, and the attendant specialization probably raised production considerably on an overall basis (Flannery and Coe 1966).

Flannery et al. (1971, pp. 159, 176) feel that the organization that preceded the Classic period at Monte Albán was of the chiefdom type. Such a feeling, of course, cannot be conclusive, but is based on the indications of rank differences (especially burials of theocratic chiefs), redistribution, trade, monuments, and specialized artists and craftsmen.

By about B.C./A.D., as mentioned above, characteristics of the civilization of the central highlands had developed at Monte Albán. The Classic phase thus not only began at about the same time as that of Teotihuacán, but for unknown reasons the demise of the two centers was also nearly contemporaneous. Coe (1962, p. 127) says that ". . . by the end of Monte Albán III-B, about A.D. 900, all inhabitants had left Monte Albán, and this and other centres of civilization in the Valley of Oaxaca fell gradually into ruin. Later peoples, like the Mixtecs, used the old Zapotec site as a kind of consecrated ground for their tombs, . . . perhaps in an attempt to establish their continuity with the native dynasties which had ruled here for over a thousand years." I can find no other contemporary instances of such disasters and no other suggestion of barbarian invasions. But since the struggles elsewhere with nomadic invaders were taking place within this same narrow time span

(700–900 A.D.), it does seem probable that the abandonment of Monte Albán was related to warfare. However, there is no evidence of earlier invasions related to the origin of the civilization; and in fact we cannot even be sure that Monte Albán was the product of a true empire similar to Teotihuacán.[8]

Kaminaljuyu (ca. 600 A.D.–?)

The importance of this site on the outskirts of Guatemala City is its very long history. The area was occupied continuously from the beginning of the Formative period into the Late Classic. It is the only true urban Mayan site that has been excavated in the highlands, suggesting that a Mayan urban and hydraulic development could have preceded and influenced the lowland nonurban civic centers based on swidden horticulture.

This does not mean that Kaminaljuyu was itself a primary center of empire. There is a strong indication of Teotihuacán influence in the style of sculpture and painting and in the architectural style (Thompson 1954, p. 74). According to Sanders and Price (1968, p. 166), this latter point is of great significance:

> The reasons for stressing the diffusion of architecture as evidence of expansion of states are obvious: a local group may well purchase portable foreign objects as exotic household furniture or even bury them with their dead but (particularly where the local society has a highly evolved religious system) such a group does not voluntarily supply the manpower required for the construction of monumental civic buildings to serve foreign gods. The introduction of large-scale ceremonial architecture of a foreign style in a local sequence, therefore, is evidence that the foreign power in some manner has secured control over the surplus labor of a local population.

These authors (pp. 168–69) argue that the site of Kaminaljuyu represents an actual colonization from the Central Plateau, including some military forces. The Guatemalan site was an un-

8. Recent work on the city of Monte Albán by Richard Blanton (1973) has revealed a defensive wall, a reservoir, and a nearby irrigation system, which he thinks indicate competition in the valley between major centers, and an attempt by the city at defensive self-sufficiency in terms of food and water. He also mentions a continuing study (unpublished) of carved stone monuments by Joyce Marcus, who finds that the replacement of local styles in Monte Albán III by one single overlay style (as well as some scenes depicting conquest) suggests a probable Monte Albán empire.

usually strategic location for controlling access to the lowlands of the Pacific Coast, so rich in the highly prized cacao. This pattern is well documented for the later Aztec's domination of the cacao trade; the Aztec could have been simply following an older arrangement first begun by Teotihuacán. At any rate, here is evidence of highland domination of at least some lowlands. As we discuss the lowlands below we must consider the possibility of lowland nonurban polities as being secondary (or, indeed, perhaps tertiary), that is, due to outside creative influences.

The Lowlands

There is much disagreement as to whether the lowlands could have developed a civilization of the pristine or primary kind. True urban centers have not been found in the lowlands, nor the various forms of water control and terracing that were characteristic of the highlands, nor specialized agricultural zones leading to a high development of economic symbiosis. Sanders and Price believe that political organization, civilization, and urbanism in the New World in general were in their origin and development functionally related to hydraulic agriculture in arid environments (1968, pp. 202–10 and elsewhere).

Michael Coe disagrees. He asserts that the "basic" Mesoamerican pattern, from the Formative period until conquest times, was of "elite centers," clusters of architectural and monumental art and religious works, and residences of ruling and priestly hierarchies, whereas the mass of the people, the swidden agriculturalists, lived in scattered villages and hamlets. This is of course the lowland pattern. Coe, moreover, believes that Mesoamerican civilization actually began in the lowlands and spread from there. Specifically, the earliest and primary source was the Olmec civilization of southern Vera Cruz and Tabasco on the coast of the Gulf of Mexico (1963, p. 83). Miguel Covarrubias also argued this in 1946 (p. 80), and according to James A. Ford (1969, p. 15), "most investigators agree that Olmec culture is the principal ancestor of later high cultural developments."

The Olmec Culture (*1500–800* B.C.) • Many Olmec artifacts and art works *are* truly distinctive and of specialized craftsmanship, and an early radiocarbon date has been established for the principal sites (Ford 1969, p. 15). The most important Olmec site of La Venta flourished between 1200 and 800 B.C. (Ford 1969, p. 188); thus, a major part of this culture is within the Middle Formative period. "There is not the slightest doubt that all later civilizations in Mesoamerica, whether Mexican or Maya, ultimately rest on an Olmec base" (Coe 1962, p. 84).

We may be having semantic troubles here, specifically as to what is meant by the word *civilization*. Sanders and Price associate it with the development of the state, recognizing at the same time the difficulties of inferring reliably from archaeological evidence the fundamental political and social distinctions between chiefdoms and states (1968, pp. 54–57). But many people, Mesoamerican archaeologists particularly, associate civilization with the appearance of only a few indicators, such as a refined art style, a specialized architecture, or writing and a calendar. All of these are, to be sure, found typically among developed archaic civilizations throughout the world. But are they found *only* among true states or empires, or can they, at least singly, anticipate the state? We know, ethnologically, that they can be found in prestate societies—in chiefdoms, that is. The chiefdoms of the southeastern United States had various kinds of monuments; the carving art of the Northwest Coast Indians was highly specialized; the Pueblo Indians had a calendar; the Polynesians' calendar and astronomy, carving, monuments, and so on, were all remarkable. All of these examples demonstrate the chiefdoms' ability to subsidize specialists and control some amount of public labor.

According to Sanders and Price (1968), agreeing in principle with my own earlier definitions (1962), the difference between a chiefdom and a full civilization is evidently a difference in degree (amount, size, excellence) in the above characteristics; the qualitative difference is the legal-repressive aspect of the sociopolitical structure. Sanders and Price see this aspect—indicative of the true state—as making possible greater size and density of population, better and larger military force, and many more kinds of products of specialization. Later in this chapter we will examine evidence against the thesis that the state was necessary for these cultural developments.

It seems that the Olmec culture may have been called a civilization because some investigators have identified a "sophisticated" or "masterful" art style with "civilization." Coe says (1962, p. 84) that "the hallmark of Olmec civilization is the art style." That art style is basically represented in stone carvings, from colossal stone heads, stelae, and altars to tiny jade figurines and pendants. The Olmec style was highly distinctive, featuring the well-known "baby face" and jaguar motifs. One problem in assessing the power and priority of the Olmecs is how to account for the later wide distribution of some of the distinctive Olmec styles and motifs: Was it due to the spread of an Olmec religious cult? Trade? Emulation? There is no answer to this except that we do know that all three are commonplace causes of a wide distribution of elements in an art style. Hence, the simple fact of this distribution cannot be considered good evidence that an Olmec "power" or "empire" caused the spread of these elements.[9]

As for the monumental civic (or "elite") centers, the largest is that of La Venta, with other smaller, more recently excavated, centers at Tres Zapotes and San Lorenzo. Excavations, surface collections, and test-samplings at these sites suggest that the Middle Formative period of Olmec populated a rather smallish district about 125 miles long and about 50 miles wide (Coe 1962, p. 86). The ritual centers, or civic architecture, at these sites are clay constructions of pyramids, plazas, tombs, and mounds. The largest monument, the pyramid at La Venta, is 240 by 420 feet at the base and 110 feet high. It is the largest of its period, but much smaller than the Pyramid of the Sun at Teotihuacán (689 by 689 feet at the base and 210 feet in height). As Sanders and Price admit, though they do not class the Olmec culture as a state, "the size and complexity of these three Olmec centers implies the presence of a well organized social system with some professional administrative and craft personnel" (1968, p. 28). But in their view (and in mine, from ethnological evidence), specialized personnel are as indicative of chiefdoms as they are of states.

In discussing the Olmec, particularly the distribution of so-called Olmec artifacts and motifs, Sanders and Price say in sum-

9. Kent Flannery (1968) argues cogently that this art style probably accompanied symbiosis in important economic trade.

mary (ibid., p. 122): "What the archaeological evidence suggests is that the South Gulf Coast [Olmec] Chiefdoms were larger in population and constructed more imposing civic centers than elsewhere in Mesoamerica during Middle Formative times. Even this generalization is subject to argument, however; and there may have been equally imposing centers on the Chiapas-Guatemala Coast, or at Monte Albán and Kaminaljuyu during the Middle Formative phase, centers whose development may have been quite independent of happenings in the 'tropical heartland.' "

At any rate, during the Formative period development of the Olmec region may well have been faster and the swidden agriculture more productive than in the arid highlands, where the greater potentiality of hydraulic agriculture had not yet been achieved (ibid., p. 134). Robert Heizer (cited by Coe 1962, p. 88) has calculated that the largest center, La Venta, required a supporting population in the hinterlands of at least 18,000, since the main pyramid alone probably took about 800,000 man-days to construct. If so, this was a very large chiefdom.

But we should refrain now from adjudicating this question, for it could go either way. An important point is that the Olmec culture needn't be classified as a state just because its art was so developed, or because its monuments were so large. "800,000 man-days" could bespeak large numbers of days instead of large numbers of men.[10] And large-scale monuments are also, of course, related to the presence or absence of building materials. As Erasmus says (1965, p. 279), "the Maya were living on a great natural erector set—their rocky limestone peninsula—and they chose to play with it."

It is possible that full civilizations occurred only in a few places in lowland Mesoamerica and then only in the Late Classic period, 600–900 A.D. (Sanders and Price 1968, p. 142). Possibly, also, the lowland societies should not be treated as examples of the independent origin of civilization, for they were undoubtedly strongly influenced by the highland empires. Nevertheless, they must be discussed, especially because of their characteristic nonurban organization and other demographic peculiarities, and be-

10. On inferences to be made from massive monuments, see Kaplan (1963) and Erasmus (1965).

cause their agricultural system was so different from that of the highland societies.

Tajín and Tikal (ca. 600 B.C.–B.C./A.D.*)* • On the Central Gulf Coast of Mexico, Tajín was the major center for a large nuclear area. This was apparently one of the first centers comparable to Teotihuacán or Monte Albán to arise in the lowland areas. Tikal, in the Petén of Guatemala and the largest of the Mayan cities, was the other possible rival to Tajín, and so distant from Teotihuacán that it deserves separate consideration.

Tajín was located in the tropical rain forest in northern Veracruz. The monumental center, constructed around 600 A.D., had a great pyramid. The center was abandoned and burned around 1200 A.D., probably a consequence of the widespread Chichimec invasions. Stylistically, the monuments and the arts show strong influence from Teotihuacán, suggesting that Tajín originally may have been a colony of Teotihuacán satellites (Coe 1962, pp. 119–23). Sanders and Price (1968, p. 142) point out, also, that its florescence seems to have taken place in Late Classic times, after Teotihuacán had collapsed and left a power vacuum. A satellite power in origin, in other words, it was able when freed from domination to itself dominate a large lowland area—an area large enough, at any rate, to supply the labor to build a huge monumental center.

Tikal, in the Petén region of northern (lowland) Guatemala, seems to have been the largest and one of the earliest of the regional ceremonial centers of the areas occupied by lowland Maya.[11] Its development occurred in the Late Formative period (600 B.C.–B.C./A.D.), so it is roughly contemporaneous with Kaminaljuyu in highland Guatemala.

The great court of Tikal—the ceremonial center—has two huge temple-crowned pyramids, at each side, together with a number of smaller temple-pyramids on platforms. For the total complex includes adjacent platforms with dwelling (or "caste"-like) compounds and still other pyramids and buildings (Thompson 1954, pp. 3, 62–64).

But Tikal lacked truly urban population concentrations. Build-

11. A smaller site nearby, Uaxactún, has the oldest dated monument but does not challenge for early status of urban statehood as much as Tikal.

ings that had possible dwelling rooms were probably the residences of a sacerdotal-temple-craftsmen class. According to Sanders and Price (1968, pp. 162–66), Tikal was in striking contrast to Teotihuacán in demographic and settlement patterns. Surface surveys showed that the population was nucleated in hamlets arranged mainly on level ridge-tops or natural terraces—with none of the overall planning that characterized Teotihuacán.[12]

Haviland (1969) estimates the population of the core area of 65 square kilometers as 39,000, which Sanders reduces to 26,000 (because the average figure of 5.7 persons per nuclear family is too high). Sanders (1972, p. 125) estimates the density of this core together with the surrounding populated area as an average of 200 per square kilometer—assuming that all of the Late Classic houses were simultaneously occupied—which is, as he says, a dubious assumption.

This is far from "urban," in either estimate. On the other hand, it is too densely settled for all the people to have subsisted by their own swidden agriculture. Either they must have been supported in part by tribute collection from a wider region (as was, of course, labor for public buildings), or else the dwelling groups were not nearly all contemporaneously occupied. But even if the elite residences of the civic center were completely occupied, they housed a population of only about two or three thousand.[13]

Tikal was the largest and most nucleated site of swidden (lowland) agriculturalists in Mesoamerica, yet very far below the size, density, and complexity of Teotihuacán. Even the civic architecture reflects the difference in population scale. The civic compound at Teotihuacán (called the Ciudadela) and market alone cover as much ground as all of the buildings at Tikal. Think of the differences if the Teotihuacán pyramids of the sun and moon and their associated complexes were added! If lowland Maya "city-states" were in fact states, they were clearly nonurban—as even the case of Tikal, the largest, attests.

12. Interestingly, Puleston and Calendar (1967) have discussed the possibility that modest defensive earthworks may have surrounded the hamlets.

13. It should be observed, however parenthetically at this point, that the lack of urbanization was probably not due to the inherent deficiencies of swidden agriculture based on root crops—for such gardening can be very productive (cf. Carneiro 1961; Bronson 1966).

How, then, to account for Tikal? Evidently the intermediate position of Kaminaljuyu in highland Guatemala was the key. This city was probably a colonylike appendage of Teotihuacán, and in turn may have formed itself as a nuclear center over a set of symbiotic regions that included Tikal and other lowland chiefdoms of the Petén. Sanders and Price believe—and this seems reasonable from ethnological experience—that groups of low-level, nonurban swidden agriculturalists can become altered structurally by becoming a functioning part of an imperial network, particularly as this might intensify any tendency toward centralization and redistribution already present. The new outside power would immeasurably strengthen the position of the local elite, and make that elite in turn receptive to the use of techniques of government that originated in a hydraulic highland civilization (Sanders and Price 1968, pp. 204–205).[14]

City, State, and Civilization in Mesoamerica

The case for Teotihuacán as an important site of the development of a primary civilization in highland Mesoamerica seems well established. The more-or-less contemporary development at Monte Albán may have been also primary and independent, or it may not, but most likely it depended on Olmec influence. There are formidable mountain obstacles between the two valleys, which also are about two hundred fifty miles apart. This problem of independence presents no major difficulty for the present, however, since the Oaxaca development does not require any modification of our generalizations about Teotihuacán. To be sure, there was one interesting ecological divergence with respect to water control, but this has no bearing on the matter of Monte Albán's possible independence: The functional-ecological significance of the form of water control is the same whether the state development was independent or not.

14. It may be remembered that after the collapse of Teotihuacán a power vacuum occurred in Central Mexico until Tula finally succeeded Teotihuacán as a controlling center. It is of interest that following the fall of Teotihuacán there was a fifty- to sixty-year cessation of building activity at Tikal (ibid., p. 206). This and much other evidence support Rathje's (1972) hypothesis of the great significance of long-distance trade in stimulating the rise of the centralized lowland polity.

The other highland site, Kaminaljuyu in Mayan Guatemala, was apparently a colony of the Teotihuacán empire. Its significance is that it demonstrates how truly extraordinary was the wide influence of Teotihuacán. Also, its presence seems to afford a plausible explanation for some of the developments in the lowland Maya region (the Petén). This should be viewed as a provisional judgment at this point, however, since we do not want such a problematical case to influence subsequent generalizations.

A major problem has to do with the relations of highlands and lowlands and with the question of donor and receiver in the origin and spread of civilization. Archeologists who have worked with Olmec and Mayan materials have, in the past at least, tended to consider these—particularly the Olmec—as the source of "high culture." The rich developments in Olmec art did in fact antedate others, and judging from the subsequent wide distribution of Olmec-like art motifs, calendar, writing, and architecture—all of which are indicative of a complex specialized redistributional government—Olmec influence must have been great and widespread. The culture of the lowland Maya also had a wide influence, and its sheer excellence is agreed upon by all art historians and archaeologists. Both the Olmec and the Maya qualify as true civilizations, except that of Childe's ten criteria the urbanism is only modest and there is no evidence of a repressive secular state apparatus.

The urbanism so characteristic of Teotihuacán, contrasting with the much smaller "elite," or ceremonial, centers in the lowlands, must be due to special local factors that do not directly bear on the question of the development of civilization. Sanders and Price (1968, pp. 235–39) conclude their important book by emphasizing that the problem of urbanism is distinct from that of state and civilization, a caution we will do well to heed.

The question of the repressive state as an important indicator of civilization is obviously a much more difficult problem. Sanders and Price accept this criterion. The distinction is in terms of the presence of a qualitative demarker: statelike means of integration, mostly having to do with repressive force. But such things are not visible archaeologically, at least in these cases, and we should be careful that we speak of something real, something other than a verbal device or guess. Sometimes something looking like violence is depicted in iconographs, to be sure, but this violence seems to be related to sacrificial victims, war prisoners, military episodes, and the like.

The rise of states in the ethnohistorical record reviewed in earlier chapters taught us, most importantly, that the uses of force in internal repression were against "princes" or other aristocratic pretenders at time of crisis or succession, and in external relations, to create or maintain a foreign conquest. There was, in other words, no evidence of violence used by rulers against a class or stratum of the original society. Furthermore, the manifested violence can be taken normally as a sign of the failure of internal and external integrative and peacemaking devices to operate effectively.

It would seem, judged only provisionally at this point, that the major differences between the important highland societies like Teotihuacán and Tula and lowland examples like the Olmec and the Maya have to do with *degrees* in the amount of urbanism, amount and distance of trade, intensity of agriculture and overall population density. Local ecological factors, as Sanders and Price emphasize, can be used to account for these. In all of the characteristics of civilization other than urbanism and the repressive state controls, however, the lowland cultures were at least the equal of the highland cultures (indeed in some ways superior). It would seem, then, that we can consider them both as civilizations. This would mean, of course, that neither urbanism nor state violence is a necessary factor in the *development* of civilization—as we have stated before.

11

The Origins of Civilization in Peru

THERE ARE SUCH important similarities between the geographic setting and the cultural adaptations and developments in Peru[1] and those in Mesoamerica that some archaeologists posit a sort of diffusional continuum between them (Strong 1951; Willey 1955; Lathrap 1966; and especially Ford 1969). But there are also significant differences that seem to cast some doubt on this proposition, especially when one tries to account for sociopolitical structural developments by reference to "contacts" that must have been indirect (Millon 1968, p. 211). Some aspects of culture are, of course, borrowed and traded over great distances, but others are more likely parallelisms or functional adjustments to similar geographical and historical circumstances. Still others remain idiosyncratic traits that characterize particular cultures

1. Peru, although the name of a modern nation, is used here to designate the locale of the cultural developments under discussion with the proviso that it should include the Bolivian shore of Lake Titicaca where the site of Tiahuanaco is found (cf. Bennett's [1948] "Peruvian Co-Tradition"). *Central Andean,* an alternative in frequent use, would omit the very important Pacific coastal area, unless a longer proviso were made.

over long periods without diffusing even to next-door neighbors or adapting to greatly changed circumstances (Service 1971, ch. 9). We should bear in mind throughout this chapter that the differences between the central Mexican and the Peruvian environment and culture may be as significant as the similarities.

The geographical similarities in the two regions are important mostly in that highly variable environments exist in close proximity in both. The Andes are very high and steep, ascending directly to tremendous heights from near sea level. Within relatively short distances are found deserts, complex river systems, and high valleys, with great differences in fauna and flora, making possible the "symbiotic regions" that were so important in the interpretations of cultural developments in central Mexico. The Peruvian landscape presents, in fact, much greater extremes for such potential ecological specialization.

But some of the differences should now be mentioned. The coastal lowlands of Mesoamerica were areas of highly productive, but extensive, rainfall agriculture, whereas the Pacific Coast of Peru was very arid (because of the atmospheric effect of the cold Humboldt Current) and the areas of useful rainfall in Peru were in the high mountain valleys. In this sense, the significance of highland-lowland contrasts for agriculture was reversed in the two regions (although humid jungles were characteristic of the eastern slope of the Andes). The coastal strip had great potential for irrigation, however, because of the frequent rivers rushing out of the mountains directly across the desert to the ocean. Additionally, the ocean and river mouths were rich in marine foods and aquatic bird-life (the guano deposits became very important for agricultural fertilizer, as they still are). The geography of Peru had, if anything, greater potential for the development of intensive agriculture than Mesoamerica, given similar technologies.

The Formative Era (1500 B.C.–B.C./A.D.)

As in Mesoamerica, the Formative era in Peru was characterized by a long period of slow growth in agricultural techniques, in number of cultigens, in sedentism, and in the size of communities. A fully sedentary "village agriculture" based on maize cultivation was established in both areas around 1500 B.C. In

Mesoamerica about 800 B.C. the great ceremonial center at La Venta (Tabasco) was created, with its associated "Olmec" art style. At roughly the same time, ceremonial mounds appeared in Peru along with the "Chavín" art style. The formal properties of the two styles are different, and the absence of either style in the areas between the two centers of civilization argues "against a close, continuous Olmec-Chavín relationship on the level of style. . . ." (Willey 1962, pp. 4–5). Nevertheless, the rise of such "fine art" so suddenly at about the same time in both Mesoamerica and Peru generates great interest.

It seems likely that the sudden appearance of such styles was related functionally to something that was occurring in both regions. This could only have been the rise of craft specialization, which itself depends on centralized administrative centers and a related redistributional network that can subsidize and reward (i.e., professionalize) full-time artisans.

In the archaeological record of the Formative era in Peru are many indirect evidences of the sudden rise of theocratic chiefdoms: status burials, ceremonial centers, and increased variety in crops probably due to regional specialization and irrigation networks. The break is so sharply evident that Ford, in his monumental comparisons of various Formative cultures in the Americas (1969), divided the Formative into two parts. The early he labeled Colonial Formative, and the later, the Theocratic Formative. We may accept this classification, but for consistency with the other chapters Ford's Theocratic Formative will be designated as a chiefdom form of organization and referred to as such, inasmuch as the structural criteria are exactly paralleled.

Ford says that the real initial impetus of the Formative in Nuclear America (Mesoamerica and Peru) occurred between 1500 and 1000 B.C., based on the diffusion of two different cultural patterns. One was the spread of maize agriculture from its point of origin in highland Mexico. This, added to the already established cultigens, made possible the population increase associated with the Formative cultural florescence. The other pattern was ideological, particularly involving religious concepts (Ford 1969, p. 180):

> . . . The sudden appearance of a religio-political group of ideas began to produce the monumental mound structures, large stone carvings, a lapidary industry for personal adornment, and the distinctive art styles

that are preserved for the admiration of the students of pre-Columbian art. The high points of his first wave of organized religion and political control were the Olmec culture . . . (1200–400 B.C.), Chavín culture . . . (800–400 B.C.), and the Poverty Point–Hopewell cultures of the Mississippi Valley (1200 B.C.–A.D. 200). These were true cultural revolutions; revolutions that apparently were not imposed by military force. Suddenly really tremendous amounts of labor were absorbed in the construction of religious edifices, and marked social stratification can be inferred from burial practices.

Ford, like Willey (1962) before him, tends to divide causality in culture change into two separate kinds: material subsistence (diffusion of maize, in this case), and "ideas" and "belief systems." Ford does mention "tremendous amounts of labor" and "social stratification," both clearly aspects of political power. But this does not sufficiently point up something we already know, that centralized political organization can be a tremendously productive material force in and of itself, and furthermore, that it generates its own appropriate ideology. The political hierarchy of chiefdoms is normally a theocratic one: It invents, extends, or develops forms of religious worship that serve to perpetuate its power by institutionalizing it. In doing this it also controls labor for making monuments for its own glory and that of its ancestors. It subsidizes religious fine arts and other forms of specialized technology, thus increasing its productivity. Perhaps most important of all, it can stimulate and control trade and redistribution on the basis of regional symbiosis (though not on such a grand basis as the later states). Because of this potentiality of chiefdoms, true imperial centers may arise at the nexus of key routes and ecological zones, so important is this economic control once such communities have become dependent on the symbiosis. And finally, the ability of a chiefdom to extend an irrigation network between communities can be a factor not only in holding or extending its power but also in causing a greater and more concentrated population.

Remembering that Olmec and Chavín art styles do not resemble each other in detail but only in their characteristics that seem "civilized" rather than "primitive," we may see them as products of similarly developed chiefdoms. What did diffuse, most obviously, were numerous agricultural crops and techniques, lapidary and ceramic methods (not particular styles), and general technologies of adapting to or exploiting nature. Sociopolitical forms, on the other hand, seem to be closely related to the organizational problems of population size, economic devices, warfare, boundaries, and so on. Let us, then, dispense for the moment with the explanation based on diffusion of "ideas" and "styles" for a closer look at circumstances. Ideas, styles, narcotics, tools, ornaments, and so on, do in fact diffuse, of course, but no such admission helps explain the sporadic and widely separated origins of the first redistributional centers in the Americas, for such centers are complicated structures of many functions, not just "styles" or "ideas."

The spread of the Chavín art style in Peru was over a greater distance than was the Olmec diffusion in Mexico, but otherwise the process was very similar. The Olmec diffusion was apparently a peaceful matter of borrowing through trade, and presumably through emulation, and so was the spread of the Chavín style. According to Ford (1969, p. 190), "the minor extent to which the ceramics and other features were modified indicates that it was accepted as a markedly new and superior block of cultural features; apparently nothing existed that offered successful competition. There is little evidence of military construction, suggesting that the adoption was voluntary. This is in marked contrast to the warfare that characterized the later Pan-Peruvian cultural horizons: the Huari or Tiahuanaco, and the Inca." Willey, in a recent summary, agrees (1971, p. 130).

There is a sense in which Chavín culture was basic to subsequent developments in Peru. Wherever it began (it is named from the type-site of Chavín de Huantar, but that is not necessarily the original site), it was undoubtedly a theocratic chiefdom, which quickly embellished its distinctive religious art and architecture through the creation of craft specialists. Probably adjacent communities were influenced to emulate not only the art and architecture but also the new form of politics; this emulation, of course, should not be construed as the diffusion of the chiefdom form of organization from Mexico to Peru.

The State

At this crucial point, when we move from the "Theocratic Formative" or chiefdom era to consider the rise of states, we must look again at what kinds of archaeological evidence can be used in inferring the presence of a state. This conceptual matter is particularly significant in the case of Peru since one authority, the late Julian H. Steward, was very interested in this question, and his views have tended to predominate. His "functional" classification of the Peruvian stages of development stresses sociopolitical and economic developments and his own particular evolutionary explanations of how they come about. Other writers also are increasingly insistent that their classifications are "functional" rather than concerned solely with pottery "horizon styles" (Willey 1948), yet none has addressed himself to the comparative study of the origins of state and empire as closely as Steward.[2] (It may be relevant that Steward was an ethnologist and the others archaeologists.)

In Steward's work we must judge two different but related theoretical matters: (1) the causal theory of the origin of the state; and (2) the classification of the archaeological data into stages, involving definitions of "chiefdom" and "state." It seems likely that the causal theory influenced the definitions; we must consider this question carefully because the classification can strongly influence our interpretations of the actual data.

The theory is quite simple.[3] Technology applied to the potentialities of a particular environment may make possible the production of a surplus of food. If it does not, the communities remain undifferentiated (unstratified) "folk" societies. With a sufficient surplus, however, full-time craft specialists and military, religious, and political classes appear. Now and then a disclaimer is made that this result is not inevitable (Steward and Faron 1959, p. 63), but otherwise the force of a surplus in subsistence is described as a powerful factor in the evolution of the state. It is not termed *the* cause, but rather a necessary condition that, when it appears, makes possible (or probable) a kind of logical or likely differentiation of the society into inferior food producers and superior nonproducers. The reader has the strong impression that this kind of social stratification appears more or less naturally. Its widespread absence, as in tropical forest environments,

2. The separate essays about this "multilinear evolution" are collected in Steward (1955). Steward's latest formulation is (with Louis Faron) in *The Native Peoples of South America* (1959).

3. It is most succinctly summarized in the section called "Surplus Production and Social Types" (Steward and Faron 1959, pp. 60–64).

is explained as due to the inability of the tribes to produce the required surplus (ibid., p. 62).

The Peruvian "state" in Steward and Faron's view seems to be simply synonymous with a "class-structured society." This conception resembles the Morgan-Engels formulation, with the implication that the state is a repressive apparatus founded to protect the ruling class from the ruled. But it is not boldly stated that repression is *the* cause.

In Peru, these authors say, the small agricultural folk villages grew during the Formative era into states. There seems to have been, according to Steward and Faron, no intervening stage.

> The Formative Era is marked by the introduction of factors that brought about the emergence of local states. A substantial number of new crops grown by means of irrigation supported an increasing population, which lived in small communities dispersed around temple mounds. The temples were the centers of theocratic states under the control of a priestly class, which coordinated the efforts of the several communities in agricultural ritual and probably also directed cooperative irrigation [ibid., p. 70].

This description (as well as a great many others) sounds very like what we have been calling chiefdoms in other chapters. Paradoxically, Steward and Faron do classify as chiefdoms the similarly hierarchical Indian societies in parts of the circum-Caribbean area of Ecuador, Colombia, Venezuela, and the Greater Antilles. It is not clear what the difference in structure might be, for the discussion of these chiefdoms (ibid., p. 200) makes them seem very similar. Evidently the hierarchical societies are "states" when found in Peru and "chiefdoms" when found in the circum-Caribbean area.

In another context, in defining the difference between *state* and *empire,* Steward and Faron (pp. 100–110) describe the state as having two functions. One, it is an agency of central coordination of activities, such as irrigation canals, that serve the needs of the people; second, it is exploitative in the sense that it demands goods and services to support the special nonproducing classes of people, such as warriors and priests. In a "florescent" era, they explain, when the economy is expanding due to new technologies and new resources, this demand on production can also expand without difficulty. But when technology is not progressing and new resources are not available, the state goes outside its normal confines to acquire wealth from other societies. Thus, in time, some states conquer or intimidate others, which become tributaries or are incorporated in a multistate *empire.* The purpose of empire-building is frankly economic exploitation.

According to these authors, the strain imposed on the state by new demands for goods and services in a stagnant economy and the necessity of controlling subject peoples results in a stronger political and legal system. Centralization of these controls leads to population concentrations that become cities. In time an empire incorporates all three stages that preceded its culmination. Steward and Faron put it this way (ibid., p. 103).

> . . . An empire represents a level of sociocultural integration that is higher and qualitatively different from the state level, just as the latter is different from the community level. . . . The folk communities form the lowest or basic level. They carry on the primary functions of producing goods for their own consumption, procreating and rearing children, and living day by day in the context of local social and religious life. . . . The multicommunity, theocratic state represents the second level. The state developed wholly new forms of religion, political and economic organization, and militarism. . . . The empire, an amalgamation of states, constitutes the third level. It is like an additional layer of culture superimposed upon the other two levels.

It now seems clear that Steward and Faron are referring to our category *chiefdom* when they speak of "states" in Peru; and when they talk of "empires," it is our category *state* that is meant (in the sense of exploitative and repressive military measures). So far, if we grant this interpretation, no difficulty is encountered in identifying the stages from their account, since the only problem is semantic.

The "empire" (or state) stage in Peru became evident in the archaeological record toward the end of the era of Regional Florescence, about 400–500 A.D. Irrigation systems had reached fulfillment in most regions, the basic technologies were established, and population was near its maximum. Militarism was very evident, and functioned not only to provide sacrificial victims but also as an "implement of imperialism" (ibid., p. 104). One of the most important and striking of the developments was that of the Mochica, which had by this time acquired hegemony over five or more major valleys in the Peruvian North Coast (Collier 1955, p. 21; Bennett and Bird 1949, p. 182). The Mochican developments deserve a more carefully focused discussion, which follows in the next section.

The North Coast Classic (B.C./A.D.–800 A.D.)

In a formulation resembling that of Steward and Faron, Donald Collier (1961) placed Mochica (and the roughly contemporaneous Gallinazo, Maranga, and Nazca) in a period he called Classic, dating from B.C./A.D. to 800 A.D. This epoch, he felt, witnessed the origin of the state in coastal Peru. His researches showed the presence of a full range of agricultural products; there were trans-valley irrigation systems, and fertilizer was probably used. Population had increased since the Late Formative; in the Viru Valley, for example, it was about five times greater. "There is ample evidence of the growth of class-structured societies and of state control over simple valleys and groups of valleys. The expansion of state power toward the end of the period was associated with intensified warfare. . . ." (p. 106).

Since the above was written, much more work has been done on the irrigation systems, especially by Paul Kosok (1965), and on demography, especially by Richard Schaedel (1966*a, b,* 1969, 1971, and an unpublished ms). Schaedel, in paricular, is directly concerned with functional and operational criteria for distinguishing states from chiefdoms in the archaeological record (much as were Sanders and Price [1968], as discussed in the previous chapter), whereas Collier's discussion above uses the concept "state" much as Steward and Faron do: that is, as though "stateness" were a normal attribute of a stratified society. Schaedel believes that settlement patterns from which population size and distribution can be inferred are of great importance; and above all, that an urban center, concentrating religious, military, political, and economic functions, would be characteristic of a true state. Note that Collier and Schaedel differ, not so much with Childe, but as to which of Childe's criteria is the more important: repressive force due to class stratification, or urbanism.

On the North Coast of Peru, Schaedel sees the eight adjacent valleys that seem to have been part of a "Mochica polity" as large or "super" chiefdoms. The political unit was now multivalley, and the population was increased. The several valleys had populations ranging from 20,000 to 87,000 (the latter, in the largest valley, which had more than twice as much irrigated, cultivable land area as the others [Schaedel 1971, p. 22]). The total population of the Mochica polity is estimated at over 250,000. These figures are based on an estimated population density of one person per acre.

Cultural evidence from graves and iconography (Mochican art was notable for its realism) indicate a warrior-priest aristocracy, an artisan "middle" class, and a lower class of worker-farmers. Schaedel says (ibid., p. 23):

> The capitals seem to reflect a society not unlike that described in the historical accounts of the Chorotegan and Nicarao chiefdoms [in Central America], the more elaborate capitals of which corresponded to the domain of the paramount chiefs (with maximum populations of 10,000) where religious rites were performed and jural rights were mediated, and the smaller village centers (1,000 population) corresponded to the subject chiefs. The major capital of the Mochica polity, although it apparently enjoyed hegemony over most of the other seven valleys, was simply larger, but not more differentiated than the ceremonial centers in the individual valleys.

In other words, the capital, if such it were, was not large enough or differentiated enough (in terms of craft and bureaucratic specializations) to suggest that the multi-functional urban nucleation of Moche had progressed far enough, especially in economic terms, to be a true civilization. Rather, the concept "extended chiefdom" seems appropriate. But this problem can be considered better when we compare the Mochica, as a kind of type case for the North Coast, with later developments that occurred elsewhere.

Relation of Highland and Lowland Developments

The most important contrast between the geography of the lowlands and the highlands in Peru is that the centralized and urbanized developments in the lowlands were based on intensive irrigation agriculture, whereas the highland developments were not—at least not during the major developmental phases. Power clusters developed in the highlands; they were great economic coordinating redistributional centers that were based on the "regional symbiosis" noted in our previous chapter as a critical factor in the florescence of Teotihuacán. On the other hand, the lowland northern coastal valleys of Peru were nearly identical to each other. Teotihuacán, in Mexico, was, of course, *both* a center of coordinated redistribution of regional symbiosis and of complex irrigational systems. In Peru, the possibility of regional symbiosis was probably greater than in Mexico, because of exaggerated environmental differences, but any such symbiosis had to involve the highlands since the environmental differences were essentially due to greatly varying altitudes.

The Effects of Irrigation • The widespread and longstanding irrigation canals in Peru formed a true system, and agriculture was intensive in the fullest sense of the word. It appears that these factors did not mark, or result from, the development of a true state. When stating that "present evidence indicates that the irrigation systems were not built until the requisite authority patterns had come into existence," Lanning (1967, p. 181) makes it clear that the authority patterns in question are those of what we have called chiefdoms. In the North Coast valleys, canal irrigation lasted from about 1400 B.C. until the beginning of the Mochican epoch at B.C./A.D., under lesser chiefdoms only. Even the societies of the next eight hundred years, exemplified by the Mochica, apparently did not reach the level of organization of states; or if they did, they certainly were not highly urbanized or politically complex. Yet the intensity of agricultural development and the canal system had reached their zenith long before the culmination of the Mochica (Classic) period, and *very* long (more than 1,500 years) before the first truly urban, fully developed empires of the Tiahuanaco.

Canal irrigation can clearly become enlarged, systematized, and controlled over a large region without an urban center of a complex state being necessary, as Woodbury has shown (1961). But as it makes possible greater production of crops and better control of that production, it also makes possible a usual (or, other things being equal, perhaps an inevitable) rise in the population density. But greater overall density in a region is not the same thing as the development of a city. A city may need greater and more controlled production to exist, true, but the city is apparently not an inevitable consequence of an increase in either productivity or population. Similarly, the rise of monumental architecture, large armies, and a class of specialized nonproducing priests and artisans will require sufficient food in constant supply, and the means to control and distribute it, but these do not come about as a simple consequence of the enlarged food supply (as is suggested in Steward and Faron's version).

Dominance of the Highland Pattern • Highland centers, of which Huari (sometimes written as Wari) and Tiahuanaco were the first of any size, may have been the first to combine chiefdom-like theocratic centralization with trading and permanent military security of the trade routes and redistributional centers. In other words, as cultural outposts of the developed coastal chiefdoms they faced the necessity of maintaining *regular* dominance over the gradually more specialized regions as they all became more involved in the symbiotic network. At any rate, it seems evident that a more "total" kind of militarism originated in the highlands, associated with distant trade and a greater urbanism having more functions (Parsons 1968*a*).

It may be that a complicated society in an area of environmental differentiation is much more inclined to dominate the adjacent regions by military means than are the peoples of a more homogeneous area. The coastal Mochica, for example, showed varying amounts of cultural influence on adjacent valleys, perhaps only involving religious cults. But since the valleys did not depend on each other economically, being relatively self-sufficient replicas of one another, their economic security did not depend on the physical military dominance of a center, like Moche, over the others—and there is no good indication that such dominance did occur.

Also, it seems possible for an urban agglomeration to appear in areas that may control goods by means of trade or plunder, even though the city may not necessarily produce very much itself.

Such a city may finally become itself a productive force, increasing by political controls the specialization and exchange of subsistence necessary for its continued growth. It is mainly in this respect that the Peruvian highlands differed from the coast. The most important difference between the Peruvian coastal valleys and the highland developments may have been that Huari and Tiahuanaco became secular, administrative power centers because of strategic locations, rather than from their ability to intensify their own production. The effects of "regional symbiosis" as discussed by Sanders and Price, and the related importance of the urban "concentration of multiple functions" suggested by Schaedel may be of significance at this point.

The trend toward secular organization in the highlands, as manifested by Huari and Tiahuanaco, spread over most of Peru, including the North Coast valleys. Goods, such as pottery, were mass-produced, urban sites were planned in grid form, and bronze metallurgy began. An art style that seems to have been first manifested at Tiahuanaco spread over the Andes and the coast by about A.D. 800, but no one is sure what this means. The movement of their style could have been caused by political influence, or even the dominance of a huge, completely realized empire. We know that the later distribution of the Chimu art style that preceded the Inca was due to its dominance as a true empire, (and in fact provided the model for the Inca), hence the probability that Tiahuanaco was a similar case. But whatever the political significance of the distribution of the Tiahuanaco art style (it was a short-lived influence), it seems evident that at least multi-valley dominance had been achieved, involving highland-coastal interrelationships that must have been economic as well as political.

Schaedel (1971, p. 25) believes that the evidence of settlement patterns reveals a complicated urban concentration, which on the coast resulted from conquest. But what he called the "true state and true urban living" developed in various places between 750–1200 A.D. The multi-valley states he proposed had populations (based on an average density of one person/one acre) of 75,000 to 160,000 (ibid., p. 11): Schaedel thinks that these "galaxies of towns" represent Huari or Huari-affiliated elites. As for the urban factor, the larger towns averaged about 10,000 persons, and the smallest about 2,000 (ibid., p. 12).

The Post-Classic Era (800–1500 A.D.)

These urban concentrations led the way, or at least provided the models, for the much greater city-states that followed the collapse of the Tiahuanaco influence. Chan Chan, the Chimu capital in the Moche Valley, was by A.D. 1200 a dense city of 50,000 that had carefully walled subdivisions, each with its own reservoirs, gardens, cemeteries, and ceremonial centers. Elsewhere a similar though less imposing trend continued; these towns also had defensive walls.

As we have seen, the older pattern was an agglomeration of chiefdoms—scattered, smaller towns and villages around elite ceremonial centers and protected by hilltop forts at strategic places. Evidently the factor of increasing warfare, or perhaps raiding, was of consequence in the trend toward larger defensive agglomerations; but perhaps, also, there was more to protect in the way of wealth and stores than formerly; and certainly the process of directing the economy must have been complicated, in order to feed so many people as well as direct their specialized and multifarious activities.

Meanwhile, the highland societies continued to alternate between polities of the size of the Chimu empire and disintegration into loosely federated chiefdoms. Apparently the empires could not maintain dominance, according to Schaedel (ibid., p. 28), because none of the mountain societies after the Huari developed a true urban center, differentiated to provide all of the various religious, political, military, and economic functions of a vigorous, well-established political state. As we have seen, Schaedel, more than most archaeologists, regards the "urban" feature in Childe's formulation as the prime mover.

The Post-Classic (Steward's "Empire" stage) was preeminently a time of expanding and competing polities, beginning in the highlands, but eventually involving the coast. True cities were formed with huge walls and redoubts, so that plainly an important aspect of the trend toward urbanism was the need for defense against siege. The increase in the amount and intensity of warfare was so great that this period was called in Steward's original formulation of stages "the era of cyclical conquests" (see table 1 in chapter 1, above).

The Determinants of Civilization in Peru

Inasmuch as urbanism is factored out, so to speak, in the case of Peru, or at least disassociated from intensive irrigation agriculture, it is much easier to see its lack of significance here than in the Valley of Mexico, where intensive agriculture, water control, and especially hinterland redistributional exchange systems were all in close association with it. Coastal Peru particularly lacked such broad "regional symbiosis." This is not to say that there was no redistributional regional exchange on the coast at all. On the contrary, from everything we know of it, a centralized redistributional system was probably the very core of the origin and development of the kind of coastal theocracies that thrived there for such a long time. The very presence of and the high development of the specialized arts, crafts, and monumental architecture bespeaks redistribution. But mere *local* specialization and redistribution can do this; a chiefdom, in other words, has the organization to extend the system widely, but will do so to an important extent only as it needs to exploit more distant regional ecological variations. The more it does this, of course, and the more necessary the exchange becomes, the more developed becomes the system and its related appurtenances such as storage centers, transportation, forts —and above all, the military might to secure, maintain, and extend the system. Something like this seems to have been the case in the rise of the wide-ranging militaristic empires of Huari and Tiahuanaco. These societies therefore developed large cities because of these special needs related to long distance ecological symbiosis.

It can be argued that imperial warfare is not simply a response to competition caused by population pressures, although such pressures must contribute. But it may be that governments which rely on control of goods over an interregional network tend to expand their network outward as they grow internally, as well as intensify their exploitation of the communities already under control. It may also reasonably be posited that a bureaucracy with economic, political, and military functions tends to aggrandize itself, normally by expanding its functions. As it expands, however, it tends to remake the communities it subsumes: Not only does it create obvious things like subsidiary redistributional centers and depots, but it may often conscript soldiers, training and creating a local military body that becomes perhaps more effective than it had ever been in the previous form of society. As we have seen so dramatically in modern times, an empire plants in its colonies the "seeds of its own destruction." We can see that the very nature of the primary empires may lead them to expand easily because of the absence of an effectively organized resistance, and then to find themselves over-expanded as the subjects acquire more effective organization, better tactics, and perhaps even new weapons, developed from the prototypes acquired from the original conqueror.

Although the rise and fall of competing empires is not our major problem at this point, we may find it useful in considering Carneiro's theory of bounded resources or "circumscription" (see chapter 2). When the populations of the coastal valleys of Peru began to grow, the irrigation system was expanded and intensified until a balance was reached. As all the valleys reached their culminating populations by Classic times, the rule of the theocracy over its subjects was made easier because there was no place for dissident groups to colonize, for outside the valleys lay nothing but (literally) desert. It is possible that in Classic times or earlier coastal groups had with some difficulty begun to populate highland valleys. As the nearby highland valleys filled up, they too would find but few intervening fertile areas. All in all, both coast and mountains in Peru provided the possibly crucial environmental factor necessary for the formation of easily governed local populations. The eventual appearance of secular violence was military, and its context was competition among different regions rather than a government's repression of its own population.

The major point to be made, however, is the contrast between highland empire and Classic lowlands: The great ecological variability in the highlands points up the probable significance of regional symbiosis and redistribution within the highlands and between highland and lowland areas. Conceivably the large Post-

Classic lowland city-state of Chan Chan was produced by highland-lowland symbiosis, but the earlier development of chiefdoms leading up to the Classic period in the coastal valleys was clearly unusual in the absence of an important amount of regional symbiosis, and this may account for the relative lack of urbanism there.

As in the case of Mesoamerica, we have here an interesting juxtaposition of variables that cast doubt on some of the most important implications in Childe's formulation of civilization. And some of these associations of variables in Peru are strikingly distinct from those of Mesoamerica. In brief, we find in both areas the same phenomenon of a long evolutionary succession in the lowlands from segmental societies to hierarchical chiefdoms (the "Theocratic Formative" period), culminating in a "Classic" stage that manifests all of the specialized excellence in intellectual, technical, and economic aspects that characterize full civilization. But in both cases of the Classic lowlands, two of Childe's most important factors are missing: urban centers and evidence of repressive violent statecraft. And one significant reversal and one significant parallel emerge in the comparison. The reversal is that the lowland Classic phase in Mesoamerica (Olmec and Petén Maya) was based on *extensive* rainfall agriculture, whereas in North Coast Peru the evolution to the Classic period (of Mochica) was based on very *intensive,* full-scale, irrigation agriculture. In both areas the urban centers were Post-Classic developments, arising first in the highlands. This urbanism seems to have been associated with regional symbiosis, extensive trade and redistribution, and perhaps defense. The evidence shows that violence seems to have been directed outward in the military conduct of foreign affairs rather than in internal statecraft, as Childe would have it.

12

The Origins of Civilization in Mesopotamia

THE GREATEST AND most obvious difference in the geography of both Mesopotamia and Egypt when compared with Mesoamerica and Peru lies in the relatively greater diversity in the latter areas. Both Mesopotamia and Egypt are basically great arid river valleys with little of the ecological variability of the New World regions. That variability, as we have seen, is due to great differences in mountain altitudes, creating cold, temperate, and tropical zones with great differences in rainfall and in kinds of native flora and fauna. But Mesoamerica and Peru had only small watersheds for their irrigation systems, contrasting greatly with the tremendous magnitude of the Nile and the Tigris-Euphrates drainage areas. V. Gordon Childe (1942, p. 106) has made a great point of the significance of these rivers not only for large-scale irrigation, but also as arteries of commerce and communication that must have stimulated urbanization.

The availability of large domesticable animals for both food and labor in the Old World is another obviously significant difference. The Mesoamericans had no draft animals, and the Peruvians had only the llama, of some use in transport in the highlands and for wool. In contrast, Mesopotamia had the donkey and ox for labor (the horse was late and not much used), while cows and calves were obviously important for milk and meat, and goats, pigs, and sheep were plentiful (Kramer 1963, pp. 109–110). As for vegetable foods, the Old World had several storable cereals of great importance, but the New World had its maize, beans, and squash complex, also storable. Cultivation methods differed in the two regions, of course, but it is difficult to see any great significance in this, since both were highly intensive.

The Formative Era (ca. 5000–3500 B.C.)

The Tigris-Euphrates lowlands (like the Nile Valley) did not have sufficient rainfall for nonirrigated agriculture, although a crop planted in an area of annual flooding sometimes could come to maturity before the soil completely dried out (Butzer 1971, p. 215). It is more likely, however, that plant and animal domestication first occurred in upland areas of greater rainfall.

"Neolithic" (early Formative) farming communities found their best environment for general overall development in the piedmont zone between the Mesopotamian lowlands and the Zagros mountains of Kurdistan and Luristan. Most of this land is in Iraq, and is called the Assyrian steppe. This intermediate zone had sufficient rainfall in winter for dry farming and large rivers for irrigation in dry seasons or in areas of insufficient rainfall, so that a transition toward irrigation, little by little, or partial, was possible. Adams (1962, p. 112) says that irrigation farming probably originated there.

It is thought that after about 1,000 years the early part-farming communities of the Mesopotamian uplands finally developed their economy to a mixed herding-farming basis by about 6000 B.C. (Hole et al. 1971, pp. 279–88). The basic products were emmer wheat, barley, sheep, and goats. The population was sparse and the communities small at first, but between 5500–5000 B.C. small-scale irrigation was introduced in some areas, which enabled more of the lowlands to be utilized (ibid., p. 308). By 4000 B.C. the basic economy of the formative Mesopotamian-Khuzistan period was evident. The probable population of "Susiana proper" (the heartland named from the famous type-site of Susa) at this time was over 15,000 (ibid., p. 303).

Although sedentary agricultural villages characteristically developed in the uplands and highlands, they took a further development as people gradually moved into the alluvial lowlands of the Tigris-Euphrates system. Apparently the lowlands were not widely habitable by sedentary groups until irrigation became fully employed and the villages were freed from a partial dependence on hunting and gathering wild food. Additionally, transport and some kind of exchange corridor had to be established in order to get raw materials like hardwoods (for boat-building) and stone from the distant highlands. But once the required developments in population size and in technology were achieved, the lowlands had enormous potential for further evolutionary growth into truly urban societies.

The aforementioned dependence on irrigation made for an obviously more intensive agriculture, and the absence of stone greatly facilitated plowing. The river systems, naturally, provided fish, mollusks, and aquatic birds in abundance, and equally obviously, a potentially great transportation system. Easy and efficient transportation has two aspects, it should be remembered; it not only facilitates the passage of goods and people, but also stimulates a wide diffusion of inventions, discoveries, and ideas in general. As William McNeill says (1963, p. 31):

> The local peculiarities of desert river banks do much to explain the direction of social evolution among the pioneer agricultural communities that penetrated the lower reaches of the Tigres-Euphrates Valley after about 4000 B.C. The larger geographical setting of this habitat also stimulated human ingenuity by both inviting and necessitating long-distance transport and communication on a comparatively massive scale. This meant that the stimulus of contacts with strangers was never long absent from the early settler's horizon. Boats and rafts could move with ease along the rivers, lagoons, and bayous of the region itself, and sail along the shores of the Persian Gulf (and beyond) without encountering any but the natural difficulties of wind and waves. Overland, too, no geographical obstacles hindered pack trains on their way to the mountains that ringed the Mesopotamian plain to the north, east, and west. The fact that the alluvium of lower Mesopotamia lacked stone, timber, and metals supplied ample incentive for travels. In proportion as the valley dwellers required these commodities, they had either to organize expeditions to find,

prepare, and bring back what they needed, or else to persuade neighboring peoples to exchange local stone, timber, or metals for the surpluses of the plains. As specialization progressed within the social structure of the valley peoples, such trade between hill and plain assumed an increasing scale and importance; and the emergent cities along the rivers became centers of communication and stimulus for the whole surrounding region.

An important difference between Mesopotamia and the Mesoamerican and Peruvian areas is the great significance of pastoralism in the Old World region (as well as the aforementioned use of oxen for plowing). The "mixed economies" of the Mesopotamian uplands used wild foods to supplement domesticated animals and dry farming. As further development went on and less-provident environments became utilized, pastoralism became increasingly a specialization in the grasslands where agriculture was difficult. Thus, as time went on, two distinct kinds of cultures became increasingly divergent. The partly independent and partly complementary nature of these cultures' association varied, sometimes characterized by trading, at other times by symbiotic relationships, and at others by raiding. Again, it is important to remember that there are two sides to a symbiosis of two such societies: Both sides are economically better off because of the specialization, and so they need each other; but pastoralism is a rather mobile way of life and leads to military superiority of a certain kind, an offensive, raiding, predatory kind of warfare—as we saw with the Ankole state (chapter 6). That "the Assyrian came down like a wolf on the fold" must have been a very significant factor in the lives of the victimized farming communities.

About 3500 B.C. the alluvial plain of Sumer in the far south fostered a rapid development of culture. The Sumerians seem to have been the first to break through to urbanization. And by about 3000 B.C. they also had developed writing—which is, of course, of great significance to us, for at that point we merge archaeology (prehistory) with documentary history.

The late Formative type-site named Al Ubaid gives us some idea of the widespread kind of Sumerian culture immediately preceding the rise of the great cities. The farming people lived in reed-and-clay constructions, huddled together in villages that were relatively self-sufficient and politically autonomous. There were no evidences of defensive fortifications, and apparently peaceful contact and trade were widespread. The date palm and fish were important additions to the cereals and goat and sheep herds; apparently holdings of cattle were centralized as the property of the palace-temple (Adams 1955, pp. 9–10).

Technological advances in the Formative bespoke a great increase in craft specialization. As McNeill describes it, ". . . The rapid pace of technical progress, the heavy requirements of time for production with existing techniques, the uniformly high artistry, and the increasingly complex, exacting, and capitalized nature of the operations argues strongly that most of them were able to devote fulltime to their specialized pursuits" (ibid., p. 11). As we have seen in the ethnological chapters, such specialization requires the kind of centralized redistributional system characteristic of chiefdoms and primitive states.

The chiefdom elsewhere is always theocratic, and this was clearly the case in Sumer (Adams, 1966, p. 121). Even at such an early stage as the Ubaid (around 3500 B.C.), the temple was the most imposing structure (or set of structures), and was not only a "house of worship" but a sanctuary, a palace, and a storage place and redistributive center. "The construction and above all the frequent re-construction of temples, which might be of very substantial size, go to show that the Ubaid people had already so to speak created the characteristic form of early civilization in Mesopotamia, the sacred city whose economic, social and religious life was centred on the temple and its priests" (Clark 1969, p. 103).

The Florescent and Protoliterate Eras (3500–3000 B.C.)

Following the spread of Neolithic irrigation farmers throughout the southern alluvium, a few special locations underwent rapid development in size and complexity. One of the most striking, and today best-known archaeologically, is that of *Warka* (Sumerian *Uruk,* Semitic *Erech*). Warka has become the type-site for the early Florescent era (3500–3000 B.C.), as Ubaid serves for the late Formative.

It is, of course, difficult (or dangerous) to estimate population figures from the size of monuments, but certainly a really great growth in the size of monuments is suggestive. Adams (1966, p. 126) estimates that the temple and mound at Warka alone was worth 7,500 man-years in the building. So much of the archaeological work in Mesopotamia has been concerned with these temples that we may as well begin with a brief description, with emphasis on Warka.

A characteristic kind of temple is the stepped platform, or ziggurat, on which a temple-tower was raised (the tower of Babel was an example). The temple and the city and its land was the property of one particular ruling patron-god (Eanna [Anu] in the case of Warka). Nearby complexes of living quarters enclosed by a wall have been suggested as evidence of a progressive detachment of the temple's personnel from direct involvement in the life of the community (Adam 1966, p. 126). This is perhaps to be expected, for we have seen in earlier chapters that with the growth of a theocracy there is a tendency toward a "separation of powers," with the priestly power increasing its social distance from the masses and from the more mundane military and economic matters, although retaining important or ultimate decision-making powers.

The artificial mound itself at Warka was forty feet high and covered an area of 420,000 square feet, dominating the flat plain for many miles. The building and walls, including the sides of the mound, were coated with a mud plaster covering the sundried brickwork, which in turn was covered with tens of thousands of fire-baked clay cones stuck into it to form complex patterns of design. This complexity is noted because it is further evidence, beyond the sheer size of the monument, of a great deal of labor and planning.

The temple continued to be the focus and organizer of religious, economic, and political life during the Florescent period. As the cities grew so too did the crafts, including pottery and carpentry, as well as metallurgy. The presence of wood and metals from great distances show the increasing ability of the administrators of the temple to collect and ration foodstuffs, to exchange with foreigners, to transport goods, and above all to store and to redistribute both finished goods and raw materials. This complex function of the theocratic chiefdom must have tremendous political significance, for it would have made both individuals and potential disruptive factions very conscious of the practical benefits dispensed by the regime—and as "gifts" of the god that the regime stood for. Adams (1955, p. 12), evaluating the nature of the monumental structures as temples, concludes that "a stage in which the economic controls of this highly sophisticated (if not quite urbanized) society were more important and more formalized than its political ones, and were primarily of a theocratic nature, can thus be isolated with considerable assurance."

Most of the important technological and economic developments had become well established by Protoliterate times (around 3000 B.C.). Writing appeared in the form of simple pictographs that were rapidly becoming conventionalized among scribes and record-keepers, thereby to undergo further development, as did the related numerical notation. The improved plow, wheeled carts, sailing rafts and boats, and the use of bronze for tools and weapons all were established early in the Protoliterate era, and remained basic to later Mesopotamian civilization.

There is a possibility that in the Protoliterate era there existed a short-lived political institution that departed somewhat from pure theocracy. Jacobsen argues (1943) from his study of early texts that the cities held meetings of an "assembly" of adult male citizens guided by a council of elders. The Protoliterate texts are difficult to interpret and too scanty for us to make very much of the above interpretation. In any event, the much more complete texts of the early Dynastic period do not reveal any important survival of the "assembly" or any such oligarchy (Frankfort n.d., p. 78). It is mentioned here with no attempt at evaluation and with the reminder that Gearing has described from ethnohistorical data a similar-sounding institution among the Cherokee (see chapter 8).

The Dynastic Era (ca. 2900–2500 B.C.)

Authorities agree that sometime early in the third millenium B.C. an increasing secular political trend grew into an established hereditary military kingdom in several of the lower Mesopotamian cities, hence their use of the label *Dynastic era*. It is also agreed that this political trend was accompanied by increased militarism and warfare.[1]

The fifteen to twenty independent Sumerian cities grew increasingly "urban," probably by concentrating defensively. Kish and Warka may have held as many as twenty to thirty thousand inhabitants (Adams 1955, p. 14). Adams feels that the origin of kingship was closely related to the demographic situation (ibid.): "Since virtually the whole of the era is marked by some evidence of warfare it may be suggested that population had expanded nearly to the limits that the land would afford by the end of the preceding era, and that what followed was a chronically precarious balance between population and food resources. Under these conditions, the rise of kingship may have been largely a self-generating process."

Adams has here, as have many others in other contexts, ascribed warfare to population pressure and competition among the independent cities, the implication being that the competition was over arable lands lying somewhere between. As an example, he cites the ". . . long history of internecine rivalry between Lafash and Umma over border territories . . . ; under such a chronic state of emergency there was neither time nor disposition for the war-leader to relinquish his powers" (ibid.). McNeill agrees that as population grew and swamps and deserts were reclaimed the buffer zones between cities ceased to exist and their lands came to abut one another's, causing "perennial friction and chronic war" (1963, pp. 41–42). A standing army, and perpetuation of the military rule, is also felt to be related to the problems of the incursions of raiding nomads. "In proportion as war became chronic, kingship became necessary. Concentration of political authority in the hands of a single man seems to have become the rule in Sumerian cities by 3000 B.C." (McNeill 1963, p. 43).

But the question remains, what means and circumstances transformed rule by a military chief into a political "kingship" with built-in guarantees of perpetuation beyond the rule of the man himself? The idea that omnipresent military threats or needs

1. Adams (1955, p. 13; and 1966, p. 133); Childe (1936, p. 125); Clark (1969, p. 106); Frankfort (n.d., p. 87); McNeill (1963, pp. 41–46). These authorities are either anthropologists, or historians (Frankfort and McNeill) who are anthropologically sophisticated.

tend to perpetuate military bureaucracy and power seems sensible, but as we have seen in other chapters (especially the case of Shaka Zulu), the consolidation of a true legal state is still difficult to achieve. Such a thought carries the further suggestion that perhaps the first dynastic cities were not yet full-fledged states. At least this question is something for later consideration.

Stratification and the State • As we saw above, Adams and others have presented the idea that chronic warfare led to a secular military rule, with the suggestion that this is the cause of the Sumerian city-state. But Adams has another theory, presented years later, which we suppose has superseded, or at least supplements the above (though he does not say so). This theory is an important modification of Childe's modification of the Morgan-Marx-Engels (and later, Leninist) theory of the origin of and nature of the state. Inasmuch as these latter were discussed in chapter 2, they will be mentioned only very succinctly here.

A crucial element in Adams's theory is the increase in "stratification." Whereas Morgan had cited the growth of private property as the cause of the state (which, according to Engels, then came about to protect the propertied class from the propertyless), Adams (1966, p. 80) emphasized "the system of stratified social relations, of which rights to property were only an expression." Adams felt that "probably most would also tend to question Morgan's implicit assumption that the substitution of territorically defined communities for ethnically defined ones was both a necessary and a sufficient cause for the growth of the institution of private property." He did agree with Morgan about "the general shift [Morgan] posited from ascriptively defined groupings of persons to politically organized units based on residence." But "class stratification," Adams feels, "was the mainspring and 'foundation' of political society."

What is meant by *stratification,* and what are the evidences for it? Apparently stratification for Adams is a synonym for *class.* This is not stated, but they are used rather interchangeably. Adams does not formally define stratification, but does define class (1966, p. 79), as describing "objectively differentiated degrees of access to the means of production of the society without any necessary implications of sharply reduced mobility, class consciousness, or overt interclass struggle. . . ." And in this sense, he says, "the early states characteristically were class societies."

Adams believes that the common citizenry of the Mesopotamian cities were organized as "conical clans," citing indirect evidence for this (1966, p. 94). The argument is even more acceptable in our present context, since our comparative study of the ethnologially known states and chiefdoms has shown the probable universality and the functional utility of what we call *ramages,* forms of kinship that involve the institutionalization of inequality by heredity. But it may be well to point out that the ramage (conical clan) is typically characterized by political, or bureaucratic, differentiation accompanied by symbols of high-low status, but with no significant or meaningful "objectively differentiated degrees of access to the means of production" among them. That is, it is typical of chiefdoms that priests or chiefs (and their immediate families) do not produce foodstuffs, but accept or require "gifts," or taxes, or tribute for partial redistribution—(a part is withheld). But this is not what Marx and Engels meant by differential relations to the means of production. They were thinking of *owners* of land or machinery, versus *nonowners* (slaves, serfs, or wageworkers). The relation of a priest-chief–redistributor to the agricultural workers in a chiefdom is best seen as a *political* power relationship, not an economic relationship that grew out of the unequal acquisition of wealth in a market economy. At any rate, there is no need to posit a class relationship that necessarily must have been founded on economic ownership. It is the power relationship itself that we are investigating, and so far it looks as if it began with an unequal power to make redistributive exchanges (and unequal access to gods rather than goods).

But let us see what evidence Adams (1966, pp. 95–110) finds for the development of class stratification. In the late Ubaid period there was little distinction in the kind of grave goods that could be taken as signifying important status differentiation. In the Warka and Protoliterate periods greater variations began to appear, and in the late Protoliterate still further differentiation was evident at the excavations at Ur, but none of these show a very complete stratification. There is more complete evidence that burials in Early Dynastic times showed status differences based on wealth.

The written records of the Early Dynastic period confirm these archaeological suppositions.

At the bottom of this society was a class of slaves, not numerous but usually working at important "semi-industrialized" tasks such as weaving cloth. These slaves seem to have been war captives, sometimes referred to as "foreigners." The bulk of the population was of various kinds of peasantry with varying degrees of control over the land they worked. Some proportion of them were still organized as primitive kinship units. Professional artisans, of course, had varying degrees of skill, and worked at tasks of varying importance, so that it is probably not reasonable to attempt a classification of them on an economic basis—it may be best to treat them as a kind of residual category. At the top of the society were the ruler and the aristocratic, or princely, families. Adams thinks that they headed "manorial estates" of varying sizes. One cannot know if they were literally manorial, meaning privately owned and administrated for private profit, since a simple political jurisdiction over a unit of *persons,* however regionally defined, could give the same appearance without any implication of ownership in the marketplace sense of the term.

We cannot disagree with the conclusion that some kind of social differentiation appeared in Dynastic times, if not earlier. But all the evidence relates to status differences, which probably were related to political or bureaucratic distinctions, not economic ones. I cannot find the "differential access to the means of production" definition a very meaningful one. Originally, I think, this definition was accepted by Marxists because of the assumption that classes "struggle" because of this economic inequity. (It should be noted that Adams does not seem firm, or even very explicit, about this—in the statement about Morgan quoted, he wanted to substitute "class stratification" for "property" as the "mainspring" and "foundation" of political society. But perhaps his first definition of class was not meant to imply that "differential access" had to do with property.)

Childe had been a strong proponent of the class oppression theory of the rise of the state in Mesopotamia, especially in his widely read and influential *Man Makes Himself* (1936). Henri Frankfort disputes this directly (n.d., pp. 69–70).

To speak of the "surplus" of food which must be produced in order to maintain officials as well as merchants and craftsmen, and to imply that the officials must have been a parasite class which kept the farmers in subjection, leaves out of account several circumstances, of which the most important is the climate of the country. Wherever there is power there is, inevitably, abuse of power. But the rich soil of Mesopotamia, if well watered, produces food in abundance without excessive or continuous toil. Labor in the fields was largely seasonal. At seed time and harvest time every able-bodied person was no doubt on the land, as was the case in medieval England. But the farmers were not a separate class or caste. Every citizen, whether priest, merchant, or craftsman, was a practical farmer who worked his allotment to support himself and his dependents. Once the seed was sown and the harvest gathered, plenty of time remained in which special skills could be developed, taught, and exploited.

It is hard to see how Frankfort knows that everyone worked in the fields, but his point is well taken that oppression, repression, or exploitation for the production of the "surplus" simply do not follow from the evidence and from the nature of the agricultural production. It is also hard to understand how he knows that crafts and home industry were not separated. But his argument has merit, judging from what we know ethnographically of simple agricultural societies. Since we do not really *know,* however, it is best to leave the question in abeyance—which means that we do not accept as a given, as Childe did, that agricultural "surplus" equals "exploitation" of one class by another, which in turn means that the state originates to repress one class in the interest of the other. Once founded, of course, a state takes on many new functions, especially self-protection, which is itself normally a maintenance of the status quo, but also takes the form of military protection against competing societies.

Competition and Warfare • There is ample testimony that the evolution of the Mesopotamian society from the time of the earliest sedentary villages to the great Babylonian empires was accompanied by a commensurate rise in the amount and extent of warfare. And, to repeat perhaps unnecessarily, the warfare was of two distinct kinds, between rival competitive neighbors and between the sedentary cities and raiding nomads. These involve distinctly different strategies and organization.

Once southern Mesopotamia became more or less "filled up" in the Dynastic period in Sumer, rival cities waged both war and peace, and both of these are simply two aspects of an external political strategy. A city defeated by another may become its tributary, but probably unwillingly and apparently for only a short time because the means of permanently consolidating or federating regions were still lacking. Probably, too, one city was not greatly superior militarily to all others until the time of Sargon. Peace was waged also in terms of alliances among neighbors against rival confederacies, but since these strategies were military only, rather than economically symbiotic, they tended to be ephemeral.

It may be an important suggestion, in comparing the Mesopotamian Dynastic era with Peruvian North Coast valleys of the equivalent late Florescent era, that the relative lack of success in both areas in uniting into larger polities was because the cities and the coastal valleys were quite similar economically to their neighbors. The larger "empires" like Tiahuanaco and Akkad (and, for that matter, Teotihuacán in Mexico) all involved geographically distinct zones so that the imperial bureaucracy could create an economic symbiosis having enough importance to confer political benefits through the planned exchanges of important goods.

The other kind of warfare, that of defense against raiding pastoralists, is of course difficult to wage because of the great mobility of the predators. It is also almost impossible to wage peace against them except for sometimes "buying them off," a chancy and short-term solution usually.

The difficulty the agriculturalists had with wandering predators was persistent in Mesopotamia. This very persistence throughout millenia undoubtedly had a powerful effect, creating no-man's-lands and buffer zones in areas that might otherwise have been economically productive. The other side of this coin is particularly important: With increasing pressure from nomads on people in the intermediate zones, they had to choose either to become nomads themselves or to join the larger sedentary polities, thus increasing the nomadic population as well as that of the cities. It may well be that the unprecedented rise of true urban agglomerations in southern Mesopotamia, which was also the first zone of fully sedentary occupation, was partly caused by the very impossibility of such a complete adaptation in the upland steppes.

(These intermediate areas in the north were in fact late to develop.) It is important to emphasize again the simple fact that military considerations influence not only the overall size of a population but its dislocation and relocation, ultimately toward a characteristic distribution.

As Adams points out (1972, pp. 61–62), there was a significant increase in the sedentary population during the Ubaid period until the early centuries of the fourth millennium. The distribution was of dense clusters of villages and towns near rivers and streams. It is not known whether this population increase was natural or due to immigration.

> In any case, the most extensive development of the urban institutions characteristic of Sumerian civilization came after this period of population growth, in the last centuries of the fourth millennium. . . . at least in a few centers like Uruk the process of growth not only was explosively rapid but was accompanied by profound structural changes, with massive fortifications, palaces, and political hierarchies shifting the emphasis away from temples and their associated priesthoods. But the important point is that this urbanization involved redistribution of the population rather than a further increase. It was accomplished, in other words, only through widespread rural abandonment and the more or less forcible relocation of former villages and townsmen in wholly unprecedented urban agglomerations.

The Imperial Era (ca. 2500–1500 B.C.)

The very geographical peculiarity of Mesopotamia that tempted nomads also led to internecine warfare and attempts at conquest among the cities themselves. As Childe explains (1936, p. 125), they all depended on the two rivers, the Tigris and the Euphrates, for life itself, and for "the importation of . . . exotic substances from common sources." And therefore,

> . . . disputes about lands and water rights were liable to arise between the several autonomous cities. Just because all relied on the same foreign trade to bring them the same necessities for industry, commercial rivalries were inevitable amongst sovereign states; the contradiction between an economic system that ought to be unitary and political separatism was made manifest in interminable dynastic wars. Our earliest documents after the temple accounts, in fact, record wars between adjacent cities and treaties that temporarily ended them. The ambition of any city dynast was to obtain hegemony over his neighbors.

The Akkadian Empire • Around 2500 B.C. the attempts at empire began to have some wide success, but they were not long-lived. Sargon of Akkad, about 2370 B.C., was apparently the first to found an imperial dynasty that lasted through several reigns (about a century). This dynasty ruled over all of Mesopotamia and apparently either subjected or overawed the upland barbarians.

Sargon, according to tradition, began his political career as a cup-bearer to the king of Kish, a city on the northern borders of the Sumer. (Sumer was the southern part of Lower Mesopotamia.) Eventually he became a successful military leader, who, after defeat in several neighboring cities, founded his own city Akkad (Agade). From Akkad, he continued his campaigns ever southward until all of Sumer was tributary to him. Such a conquest was not new to the Sumerians, but all previous incursions, like their own internecine wars, had been rather ephemeral in their results.

Akkad was founded in a strategic military position in the transition zone between the barbarian steppes and the civilized south. It is likely that it is for this very reason that Sargon was so successful; he was able "to unite barbarian prowess with civilized technique" forming a combination superior to either (McNeill 1963, p. 46.) Sumerian culture had influenced the middle and upper regions of Mesopotamia without conquering them, so the new city that Sargon built in Akkad had an important Sumerian foundation, but without the rigid priest-and-temple structure of the old Sumerian cities. Priests and temple communities existed in Akkad, but since the city was created by the military, the secular and military parts of the society were ascendent and remained so.

Another possibly important feature of the rise of the Akkadian empire lay in the differences in the original cultures of the northern Semites and the southern Sumerians. The Sumerians had been sedentary irrigation agriculturalists for many hundreds of years. Many of the Semitic-speaking peoples of the upper rivers and steppes had been nomadic herdsmen, and even after they adopted irrigation farming (around 2500 B.C.) they still had an important symbiotic connection with the neighboring herdsmen. Thus, united Mesopotamia held two subcultures, the older, aristocratic, sophisticated, theocratic cities of Sumer and the newer, powerful, more secular fortresses of the northern frontier. McNeill feels that the pastoral heritage of the Semites was a powerful factor in causing the transition to irrigation farming to take a new form (1963, pp. 46–47):

> No doubt the obvious rewards of irrigation induced this change; but it occurred within the framework of a social system which had developed to suit the needs of pastoralism. Above all, this meant a society led by tribal chieftains, whose function it was to direct the co-operative effort needed to safeguard the flocks and move them from pasture to pasture. As irrigated agriculture took root in Akkad, this sort of traditional authority was extended and transformed: chieftains began to mobilize and supervise the work gangs needed to build and maintain irrigation works.

It has been noted how often an older set of cultural forms and institutions takes on new life when transplanted to a new locality and taken up by a new people. There seem to be two related reasons for this: The borrowers are likely to choose only the obviously best of the range of variations in such things as irrigation techniques; and (2) the borrowed elements may find themselves adapted to unfamiliar uses and means, which may (or, of course, may not) give rise to new combinations of greater evolutionary potentiality. Both of these factors appear to account for the ascendency of Akkad, particularly in that the adaptation of farming was related to secular rather than religious management. This and the pastoral military heritage created not only a stronger city but also one more purely a secular state rather than an elaborate chiefdom or theocratic near-state. McNeill summarizes this development as follows (1963, p. 50): "The successful transplantation of Sumerian high culture up-river among the Akkadians marked an important stage in the expansion of civilization. The sociological barrier which had hitherto restricted civilized life to communities organized and led by priesthoods was for the first time transcended."

The Akkadian secular rule of the military, the economy, and the irrigation system was able to expand much more easily into the up-river hinterlands. And probably of great significance was a new role Sargon invented for himself: He made it possible for his name to be invoked along with the gods in the swearing of an oath upon an agreement. At first glance, this looks like an attempt at self-deification, to reestablish an important theocratic feature—and perhaps this is so. But the practical significance was that if an agreement sworn on such an oath were broken, or perjured, the ruler was committed to uphold the right of the injured party. This amounted to Sargon's constituting himself as a court of appeal for the whole land, independent of the cities. This was an important step in the development of a true code of law, law whose origin was political, not religious (Frankfort n.d., p. 86).

The Sargonic empire lasted through four generations until it was successfully overthrown by an invasion of Gutians, who themselves ruled a loose empire for about a century until overthrown by internal revolt. The Third Dynasty of Ur ruled Sumer and Akkad for another century, after which a complex series of disorders and wars beset Mesopotamia until about 1700 B.C., when Hammurabi united the country from his own city of Babylon, still farther to the north than Akkad. But Hammurabi's dynasty, like the others before him, had a life-cycle of only about a century before it succumbed to new barbarian breakthroughs. So repetitive was this rise-and-fall that it helped precipitate the many cyclical theories of the state alluded to in chapter 2.

The Structure of Empire • But despite the disorder—and in some respects because of it—Mesopotamian civilization underwent certain structural and institutional developments that were to provide the foundations of empires and cities throughout the Near- and Mideast (and possibly beyond) long before the Christian epoch. Beginning in Akkadian times, first of all, the political trend was toward ever-larger territories that experienced, apparently (or even necessarily), a slow development of the political, bureaucratic, and military means of control. Writing and mathematics continued to develop in connection with statecraft, while economics, law, religion, and ideology were modified also in accordance with new political demands. Related to all of these was an increase in the scope of the economy, especially in the movement of goods and materials.

For the trend toward larger polities to succeed, it had to involve a transfer of some political loyalties, at least of some bureaucrats, from local cities to the larger polity. One obvious way to encourage this was to supplant some of the local higher officials with foreigners loyal to the emperor. Naram Sin (grandson of Sargon) replaced local rulers and priests with his own relatives; and in time, as his royal officialdom proliferated, it may be supposed that bureaucratic personnel became more and more professionalized—increasingly loyal to their own organization and its purposes, which of course were also mainly the purposes of the empire.

The bureaucracy—secular, priestly, and military—must have been immensely aided by written communication and numerical notation. Simple pictographic writing and numerals had been used in Sumer to keep temple accounts and to record economic contracts. With the growth of the empire came a greatly increased need for writing and arithmetic, and so their development expanded. Politically, the significance of the writing of law codes must have been of tremendous importance. Establishing a uniform system of royal justice throughout the realm brought the representatives of the imperial court into direct contact with the affairs of local persons and groups, and in time made the bureaucracy, in its legal aspect, ever more useful and necessary. It could in this way undermine local leaders who formerly administered mere local customs, rather than the law of the land (cf. McNeill 1963, p. 54 and *n.* 38). (We may suppose, with McNeill, that there were royal law codes antedating the famous one of Hammurabi.)

The political significance of writing, as we have noted before, extended to ideology. Religious mythology when transmitted only orally was subject to unconscious, unintentional change, but when written it became codified and "official." Changes could be made for political reasons—to lower the status of one local god or raise that of another (as in the famous *Epic of Creation,* which elevated the Babylonian god, Marduk, to supremacy).

The increase in economic activity in the Imperial era poses a problem in interpretation. There are those who see any evidences of movements of goods as "commerce," from which it follows that private entrepreneurs had appeared to become a "merchant class." The famous economic historian Karl Polanyi (in Polanyi et al. 1957) tellingly disputes this simplistic, ethnocentric interpretation. Carriers of goods, bureaucratic representatives of the empire, even ambassadors of a sort, all may be empowered to negotiate exchanges and determine equivalencies and quality, but no unearned middle-man's increment remains in their coffers. An appointed carrier-representative may operate on commission, or salary, but in any case the "price" will be a politically determined, bureaucratically negotiated one, not the product of supply-and-demand fluctuations in a free market. It is only in this latter sense that a "merchant class," by profiteering, could become wealthy and politically powerful and thus influence the nature of the political state in the Marxian sense.

This is not to say that there was no "market" in another sense of the word. A peasant village's "market" is preeminently a meeting *place* rather than a price-determining institution like the stock market. Such a place is useful for people to come together to exchange the surpluses of their own household economies. No city or village bureaucracy can easily regulate such a complex yet picayune affair, and probably few even bothered to try—though they probably did try to police it, tax it, settle disputes, and so on. But even if the prices are mostly determined by haggling, supply-and-demand, or irrational ideology—if prices that is, are unregulated by bureaucracy—this does not produce "merchants" powerful enough to be politically significant as a "class." It is undoubtedly the insignificance of these exchanges that allowed them to be so unregulated.

But neither the presence nor absence of a propertied merchant class by the time of Hammurabi can be proved. To me it seems very doubtful that such a class existed, but for our present purposes it is irrelevant: We are concerned with earlier times, the Dynastic era of Sumer and the early Akkadian period, in order to judge the significance of the "class" or "stratification" factor and to discover its nature, and clearly its origin in those times was not entrepreneurial.

Adams says (1966, p. 155) that for the Early Dynastic period of Sumer "much of the intercity trade was either subject to royal demand or under direct royal control." The agents responsible for the exchanges were officials, not free entrepreneurs, and were organized in a hierarchy. This does not mean that those same persons could not have engaged in some private trade, but only that their power, whatever it was, arose from their bureaucratic position, not from their private wealth gained through trade. In the Akkadian times of greater military endeavors, ". . . patterns of trade probably were still closely interdigitated with exactions of booty and tribute within the spreading realm of Akkadian control" (ibid., p. 156).

It seems evident that although a strong case can be made for the economic significance of the exchange of goods in relation to the bureaucracy, this very exchange did not create a *class* of entrepreneurs of any political significance. If anything, a case could be more easily argued that the development of government made possible an increase in the amount of distant exchanges of goods, rather than vice versa, and that the exchanges reciprocally strengthened the bureaucracy engaged in them. But it should be emphasized that this claim is being made for the political significance of *distant* and *important* exchanges of goods, for it is these that must have been officially planned and managed—not the petty exchanges made for general household requirements by private individuals. But even if the whole population of a city on market-day act like "penny capitalists" (Sol Tax's phrase for his Guatemalan Indian villagers), this should not create a *class* of rich entrepreneurs as the basis of a repressive state in ancient Mesopotamia, any more than it did in a modern Guatemalan village.

The First Urban Civilization

Just as in Mesoamerica and Peru, Mesopotamia exhibits a long developmental period of theocratic rule leading to a "classic" period, followed by an increase in warfare and the successive rise and fall of military empires. And, as in the preceding cases, an increase in the size and numbers of cities accompanied this development—but without the "regional symbiosis" that seemed so fundamental in the New World regions. In the Mesopotamian lowlands the specialization was more technological than ecological.

The size of the individual Mesopotamian cities poses the problem of cause-and-effect in the development of governance. Did they require controls because of their size, or did the presence of the military and the protection of the cities foster their growth? Certainly the two grew together, but it seems likely that the two distinct kinds of military problems, protection against nomads and against rival cities, must have been a prime factor in the growth of the cities. We must also recognize, of course, that intensive plant and animal domestication had to accompany the growth of urban centers.

But, as we have also noted in earlier chapters (especially with respect to Teotihuacán), not only does military pressure tend to make the city population grow, it discourages political dissidents from leaving. Thus the rather normal centrifugal tendencies in any large polity tend to be overcome by the centripetal force of the beneficial features of membership in the polity—especially the benefits of its protection.

This is again a case whereby Carneiro's (1970) circumscription hypothesis needs amending. I believe that when geographic circumscription is present the political effect is as Carneiro says—but I would call it another instance among several of the factor of governance by benefit. This general factor is, so far as I can see now, a universal in the formation of all persevering power relationships. Redistribution and economic well-being in general, priestly intervention with the gods, protection, and so on are all helpful in political integration when it is apparent that they are superior benefits compared to the alternative of moving away (or, as in more modern politics, of overthrowing the government). Carneiro emphasizes only one of these factors, the geographic isolation of the ecologically well adapted, highly productive society. But, we should add at this point, another sort of ecological factor is the military adapation of nomads and settled intensive agriculturalists. Their competition creates a polarizing tendency, with some of the societies becoming increasingly nomadic and aggressive, on the one hand, and others increasingly intensive farmers with a sedentary defensive strategy, on the other hand. This results in the appearance of geographical isolation, as in part it is; but it is caused mostly by military specialization, and relatively empty intermediate no-man's-lands might therefore appear to be more unproductive than they really are.

The other form of warfare, between the cities themselves, resulted eventually in forms of statecraft (governance by force or threat of it) that were developed in external affairs, culminating in Sargon's empire and the various successors. But Mesopotamian *civilization* preceded these developments, just as the military empires of Mesoamerica and Peru were preceded by civilization there. And, it seems evident, successful conquest to be made permanent depended on not only military might, but on the prior development of a governmental bureaucracy capable of undertaking new tasks.

13

The Origins of Civilization in Egypt

IT HAS BEEN EMPHASIZED in the previous chapter how wide-ranging was the transportation network out from Mesopotamia, particularly after rafts, barges, and true ships became propelled with sails. There is no doubt that the whole of the so-called fertile crescent from Mesopotamia to the Nile was heavily influenced by diffusion from and emulation of Mesopotamia. The rise of civilization in Egypt, therefore, may well have been related in some respects to that of Sumer; it was nearly contemporaneous. Keeping this in mind, it will still serve some purpose to treat Egypt separately, for there are some interesting differences and peculiarities in geography and in the development of the sociopolitical structure.

There are, to be sure, evidences of early contacts of Sumer with lower Egypt, and certain Sumerian inventions, such as the potter's wheel, bricks, cylinder seals, a few art motifs and stylistic peculiarities, and evidently the stimulus, though not the model, of writing and numbering. But Henri Frankfort (n.d., p. 97), a specialist on these matters, does not see this contact as affecting the "social and political sphere" that concerns us as it concerned him. He finds that "the autochthonous character of the Egyptian development is unmistakable." Furthermore, he states that "the basic structure of the society which emerged [in Egypt] was the direct opposite of that which came into being in Mesopotamia."

Like the Tigris-Euphrates alluvium, the Nile Valley of Egypt lent itself obviously to intensive irrigation agriculture and to massive riverine transport. But there were some important contrasts. The Nile Valley, unlike Sumer, is exceptionally well cast as an instance of a highly productive agricultural area bounded by (and protected by) areas of very low productivity. On both sides, the valley is bounded by deserts, the Libyan on the west and the Arabian to the east. The great delta to the north was, of course, open to conquest only from the sea, which would have been difficult since it had no natural harbors. To the south were the Nubian Desert and the enormous cataracts of the Nile. Egypt was thus remarkably sheltered from the incursion of nomadic pastoralists or such rival foreign ethnic groups as the Sumerians and Semites.

Longtime political stability was one important consequence of the isolation of the Nile Valley. And the problem of countering the normal internal centrifugal tendencies was simplified because the territory was bounded by deserts so impossible to cultivate (especially by Egyptian standards) that dissident elements simply had nowhere to go, a circumstance which Robert Carneiro believes was a very powerful environmental influence in the origin of all primary states. Egypt was a remarkable example of this geographical circumstance and it seems likely that it worked as a powerful restraint against any political dissidence. Carneiro is certainly vindicated in this case, though for others an important amendment has been suggested (chapter 12): that the fear of raiding predators, especially as in the case of Mesopotamia, leads to a polarization of defensive large cities and pure nomadism, thus creating a no-man's-land that looks like geographic isolation but is actually caused by military tactics. Egypt's remarkable development without urbanism must be directly related to the lack of military defense against nomadic raids during the third millennium. The ease with which the nomadic Hyksos finally occupied Northern Egypt (around 1600 B.C.) certainly supports this proposition.

The institutions of the Egyptian civilization were also distinct from those of Mesopotamia in some salient respects. For our interests, the most unusual was the early and rapid imposition of political controls over a region that incorporated many hundreds of communities. In other words, the highly urban, independent cities of Sumer did not appear; the origin of civilization in Egypt was not a good instance of Childe's "urban revolution." The other surprising feature is the equally sudden appearance of a ruler who functioned as both secular king (or emperor) and deity, in contrast to the trend elsewhere toward a "separation of powers" in which, usually, the priestly hierarchy became increasingly removed from mundane secular affairs, especially the economic and military.

The Formative Era: "Badarian" and Predynastic Periods (ca. 4000–3100 B.C.)

One of the unusual characteristics of the Nile River is the regularity of the annual flooding of its valley (before the building of the Aswan Dam). In its flood the river rises slowly, to spread gradually over much of its valley for about two months, and finally to recede slowly, leaving a deposit of fine silt that is free of salt and that completely renews the fertility of the soil. This has happened over so many thousands of years that the flooded land became almost perfectly flat long ago; thus no, or very little, surface erosion has occurred. The timing of the flood is also very important: It begins in later summer after the harvest and withdraws in the fall in time for the sowing of the winter crops. The soil retains enough moisture so that as the winter crops mature their roots can keep growing downward to retain contact with the slowly receding moisture table. Spring-summer crops were watered by canal irrigation in Dynastic times, but apparently the earlier farming communities depended on the annual flood alone (Woolley 1963, pp. 111–12).

By about 4000 B.C. sedentary villages living by floodwater farming were scattered throughout the Nile's flood plains. Cereal grains, most importantly, and various legumes and other vegetables were planted on land plowed by oxen. Goats were common, but not sheep, during the early period. Dogs, donkeys, pigs, geese, and ducks were also domesticated early, but neither the horse nor camel was used in the Nile Valley. Not much is known in detail about early food production in Egypt because the deep layers of silt in the Nile Valley and the fact of continuous occupation have hindered the discovery of more than a few early village archaeological sites. But it seems evident that between 4000 and 3000 B.C. there was in Egypt, as in Mesopotamia, a growing population and increasing craft specialization—at least a growth of greater skill in technology. An increase in luxury items like precious ornaments in some burials indicates the probable development of sociopolitical status differentiation.

River transportation was by boats made of bundles of reeds, propelled by oars and sail. Overland transport was by oxen and donkeys, but there were no wheeled carts until much later. Egypt was much more of a self-contained economic entity than was Sumer, for the Nile River integrated the valley early and easily, as far as the movement of goods and raw materials was concerned. And this provided a kind of natural foundation upon which a political unification could be erected.

Perhaps the ease with which the unification of Egypt was later to take place was related to the absence of urban power centers that could resist incorporation. The local districts, called *nomes,* later became administrative districts, but in Predynastic times they were probably autonomous. ". . . But the authority exercised locally by priests, chieftains, or priest-kings must have been undeveloped and flimsy in prehistoric Egypt as compared with the authority of comparable rulers in Sumer" (McNeill 1963, p. 71). The nucleus of each nome may have been a temple with temple estates, but religion did not work in such a way as to create local loyalties; the local chieftain was not the earthly representation of the local god. This was another trait that presumably eased the path toward centralization in Egypt. The Pharaoh of Dynastic Egypt was accepted by the people as *the* god of the whole land, rather than a representative of one of several local city gods vying for supremacy, as was the case in Sumer.

Apparently the villages of Predynastic Egypt were small and scattered, and were normally unwalled (Woolley 1963, p. 129). The Predynastic period was evidently like late Formative periods elsewhere, with the basic economic and technological foundations developing within the political order of a purely theocratic chiefdom, with neither warfare nor other secular matters having become important enough to lead to the separation of priestly from secular powers. There was apparently as yet no important long-distance trade that required deputized professional carriers, bureaucratic planners, or other such secularized officials, or "merchants" (Woolley 1963, p. 323).

The Old Kingdom (ca. 3100–2200 B.C.)

The beginning of the Egyptian civilization—and the early dynastic society should indeed be called this—was tied to the conquest of the "northern land" (the lower Nile) by the southerners (of the upper Nile). Later mythological literature attributes this conquest to Menes, a chief of This, near Abydos in Upper Egypt. There is some archaeological evidence for such a unification made by military means, but the mythological account is probably foreshortened, and Frankfort (1948, ch. 2) believes that it attributes to a single person a feat which probably took two or more generations. Not much is known of the first three dynasties (3100–2650 B.C.); but the Old Kingdom was at its height under the Fourth and Fifth Dynasties (2650–2350 B.C.) and most of the following discussion refers to that period. (The Sixth Dynasty disintegrated into a kind of disorderly feudalism around 2200 B.C.)

In certain respects the new united Egypt was ruled by the simple addition of a kind of Sumerian temple chiefdom on top of the scattered smallish nomes. It could even be argued that as a government Pharaoh's temple was no more than an elaborate chiefdom that somehow, for peculiarly local reasons, was able to hold in thrall a hinterland that was tremendous in size for a chiefdom.

McNeill (1963, p. 72) considers the Egypt of this period "like a single temple community writ large. It was as though the first rulers of united Egypt had taken the social system of Sumer and improved upon it by enlarging the territorial base to include the entire navigable length of the lower Nile, thereby automatically solving the political problem which arose from conflict between adjacent states in the older land."

The source of the temple-like theocratic political hierarchy was the royal family itself. Pharaoh ruled, but more importantly, he symbolized the society in both its spiritual-intellectual and its temporal aspects, so that "for the Egyptians, civilized life gravitated around the divine king" (Frankfort n.d., p. 99).

Pharaoh was the source of law, governing by inspired decisions. The bureaucracy of the government had a patriarchal character, with sons and close male relatives of Pharaoh as principal figures, and more distant relatives in more minor posts. Thus a familistic aristocratic theocracy, very characteristic of all the chiefdoms we have discussed, stood at the apex of the society—distinguished from the others, to repeat, not so much in content as in the size of the domain. There was no clear administrative separation of powers of the theocracy until the Fourth Dynasty, when a grand vizier was introduced as a kind of chief justice and prime minister.

The administration under the vizier had several departments. One important one was the treasury, a central depot for all imports and duties, with branches and storehouses throughout the country. Troops and ships were also administered by the treasury for the royal trading expeditions to foreign lands. A second important department head was the "chief of the fields," whose domain was agriculture, and another was the "master of largesse," whose concern was livestock. All of these ministries employed men who moved from post to post or up the hierarchy, independently of any local ties. The bureaucracy, which began with Pharaoh's descendants and relatives, became very large, and a *pure* centralized bureaucracy, whose affinities and interests were entirely with the court (Frankfort n.d., p. 101).

The bureaucratic centralization was particularly manifested in its control of trade. Sir Leonard Woolley (1963, p. 322) concludes that "in Egyptian texts, down to the end of the second millennium B.C., there is nowhere any mention of merchants."

This silence does not mean, as some authorities have assumed, that commerce was nonexistent, but it does imply that private merchants, even though they existed and might become wealthy, yet enjoyed no such social rank as would enable them to build rich tombs for themselves and thereby leave a memorial that could endure to our time. We have no knowledge of any Egyptian laws regulating trade, and this again tends to show that the private trader played no very important part in the land's economy. The fact was that all commerce was in the hands of Pharaoh, and the divine Pharaoh was, of course, a law unto himself.

Raw materials obtained from foreign areas included copper from Sinai, gold from Nubia, ebony, perfumes, and spices from Arabia or Somaliland, magical gums from Asia—all acquired by state expeditions (Childe 1942, p. 115).

According to Frankfort (n.d., p. 117) trade was a subordinate part of the country's internal economy. Individuals bought or exchanged the goods their households produced. The common tillers of the soil were liable to *corvée* for military service and service in labor corps for public works such as maintaining canals, quarrying stone, and building temples and tombs. Some of the cultivators also worked temple estates and the royal domain. The hamlets and villages worked their lands collectively under a headman who was responsible for turning over stipulated amounts to the state. Craftsmen were organized in groups under a foreman who received and distributed their family rations of food, clothing and raw materials, and who disposed of their finished products.

The complexity and size of the redistributional bureaucracy must have been enormous.

> It has been said that Pharaoh was the only wholesale merchant in Egypt and that foreign trade was a royal monopoly. But the implication of profit-making and exploitation is inappropriate. It was merely due to the complete consistency with which the Egyptians had organized their community as a centralized monarchy that they supplied themselves with the foreign materials of which they stood in need by means of royal expeditions. It is curious evidence of the practical effectiveness of Pharaonic rule that the absolute monarchy did supply essential commodities, whether imported or produced at home, to the people as a whole in sufficient quantities; the distribution took place "from above," the king making gifts and allotments to his officials who in turn rewarded their retainers and so down the social scale. And in the First Intermediate period, when royal power suffered an eclipse, the texts contain a complaint that there is no wood available for the making of coffins [Frankfort n.d., p. 119].

If there was no important trade that was not both administered and redistributed bureaucractically, what can we say of the *class* structure (or "stratification")? Childe, who has elsewhere made much of the economic sources of class differentiation, has said (1946, p. 125) that "under the totalitarian regime of Old Kingdom Egypt merchants had little scope." But certainly the differential ranking of persons persisted and was probably extended widely. Is this an impulse for the creation of a repressive state—to protect this differentiation—or is it a product of the very development of the bureaucratic order? In Egypt, it is apparent, the bureaucratic order extended its benefits as its own structural development proceeded, and must have *itself* been the source of differential ranking. If there was stratification, we must be careful how we define it, and what political consequences we attribute to it.

Woolley finds that "class distinctions" in the early dynasties of Egypt amount to two classes—"the government and the governed" (1963, p. 171).

Pharaoh as god was a being apart, incomparably superior to any mortal; but Pharaoh as ruler had to have associated with him officials to whom could be entrusted the executive functions of rule. The unification of the country had been effected by war; the old governors of the northern nomes, therefore, had been replaced by Pharaoh's nominees who, as his representatives in the provinces, kept their own almost independent courts and had their forces of armed retainers held at the disposition of the supreme ruler; these "monarchs," together with the great functionaries of the royal court, the members of the royal family (for the sons of the Pharaoh took a prominent part in affairs) and perhaps also the officers of the royal bodyguard, "the followers of His Majesty," formed the aristocracy of the Old Kingdom. Even as late as the Middle Kingdom the priesthood was still merely an incidental office held by a layman; the lower orders of officials, a few artists, highly skilled craftsmen and merchants might claim a superior status to that of the artisan or the agricultural labourer, but in reality all alike were indiscriminately Pharaoh's serfs.

If such rank or status differentiations, however overweening, are to be called *class* or *class stratification*, then what about the usual Marxist definition of class as "differential relations to the means of production"? There seems to be, surely enough, a differential manifested here, but it is a matter above all of official stewardship over persons, and of guidance of their activities by the political power or authority—a matter, in short, of pure bureaucracy. It is not "ownership," or merchants' profit-taking (which makes wealth, which in turn makes power), as in common capitalist ideology. It is the plain power that accrues to theocratic officialdom.

There seemed to be no permanent military bureaucracy nor standing army, presumably because Egypt was so safely isolated during Old Kingdom times. Such expeditions abroad that needed troops had them called up as required. Much later, in the Eighteenth Dynasty, imperial commitments made a standing army necessary (Woolley 1963, p. 172), but this is beyond the historical scope of our discussion. Similarly, slavery never was important economically (ibid., p. 175), so that owners and slaves were not themselves part of a class system. The economy, in short, was simply collection and redistribution, possibly on the grandest and most complete scale that ever existed anywhere in the ancient world.

Such highly centralized and overwhelming redistribution must have been in large part responsible for the great amount of internal political stability. The monolithic nature of this bureaucracy was matched by its ideology, especially its religious ideology. Pharaoh was the living god of Egypt, which must have given him a hold over his subjects' minds that matched his economic significance. Since he was a god, he had to be immortal, and somehow he was able to confer immortality on his officials if they pleased him in his service. "Who would wittingly incur the god-king's wrath when penalties for disobedience were so drastic, and the rewards for good behavior seemed so sweet? Here, surely, lay the secret of the Old Kingdom" (McNeill 1963, p. 74).

With the concern for immortality came the related concern for preserving the body and it abode, which in Egypt led to the building of the great pyramids. Here again we see the conjunction of the bureaucratic command of labor, wealth, and religious belief—all joining together in one grand enterprise at the apex of the theocracy, the royal household. The first true stepped pyramid and the temples around it, all constructed of stone, were those of King Zoser at Saqqâra, in the Third Dynasty (ca. 2700 B.C.). Within about a century and a half after this, the largest of all (Cheops) was built, and by then the Egyptians had fully demonstrated their extraordinary skill in architecture and masonry. As

Woolley has said (1963, p. 248), ". . . it is indeed no exaggeration to say that the workmanship of the pyramid builders has never been surpassed in any country." But it should also be stressed that these were monuments to a tremendous strength of organization.

At the same time all this was going on (roughly 2700–2550 B.C.) many other aspects of classical Egyptian culture were reaching fulfillment. Sculpture and painting, ornamental metallurgy in gold, silver, and copper, the carving of stone vases, carpentry, boat-building, weaving (of flax)—all of very high quality—were all completely specialized by then. Artisans and craftsmen were organized in craft guilds that were apparently fully hereditary (Woolley 1963, p. 298).

It would seem that a bureaucracy that could organize such a technology, an economy, and a religion could not possibly do so without a system of written communication and record-keeping by professional scribes. Hieroglyphic writing appeared before the beginning of the Dynastic period; it may have been stimulated by experience with the Mesopotamian cuneiform. It was thus not so much a great single intellectual achievement as a reaction to the bureaucratic need for a system of professionalized record-keeping, a need that grew increasingly complex as the bureaucracy itself grew.

The Middle Kingdom and After (2050–1800 B.C.)

The Old Kingdom of Egypt is noteworthy for remarkable political continuity. The six dynasties it comprised lasted more than eight centuries (3100–2270 B.C.), without any apparent disorder or severe repression of dissident factions or localities. Nor was there any evident foreign threat of any significance. But nevertheless some kind of disintegration began under the Sixth Dynasty (2350–2200 B.C.), culminating in an unruly epoch called the First Intermediate Period (2200–2050 B.C.). During this period there was no royal household functioning long enough to administer the whole of Egypt and the various arts and crafts degenerated, although they were still being produced.

The Middle Kingdom was created when a local lord of Thebes

in Upper Egypt defeated all rivals and united the country under his new dynasty (the Twelfth). It may be observed that this unification somewhat resembles the original one of Menes, who also came from the south, which was a relatively backward area. These, together with the instance of Sargon's conquest of Mesopotamia, illustrate the advantages that seem to come to a marcher (borderlands) lord in the power struggles of petty states (McNeill 1963, p. 81, *n.* 22). If we take as rather similar instances the imperial success of Tiahuanaco in highland Peru, Tulu, and then the Aztecs in central Mexico, perhaps we are witnessing the workings of a kind of process of evolutionary potential in the political aspects of culture (Service 1971, ch. 3). The secondary, less-adapted, less-specialized societies of the hinterlands have more freedom to accept solutions from among more workable alternatives than the societies of the classic archaic style.

In any event, the classical simplicity of the Old Kingdom was not repeated, especially in the degree of royal centralization. Local magistrates and hierarchies of priests remained powerful and rather independent, even the art styles showed more regional differentiation than ever before, and the central authority was less exalted and less absolute.

By about 1088 B.C. the kingdom was disintegrating again, and for the first time found itself unable to resist foreign invasion, which its relatively protected position had made an easy task earlier. A people known as Hyksos crossed the Sinai Desert, overwhelmed the northern areas of Egypt, and established themselves as rulers. Naturally enough, the proud Egyptians hated to be ruled by crude barbarians and eventually they reunited under a new king (again from the southern frontier), in about 1570 B.C.

But the Near and Middle East were in a new ferment in those days, with barbarian hordes on the move, new empires, and new centers of commerce and power being formed. Although the Egyptians successfully expelled the invaders, they no longer felt as secure as before, and they prepared themselves to confront the world. In particular, "the Egyptian rulers entered upon a cosmopolitan career in direct contact with and competition against the other great Middle Eastern river valley civilization, the Mesopotamian" (McNeill 1963, p. 82).

The Evolution of a Super-Bureaucracy

All of the researchers on Egypt that have been mentioned so far are agreed that although Mesopotamia apparently reached the thresholds of civilization slightly earlier than Egypt, and that there are evidences of trade or some kind of diffusion between them, yet Egypt's sociopolitical structure was actually so distinct that it should be treated as a primary autochthonous development. Of particular interest is the association of cities with Mesopotamia and their absence in Egypt.

A growth in overall population accompanied the transformation of Formative theocracies to civilizations in all our examples. Population growth after a certain point probably requires more and more authoritative controls of the more impersonal kind. And of course a successful polity may acquire a larger population by accretion of a voluntary kind as well as by conquest of neighbors. Probably the Nile Valley was united in both of these ways. Evidently, however, this unification took place before there were any large cities, and after unification there was no need for them for most of the third millenium, at least during the era of the Old Kingdom.

As we have seen, Childe felt that "urban revolution" was a good name for the secularizing political and economic processes that accompanied the rise of civilization. Here, as with Mesoamerica, Peru, and Mesopotamia, it must be deemed as misleading, for urbanization accompanied civilization only in some cases, notably Teotihuacán, Chan Chan, and Sumer. All of those large cities were walled and otherwise fortified, for all arose in times of warfare and turmoil. It may be suggested that those classical cities represented a *defensive* way of life. But once in existence a city can take on many functions or characteristics that may have had nothing to do with its origin: It may come to monopolize commerce and redistribution, become a center of theology and learning or of arts and crafts, and so on, continuing to grow for these reasons as well as for military defensive tactics. In Egypt true cities never developed until late in the second millennium B.C., after a long period of invasions as well as internecine warfare. The Old Kingdom, after the original unification, was a notably long peaceful epoch, and hence it had no need for a defensive posture—especially against raiding nomads like those that harassed Mesopotamia.

The so-called "vertical economy," the regional symbiosis of micro- and macro-ecological variation that may be an important functional aspect of urbanism, was also largely missing in Egypt. The villages and towns strung along the Nile were largely homogeneous replicas of one another except for craft specializations. Yet Egypt developed rapidly into the most thoroughly bureaucratized, and thus the most completely redistributional, economy ever known to history. Obviously, the relationship between regional symbiosis and redistribution is not a necessary one, nor is urbanism required for the development of either.

Egypt's route to economic redistribution was clearly the division of labor in personnel rather than by regions. The division of labor was subsidized and guided at all important points—"a temple economy writ large." Mesopotamian towns apparently began their redistributional economies in the same way, with the temple economy being basically a subsidized division of labor. But once in career, a temple economy can grow into a larger, more widely effective redistributional system that can create a quite effective symbiosis of distant regions where it had not done so at first. It seems evident that there is a strong tendency for such a system to extend itself, for its increased size and effectiveness is, in effect, a guarantee of its own survival. Egypt's bureaucracy directed an economy that ran more intensively and purely to craft specialization and mass labor projects; Mesopotamia's economy was finally mixed, involving both specialized skills and differing regions; while the economy of Tiahuanaco in the Andean highlands was based more completely on regional specialties.

14

The Origins of Civilization in the Indus River Valley

For about one thousand years, beginning about 2500 B.C., a civilization of the classic type prevailed over the valley of the Indus River and its tributaries. It had writing (as yet not deciphered) and a decimal mathematical notation, specialized skilled crafts (including metallurgy in bronze), two planned cities as large as any in Sumer, irrigation and flood control, monumental architecture, vast systems of transport, all of which were similar to those of Sumer and at least as good. The valley succumbed to invasions of barbaric pastoralists (believed by some to be "Aryans") around 1500 B.C., never to recover its independence.

The Formative Era

As in the case of Egypt, we are confronted with a "precocious" development in the Indus Valley, the antecedent stages of which are not well known at yet. Malik believes that recent archaeological evidence shows that the Indus development was probably indigenous (1968, pp. 11–112). But as in the case of Egypt, there is evidence of trade with Sumer, so again there is the problem of how to assess the degree of independence of the Indus civilization. It is possible that its rise was rapid, like Egypt's, because the Sumerian civilization provided models that could be adapted to the conditions of the Indus River Valley. But the basic traits were distinctive.

The Twin Cities (ca. 2500–1500 B.C.)

The Indus Valley civilization occupied a larger territory than either Egypt or Sumer. The two large cities, Harappa and Mohenjo-daro, were about three hundred fifty miles apart, and the most distant lesser sites were about a thousand miles apart. The valley was similar to Mesopotamia in that low rainfall necessitated irrigation, but was unlike Egypt in that the flooding of the plains was not regular. Hence, it could not be occupied successfully except on the basis of manmade irrigation. For this reason alone, a Formative stage of development, in which an irrigation system grew to near-maturity, must have taken place elsewhere before the plains were occupied. The Indus Valley dwellers would have needed such a system not only to irrigate crops, but also to control the irregular floods.

Further indirect evidence strongly supports the theory that a full-fledged culture was imported to the valley of the Indus. From top to bottom (over a thousand miles) and up the five tributaries, the occupied area is uniform in culture, even in minor stylistic features (Allchin 1968, p. 136). Moreover, the large cities apparently were geometrically planned and then built to the plan, rather than growing randomly by accretion like the Mesopotamian cities. As McNeill points out (1963, p. 85, *n.* 31), this difference can be noted today in contrasting the regularity in layout of Washington, D.C., Canberra, and Brazilia with the irregularity of London, Paris, or Lisbon. At any rate, we should not be surprised that the evolutionary potential of such a development as irrigation agriculture became suddenly greater as it spread to a new area than it was in the region of its original development. This was somewhat evident in Mesoamerica and clearly so in Mesopotamia (though not clear in Egypt). The Indus River development was unusual only in the apparent rapidity of its appearance.

It may be remembered that Sumer itself underwent rapid development only after most of the important elements of its civilization had been developed elsewhere, most likely from the uplands to the east. This same source may have generated important elements of the Indus civilization as well. That is, instead of attributing the civilizing inspiration to Sumerian influence, it might be more proper to imagine a very generalized common source for both of them. This would help explain why, although Sumer and the Indus Valley shared generalized traits like writing and mathematics, monuments, bricklaying, copper and bronze metallurgy, and so on, the two civilizations had diverged through time to have characters of their own, distinctively Sumerian and distinctively Indian (Woolley 1963, p. 88).[1]

The two large cities (Mohenjo-daro covered at least one square mile) were built almost entirely of kiln-fired brick. The kilns must have used tremendous amounts of wood for fuel, and a great amount of labor must have been expended in transporting the wood as well as constructing the cities (Childe 1946, p. 118). The alluvial plain of the Indus slopes to the sea much more steeply than does the Euphrates delta and nearly twice as much as the Nile delta (Woolley 1963, p. 151). This makes the engineering of a canal system much simpler and water can flow much farther, making an extensive system possible. The canal systems needed to irrigate such vast areas as were evidently under cultivation must have demanded centralization on a grand scale. The flooding occurs from May to August, so that (as in Sumer) canals had to be constructed for perennial irrigation; natural flooding could not be depended on.

The great uniformity in architecture and decorative styles over the whole area implies a political unification similar to that of Egypt. And Woolley suggests also (ibid., p. 152) that ". . . if the

1. Recent archaeological investigations in ancient Persia suggest that the early Mesopotamian developments that began in Elam (Susa and Sialk) culminated in the fourth millennium B.C. about five hundred miles farther east in Tepe Yahya, about midway between the Mesopotamian cities and the Indus Valley. The excavators of this site suggest that it was the immediate stimulator of the Indus civilizations' rise to prominence in the third millennium B.C. (Lamberg-Karlovsky 1971).

striking similarity in the planning of Harappa and Mohenjo-daro justifies us in regarding the two cities as twin capitals of the same ruling power, then their existence is fully explained by the difficulty of controlling from a single administrative centre the irrigation of an area so immense as that of the Indus valley."[2]

But we cannot be sure that the irrigation system was such a large-scale one. Malik (1968, pp. 97–98) believes that it is more likely that there were numerous small canal systems, rather than one system, centrally managed. There is no archaeological evidence for the large systems, and throughout the known history, even to today, small village systems are adequate. The fact that a city such as Mohenjo-daro lay at the heart of a cluster of smaller settlements further suggests that irrigation was probably small-scale and local.

The cities were not walled or otherwise fortified, except that they each had a raised citadel or acropolis on the outskirts, which might have been the residence of "authority" (Malik 1698, p. 82). Otherwise, there are few evidences of warfare or defense against attack. "Hence not a military empire, like Sargon's, but a priestly state, like the Egyptian Old Kingdom, seems the likely political pattern" (McNeill 1963, p. 86).[3]

Small villages and towns were scattered around the countryside in a pattern that suggests peace rather than war, or even any expectation of war. Had there been internal war, the population of the countryside would have been more defensively agglomerated. A fear of raiding nomads would have caused similar clusters together with the polarization of nomadism and sedentism that makes for no man's land at the borders, with perhaps occasional marcher fortresses. If such things occurred, it would seem that some evidences would have been noted.

Redistribution must have been very extensive and highly organized. The urban sites had huge granaries, suggesting highly organized collections and delayed distributions. Maritime as well

2. Raikes (1964) believes that Harappa actually replaced Mohenjo-daro as capital after a disastrous flood of the lower Indus River.

3. Fairservis (1961, p. 18) definitely believes that the cities were chiefly ceremonial centers. Wheatley (1971) says that this was true of all of the cities of the primary civilizations.

as riverine trade was very extensive, as indicated by trade objects and scarce precious stones like jade (found only in Mysore), copper and tin, gold and silver. Such evidences as these, together with the recent excavations of sites with typical "Harappan" features, show that the Indus civilization extended eastward at least to Surat, only 175 miles north of Bombay (Malik 1968, pp. 82–83). The indications are that it was not canal systems that were organized by the centralized authority, but a truly extensive redistributional system.

Writing was present, but evidently confined to economic trade and record-keeping, rather than literature, ideology, or education. Again, it would seem that script and number are closely allied in origin and the origin is likely to be simply a mnemonic device necessary for record-keeping in a complex system.

Childe (1942, p. 119–20) notes storage places and varieties of highly skilled crafts, and concludes that the Indus was a "class" society composed of rich merchants and laborers and artisans. But this is an unwarranted inference. Chiefdoms and primitive states with completely regulated redistributional systems may have highly differentiated statuses and sumptuary rules for their aristocracies, but the aristocracies have a political foundation rather than an economic one. Woolley, on the same evidence, thinks that the Indus civilization must have been a conquest state (1963, p. 157). Everyone agrees, however, that the complex geometrical plan of the cities requires the presence of a truly effective and centralized authority system.

Malik (1968, pp. 99–110) argues that the Indus River systems were chiefdoms rather than states. This argument rests largely upon the absence of evidences of a coercive state, and thus cannot be conclusive. In favor of Malik's view, however, and a point he does not bring up, is that the overall cultural coherence over a long time-span, with no (or little) evidence of warfare or other disturbances, remind us of both Egypt and the valley cultures of coastal Peru. In both of those instances, we have pointed out their differences in comparison with Sumer and Tiahuanaco, and raised the possibility that they were chiefdoms rather than states.

In this context, Malik brings up an interesting discussion of the possibility that the extensive chiefdom system in the Indus River Valley created the basis of the caste system so characteristic of later Hindu society.[4] Chiefdoms have many obviously caste-like characteristics; if a chiefdom is "writ large," and lasts long enough to crystallize its tendency toward endogamy and toward an increasing specialization of both regional and craft labor, it would surely deserve the label "caste society." Such a view makes much more functional-historical (or evolutionary) sense out of the origins of caste than the more prevalent view, which finds those origins in racial conquest and endogamy imposed to prevent racial or ethnic miscegenation (although, to be sure, a functioning caste system if diffused widely could come to have such additional functions).

As we have seen, hereditary inequality originated with chiefdoms, first of all familistically out of the kinship conceptions of tribal society. Inequality then became pervasive, but with broad classes of status as well, normally buttressed by ideology, ritual, and sumptuary rules. As the tendency toward endogamy, probably begun by the upper stratum, became fully hereditary, the inequality became "frozen" through time—one of the salient features of the Indian caste system.

The beginnings as well as the subsequent development of chiefdoms are closely related to specialization in skills and of regions, which also tend to become hereditary as they become customary through time. Our usual preoccupation with this aspect of chiefdoms is because of the association of the specialization with redistribution, which in turn strengthens the central authority system. (It should be noted that once the specialized parts are fully structured they can engage in reciprocal services and exchanges among themselves, another frequently described characterestic of small village caste systems).

A third usual feature of chiefdoms is the theocratic nature of the authority system. Religious conceptions are, of course, a prominent buttress to the traditional caste system of Hindu India. Such conceptions and rituals, and the myths associated with them, not only provide the rationale for the system but also help pattern it into a shared system over wide regions.

It seems conceivable that once bureaucracy has achieved order and direction over a wide area and once the fully organismic inter-

4. Childe earlier (1953, p. 121) also proposed that the Indus civilization, rather than "Aryan invaders," laid the basis for modern Hindu-Indian culture.

dependence of parts is achieved, together with a pattern of hereditary statuses and occupations, that coercive force and negative sanctions might not be in great need most of the time. Such a system, once hereditary, can become so internalized through the benefits it brings—that is, by positive reinforcement—that individuals and local groups are not inclined to rebel. Such a society can be very stable, and probably even satisfying. Ralph Linton put it this way in a well-known passage (1936, pp. 130–31):

> Americans have been trained to attach such high values to individual initiative and achievement that they tend to look down upon societies which are rigidly organized and to pity the persons who live in them. [However] . . . It would never occur to an orthodox Hindu that he was to be pitied because he could not change his caste. . . . His religion provides him with rationalizations of the whole system and with an explanation of his presence in the caste as a result of his soul's evolutionary status. . . . Membership in a rigidly organized society may deprive the individual of opportunities to exercise his particular gifts, but it gives him an emotional security which is almost unknown among ourselves.

The Demise

The *Rig Veda* is the oldest surviving Sanskritic literature, and describes (from the Aryan point of view) the conquest of the dark-skinned natives by light-skinned Aryan-speaking invaders. The archaeological evidence, however, suggests a sort of decay before 1500 B.C., which has led some to postulate "natural" causes like climatic changes—but there is no actual evidence for such a cause except for flooding at Mohenjo-daro. At any rate the same climatic change (or flooding, or dessication, or whatever) would not affect such a vast region equally.

Malik shows that none of the postulations about the "end" of the Indus civilization, whether by reason of climatic changes or invasions,[5] are based on good data or a realistic view of the behavior of societies (1968, pp. 118–21). The signs of "decay" at the civic centers of Harappa and Mohenjo-daro—the lack of coherence in replacing buildings, poorly built houses, the use of old bricks, etc.—support only the idea that the central authority was not in firm control, that some *political* disintegration had

5. Or, some would say, earthquakes (Raikes 1964).

occurred, and not the notion of a wholesale destruction of a people or their departure, even though eventually the cities were abandoned. (This problem is reminiscent of the speculations about the demise of the "Old Empire" of the Petén Maya.)

City, State, and Civilization in the Indus River Valley

The primary problem in this chapter is that, because of the lack of conclusive data, one is tempted to interpretation by extrapolating from previous chapters. If these interpretations are then used as though they were now further instances of the phenomenon, then we would be guilty of circularity. On the other hand, one of the virtues of a broadly comparative method, such as the present endeavor, is that knowledge of better-documented cases can help in interpreting the less-documented. Therefore, our task is to proceed with a tentative interpretation of the Indus culture, but taking care that we do not lend the interpretation more certainty than it deserves.

The salient fact about the twin cities of Harappa and Mohenjo-daro is that they were meticulously planned, and the population evidently installed in them, until they reached a size of about one square mile. This is in direct opposition to the notion of Childe, and others after him, that the growth or development of urbanism is the matrix for (if not in certain respects the direct cause of) many of the characteristics of civilization such as literacy, art and craft specialization, monumental architecture, science, and so on. It seems evident that the potentiality for civilization in the Indus Valley was created in advance of urban demography and that the civilization thus achieved was the cause of the cities, not the other way around. A good guess might be that the cities began as civic-ceremonial centers only. As their political significance grew so did the bureaucracy, which began to plan for the probable rapid growth of itself and its satellite families of servants, custodians, artisans, economic distributors, and so on. As in Egypt, there is no evidence of the use of secular force.

Piggott's opinions based on the unusual characteristics of the Indus urban centers are that the civilization was thoroughly theocratic (1950, pp. 150–51):

The archaeological evidence of continuous occupation of the city-sites over centuries, with at Mohenjo-daro at least the preservation of the initial street-plan from first to last, with practically no encroachment on the building-lines of houses where they faced upon main streets or subsidiary lanes, shows that continuity of government was somehow assured throughout this long time, and that whatever the changes of dynasty or of individuals in power, the tradition was transmitted unimpaired and of constant validity. While it is dangerous to make deductions from the evidence with any confidence, one can nevertheless suggest that such a continuity over generations is likely to have been enforced by religious sanctions, and that, in its remarkable conservatism and scrupulous preservation of even the details of everyday life intact for centuries, the texture of the Harappa civilization has a strongly theocratic tinge, and surely implies a social system wherein the unchanging traditions of the temple were of more account than the ambitions of an individual ruler or the secular instability of the court, and in which the form of land tenure was dictated by the priestly hierarchy.

In summary, all that we know of the Indus River Valley culture points to an Egyptian style in contrast to the Sumerian. It was a spread-out, relatively secure (and thus unwarlike) highly bureaucraticized (attested to by the extraordinary city planning), stable society. We have no certain evidence that it was as intensely theocratic as Egypt, but it does seem that Malik is probably correct in judging that this was India's ancestral caste society, and that mythic beliefs and religious ceremony were its buttress rather than coercive force. But there were apparently no great temples or tombs in the Egyptian fashion.

The main point that the Indus River society confirms is that urbanism is not necessarily the concomitant of a developing civilization. The evidence in this case is clearly that it was the developing civilization that later made possible the relatively small amount of urbanism, rather than the reverse.

15

The Origins of Civilization in China

CHINESE BRONZE-AGE civilization began at the middle reaches of the Yellow River (the Huangho) of North China, in the area usually called the Great Bend. In general, scholars seem to agree that the total pattern of civilizational developments in China was strongly autochthonous, and that China deserves separate consideration as one of the primary civilizations. Writing, art styles, clothing styles, religion, and ceremony seem to have been "Chinese" from the earliest times. Certainly there was no civilizational model for the Yellow River people among any neighbors that were close enough to be observed.

The habitat in the Great Bend region of the Yellow River is characterized by a distinctive loess soil that is easily worked with primitive hand implements. This deep wind-blown soil is free of stones and has no tracts of heavy timber. The porosity of the loess causes it to absorb water rapidly without runoff or erosion, and the water is drawn naturally again to the surface to nourish the plants. The rainfall is usually sufficient, but irregular; there was probably a use for the simple and small beginnings of irrigation in the region, and since the soil is so easily dug into channels it needed no special tools or skill. But as Owen Lattimore put it (1940, p. 33), "[more sophisticated] control of soil and water in combination lay only within the reach of groups of people, helping each other to dig larger channels and perhaps to build embankments that would keep flood water out of the bottom lands." Bodde (1956) has argued that it was flood control rather than irrigation that was of the greater importance. In either case, it is control of water that makes possible a greater intensification of agriculture—as we have seen before.

The Formative Era

Chinese traditions tell of a succession of seventeen or eighteen kings called the Hsia dynasty, supposedly ruling in northern China from 2205 B.C. until 1766 B.C., when it was overthrown by T'ang, the founder of the Shang dynasty (itself to be overthrown in 1122 B.C. by Chou). Scholars conclude, on the basis of a study of the earliest Chinese writings, that there probably was a culture somewhat resembling the legendary one, and that it was the prestigious leader and originator of the earliest Chinese civilization.

There has been enough archaeological investigation of the Neolithic cultures, dating from around 2000 B.C., to assume now that the Lung-shan culture was a local development, and to consider it ancestral to the later Shang dynasties. The Lung-shan villages were based on intensive gardening and were quite populous, but also rather typically Neolithic in their apparently egalitarian social organization and undeveloped craft specialization.

The transition of the formative Lung-shan culture into Shang looks like a gradual building up of a hierarchical society out of a more egalitarian, less complex society. In the terms used in this book, we could guess that the Shang "dynasty" began as an aristocratic chiefdom that continued its development into the period of the Chou dynasty that followed. There also appears to have been a development toward somewhat more warlike, "feudal" societies; perhaps more complicated, larger, and more powerful. Let us not treat this guess as a conclusion, however. Treistman (1972, ch. 5) thinks that there were statelike beginnings in the transition from Shang to Chou. A foremost expert on China, however, considers the Shang the first civilization in China (Chang, 1963, ch. 6). The problem here is reminiscent of whether Chavín and the Olmec in the New World qualify as civilizations. We will treat the Shang and Chou developments separately, and as descriptively as possible, so that we can see more clearly which characteristics the two have in common and which are distinctively Shang or Chou.

Such theory as will be introduced in this chapter will be Owen Lattimore's (1940, ch. 4; 1962). His explanation is given in functional-evolutionary-ecological terms, and concerns the interrelated rise of intensive and extensive adaptive modes, modes which finally polarized into symbiotic but increasingly distinct specializations. But this is not so much "theory" in the sense of guesswork as it is a highly sophisticated interpretation of the early history of North China. Let us briefly consider the essentials of this interpretation and then follow with a description of Shang and Chou developments.

A range of economic variation in North China corresponded roughly to a geographical gradient that ran from river-valley loess to increasingly dry zones, culminating in the arid steppe of Mongolia. In the valleys, water control made possible the most concentrated and sedentary populations and the most intensive form of agriculture; these areas finally lost all or most of their dependence on herds of grazing animals. Pastoral nomadism, on the other hand, was the most extensive economy, with the society widely dispersed in the steppe. Intermediate forms were "mixed economies," having rainfall agriculture and depending to some extent on domestic herds. As in the Mesopotamian uplands, the mixed economy was probably the earliest. But this early farming, which was widespread in the Neolithic period, did not prevail. Instead, the steppes of Mongolia became dominated by pastoral nomadism, while agriculture in the valleys of North China became increasing intensive, with a commensurate decrease in the intermediate forms.

As the polarization sharpened at the two ends of the gradient, it was the earlier mixed economy that became increasingly marginal—in some senses inferior to the nomadic society as well as to the sedentary society. The superiority of the pastoralists was mainly military, since (as we have seen with modern African tribes) nomadism developed an increasing mobility and an affinity for predatory raids. Eventually the nomads became horsemen, and with the use of the compound bow, a true and highly proficient cavalry. Under these conditions the scattered villages having a mixed economy were easy targets for the nomads' raids, and were dominated by them. Increasingly, villagers tended either to join in a fully nomadic way of life, or to move to the valleys in search of the protection afforded by the developing cities—whose defensive arrangements were becoming increasingly effective. Finally, it appears, two distinct kinds of societies coalesced, their modes of life irreconcilably opposed.

The economic polarization—extremely intensive use of land versus extremely extensive use—was therefore paralleled by a contrast in military modes: In the agricultural communities, defensive arrangements were primary, whereas the nomads concentrated on offensive raiding. These differences encouraged demographic and sociopolitical distinctions as well. The defensive style encouraged the growth of densely occupied cities, and the offensive, a greatly extended population. A purely political point may also be emphasized: The denizens of a city in such a case are more easily ruled; centrifugal tendencies are overcome by the benefits of the protection of the city, compared to the alternatives.

But such a polarization in the two economies may have a symbiotic as well as competitive side. The most extreme instance of regional symbiosis and related redistribution is the necessary economic interrelationship between the extensive pastoralists and the intensive agriculturalists. The pastoralists' products, meat, wool, and skins from sheep and goats, were always welcome to the agriculturalists, who could not keep many of these animals. The pastoralists needed, above all, the craftsman's specialties, especially bronze weapons and tools and ever-welcome grains (also vegetables to be consumed quickly; grain was more desirable because it transports easily and keeps well). This polarization and specialization occurred mainly during the Chou period.

The fact that relations at any given time between some agriculturalists and some pastoralists were warlike does not mean that there was no important trade, for warfare was sporadic and trade was continually necessary. The walled cities were the safe place for such trade, and they were also the location of the granaries and handicrafts that were produced for the trade. A walled city with its symbiotic relationship with pastoralists was relatively self-sufficient otherwise, for the landscape within the Shang-Chou territory was quite uniform and the various cities closely resembled one another. Exchange and redistribution, other than with pastoralists, was at short range. Peasant villages were the units of agricultural production, with the surplus concentrated in the city granaries. A few things, however, like salt, silk, iron, and tea, were products of limited areas and traded at long distances as "tribute-trade"; however, this form of "trade" is also controlled politically rather than by entrepreneurs (Lattimore 1962, pp. 482–83).

The Shang Dynasty (1766–1122 B.C.)

That legendary Hsia were ancestral to the Shang has long seemed problematical. Excavations of the legendary Shang capital city of An-yang in the years 1928–1936 seemed to show too sudden a local transition from the known Neolithic sites to the Shang culture. The refined arts, particularly the bronzes, the unprecedentedly large, complex, planned city, the royal tombs, all suggested the intrusion of a foreign civilized people into the area.

Since about 1950, however, much more has been discovered about the widespread Lung-shan archaeological period, the Neolithiclike culture probably connected to the legendary Hsia. Other sites of Shang culture besides An-yang are now known. They range from the early Lung-shan type through developmental stages to the full-blown manifestations that were found at the later site of An-yang. There is no longer any doubt that Shang culture is an autochthonous North China development rather than a culture foreign to that locality.[1]

Many characteristics from the Lung-shan period and earlier remained in the recently discovered Shang sites. The new features of the Shang culture, in fact, were mostly in socioeconomic aspects of the society rather than in traditionalized items of culture. The most important were, in brief: a more "mature urbanism"; class differentiation (aristocracy, farmers, and craftsmen were more sharply differentiated); new economic patterns based on conquest, tribute, and redistribution; wider trade; intensified warfare; and

1. The following brief discussion of the Shang culture is after Chang (1963) unless otherwise noted.

a more intense specialization in crafts (especially manifested in the superb developments in bronze metallurgy, writing, stone carving, and pottery).

A predominant new feature of Shang life was that individual villages became organized into intervillage networks having economic, administrative, and religious aspects. Prominent sites such as Cheng-chou had walled-in political-ceremonial centers where the royal family and nobles resided. Around this nucleus were found the neighborhoods and hamlets were the craftsmen and their families lived, and then came the nearby farming villages. The administrative-ceremonial center was also the redistributional center. These Shang cities were not as large as Ur, Mohenjo-daro, or Teotihuacán, but they did have the same functions of those more urbanized civilizations—and they were destined to become larger. But above all, the interdependence among specialized communities was a most distinctive characteristic.

There is abundant evidence, from archaeological work, inscriptions, and historical records, that Cheng-chou and An-yang were the seats of powerfully centralized governments controlling a number of more scattered villages in North China. At the apex of the society was a grand lineage that was the center of the political, economic, and ceremonial structure—the Shang were a thoroughgoing hereditary theocracy, in short. The lords who administrated the settlements of the various localities were relatives of the ruler, high administrative officials, and native rulers of more distant localities that paid tribute to the central government.

High status was inherited by primogeniture in a system of patrilineal lineages. This yields, of course, the ramage system of kinship so widely found among ethnologically known chiefdoms. The theocratic buttress of the ramage system everywhere is ancestor-worship, and China may well have acquired in Shang times this long-lasting culture trait so characteristic of it even in modern times.

The high development of the arts and crafts—especially in bronze metallurgy, which Woolley (1963, p. 313) says are the finest ever made in China—attests to a highly organized subsidization program. As we have seen in other examples, this must mean that centralized planning and redistribution were of a highly bureaucraticized order. Chinese calligraphy was also highly specialized and clearly a professionalized activity on a par with other kinds of art. It could be said to incorporate literature as well as painting.

The Chou Dynasty (ca. 1000–256 B.C.)

The Chou are frequently said to have been "barbarians," and perhaps in contact with central Asia. Lattimore (1940, pp. 307–308) disputes this, finding it more plausible to consider the Chou as neighboring participants in the development of the Yellow River culture, perhaps beginning at a lower level, perhaps somewhat provincial, but finally strong enough to take charge of the area. Creel (1954, p. 51) agrees that although the Chou people may have built up the "Hsia myth" (of their cultural precedence over the Shang) in order to claim legitimacy over the area, they were probably not an un-Chinese barbarian people. (Later in Chinese history the conquest of the empires by nomadic barbarians became almost commonplace, but that is no reason for assuming, in the absence of any evidence, that it began with the Chou.) In any event, the period of the Chou dynasty was the classic period in the development of Chinese civilization, when the basic characteristics of Chinese life took their definite form (McNeill 1963, p. 223).

The rule of the Chou falls into two distinct periods. At first, for over two centuries, the Chou capital was in western China, having military, and presumably political, ascendency over most of North China. But in 771 B.C. the capital city was destroyed (it is not known how). The Chou reestablished themselves farther east and ruled again until 256 B.C., but this second reign was relatively ineffective, and power was dispersed among noble or princely houses. In the fifth, fourth, and third centuries B.C. there were wars of ever-increasing intensity, which culminated in the replacement of the faltering Chou by the newly strong Ch'in. The latter had developed alongside the Chou much as the Chou themselves had participated in Shang culture and finally overthrown it (Lattimore 1940, pp. 356–57).

The phenomenon by which newer groups displace older ones has been noted in previous chapters. It may be recalled that McNeill described it as due to the increasing military strength of "marcher states"; that is, societies in frontier districts that can participate in the diffusion of the classic culture, but at the same time are forced to be militarily strong and alert. To this we might add that the marcher states are *newer,* and thus able to accept only the newest and most effective of cultural (especially military) developments, whereas the original classic center remains relatively somewhat burdened by its own past history. Such classic societies in effect become increasingly overspecialized, less and less able to adapt to changing circumstances.

We must note again, in this context, Lattimore's refutation of the widely prevailing notion that the rise and fall of these Chinese dynasties was due simply to "barbarian pressure." But this interpretation does not take into account the growth in numbers and power of separate newly civilized societies in China. These were made possible by an increasingly adept intensive and exclusive agriculture that developed out of the older, loosely distributed mixed agriculture at the same time that the other mode, the pastoral, became increasingly nomadic. Thus, fluctuations in the territory occupied by "barbarians" meant fluctuations in the territory dominated by agriculturalists. These were quite different from the common picture of " 'waves' of barbarian attack seeking to penetrate and overwhelm the orderly domains of the Chinese" (Lattimore 1962, pp. 361–62).

This is not to say there were no dangers from, or attacks by, the barbarians, but rather that it was a two-way process. Furthermore, the growing civilized societies not only applied pressure on barbarians, but also moved against each other. Although McNeill (1963, p. 223) has described the destruction of the western Chou in 771 B.C. in terms of a barbarian invasion (". . . Barbarians sacked the capital, killed the reigning emperor, and shattered the central power"), Lattimore says that "the eastward move of the Chou in B.C. 771 was probably due more to the rise of new Chinese states than to 'barbarian pressure' " (Lattimore 1962, p. 363). One thinks back to the strikingly parallel developments in Mesopotamia and the connected rise of nomadic horsemen on the arid steppe and of new marcher states: Lattimore's analysis might make equal sense applied there.

To return to the beginning of the Chou dynasty: McNeill

does agree with Lattimore (and others) that the Chou usurpers were not themselves barbarians.

> When the Chou conquerors first overran the centers of Shang civilization, they were rough and ready warriors, trained in a hard school of frontier fighting against the outer barbarians who surrounded the Chinese world. Indeed, the Chou used barbarian tribes as allies in their conquest of China. Yet, like many another marchland people, the Chou had been tinctured by Shang culture even before they conquered Shang territory; and under their rule, Chinese civilization continued uninterruptedly to elaborated itself [McNeill 1963, p. 224].

The fact of diverse river valleys interspersed by plains makes for intensive land use and rather small cohesive polities confined mostly to the valleys, but tied into a larger polity or empire only loosely, perhaps only intermittently. It is for this reason that most authorities consider the Chou period one of "feudal monarchies."[2] Lattimore stresses geography and uneven development of the petty principalities as difficulties in achieving a larger coherence, although they participated in the same general culture (1940, p. 368).

> It is evident that the Chou 'dynasty' cannot have ruled a centralized empire containing such diverse regions, inhabited by communities developing at different rates of growth. The 'empire' must have been of a feudal kind, its emperors holding great power at first but later falling into pathetic insignificance, while the descendants of various powerful feudal nobles gradually developed into the royal sovereigns of independent states.

Thus, in Chou times, a kind of feudal monarchy appeared at first simply because the victorious ruler did not have well-devel-

2. European feudalism is so often taken as the type case for feudalism anywhere, and the definitions of it vary so, that we must be wary of its use. I take it that looseness of confederation, combined with considerable local self-sufficiency in economic and political life, are the parallels seen here. But often, too, "feudalism" refers to a special type of relationship of peasant to land, peasant to lord, and above all, lord to lord in a voluntaristic hierarchical relationship—a system of particular kinds of rights and duties. This is much too specially European to expect an exact parallel in China. But Creel (1970, pp. 420–21) attributes the general emphasis on *personal* relationships to the Chou period, and terms it feudal. We may retain this meaning here, remembering its looseness.

Wheatley (1971, pp. 124–25) likens the Chou economy to a feudalistic manorial type featuring lord-serf relations.

oped means of unifying the whole area. Probably the conquered population continued to live as before, growing their crops and paying tribute through their own village leaders. Just as in feudal Europe, there was no territorially demarked "nation-state," but only a series of separate more-or-less powerful domains belonging to feudal lords. The emperor was at the center of a culture rather than a government; that is, he did not rule an integrated society by interfering in local administration. Taxation, adjudication, public labor, and military service were autonomously directed in each holding. "The Chou rulers also had their own personal domain which they administered not as emperors but as great feudal nobles. As an emperor, therefore, the Chou ruler had only the strictly feudal status of *primus inter pares*" (Lattimore 1940, p. 391).

Creel's latest work (1970), based on newly discovered bronze inscriptions, modifies somewhat this view of local Chou self-sufficiency. The Western Chou apparently did have standing armies, and a government that was centralized enough to be called "royal," and there was some kind of central legal system. But the nature of the controls remained basically personal, and even the beginning bureaucracy was a hybrid of personalism and officialism (Creel 1970, pp. 420–24).

Trade was apparently less significant in China than in other classical civilizations. The landscape was relatively uniform and the crops similar. Only a few items like salt, iron, tea and silk were widely traded, because they were products of limited areas. Otherwise, the local principalities so resembled each other and were relatively so self-sufficient that Lattimore (1940, p. 395) calls them "cell-like." Each had its central walled city with its garrison, granaries, artisans, scribes, priests, and administrators; outlying villages provided the basic agricultural production. One may surmise that the redistributive mechanism, and the other benefits of the city, enabled it to be coherent and easily governed. The whole empire, on the other hand, was only loosely connected because of the relative absence of important trade, redistribution, and other overall benefits.

Perhaps the lack of centralization in material matters was responsible for new emphases in the ideology of politics and religion. Of particular relevance is the Chou promulgation of the belief that heaven had conferred a mandate upon the political authority to rule as a universal authority. As "Son of Heaven," the ruler should be deferred to by all people, Chinese and barbarian alike. "This frame of mind enormously facilitated imperial consolidation under successive dynasties and kept the country far more consistently united than the naked balance of military forces could ever had done" (McNeill 1963, p. 226).

The political aspects of this idea were part of a complex cosmological system. The earth was supposed to reflect heaven, the abode of ancestors and of good order. The emperor, as Son of Heaven, was the link between heaven and earth. These beliefs were an overlay of, not a replacement for, the older religion of local spiritism and cults. But they became of great importance to the aristocracy, who were linked to the emperor as varyingly lesser representatives of similarly powerful ancestral spirits of heaven. Each noble, like the emperor himself, thus presided over his own political territory simultaneously as war leader, secular chief, and head priest.

Some of the looseness so characteristic of a feudal system was overcome by a kind of aristocratic educational system, unique among the early civilizations. In this practice, the eldest sons of the important nobles were sent to the capital for a training period that lasted ten years. The heir of the emperor was also attending the school, which must have created friendship and trust between the heir and his chief vassals-to-be, as well as a general sense of aristocratic solidarity. The younger sons of the chief nobles and the eldest sons of lesser nobles attended provincial schools. All followed a fixed curriculum of training in military skills, religion and ceremony, arithmetic and writing. So strong was the felt association between aristocracy and moral education (with its uniquely strong emphasis on literary) that it continued to characterize Chinese culture even until today, when the original class system has completely disappeared.

By 771 B.C., however, effective political sovereignty was held by more than a dozen scattered princely houses, in spite of the continuing beliefs in the emperor as Son of Heaven. The rulers who became powerful and independent illustrate the evolutionary potentiality that comes from occupying a frontier position, for all of them were located on the margins of the Chinese world. As McNeill points out (ibid., p. 228), the lords on the borderlands conquered the barbarians around them and brought them Chinese culture. These marcher states grew so large and powerful, and so practiced in military affairs, that they overshadowed the more civilized, but older, polities nearer the center.

In the sixth century B.C., warfare became chronic and more intense. But this disorder resulted in an outward geographical expansion of Chinese culture. Defeated or dissident elements, adventurers, the uprooted of all kinds, were conquered or were assimilated among the neighboring barbarians. The Shantung Peninsula and the coastal plain to the northeast became culturally parts of China, as did the more northerly and westerly borders of China. Most important for subsequent history was the expansion to the south, to the great valley of the Yangtze and its delta plain, where Chinese culture and society became organized in the fashion of the Yellow River region.

Meanwhile, as the border areas began to prosper, the original civilized society of the Great Bend region waned in relative influence. The educated classes thought more and more of the good old days when their imperial power was paramount. Such nostalgia was an important ingredient in the thought of the great Confucius (551–479 B.C.).

Apparently the loss of power and prestige of the Chou was accompanied by a breakdown in general morality, ethics, and good government. The mandate of heaven was not working very well. It was Confucius's role to try to reintegrate the empire by ideological means, chiefly by persuading the people themselves to behave properly, in the manner of nobility or gentility—whether low-born or high-born. According to this ideology, good government was matched by individual morality in the golden age of the successful empire. In later days, perhaps successful government could be achieved again if *all* the people, aristocracy, politicians, and the masses as well, behaved properly and honorably. To teach this, Confucius had to break with the past in one important way. He had to teach that nobility was achievable, rather than being inborn in the aristocracy. Above all, however, he taught that the greatest reward for a self-cultivated, virtuous person was to govern.

Confucius also departed from some of the older aristocratic dicta by playing down the military virtues and by accentuating the idea that good governance was a matter of decorum, of gracefully giving way when necessary in accord with traditional rules of etiquette and propriety. He believed that the alternative form of governance, by coercive force, would engender counter-violence, intrigue, and civil strife—as was evident in the society of his day.

Confucius himself was not successful in his attempts to get contemporaneous governments to accept his principles. But there was fertile ground for subsequent successes by his disciples. His significance lies in the fact that he was a product of, and the conserver of, the best governing ideas of feudalism—and at the same time, the prophet of a new order that would supersede it (Lattimore 1940, p. 397). Essentially, he recognized that government should be centralized and that a skilled professional bureaucracy should replace the unruly hereditary feudal warrior-nobility. And like other messiahs in history he aimed at a true universalism for his philosophy of just and good government and conduct. And in fact he did have a very widespread and long-lasting effect, comparable in the Far East to that of Jesus in the West.

The First Chinese Empire (223–206 B.C.)

The sixth and fifth centuries B.C. were periods of turbulence that eventually saw the emergence of the Ch'in as the dominant power. The Ch'in were from the northwest loess country, again an example of the emergent power of borderland states. The Ch'in may be said to have begun the Imperial epoch because they inaugurated several military and political policies that changed China from a kind of feudalism toward a much more centralized and powerful government.

First of all was a change in the very nature of warfare. The earlier feudal aristocrats waged a kind of "polite" ritualized warfare that never resulted in permanent subjugation of the vanquished. The defeated ruler would acknowledge his defeat and agree to pay ransom or a periodic tribute, which he himself raised from his subjects. He remained as ruler of his territory, having only "joined" the victor as a subordinate satellite. But this might be only temporary, for he might rebel and join forces with a rival state. Just because warfare was not conclusive, shifts of power by alliance caused a nearly permanent state of unrest.

The new form of warfare was designed to destroy the whole political structure of the conquered side. The Ch'in not only massacred the ruling family, but tried to destroy the defeated army by paying a bounty for enemy heads. The surviving population was incorporated into the victorious society, under the direct administration of the Ch'in. This policy horrified rival states and probably made them more willing to join or ally themselves with the Ch'in.

Another change from feudalism in the fourth century B.C. was the rise of a new class of men who made it their careers to sell their skills in political administration and war. These men were from the minor feudal nobility but had divested themselves of their local feudal loyalties to serve the central administration. (Confucius was an early example of just such a professional administrator.)

Under efficient administration the Ch'in society was able to promote and improve irrigation systems, and to command regional labor forces to the extent of building the stupendous Great Wall. More difficult, probably, was the installation of a taxation system that made the individual family head the taxable unit. Earlier, lords and their subnobility had collected taxes, an inefficient method that was really nothing more than tribute-taking. The public labor on irrigation systems was also directly administered, along wih military service, and like the taxing system required efficient record-keeping and censuses. All of this effectively destroyed the protective sanctions and privileges of feudalism.[3]

The process of creating a true imperium did not proceed without resistance. Also, as the Ch'in were consolidating the Yellow River area, another great empire was being formed by the Ch'u in the Yangtze River Valley to the south. These two fought for several decades, but the Ch'in finally prevailed in 223 B.C. Now the Ch'in ruled the steppe borderlands, the loess region, the Yellow River Valley, the great Yangtze Valley, and above all, the tremendous delta of the Yangtze with its complicated and productive system of canals for boats as well as irrigation. The ruler of the Ch'in became the first emperor of a new China.

We must not lose sight of the source of the power that enabled

3. This section follows Lattimore's interpretations (1940, pp. 399–406).

the Ch'in to defeat what seemed like an equally powerful polity, the Ch'u, who were in their own homeland. The biggest difference was that the Ch'in were a "marcher state" in the first place, in contact with "barbarians," while the Ch'u originated far to the south, with little consistent danger from nomads. As the Ch'in expanded, they conquered not only the civilized states to their south and east, but also subdued barbarians. This latter movement resulted in a rapid enlistment of new barbarian subjects, and these were an important part of the Ch'in armies, particularly as cavalry. (The barbarian element in the Ch'in society was the foundation of a permanent historical tradition in China of dislike for barbarians as destroyers of feudal, conservative, "high" culture.)

Although the Ch'in dynasty fell after only sixteen years, and the succeeding Han (who governed until 220 A.D.) might seem to be more truly the first successful and creative empire of China, it was the Ch'in who first governed China and left as a legacy ". . . the concept of a unified empire, not as something to be attained but as something to be recovered and restored. . . " (Lattimore 1940, p. 424).

The tremendous army that the Ch'in had created was not like a feudal army that could quickly disband and go home to the harvest. It was a professional army, and once the conquests had been made there was little for it to do. Insurrections among them and a series of terrible wars began in 209 B.C. They may be seen as a consequence of excessive overdevelopment of the military, development that contrasts with the relative inefficiency of the economic and administrative branches. At any rate, the fall of the Ch'in did not result in a return to the feudal autonomy of the original petty states. The Han reintegrated the former empire and set about creating the kind of administration that could maintain it. This was a success, and the Han empire quickly flowered into a great interregional culture reminiscent of the influence of the Roman empire.

Under the first rulers, the Ch'in, the greatest threat to unity was probably overexpansion. More specifically, the expansion of the Ch'in from the Yellow River region to the Yangtze (the Ch'u empire) meant the incorporation of a polity and economy of great complexity and power. The Ch'in empire thus had two great power centers, both of which could govern themselves better separately than together. Above all, the former Ch'u empire was undoubtedly difficult to administer and govern from a seat of government in the far north.

It is suggestive that of all the contenders for power after the breakup of the Ch'in, the final victor—after prominent noble leaders of the Ch'u, in particular, had exhausted themselves—was Liu Pang, a native of the Huai area, which lies between the Yellow and Yangtze rivers and had been influenced therefore by both the northern and southern cultures. In a sense, the balance of power lay exactly there, and Liu Pang was able eventually to take advantage of it. He worked a balance of power politics in another way, as well. He was not of noble origins, nor basically a military man, but a minor official who, because of the overlapping influences in his region, was able to resolve difficulties insightfully and to create a balance between the military, the hereditary nobles, and the professional administrators.

It was as an administrator of administrators that Liu Pang made his success. At first the basis of the new bureaucracy was formed with his old trusted comrades-in-arms, but he also freely recruited able men. In time these bureaucrats formed a kind of nobility, a literate gentry, trained in Confucianism. It is possible that the Han were able to rule so peacefully, almost "philosophically," because the disorders and terrorism of the Ch'in epoch and of the wars that established the Han remained fresh in peoples' memories.

Some changes had taken place in external affairs, as well. During the disorderly period the pastoral nomads had made some incursions into the marginal territory near the Yellow River, from which they had been excluded when the Ch'in made the Great Wall. (The wall was actually built by piecing together lesser walls that had been constructed by the smaller feudal principalities). While the Ch'in had been preoccupied in the south, a great confederacy of nomads led by the Hsiungnu had been formed, and in their waxing strength the nomads finally crossed the Great Wall and occupied territory they had been formerly excluded from. Such a successful confederacy, led by a war chief (a "khan"), was subsequently to have a consistent effect on Chinese polity, as of course did the new Chinese polity have an effect on the nomads.

The effective rule of the Han was restored in the north at the fixed frontier marked by the Great Wall. This frontier was a boundary between steppe and agricultural societies, but also a rigid political and cultural boundary. There is no doubt it "did something" to reinforce the unity of a people, like the northern Chinese, to have this sense of continual menace.

To the south, according to Lattimore (1940, p. 472), the Han expanded in a very different fashion. The land was a wilderness that became gradually converted into a typical Chinese landscape, without the mutual recoil and polarization of culture that had occurred in the north as agriculturalists encountered the powerful "barbarians" there.

Most of the subsequent rather rapid expansion of the Chinese empire was in the southern areas. But this "frontier" yielded easily to Chinese settlement, much as did the Western frontier of the United States: There was some fighting, to be sure, but the southern frontier had very different political effects from the frontier of the Great Wall. It may be for this reason that the capital of the Han did not remain in the Huai area of its homeland, but established itself in the north.

But some of the expansion of Chinese power was by pure military might. During the reign of Wu-ti (140–87 B.C.), his armies conquered central Asia, opening up the grand caravan routes that connected the East with western Asia. The Chinese penetrated Korea and, indirectly, Japan was affected by Chinese culture about this time. During the first century B.C., China had achieved such a stable and effective state that it had nearly reached its later traditional boundaries and areas of direct cultural influence.

City, State, and Civilization in China

Aside from the decided variations in the kinds and degrees of urbanism[4] in our examples, the northern Chinese career to civiliza-

4. Wheatley's (1971) large-scale and definitive study of ancient Chinese cities concludes that the usual ascription of urbanism to a level or stage of social evolution to be unfounded and quite ethnocentric. He says of his comparison of China with other early civilizations (p. 480): "I have been unable to correlate the advent of the compact city with, for example, any change in political status such as the expansion from city-state to territorial empire, or with any mutation in the organization of government

tion was remarkably parallel to the important and better-known cases of Mesoamerica, Peru, Mesopotamia, and Egypt. It seems definitely established that the early segmental-egalitarian (Neolithic) society began to change during the period of the legendary Hsia dynasty, when it came to assume the characteristics of chiefdoms. The Shang stage saw the grand movement toward the accomplishment of all of the cultural developments that have been attributed to the archaic civilizations elsewhere. The succeeding period of the Western Chou maintained these developments. It is difficult to say that the Chou dynasty added anything important, but it has left more of a literary as well as an archaeological record. The Han should be credited with having caused the first consolidation of this civilization over a huge area.

We should be wary of the tendency to think of two distinct cultural types, periods, or stages—Shang and Chou—just because two different names were historically attached to them. There was certainly a basic cultural continuity, and probably also some further development, but as far as can be told it was along a cultural continuum. Above all, that the Chou replaced the Shang dynasty by military means is no reason to believe, without other evidence, that the Chou inaugurated a repressive secular state. It seems better to maintain Lattimore's frequent usage and think of a single cultural entity called Shang-Chou, the two dynasties together forming the Classic era of the precocious Chinese civilization developments.

And eventually, just as in the other classical examples, the new civilizations extended their powers outward: They became empires, inaugurating a warlike, competitive era that was very distinct from the Classic—as is suggested by Steward's apt designation of the period as "the era of cyclical conquests." This phase is of such intrinsic interest—although it postdates the temporal focus of this book—that I will take it up at greater length in the epilogue.

---

such as that from religious oligarchy to kingship. Nor does it seem invariably to be directly or clearly related to any specific methods of warfare, or somewhat surpisingly, to specific advances in transportation technology. Possibly it may in some instances reflect the emergence of a new mode of economic exchange, but this topic is at present so obscure that it requires a study to itself."

IV

Conclusions

16

Conclusions I (Negative)

So MANY inadequate ideas have been proposed about the origin and nature of the state and civilization, by so many very influential thinkers, ancient and modern, that we should first criticize the most important of their arguments in this chapter, before proceeding to the happier task of describing the positive results in the final chapter.

These negative, critical conclusions will not so much correct downright errors, however, as suggest changes in emphasis and note complications. In fact, most of the criticisms are of oversimplified causal theories. The most troublesome oversimplifications result from the evident correlation of the rise of formal governments with certain other features that, being outside government, suggest that they play a causal role. Also, these causal theories seem based on a notion that since a bureaucracy is somehow a "structure," and thus passive, it is created rather than creative. These are all easily criticized as oversimplified, and some of them mistake concomitant dependencies and enablers for causes, but they cannot be said to be simply or plainly wrong.

Chapter 2 presented a chronological ordering of the various major theories of the origin and nature of government, state, and civilization. To set the stage for the present critical chapter, we may briefly review the classic theories, but more in terms of the actual stages in the evolution of political thought, which tend to cross-cut the chronological order to a certain extent.

A Brief Review

As we noted in chapter 2, many of the more philosophical of the writers on the political problem equated the *state,* as a means of creating social order, with society itself—all before was anarchy. Individual men, acting rationally, came together to create law and government. As modern anthropologists we know this cannot be true, for an ordered society long antedated such formal institutions. It is the actions of *groups* of people—social classes, economic systems, primitive tribes, or societies of one sort or another—that must concern us, not the actions of discrete individuals. A good many of the classical Greek and Roman philosophers therefore might be dismissed out of hand—Plato and Aristotle, for example.

The social-contract theorists of the European Enlightenment also assumed that individuals would make rational choices to create their own society. There were, of course, important differences among them, polarized by the contrary assumptions about human nature made by Hobbes and Rousseau. Hobbes believed that the original coercive state was created by the decrees of individual men wearied of strife. Rousseau thought that humans were more naturally pacific and that nature would help create an ideal government reflecting the general will. But these were both still only hypotheses about human nature and individual desires.

Rousseau *was* right, in part, in his belief that a society could (and ought to) so educate and benefit its people that repressive sanctions would not be necessary. We have reviewed numerous instances exemplifying the efficacy of such positive reinforcement toward acceptance of the regime. But—and here is the main problem—none of these reinforcements, nor for that matter repressions, take care of the major problem of *external* politics, the waging of war and peace with other societies.

Hobbes *was* right, in part, in his argument that a society is subject to serious strain because of individual contentiousness, egotistical strivings, and so on.

And, as we have seen, all societies have had to shore up their positive reinforcements sometimes with some kinds of coercive, negative sanctions. The relative proportions of these in the political mixture have varied, depending on the internal stresses and strains—especially as related to the size of the society—so that we must conclude not that Rousseau was more correct than Hobbes, or vice versa, but that human nature, a constant, is to be freed or constrained in particular ways depending on factors that lie beyond the natural propensities of individuals.

Ibn Khaldun, in the fourteenth century, may have been the first to emphasize the conflicting relations of whole societies, and the impact of other influences, chiefly geographic, from *outside* the society. More specifically, he discussed the role of climate and land in bringing about competition between nomadic and sedentary societies. This was the original conflict theory (or better, conquest theory), focusing on a situation in which victorious nomads settle permanently among sedentary villages as overlords. Jean Bodin, later but independently in Europe, argued similarly. As we have seen in the case of China in particular, their views of competition did not take into account situations of (at least partial) cooperation among victor and vanquished, nor internal factors within the bureaucracies of sedentary agricultural societies.

Of later Enlightenment writers, Montesquieu seems the most modern in scientific temperament, particularly more so than the popular Rousseau. The latter was enormously influential in France, but his prescription for a society to be based on moral training was essentially utopian and impractical. Montesquieu, on the other hand, was very influential abroad, especially among the Scottish philosophers. Adam Ferguson drew heavily on Montesquieu's work; he extended the idea of a comparative inductive approach to include more than just the civilized nations. He also drew upon missionaries' and explorers' accounts of primitive peoples—"men in a state of nature"—in an attempt to describe human nature in general. Ferguson contributed two important items that hold up well in terms of our investigation: (1) Conflict and competition can have the positive function of aiding state organization, inasmuch as conflict, danger, and the hostility of outsiders strengthens the internal subservience to the collectivity; and (2) an increase in the division of labor in a society increases its prosperity and its size and complexity (and also sometimes its problems). Ferguson thus logically extended the range of Montesquieu's interests and (as did his friend Adam Smith) placed emphasis on sociological and economic factors as determinants of legal and governmental structures, rather than ideologies, "mind," and morals. This may have been the first truly modern challenge by "materialist" theory to the prevailing "idealist" perspective. Ibn Khaldun, Bodin, and Montesquieu, in their turn, had helped the theory to arrive by looking *outside* the society, comparing whole societies in their different geographic settings. Ferguson and Smith refined this perspective almost to its modern form by including a sophisticated economic theory.

The materialistic emphasis on economics reached its apogee with the advent of industrialism, which influenced the thought of Marx and Engels to the point that they made technology and economics (the "mode of production" and the "mode of exchange") the prime movers of cultural evolution. With this emphasis on materialism they combined atheism, determinism, and anti-utopianism. When the findings of Lewis H. Morgan on primitive society were combined by Marx and Engels with their own theory based on European history, they created a full-fledged, very specific theory of how the state, as a repressive institution based on force, actually originated (Engels 1891).

In essence the Marxian chain of cause-and-effect followed this order: (1) *Technological* progress improved production in some primitive-communistic societies, so that a surplus became available for trade; (2) increased trade led to *commodity* production instead of production-for-use; (3) commodity production led to entrepreneurs, and to the formation of *classes* of rich profiteers and poor workers; (4) the *state* came about as a structure of coercive force to protect the rich from the more numerous poor—i.e., the state is a product of the "class struggle." As we have seen, it is only the last of these aspects of Marxism that has much currency today. As a special form of conflict theory it has had an effect on all of the modern theories to be discussed in the following sections.

Warfare and Conquest

The rise in the frequency and intensity of armed conflict, as well as more effective war-making, seems obviously to have been closely associated with the evolution of government. But an association or correlation of two things does not assign causal priority to one over the other. Furthermore, it is plain in the historical record that there are very different forms of conflict having highly varied causes and results. We should consider these variations, but first let us reconsider the most general and usual of the conflict theories.

Conflict theories should be disentangled so that the several meanings can be considered separately. One is the Bagehot-Spencer form of "Darwinism," holding that societies that are governed best will survive the competition of war, thus positively selecting for good government. Another, held by Spencer most prominently, is that the successful conduct of war leads members of a society to cooperate and to learn "subjugation to imperative command," and also that successful and frequent warfare leads to "permanence of chiefship." (This will be discussed in a later section, "Growth and Development.") A third form of conflict theory could better be termed *conquest* theory. Its most specific form was argued by Ibn Khaldun, as we mentioned earlier, that the state resulted from a permanent subjugation of sedentary agriculturalists by nomadic herdsmen. The conflict school of sociologists (Gumplowicz, Oppenheimer, Small, and Ward) also held that the state was a result of conquest that permanently subjugated the losers, with military use of organized force thus adapted to peacetime. This latter form of conflict theory found little support in anthropology.

Nowhere, in fact, do our data lend support for any of these specific theories. The most plausible, at least in part, is the Bagehot-Spencer argument that the well-governed societies will survive the competition of war better than others (in Bagehot's happy phrasing: "The tamest are the strongest"). But this gives priority to good government as causing superior war-making, rather than war as a cause of superior government, and we should reconsider the point positively in the next chapter. As for the theories of conquest, the only instances we find of permanent subordination from war are when the government already exists. The best examples, Ankole, Zulu, and Nupe, were superordinate over others by conquest, but in a historical continuum of long-standing military states and empires, and as we have seen, a complex of other factors had to be present before even such a fully conquering power as the Zulu was consolidated. We must agree with Fried (1967, p. 216) that "rather than war and military roles being the source of stratification, it seems that stratification is a provoker of war, and an enhancer of military status." (His use of "stratification" here is synonymous with "state.")

A chiefdom, because of its centralized authority, can obviously be a more effective war-maker than the more or less voluntary bands of hit-and-run raiders of egalitarian society. At the same time we must realize that chiefdoms have greater potential for making peace, as well. Segmental societies have existed in Hobbesian circumstances (notably in New Guinea, the Amazon Basin, and the North American Plains), permanently threatened with intertribal or intervillage violence. Threats, raids, counter-threats, and counter-raids—no matter how deadly—seem more frequently to result in an equilibrium of violence rather than a "just peace." Bohannan (1963, p. 305) appropriately contrasts this with true warfare: "War is, on the other hand, a contest having as its aim a peace in which the balance of power is shifted."

But the question remains as to the direct effect that warfare or military organization has on the development of a state apparatus. It is evident, certainly, that an increase in warfare usually accompanied the later stages of development of the historically known primitive states as well as the archaic civilizations, with the exceptions of the Egyptian and the Indus River Valley civilizations. We must remember that there are at least three distinctly different kinds of wars, with probably very different political consequences: "civil" wars, most usually over dynastic succession or distribution of power; wars among roughly equivalent societies that are competitors in a region; and the wars between settled agriculturalists and nomadic raiders. (Nowhere among the archaic civilizations or our sample of primitive states is there any evidence for "uprisings" of workers or peasants or of the poor and oppressed.)

But our conception of law and government should not simply be defined by the use of force, since conflict and warfare exist at all levels of society: Whenever authority and custom fail, in any kind of society, force may be attempted in order to compel obedience.[1] Even the most Marxian concept of the repressive *state* understands it as legitimized and legalized by authority. For example, Shaka Zulu, a successful warrior, could not hold his society together by force; it was not until King Mpande's time that the Zulu could be reasonably said to be governed. A nearly continuous condition of terror, anarchy, and civil war, however, did not *cause* the Zulu state. External conditions had changed, and the positive effects of these will be discussed in the next chapter.

The Zulu case is also instructive in the instance of the second kind of warfare. The Zulu fought their rather similar neighbors and conquered them in "total war." Then Shaka attempted to rule them by benefits, as allies, as well as by terror. But, again, this was not yet a successful state, for the apparatus of ruling was only personal whim, not law. The only instances that might have been successful conquest states created from prestate elements are those of herding-agriculturalist symbioses, like Ankole, and the slave-trading West African states like Kongo, Ashanti, Dahomey, and others. However, all of these were created in such unusual historical circumstances of European penetration that it is hard to know what to make of them. But at any rate, it is not simply the use of military force and the fact of conquest that created states in these cases. The critical causes of the origin and persistence of civilizations in particular are beyond the simple military expedients of conquest, although a case can be made for the significance of warlike competition as an important environmental factor in some cases.

A similar problem exists with respect to the relations of raiding nomads and settled agriculturalists. It is evident that these relationships were very important in the rise of civilization in Mesopotamia and northwest China. But this is not yet a simple

1. Even, as we well know, in the domestic family. The relations of parents to children must be—at some stages—the most purely authoritarian human institution, simultaneously the most repressive and the most altruistic. But certainly the use of parental corporal punishment not only does not define it; it denotes a failure of its basic principle, authority.

causal relationship. It may help to account for some of the "urban" characteristics (e.g., the walled cities) and the increased intensification of agriculture in these societies, and must be considered as a special factor in the environment, but always along with several other aspects of adaptation.

Irrigation and Intensification

As we have seen, all of the archaic civilizations had some kind of water control system, with the one exception of the lowland, swidden horticulturalists of Mesoamerica. We have reviewed Karl Wittfogel's beguilingly simple argument (in *Oriental Despotism,* 1957) that social systems, and despotic control over those systems, could only have come about through the development of bureaucratic power over the hydraulic (water-control) system. That bureaucracy, in planning the uses of the hydraulic system and employing manpower in its maintenance, had great control over the means of subsistence of the society, thus discouraging any rebellion, or even minor disobedience, of the subjects. The power center could by this means control a very large mass of people, and more thoroughly than any other political-economic system. (Wittfogel obviously presents his thesis in the larger context of Marxian class conflict.)

Woodbury (1961) has presented us with a negative case. The extensive Hohokam irrigation system of the Salt-Gila river valleys in Arizona seemed clearly to have been built by accretion, on the initiative of individuals, and extended by cooperation. The remains of the villages there show no good evidence that the society was particularly stratified, much less governed by any Oriental-style despotism.

Our very first archaeological case, Mesoamerica, has provided some interesting data on this point. The densely populated Oaxaca Valley was also an example of an irrigation civilization, but only in a qualified sense. Because of the height of the water table, shallow wells sufficed, and the crops were hand-watered as a form of "pot irrigation."

The North Coast of Peru is also an interesting case. This area is a true desert, almost totally arid, and hence there was no way to grow any crops except by irrigation. The irrigation canals in the Peruvian valleys formed a true system. But these systems began at least as early as 1400 B.C. and were used by both segmental societies and chiefdoms. Thus the intensification of agriculture and the canal system had reached its zenith long before the Classic period arose in B.C./A.D. And it was fully 1,500 years before the formation of the first fully urbanized empire of Tiahuanaco, which itself may be seen as dependent mostly on its exchange and redistributional systems and strategic location rather than an irrigation system. Clearly, Wittfogel's idea that political power was closely associated with water control is again at variance with the data.

The lower Mesopotamian floodplain is similar to Egypt's in that annual flooding made the area productive and also suggested obvious recourse to canalization for greater control and extension. Once centralized government came into existence, it could obviously plan canals and connect them over a wide area. But in such a case, it is the political system that created the system of canals, rather than vice versa. But the control of canals could, of course, have played a role in the bureaucracy's acquisition of power.

Lattimore has adduced the priority of family and neighborhood control of canals over bureaucratic control in the Yellow River Valley in China. A political system can tie them together, but here again it was a case of the creative effect of government, not of irrigation. Malik (1968, pp. 97–98) has argued similarly for the Indus Valley civilization, pointing out that small-scale local systems are the mode in the region today, so why suppose—without evidence—that there was a greater system during earlier and simpler times?

In short, nowhere do we find good evidence for a coincidence between large-scale hydraulic systems and large-scale "despotic" political systems. In Peru, large-scale irrigation systems long antedated the urbanizing empires, whereas in other cases large-scale systems originated after the political developments.[2] In other words, where there was any connection between the two large systems it was the political system that was the creative agent.

2. See Adams (1960) for a discussion of Mesopotamia, Egypt, Mesoamerica, and Peru, in a rebuttal of Wittfogel.

And again, as Adams (1960) has written, it is the *intensification of production* (and labor) that is the significance of irrigation. But this intensification can occur with small-scale systems as well as large, as in today's Indus River region, the Mexican *chinampas,* Oaxaca pot irrigation, and the predynastic Nile River Valley. The intensification of production, by small- or large-scale means, does not signify any direct political effects. Rather, the more direct effects are on regional demography, urbanization, craft specialization, and so on—and these effects merely *enable* change in these aspects; they do not cause change.

Growth and Development

In Herbert Spencer's view, it is a universal aspect of the evolutionary process that growth in societies is accompanied by "development," a differentiation of parts in the structure. But the system that regulates the structure is created predominately by warfare (1967, p. 215): "In primitive headless groups temporary chieftainship results from temporary war; chronic hostilities generate permanent chieftainship; and gradually from the military control results the civil control."

It goes without saying that all the various conflict and conquest theories cite the performance of the military aspect of transitional societies in bringing about the state structure. Some would phrase the transition from chiefdom (or theocracy) to state (or secular rule) as the consequence of a struggle between the two power centers, such as a warriors vs. priests rivalry, as in Gearing's account of the Cherokee (chapter 8) and in Adams's discussion of the Mesopotamian "career to statehood" (chapter 12). This theory has considerable plausibility. One trend we have indeed noted in the historical transitions to statehood is a sort of Spencerian specialization and separation of powers. The priest-king tended toward personal isolation and specialization in high-priestly activities, delegating stewardship over military, economic, and legal matters to others (or perhaps sometimes accepting their claims to certain realms of authority).

But there is another way to look at this phenomenon. It may well be that conflict between the military or secular organization and the priestly hierarchy is not the cause of the change from chiefdom to state, but only an aspect of the breakdown of the theocracy in one particular context—foreign affairs. A developing bureaucracy does tend to subdivide and specialize in its administrative functions, of course, as Spencer and Weber have elaborated. When warfare becomes prevalent (as we saw particularly in the Cyclical Conquest or Imperial eras), the successful military or secular arm may appear to have gained power at the expense of the priesthood. But it may be more accurate and useful to regard the theocratic rule based on the power of authority alone as having become ineffective in foreign affairs, which had become so persistently competitive and warlike. But this need not necessarily characterize the form of the government in its keeping of internal order.

In the writings of some evolutionists the problem of the relation of population growth to social complexity is reminiscent of the emphasis on economic surplus. Sometimes the confusion is of the same order; that the enablers, like sufficient amounts of food and certain population size, are mistaken for agents of causal priority. The reader may recall at this point Steward and Faron's discussion of Peruvian developments (see chapter 11): Technological improvement in relation to a particular environment may bring about a surplus of food; the surplus enables military, religious, and political specialists to appear, forming an upper, ruling class; as population increases in the nonproducing class the state gets more exploitative, even to the point of conquering neighbors for economic reasons. There seems to be no further explanation for the origin of complexity, or the state in particular, other than as an apparently "normal" functional accompaniment of an increase of food and the resulting population increase. As argued in chapter 11 (and see also chapter 2, in the discussion of Childe): An enabler is not a cause, for if states were actually brought about by a surplus of food, there would be many, many more states.

A few more sophisticated discussions of growth and complexity have appeared in the recent anthropological literature. D. E. Dumond (1965, p. 320) cautiously points out that "population growth appears favorable toward—although not sufficient cause for—a degree of social centralization sufficient to serve as a stimulus to further population growth through increased stability and the maintenance of internal peace." The relation is thus reciprocal rather than one-way.[3] Robert Carniero (1967) and Michael Harner (1970) have presented rather more specific and more complicated discussions of the correlation between growth and complexity. Let us consider them briefly in turn.

After clearly demonstrating (by scale analysis) the correlation of population size with social complexity, Carneiro states (1967, pp. 240–41) that ". . . the elaboration of social structures is the response to the stresses occasioned within it by the multiplication of its units. As human numbers increase, they stretch the capacity of the existing structure to accommodate them, and when this pressure exceeds the 'elastic limits' of the system, it responds by giving rise to new practices and institutions; in a word, by developing." He exemplifies this point by showing that the large aggregations of Plains Indians that formed during the summer buffalo hunt instituted councils and paramount chiefs and police societies, all of which were designed to solve organizational problems and were discontinued when the tribes broke up into their smaller constituencies for the rest of the year.

There can be no question that any society, but particularly one that has chiefs, councils, or some other form of centralization, can institute solutions to organizational problems, and that new organizational problems arise with increases in population. The only objection to Carneiro's thesis is that the other side of the coin needs special emphasis: that political institutions which come about to serve a perceived purpose (like the Plains police societies) later come to serve much more important integrative functions —functions that were never contemplated at first. Because our data indicate so thoroughly that this is so, particularly in regard to the origin and development of the later manifold functions of the original redistributional bureaucracies, we must modify

3. Dumond has recently modified this point further. In comparing the Valley of Mexico and Susa (Mesopotamia), he concluded that the archaeological data "accord poorly with theories of state formation that seek causes directly in simple population growth and processes that are taken to be automatically attendant upon resulting struggle for resources (as, especially, Carneiro 1970; also Sanders and Price 1968; cf. Dumond 1965, 1972). For the unmistakable conclusion is that nucleation did not result from simple competition for resources, either at Teotihuacán or at Susa."

Carneiro's causal chain to include the very important possibility that organizations related to such matters can take up others, such as extending the irrigation system, or increasing economic specialization. Thus a bureaucracy can literally create "surplus" and increased population, rather than merely responding to such things. But this argument must be made at length and we will develop it further in the next chapter.

Michael Harner (1970) has proposed that increases in population lead to the relative scarcity of subsistence resources, which intensifies competition. Competition for control of resources leads to unequal successes. With further competition, inequality increases, leading to "hereditary class stratification" and "centralized military-political organization" (p. 69). This argument has the virtue of using a more precise term, "population pressure," rather than the simple "increase." But the basic assumption is simply the usual unexamined given: "that the ownership or control of means of production is closely related to the power structure and stratification of a society" (p. 70). This is again a derivative of Marxism. Suffice it at this point to repeat that the redistributive bureaucracy *is* the power center and the upper stratum, so that Harner's statement does not really tell us anything about that bureaucracy's origins. Those origins are certainly not accounted for by "ownership of the means of production," for which there is no evidence whatsoever in any of our data. "Control," of course, is control of the whole society, including the means of production —and the problem of *its* origin is the question being asked.

It may be agreed that Harner's concept of population pressure leading to resource scarcity and conflict seems much more plausible and realistic than the various naive surplus theories. But does increasing pressure on resources necessarily lead to competition, conflict, or class struggle? It seems as likely, judging from well-known characteristics of primitive life, that scarcity could increase the amount of sharing and cooperation, and eventually to redistributive planning, intensification, and specialization.[4]

A redistributive bureaucracy is a powerful economic body

4. Boserup (1965) has cogently argued that population pressure has indeed been an important factor in creating increased technological innovation and intensification in agriculture (but, for the record, I would suggest some qualifications [see above]). Geertz (1963) has usefully discussed the same phenomenon as "agricultural involution."

that also can be powerful in other forms of leadership, including theology. As it does what it does, is it "exploiting" and "competing," or is it making possible specialization—a form of "cooperation"? Perhaps arguing this way—competition versus cooperation—is to oversimplify as well as to mislead. A redistributive system is what it is. In some unusual cases, as in the intergroup reciprocities of the Northwest Pacific Coast potlatch, would-be chiefs did compete (with one another)—but they were competing with their powers of inducing *cooperation* among their constituencies for the sake of subsequent redistributions of goods. Presumably, the people in the upper stratum of any chiefdom or primitive state enjoy their high status and might compete to raise it, but it seems evident that the lower subjects must regard their successful chiefdom as beneficial to themselves, and worth their own cooperation.

But the explanation should not focus on attitudes, or consciousness, especially on base motives of an "exploitative" upper class, when we do not really know what they were. We do know how a redistributive *system* works. As Isaac (unpublished ms.) says:

> We may need to recast the whole problem, taking it out of the framework of "cooperation and competition" and putting it squarely in the more general framework of "adaptation." Perhaps cultural anthropology is presently at the same stage that biology was at during the last century, when nature was red in tooth and claw. Perhaps we, like the biologists, will come to speak more and more in adaptational terms, rather than in such shopworn and loaded terms as conflict and competition. It has been pointed out that an emphasis on cooperative models of social evolution "sounds good and also appeals nicely to our American prejudice toward cooperation and constitutionalism" (Webb 1967:6). Perhaps we have an equally strong tendency in the opposite direction, one that appeals to another Anglo-American prejudice—competition.

It seems impossible to make any case for demographic pressure as leading to the sort of conflict that could cause a repressive state. The given in that case is the assumption that government has its origin in conflict, an unwarranted assumption to say the least, and the further assumption that population pressure causes the conflict, also unwarranted. Conflict is a relative term, but it seems evident that it has existed throughout the evolution of culture, taking various forms and intensities and being resolved in various ways—all depending on adaptive circumstances and the stage of political evolution. Population "pressure" is also relative, just like "scarcity" and "surplus." It can as well be argued (though no more easily proved) that population increases were one of the *results,* both direct and indirect, of the ability of political institutions to keep and extend the peace and thus to enlarge their jurisdictions.

At this point we may quote with approval the summation Robert Stevenson gives in his exploration of the relationship between population density and state formation in Africa (1968, p. 232). After stating that increased population density typically does accompany increased political complexity (countering the argument of Fortes and Evans-Pritchard [1940]) but that it is not directly causative, he concludes: "Rather, in far the majority of cases the process involved at least a threeway nexus between developing trade and trade routes, developing political and economic organization, and higher population densities, all reciprocally interacting and feeding back upon each other."

Population increase sometimes takes the form of very dense "urban" agglomerations. These cities are treated differently from overall densities in most evolutionary schemes, and hence we will treat them separately now.

Urbanism

To briefly repeat what was discussed at some length in chapter 2, it was V. Gordon Childe who modified the Morgan-Marx-Engels class-conflict theory into a more sophisticated anthropological theory. This view was expressed in a definition of civilization, involving several criteria that seemed to occur together visibly in the archaeological record. "Urbanism" was the basic trait Childe used to epitomize civilization. But since he also called the movement from Neolithic villages to civilization "the urban revolution," many accepted the implication that urbanism was not only an important indicator of civilization, but somehow causal as well. It is not fair to Childe to treat urbanism in his theory in this way. For example, in the article that many consider his most definitive statement on urbanism (1950) he says that "the aim of the present essay is to present the city historically—or rather prehistorically—as the *resultant* and *symbol* of a 'revolution' that initiated a new *economic stage* in the evolution of society [italics added]." This populational change, according to Childe, was the culmination of a progressive change in the "economic structure and social organization" of communities. Nevertheless, "urbanism" is equated with "state" and "stratification" by so many people that, whether or not a causal priority is always actually posited, the association still needs to be discussed.[5]

First of all, we have seen in previous chapters that there are several likely determinants of nucleation, and that they do not always go together—that is, there is no single generic kind of urban population. A very common form is the smallish ceremonial center, with the basic supporting population sometimes scattered thinly at considerable distances, coming to the center only on special occasions. Sometimes these centers have a larger live-in population. Wheatley (1971, ch. 3) argues cogently that all of the classic archaic urban developments were originally ceremonial centers, though obviously such centers frequently lent themselves to other uses. They could serve as convenient storage and redistributional centers ("central place exchange"); as gathering places where people made direct exchanges of the petty products of household production (the "penny capitalism" marketplace); and as residing places for craftsmen as well as officials.

And sometimes, very importantly, the city was fortified, perhaps by a redoubt. If food production were intensified because of the need for defense against raiders, the city could become very large. Such a defensive city, needing to accommodate all the people

5. Frequently it is thought that because a certain population density *requires* certain integrative devices if the society is to hold together, that it will somehow call them into being, as implied in Spencer's concept of "development." Sanders and Price for example say that of a "critical mass" of about 10,000 persons, "other means [of integration besides kinship] must be developed, and the result is the social-economic-political hierarchy characteristic of civilization" (1960, p. 229). At this point, let us say that this sounds plausible, but that our data suggest that the causal chain should be reversed: that the political hierarchy actually created this "mass."

at certain times, would have to provide all of the other functions as well—a further impetus to growth. Teotihuacán, Chan Chan, and the Chinese and lower Mesopotamian cities apparently were of this combined sort.

But certainly some archaic cities remained ceremonial only, having relatively dispersed populations—like most of the Mayan, Olmec and Chavín centers. Some others were ceremonial centers with separate, independent villages of craftsmen, as in Egypt. Still others combined a ceremonial and administrative center with markets, storage, and so on, achieving an imposing size, without any very evident defensive measures, as in the case of the Indus River Valley cities.

The tremendous variations in both size and type of population nucleation in the archaic civilizations certainly demonstrates that "urbanism" is not causal, nor even a good indicator or "symbol" of civilization. It is a resultant of many kinds of factors in complex interplay, one of which is of course the ability of the government itself to create for its own use a complex ceremonial, administrative, economic, and defensive center (Trigger 1972). Furthermore, the layouts of many of the large cities that combined all of these functions were clearly planned, which means of course that in these instances at least it was the prior development of the political system that made the city possible, not vice versa.

Robert McC. Adams has said (1972, p. 73) that "truly urban agglomerations depend upon the institution of the state as a political form, and the emergence of the latter is but an aspect in turn of the formation of stratified class societies." This statement sums up a view that we may take as a good counterbalance to the notion of urbanism as causal. But it also returns us to a purer version of Childe's modification of the Marxist class-conflict theory of the repressive state.

Class Stratification and Repression

The Morgan-Marx-Engels theory of the origin of the state was derived from what they believed to be the basic function of the state, which is to preserve the exploitative dominance of the ruling property-owning class over the rest of the society. As such, it is a variant of the general category of conflict theories, but it is so distinctive and has dominated the discourse of social science for so long that it should be given special treatment.

To review the theory briefly: The Marxists believed that the inequality in society that culminated in the class system and the state was the result of a system of production-for exchange, which superseded the earlier production-for-use economy. The unearned increment of the merchants (the "middlemen"), the varying efficiency of producers, luck, and other such factors resulted in wealth differences, which in turn begat still greater differences because of the advantages and power that accrue to the possessors of greater wealth. Eventually the rich became owners of the basic means of production, maintaining workers at a mere subsistence level. The repressive state was created to insure the survival of this economically divided structure.

But there is absolutely no evidence in the early archaic civilizations themselves, nor in archaeologically or historically known chiefdoms and primitive states, of any important private dealings —i.e., evidence of the dominance of capitalism. There are, to be sure, important exchanges of goods, but these are accomplished by primitive reciprocities and complex redistribution, not by entrepreneurs. The bureaucracy itself manages the important production and exchange, and of course uses a proportion of the production to maintain itself and to subsidize its own court-temple economy.

It is rare that anthropological specialists in the archaic civilizations since V. Gordon Childe upheld the private property aspect of the Marxist thesis of class exploitation, so we may drop it without further discussion.[6] But an important residue of the theory remains: that the archaic states, though perhaps not capitalistic, were nonetheless somehow economically *stratified,* suggesting the probability of "class struggle." This thesis still could justify the argument that the state was formed to repress the masses and

6. I can think of only one modern anthropologist who follows Childe in this belief, but only in part, and he is not a specialist in the archaic civilizations. Darcy Ribeiro's *The Civilization Process* (1968, p. 44) divides the urban revolution stage of archaic states into two kinds: the *privatistic,* with the upper stratum composed of the owners of land, cattle, and instruments of labor; and the *collectivist,* based primarily on irrigation agriculture and state ownership of land.

maintain the aristocracy in power. We saw this (see chapters 6 and 7) in one version of the Oberg and Nadel conquest theories. Robert McC. Adams (as discussed above in chapter 12, "Mesopotamia"), who has also frankly given up the entrepreneurial aspect of the Marxist position, also retains the stratification form of the class-struggle argument.[7] Morton Fried has argued this thesis at greater length and in a more general context (see chapter 2).

This conception of stratified societies, however modified, retains one of the essential ingredients described by the Marxist view of capitalism; that an upper class somehow in control of the society's subsistence exploits the labor of the working class. Fried's formal definition reads (1967, p. 186): "A stratified society is one in which members of the same sex and equivalent age status do not have equal access to the basic resources that sustain life." Those families that have direct or superior access to basic resources are enabled to require payment for access by the others in such terms as personal services, military assistance, or drudge labor.

"Variable access" to basic resources must involve some kind of proprietary rights—though not necessarily ownership in our modern sense, which connotes rights of disposal or entrepreneurial exchange. What are the conditions that bring about these differing rights? Fried (ibid., p. 196) lists the following: population pressure, shifts in postmarital residence patterns, the contraction or sharp natural alteration of basic resources, shifts in subsistence patterns arising from technological changes, and "development of managerial roles as an aspect of maturation of a social and ceremonial system."

A growth in population and increasing nucleation and complexity of society, without any doubt, accompanied the general evolution of culture. We cannot fault Fried for his emphasis on these factors. But note that he is talking about population *pressure* —as, for example, when a group that at first occupies only the fertile bottomlands finally has daughter villages, or perhaps when

7. In a recent personal communication (1974), Adams has indicated a further modification: ". . . My present tendency would be to place greater stress on non-'systemic,' consciously goal motivated patterns of cognition, action and conscious aspiration."

newcomers occupy much more marginal sites—so that eventually there are independent villages and somewhat dependent villages. It is possible, as indicated in chapter 4, that such varying ecological adaptation could indeed lead to a sociopolitical development, the institutionalization of inequality. But I do not agree with the notion that these inequalities were a naked exploitation of the disadvantaged by the advantaged, with institutions based on physical violence arising to protect this stratification. Indeed, chiefdoms lacked such repressive forces. However, the immense benefits of fitting such different niches and skills into a centralized redistributional system are evident in any and all accounts of functioning chiefdoms, and *social* (or political) inequalities did probably result.

"Shifts in postmarital residence patterns," "alteration of basic resources," "shifts in subsistence," all may have effects similar to those of population pressure: They may cause some people to be advantaged over others with respect to access to some basic resources. But Fried can only exemplify these in the ethnographic record (a record, incidentally, of enormous dislocations and adjustments in the primitive world caused by European economic and political expansion) in the terms stated: varying states of advantage and disadvantage. None are good examples of society-wide stratification, only "incipient" stratification; but only incipient if you truly believe that these differences are the *causes* of stratification—i.e., that stratification is bound to result from the advantages. The argument is unconvincing and so are the data.

A final, brief, but telling point: In all of the archaic civilizations and historically known chiefdoms and primitive states, the creation and extension of the authority bureaucracy was also the creation of the ruling class, or aristocracy. The "stratification" was thus mainly of two classes, the governors and the governed—political strata, not strata of ownership groups. And nowhere in the cases discussed do we find the power of force used in the maintenance of the position of the governing strata over the ordinary masses. At least this is not recorded in the historical cases, nor is it visible in the archaeological record. In other words, there apparently was no class conflict resulting in forceful repression.

In the historical cases reviewed early in this book, the violence that attended what has been called the "origin of the state" seems to have been simply the sudden blow-up of an unprecedentedly "total" warfare, of conflicts much exaggerated by the disorders created by the influence of Western civilization's new weapons, slave trade, population displacement, and so on. But these were violent episodes having to do with attempted *inter*-societal conquests, not conflicts of class against class. Even the few cases of "civil war" were wars over succession to power of rival claimants among the aristocracy, "wars of princes," not of classes (Walter 1969, ch. 14). We know less about the archaic civilizations, but when they did evidence periods of violence, it was external warfare. Even those with the best claims to repressive statehood, like Teotihuacán, the Western Chou, and Tiahuanaco, were actually would-be empires: That is, the violence and repression was military and directed at neighboring ruling-class rivals, not at a class or segment of their own original population.

A still more potent rebuttal to the stratification/conflict theory exists, however. A counter-argument about the rise of classes, it has to do with the origin and evolution of bureaucracy. We will summarize this argument in the next chapter.

Radicals and Conservatives

The mere mention of "the evolution of bureaucracy" in the context of "class struggle" immediately causes a social scientist to think of Max Weber's long-lasting opposition to Marxism, a theory he considered simple-minded, unscientific, and nothing more than the product of a particular political milieu.[8] And this thought in turn may remind us of the warning given in chapter 2 against the assumption that knowledge about the *origin* of civilization, or the state, or society—or our present civilization—somehow reveals that entity's *true nature.* This kind of assumption means that a modern political dogma or a possibly ethnocentric conclusion can become an *a posteriori* distortion of history.

For of course the rewriting of history (and of ruling-class genealogies) has forever been stimulated by revolutionary as well as conservative governments, and by *arrivistes* as well as old aristocratic families; it seems almost natural the politically moti-

8. See the discussion of Marxism in terms of the "sociology of knowledge" by Karl Mannheim (1936).

vated people find some "uses of the past" in justifying themselves. Even Polybius, the first of Western civilization's historians to be consciously a methodologist, frankly wrote his massive attempt at universal history in order to make a political argument (defending the Scipios' rule of Rome). Even the great classical thinkers, Plato and Aristotle, the Stoics and Epicureans, and the Renaissance and Enlightenment philosophers, all had political messages to tell in the guise of scientific theories of the origin of the state or civilization. The modern social-scientific version of this tendency still exists in the writings of the highly successful Marxists and their latter-day epigoni, and certainly among anti-Marxists as well. We are all today somehow, and in some measure, legatees of the Marx-Weber dichotomy.

This is not to say that these are always conscious biases, and we cannot certify that any particular individual truly holds them, unless he says so (as did Marx and Engels, and frank anti-Marxists like Weber on anti-Morganists like Robert Lowie). But the point is that there exists such a tendency because of the very politically significant nature of the questions about the origin of the state. It may be well to explore the subject of political bias briefly, not to point the finger at someone else but rather to inspect our own political thoughts, perhaps better to clear our own heads.

Politics, defined in terms of the distribution of power, wealth, and privilege (or "who gets what, when, and how") is a characteristic preoccupation of a burgeoning capitalistic-industrial society that changes so fast that most of its citizens do not know their hereditary places, a society wherein changes of social place and political power depend so largely on variations in the control of wealth. Many scholars in the social sciences tend to polarize into advocates and condemners of our "system" and its inequalities of wealth and (money-based) power.

Gerhard Lenski's *Power and Privilege* (1966, pp. 14–23) spells out the several ways in which "radical" social scientists differ from "conservatives," especially when dealing with theories of social inequality. Essentially, the difference between the two is whether one thinks that such inequality arises out of the selfish aggrandizing, anti-social desires of individuals, or out of the functional needs of society. They are conventionally labeled radical and conservative, probably because the radical view is normative, somehow *against* such elites, while the conservative view is concerned with how the classes function in the social system rather than in the mean calculations of bad men. Kingsley Davis summarizes the functionalist ("conservative") view succinctly (1949, p. 367): "Social inequality is thus an unconsciously evolved device by which societies insure that the most important positions are conscientiously filled by the most qualified persons." Within sociology, C. Wright Mills was the best-known proponent of the radical position. His book *The Power Elite* (1956) is simply Marxist conflict theory modified to include a more sophisticated analysis of the complexities of a "ruling class" that now includes members of certain powerful bureaucracies (military, governmental, and industrial) as well as the rich stockholders and owners who were the former villains.

But to Mills the power of that class is not just a function of society as such, but a means of holding onto, by a sort of closed conspiracy, what the "in" group wants at the expense of others (indeed, at the expense of the society itself). A surging indignation pervades the book, so it sounds more like a rousing populist tract than a sociological analysis.[9]

But the point at issue here should not be whether the radical or conservative position is morally right or not, but whether scientific comprehension is fostered. Both radicals and conservatives deal with aspects of reality: Human beings do have varying abilities directed and powered by different motives and values (ideally they would be self-serving at the same time that they are socially useful); but the high offices and positions of power, wealth, and authority as institutional *structures* are real, too, and we need analysis of their evolution and functional connections and purposes. Both radical and conservative positions are important and interesting and in our case it would be nice to know the rulers' ego-structures as well as the social structure. The trouble is, we can only infer personal motives and abilities from what happened in the institutional context.

Here we may be reminded again of the abrupt Hawaiian "cultural revolution," and also of Shaka Zulu's remarkable exploits in Africa. King Liholiho and Shaka were certainly power-hungry,

9. For a bitter analysis of the conservative-functionalist political attitudes shaping social science, see Andreski (1972).

and they intelligently and ruthlessly went about altering their political systems. But as we analyzed the evolution of the two states, we found that understanding was not furthered greatly by concern over Liholiho's or Shaka's great abilities or their egotistical, selfish motives. The changes in the sociopolitical structure can best be analyzed in their own terms, if explanation is to be the aim. To guess at the underlying motives and personality of leaders, and then offer the guess as an explanation, is to be reductionistic. Such an explanation is also tautological in the sense that the rise of all social statuses and offices may be presumed to have a subjective aspect; that is, they rise together, the objective and the subjective, but it is the objective and the environmental that are the variables in cultural evolution, whereas the subjective is "subject." Since the subjective changes are only inferred from, or implied by, the objective, they cannot explain the objective. Let us then, at this point, desist from Hobbesian or Rousseauian guesswork about the bad and good in human motives, to reconsider the origins and development of the governing institutions themselves. Above all, let us set aside as irrelevant our political feelings about our present state.

17

Conclusions II (Positive)

Our positive conclusions basically have to do with the relation of distributive systems to political institutions. We have long been accustomed to a society that distributes wealth unequally, with the consequence that, ultimately directly and indirectly, power and privilege are also conferred unequally. When this does not fit the case of particular individuals, it does seem applicable to classes, or at least categories, of elites. Thus a certain form of economic inequality seemed basic to the development of varieties of political power structures. Our findings now contradict this opinion, and in fact, reverse the order of precedence with respect to the origins of civilization.

A closely related problem is that of the causal assumptions in theories of the origin of civilization. The phrase "forms of economic distribution" connotes some dynamism, or some potentiality for change; but "political power structure," like "state apparatus," sounds like a resultant, or consequence, of something outside itself, of some external cause. Perhaps partly for this reason we have not sufficiently understood that the hierarchical apparatus of political power had itself undergone an origin and an evolutionary development along a causal trajectory that now seems to have had its own built-in gyroscope.

The Origins of Inequality

There is an important sense in which it can be said that in all societies there inevitably are personal inequalities in status caused by differences in individual skill, intelligence, energy, beauty, strength, luck, and so on. And it seems quite normal to human society, and especially notable in very primitive societies, for the ordinary people to confer statuses on superior persons that would even seem to exaggerate their superiority (although, in the view of egalitarian societies, the superior ought to be self-effacing in demeanor). But these are individual inequalities. In small primitive societies such high statuses do not confer greater privilege or wealth, and such power that the superior person possesses is a highly personal kind of influence, wielded in a certain few contexts only. Thus in the absence of permanent classes or hierarchies of family power, we have called such primitive societies *egalitarian* and *segmental* (this latter in the Durkheimian sense that the basic parts of the society, like lineages or clans, are similar to each other and capable of independent existence).

But it is a fact that segmental societies, however equal their parts, do exalt individuals. They follow war chiefs, accept advice from wise men, and believe in the unequal access of persons to supernatural power. And this proclivity sets the stage for more permanent hierarchies of differential power. There are political "jobs" to be done in any society, however small and segmental it may be, for there are always problems and fears of great magnitude. A leader may therefore arise, with ability and luck, to take charge and save the society from what are thought to be dire consequences. He even may combine war leadership with general wisdom to achieve such overall eminence that he becomes a mediating and administrative leader in peacetime. His successes could therefore result in considerable exaltation of his status in the minds of his followers.

The foregoing is not mere speculation, for as we have seen there are many examples of such situations in the ethnographic literature. Of particular interest are the accounts of the so-called "big-man systems" (see chapter 4), which call attention to the power struggles among would-be leaders, and to their means of acquiring and validating status by means of redistributive feasts.

The amount of redistributional exchanges mediated by a central agency, is, like the amount of reciprocal exchanges, and like trade itself, extremely varied and sporadic in the primitive world, depending on adaptive circumstances. But probably all societies have supplemented reciprocal gift-giving with redistributional exchanges at some time, and some societies do so frequently. The circumstances favoring redistribution are those that create a number of specializations, either with respect to a variety of local ecological niches, or because of a division of labor involving a collaborative effort (as in a game drive, or in the varying special activities during a harvest of spawning salmon, or some other all-hands activity). To exploit fully the potentialities that inhere in increasing specialization, either of differing localities or of skills, a society must have confidence in the fairness and judgment, in the administrative skills, of the redistributor—who is normally therefore the leader of greatest influence in other respects. Successes in the redistributive process are tremendously supportive of the bureaucracy and lead to further development of specialization —a snowballing effect—inasmuch as the effectiveness of the system is increasingly obvious.

It has been noted that some of the most highly integrated redistributional systems have begun in areas of diversity in natural products, like the varying ecological niches of central Mexico, a situation which tends to produce regional symbiosis. But it is apparent that once such systems are in operation, sustaining and increasing a redistributor's leadership, a further specialization of skilled occupations can be created—even in new habitats of relatively homogeneous resources like lower Mesopotamia.

Long-distance exchanges of useful goods or raw materials also are more likely to occur successfully when they can be arranged and administered by a leader. As we have seen in numerous cases, this kind of exchange, normally directly reciprocal between leaders of the exchanging societies, becomes redistributional finally in the fullest sense: The leader acquires from his people the goods to be exchanged, and later allocates to them the goods he received in his exchange with the outside society. It could well be, also, that a redistributing leader acquires some power to reward or punish individuals because he can give out or withhold varying amounts of the goods. Much more evident is the obverse factor, that the leader's position is strengthened by his doing the job well and fairly. In such early stages in the creation of a redistributional structure, the leader is very "accountable" to his followers (that is, to the leaders of subsidiary groups), and the benefits that accrue to them, if he is a good leader, are highly visible and easily comprehended.

So far we are discussing a situation wherein a would-be leader can enhance his political position because of an economic circumstance. But note that this is not economic power that results from ownership, or even close control, of wealth: It is, rather, the result of a form of dependence that in primitive society results from generosity, from favors given. That is to say, in important senses, that a leader is created by his followers, not by their fear of him but by their appreciation of his exemplary qualities.

As Malinowski put it, the above activities of the big-man are the amassing of a "fund of power." And with this personal influence he can direct political, ceremonial, and military matters—promoting his society's interests and widening its organization beyond the local, segmented, kin groups.

But even when the leader is a very good one with a pleased constituency of loyal followers, the system is inherently unstable. His successes may cease; he may become ill, or die. Basically, the problem is the bureaucratic one of how to transform charismatic hierarchies of leadership into institutionalized, permanent positions—*offices*. The most important circumstance obviously involves the transfer of the personal power from the holder to his successor. Unless this is done successfully, anarchy results. But also it is the case that the power *is* sometimes successfully transferred, probably much to everyone's relief if the leader was a successful one; and most usually, because it is the most natural in patrilineal societies, the transfer is from father to eldest son (or to sister's eldest son in the rare matrilineal chiefdom).

Such transfers of power became characteristic of true chiefdoms once they were accomplished successfully, and successively, over enough generations for primogeniture to become a binding custom (or perhaps more properly we might call it a *law*?). At any rate, big-man systems did in fact sometimes turn into hereditary chiefdoms, and undoubtedly those that were so successful because of centralized permanent leadership were widely emulated, or they transformed others by dominance or absorption.

We must also agree with Bagehot's insistence on the military significance of successful peaceful hereditary succession to office, that truly "the tamest are the strongest." The equally important obverse is, of course, that societies rent by civil strife or disobedient factions are the weakest.

The institutionalization of power became, therefore, a form of hereditary authority, and it also became an institutionalized form of *inequality*. As such a society grows, so does the chief's family and its bureaucratic offices and functions, until through advantageous marriages and internal growth the whole governing group becomes an aristocracy of hierarchically ordered ranks and privileges, standing over and above the ordinary people. In this process the redistributional system acquires new functions: It plans for such adventures as foreign war and trade, and engineers the consent of the governed by the adroit use of supernatural powers. Some of these are perfectly obvious to the mass of the people, others are positive sanctions or rewards that may not be direct or consciously noted. These latter are likely to be mostly in the realm of the supernatural and ceremonial, but these "blessings" may nevertheless be very supportive of the society and its governing regime.

We have usually identified chiefdoms and distinguished them from states by their relatively peaceful theocratic mode of rule; states, on the contrary, we have thought of as having more prominent secular sanctions backed by force or the threat of it. If, as stated above, chiefdoms seem relatively uncoercive because the society is well integrated by the successful prosecution by the bureaucracy of its various duties—by its benefits—then it could be guessed that the addition of the use of coercive force might be a sign of the weakness, or failure at some point, of the chiefdom's apparatus. This point will be reviewed in later pages.

The chiefdom's structure of centralized authority provides a number of ways it can act to protect itself. The most obvious is the *lèse majesté* type of rule prohibiting actions that threaten the person or the authority of the ruler. In chiefdoms, since the ruler is normally a god or highest priest, the punishment is by threat of supernatural action. Another lies in the efforts of a ruler (or his representative) to prevent feuds by mediating quarrels between kin groups.

The above two kinds of actions are possible beginnings of "law-stuff," or in Pospisil's definition, true law (see our chapter 4). As with so many other characteristics of civilization, we note that law, at least in an incipient or inchoate form, made its appearance at the chiefdom level. This fact is clearly related to the existence of a central authority system: The authority system needs rules of social control to safeguard itself for efficient operation in running the society, and the people themselves need help for solving the most pressing problems of their own social life, the quarrels between the kin-group segments.

It seems very likely that *lèse majesté* public law was the first to be formalized by the central authority with explicit negative sanctions (which were likely to be supernatural rather than secular and physical). There are two reasons for concluding this: ethnographic data and political logic. All of the chiefdoms and primitive states reviewed earlier had at least an inchoate version of laws that protect the persons in authority, or the symbols of the authority (etiquette tabus, the cults of the royal drums and stools, and so forth). In terms of logic, what could be more expected? On the other hand, private law in the ethnography of both chiefdoms and primitive states is usually only of the self-help variety. Even when some kind of mediation is clearly demanded to save the society from feud, the mediator is still often an arbitrating kinsman of the contending parties, so that mediation is of the "domestic" or "familistic" rather than that of a true "law-judge." (That true law is nondomestic is an amendment to Pospisil's criteria of law we proposed in chapter 4). And this is as it should be in terms of political logic. For the central authority to intervene in domestic quarrels and feuds between kinship segments is to court danger to the regime, for one side of the quarrel (if not both) is likely to be offended. This logic is based on the assumption that new or simple governments do not willingly and lightly undertake tasks that risk their power of authority. But more important than this assumption is the ethnographic preponderance of public law-like actions over private law-like mediations by the central authority. (For that matter, it is preferable in any society, probably, that domestic quarrels and feuds be settled out of court.)

But this talk of law, especially of public law, as a means by which a regime protects itself by negative sanctions, may give a misleading notion of the way this power is applied. We have noted frequently that chiefdoms seem relatively peaceful, lacking physical repression. But this should not be taken to mean that there is no coercion whatever. All chiefdoms are theocracies and an important aspect of the bureaucracy is its function as a priesthood. Priests know how to scare people; priests have knowledge of the supernatural and are thought to exert some control over it and therefore to control the fortunes of ordinary people. In most societies there are also witches and sorcerers, and they too may serve the authority structure by threatening supernatural harm to political malefactors.[1] There are positive benign aspects to a priesthood, as well. A priest-chief can be an awesome figure, his own supernatural powers augmented by the powers of his ancestors who are now gods in an hierarchical pantheon—and thus potentially frightening, to be sure. But this makes him formidable also as a power for good. He can bring rain and fertility through ritual, smite enemies with his curse, and govern justly and wisely under divine guidance.

The fact that the supernatural and his closer relation to it permeates all the priest-chief's activities should be emphasized. It is later, in complex civilizations, that we find the beginnings of a differentiation in the bureaucracy between secular and priestly functions. In smaller chiefdoms this seems not to be so, and it may be one of the reasons the governance seems so uncoercive. It may be, as well, that secular construction like the building of irrigation canals, usually thought of as compelled by the coercive power of government, is apparently as willingly undertaken as

1. It may be well to repeat here that this is in line with another amendment made to Pospisil's definition of law. He wants to restrict legal sanctions to a secular context (as usual in modern society), but I strongly feel that the religio-supernatural context must be included. In fact, there is practically no other context for *any* activity of the authority in such societies as the Mayan, Mesopotamian, and Egyptian—and, I would guess, all the other archaic civilizations.

the building of temples and pyramids, since the same theocratic authority hierarchy presides equally over both.[2]

Thus a chiefdom creates a religious overlay above the familistic and local segmental cult levels that is society-wide, encompassing all activities. This religion worships true gods, not just vaguely defined spirits. The public monuments and temples where the ceremonies take place pertain to the society as a whole, and are built by society-wide corvée labor. The bureaucracy in its priestly aspect mediates with these gods. Great joys as well as great fears can be created in a society that is so pervasively religious. In the ethnographies of enduring chiefdoms, the reader realizes that of course the redistributional system must have worked, of course the wars must have been won and the ditches dug—in short, the secular duties of the bureaucracy must have been successfully accomplished; but the strong feeling persists that positive and negative conditioning in the religious context was by far the most direct and pervasive cause of the "consent of the governed." And it could be that our hackneyed phrase is applicable; that it is in this religious context, more than any other, that it was possible for the rulers to plan and scheme—for the consent to be "engineered." How comfortable it must be to know that your own society's gods are the greatest in the universe, and that their representatives on earth are holy, for then you are truly a chosen people. But also, so obvious to a ruling group how convenient such beliefs would be!

Environment and Benefits

Political evolution can be thought of as consisting, in important part, of successfully "waging peace" in ever-wider contexts. The successful wars—or internally, the successfully applied deterrents to feud, revolt, or other disorder—are only sporadic episodes that spotlight the failures of the political system to sufficiently con-

2. A. M. Hocart makes this useful point (1936, p. 217): "It would be an error to put such works [as irrigation canals] in a category by themselves as 'utilitarian' in opposition to 'religious' works such as temples. Temples are just as utilitarian as dams and canals, since they are necessary to prosperity; dams and canals are as ritual as temples, since they are part of the same social system of seeking welfare. If *we* call reservoirs 'utilitarian' it is because we believe in their efficacy; *we* do not call temples so because *we* do not believe in their efficacy for crops."

trol the behavior of its own and other groups. After winning a war, or after the suppression of an internal rival, a maintenance regime must begin to govern, or resume governance. It is plain that this is not easy to do. It is especially difficult to continue in peace time the contrivance that is military rule of the state, for the military state seems to have been born in conflict and disorder out of a failure of governance.

The historical and ethnographical cases of state formation reviewed in earlier chapters were societies terribly disrupted by the conflicts caused by the historical circumstances that were usually connected with the expansion of Western imperialism into their territories, or related factors such as the introduction of guns, slavery, plantation systems, and the like. The archaic civilizations, on the contrary, seem to have expanded and developed rather gradually, at least in their crucial early stages. But they were only rarely to maintain themselves long enough for us to know them well archaeologically. Success was contingent upon the existence of certain environmental features, features that were helpful in the mutual adaptive responses of society, polity, neighbors, and nature.

Some environmental characteristics have the property of strengthening the coherence of a collectivity by making plain to its members the benefits of being part of it, as opposed to the obvious disadvantages of being outside it. There are two main aspects of such threatening environments: geography, and the presence of enemy societies. The first of these has been emphasized by Robert Carneiro in his theory of circumscription (see chapter 2): Dominated or conquered groups cannot easily retreat to another area if the society is bounded by desert or ocean, for example.[3] Such circumscription must have been especially important in the case of Egypt, where the very rich irrigated soil of the Nile Valley was surrounded by much less habitable desert. The Peruvian coastal valleys provided nearly as complete cases of circumscription: Irrigated land was bordered by pure desert, with ocean and steep mountains at each end. There is no rebuttal possible to the argument that powerful integrative forces reside in this geographic isolation. In these two cases, it is interesting that

3. Recall that Carneiro also proposed that "social circumscription" might operate when a group could not retreat because the adjacent areas were already occupied.

the long period of the Old Kingdom in Egypt and the equally long development in the North Coast of Peru appear to have been relatively peaceful—a likely testimonial to the political significance of such extreme geographic circumscription.

There is another way to put it: that the *benefits* of being part of the society obviously outweighed the alternatives. This terminology is more generally applicable, because not all of our instances had such powerful geographical deterrences to separation as the circumscription by surrounding desert. Yet *all* cases had external problems, and the benefits of membership in the society must have been very obvious, probably with much the same political effect as in the cases of the Egyptian and Peruvian isolation. The nongeographical factors were the consistent presence of outside enemies, against which a government could afford protection.

There are two basically distinct kinds of outside enemies, having different political effects. In one case, a society has potentially rival neighbors of a culture roughly similar to its own, as with the independent city-states of lower Mesopotamia or the parallel valleys of coastal Peru. In the other kind, settled society is beset with raiding nomads, professional predators and thieves that keep the society in a continual state of apprehension or near-siege. The simultaneous rise of defensive city-states and nomadic pastoralists in northern China as described by Lattimore (see chapter 15) is the best example of these latter circumstances. In both kinds of warfare, the collectivity is strengthened by the presence of outside dangers, but there the resemblance ends.

Competition and rivalry among similar neighbors, as in the first case, are dealt with politically—the leaders make peace, bargains, alliances, and sometimes war. The perception of the details of this activity cannot be very clear to the peasantry and a persistent sense of benefit probably would not be felt, although it probably would be more noticeable to their local leaders. But the benefit of being protected from nomadic raiding bands of predators would be obvious, persistent, and necessary to all, particularly to agricultural villagers. Thus the Mesopotamian and northern Chinese city-states, Mexico's Teotihuacán (and possibly Tiahuanaco and Huari in Peru) had some defenses and means of warning and protection against raiders, and the people had every reason to count it as a blessing that they were well protected.

This continuous need for defense against raids is likely to have led to permanent installations like hilltop forts, citadels, and walled cities, and in the salient case of China, to the building of the Great Wall. That the threat persisted is an important fact; it is most difficult to maintain treaties, alliances, or even peaceful trade with mobile groups that combine and subdivide, join new leaders, and in general are not under stable government themselves. But most importantly, the continuous presence of the threat of raid encouraged not only an increased defensive urbanism but also the intensification of agriculture.

The Maya, as usual, offer an interesting case. The long classic period in lowland Guatemala was apparently relatively peaceful. There were no raiding nomads, and so no need for "urbanism" in the defensive sense, or for intensification of agriculture, or for fortifications. (In only one instance, Tikal, has anything been excavated that could be interpreted as having some military function, but even this is problematical.) Over a vast area, the Maya were remarkably alike in race and culture, and evidently not crowded or otherwise forced to compete for resources. What was there to fight about? Probably there were quarrels and feuds, but chiefdoms can settle such things and the Maya undoubtedly did so. At any rate, the nonurbanism of the Maya is suggestive of the role—completely negative in this case—of persistent threat by nomadic predators. It should be noted as well that no Mayan chiefdom was geographically circumscribed in Carneiro's sense. The unusual absence of almost any degree of either of these factors must be the reason that the Maya were so remarkably unurbanized, in spite of a high degree of civilization. Probably, also, their chiefdoms were not usually very large, because the centrifugal tendencies of their subparts were so largely unchecked.

So far, we have spoken of the various kinds of benefits as though they were importantly matters of an individual's perception and decision, but now it is time to venture some important qualifications. First, the individual peasants probably did not act for themselves. Not even as a mass did they have any franchise in any case reviewed in this book. They were ruled in small localities by their local members of the aristocracy, who in turn were ruled by the next higher in the structure. Centrifugal tendencies were largely caused by the disagreements and feuds of local lords and members of the higher aristocracy, quarreling over such matters as rights to succession.

Similarly, the perception of benefits was not what prevented "revolts of the masses." The chiefdoms and archaic civilizations were *caste* societies in the fullest sense of the word. Peasants, artisans, and rulers were all in their hereditary occupations and statuses. It is inconceivable that any peasants would have considered bettering their lot by their own political actions, for this would have to be done for them by their own hereditary rulers. It seems much more realistic to think of the push and pull toward integration and disintegration of the hierarchical society as being confined to the bureaucracy itself, with the "people" passively doing as they were told.

It seems evident also that the lower orders of the hierarchical society had no "freedom." As Eisenstadt points out in his huge study of archaic and classical empires (1963, pp. 363–68), the imperial power has two aspects, which need not be closely related: (1) its arbitrary discretion over the lives of its individual subjects —its "despotism"; and (2) the "generalized" power that has to do with mobilization of resources, as in implementing long-distance trade, building public monuments, and so on.

The first aspect of power, the "despotism," is difficult to assess because we normally think of freedom or its absence as pertaining to the relations of the state with its individual citizens. But as we have noted time and again, the pressure on individuals to conform is a property of the local kin group—at least in any primitive or peasant society, including the primitive states and archaic civilizations. The considerable conformity is to the norms of the traditional folk society, and not necessarily something imposed by a despotic state; the state rules through intermediaries and the face-to-face "despotism" is simply that of the communal kin group under the aegis of its local priest-chief. As the secular use of coercive force makes its appearance along with the state, the threats and other coercion are directed from the center to subsidiary chiefs, not to peasants either as individuals or masses. The threat to the integrity of a new state is from the important components, normally the larger chiefdoms, whose chiefs or war leaders may not have fully accepted the authority of the center and might wish to break away from it or take it over or otherwise resist it.

It is mostly the second, the "generalized," aspect of power that grew in complexity during the development of government, especially in the movement from small to large, or classic, chiefdoms. The normal bureaucratic tendency to become autonomous and to take on more and more functions was strengthened by the growth of this aspect.

Eisenstadt thinks that there is a tendency toward self-limitation in the use of generalized power, and he may be correct with respect to the classic archaic civilizations. This may be the reason for their apparent fulfillment and eventual stagnation (perhaps "self-limitation" is just another way of referring to it). However, the earlier origin of institutionalized power and its development en route to the classic forms was clearly associated with increased bureaucratic mobilization of resources in several ways, but most striking in creating specializations (of skills and of regions) in an organismic redistributional system that so typically involves complex administration.

Similarly, long-distance trade under archaic conditions could only be undertaken by a governmental organization. The "prices" (the amounts and kinds of goods to be exchanged against each other) would have to be arranged, as would the carriers or shippers, and protection for them. Trade in archaic times might deal in necessities or only in luxuries, probably both usually, but in any of these an important part of the earned increments remains in the court, or temple, and can be used to subsidize all sorts of activities. Trade helps the government by ensuring a large number of benefited, hence loyal, followers among leaders of the component formerly independent chiefdoms. In some instances the wealth could support mercenary soldiers, and presumably a part of it sometimes could be channeled through the administrative hierarchy to reach the populace at large.

In some salient instances, natural resources were so distributed in distant and scattered niches that the function of the centralized bureaucracy in organizing the exploitation and exchange of the products resulted in a very large urban center. Teotihuacán, as described by Sanders and Price (see chapter 10), was a good example of an authoritarian power related to such centralized redistribution. Apparently Tiahuanaco and Huari in highland Peru were also of this sort. Once such an organismic system gets under way it quickly can become more complex and more necessary to all the people, but especially and obviously necessary to the chiefs of the specialized satellite regions.

It is when (for whatever reasons) the system malfunctions and centrifugal tendencies prevail that physical coercion is used. It may be that at the level of primitive, incipient states the beginnings of the coercive system might seem like a patchwork of wild, hasty expedients of terror. The use of force might seem untoward, an awkward and desperate effort to keep a system together that ideally should function smoothly as a theocracy. And truly this situation does seem characteristic of the transition from chiefdoms of the classic variety to the more violent expansive primitive states, as historically known. And as we have seen repeatedly, the resort to violent coercion was nowhere a true solution. Whenever a new government succeeds in maintaining itself, this very success results in reduced violence—so that a "good government" begins to look like a peaceful theocracy again.

The Road to Civilization

We have now arrived at a logical place to sum up our findings about the stage-stops along the road to civilization. Some time ago, from an evolutionary perspective based on ethnology, I found the following stages of social-political development to be well suited to the available data: bands, tribes, chiefdoms, and primitive states (Service, 1962). While this classification may still have its uses in characterizing contemporary (or historically known) primitive societies, it does not seem so useful for prehistoric archaeology. This is because the adaptive environment faced by most of the primitive societies described ethnographically included many drastic effects of the dominating spread of Euro-American civilization. Those primitive societies that survived the depopulation due to new diseases, the deadlier weapons, the unprecedentedly intense wars, the new forms of exploitation such as slavery, the population displacements due to rubber booms and gold rushes, and so on, found themselves in new or radically different kinds of social-political circumstances. This point has been developed at some length elsewhere (Service, 1971, ch. 10). In the present instance, we must consider particularly that the violent military states so numerous in our present ethnographic sample took a form that was directly and indirectly related to the thunderous impact of European influences on what previously had been simple theocratic chiefdoms.

For the purpose of demarking stages based on archaeologically discernible forms of political integration, a single segmental stage seems preferable to the division into bands and tribes. (It may, of course, be useful for many purposes to subdivide this stage into foraging, incipient agricultural, pastoral, and fishing types; simple and complex; large and small, and so on.)

"Chiefdoms" seem to be clearly distinct from segmental societies. Archaeological deposits very visibly reveal, for instance, the hierarchical nature of such societies in their status burials, the subsidized specialists in the fine arts, the theocratic aspects of many of the public monuments, and the granaries and foreign trade items that bespeak redistribution. But there seems to be no way to discriminate the state from the chiefdom stage: Some evidences of military action or violence of some sort will not do since these may be found sporadically at any evolutionary level. It is possible of course that government in some archaic civilizations did institutionalize repressive physical force. And it is possible that the evidence of military action in, for example, North China, is evidence of a state apparatus. But we cannot get the sort of conclusive evidence on this point for archaic civilizations that we can for modern primitive states. And because the modern states were "contaminated" by European contact, we cannot assume without better evidence that the archaic civilizations went through the same stages as the modern states.

It is interesting that one of the most ambitious archaeological attempts to apply the band, tribe, chiefdom, state scheme on a broad scale, Sanders and Marino's *New World Prehisory* (1970), found the same difficulty. They say (p. 9):

> The most difficult problem of identification lies in the attempt to separate chiefdoms from states. . . . Differences between chiefdoms and states are as much quantitative as they are qualitative. Our major criteria here will be found in the number of levels of community

stratification and in the size, quality and complexity of function and plan of the public architectural complexes of the largest centers known for a period of an area.

Sanders and Price have labeled the more advanced level a state, but I think that given our lack of good evidence that they were states in the classic sense, we should not attach so misleading a label. The term I have used—"archaic civilizations"—suggests the qualities of the advanced stage of primitive development. There was a point at which some few of the relatively simple hierarchical-bureaucratic chiefdoms grew, under some unusual conditions, into much larger, more complex bureaucratic empires. There seems to be no practical difficulty in the archaeological discrimination of the original archaic civilizations from the previous developments. At least, there seems to be no fundamental disagreement among archaeologists and historians as to the identity of the full-fledged developments, with only a few arguments about whether to include early forms such as the Olmec or Chavín. It may be that there is not even any great problem as to what to call the stages.

The evolutionary route from big-man society through chiefdom to civilization, as now proposed from an ethnohistorical perspective, conforms almost exactly to the archaeological classification used by Steward (1949) and others. Most saliently, the Formative era (or Ford's "Theocratic Formative" [1969]) can be equated with the chiefdom stage; the era of Regional Florescence (or "Classic" era, for many archaeologists) is what we have here called civilization. The era of Cyclical Conquests (or "Post-Classic" period) has been noticed only briefly so far, but it will be discussed in the epilogue. All of these stages have the great virtue of not specifying as an indicator some kind of supposition, such as repressive law, which is invisible in the archaeological record.

Civilizations of the classical type were not created *de novo;* their basic characteristics were all foreshadowed in earlier stages of society. The term civilization is thus a relative concept and should not be defined in terms of the appearance of some single attribute; not violence certainly, nor even writing, or fine arts. From an evolutionary standpoint, the relativity is achieved by thinking not in terms of arbitrary demarking points but of a continuum of directional change. (This does not mean that the changes are necessarily gradual.) Then the key becomes concerned with "more" or "less" advancement along the directional line. The most commonplace, because most obvious, notion of the direction cultural evolution has taken is from simple to complex cultures, or the corollary, small to large societies. Admittedly, however, these indices are only very broad-gauged.

Simple cultures normally belong to small societies and complex ones to large. This is because, as argued at such length in previous sections, centrifugal tendencies are great in segmental societies, and are overcome only gradually as various integrative means appear. The integration of various families into lineages or clans, and the integration of these segments with each other, are accomplished by means of the ideology of consanguinity and affinity and the rules of marriage, along with the numerous socio-psychological attractions that inhere in familistic religious ceremonies and life-crisis rituals. It is evident from all ethnographic accounts of segmental societies that the functioning political entity is never very large or even constant in size. Probably some 99-plus percent of human history was spent in various versions of small segmental societies.

It can be argued sensibly that such societies last so long and are so prevalent because they are evolutionary dead-ends (Kirchhoff, 1959). Very nearly all were, but somehow eventually in a few of them the circumstances that caused occasional redistribution from a center to become more permanent led to a rather more stable all-round chieftainship that could take on further functions.

Max Weber (1946, 1947) deserves great credit for his theoretical elaboration of how bureaucratic organizations developed, particularly for emphasizing the stages of their legitimization, from "charismatic" to the "traditional" to "legal-rational." But with modern comparative ethnography we can see more clearly than he the evolutionary significance of the chiefdom's redistributing theocratic bureaucracy. The "road to civilization" was the developmental career of a few bureaucracies, which under rather unusual environmental conditions fulfilled themselves eventually in ruling what finally must have been hundreds of former petty chiefdoms.

The main purpose of any bureaucracy, its own teleology, is simply to survive. Weber's "legitimization" ensures the bureaucracy's and the society's survival (and its growth, if successful) by adding to its functions, and consequently to its greater autonomy. Its survival is also dependent on peaceful successions to office. This first occurred when the big-man (or "charismatic") personal style of redistributional leadership became hereditary, that is, permanent and official—thus beginning an aristocracy as well as a ("traditional") bureaucratic hierarchy of instituted political power.

When a power institution of this sort lasts long enough to prove out, we may call it a true government. But the classical forms had one particularly salient characteristic that we should never underestimate, a thoroughly theocratic nature. Economic and political functions were all overlaid or subsumed by the priestly aspects of the organization. As Hocart so cogently pointed out, the building of an irrigation canal was not "utilitarian" and a temple "religious"; both were efficacious, practical, and necessary, and both probably seen as equally significant ritually. Obviously the perceived benefits and other forms of reinforcement of such a theocracy can enable it to govern large aggregations without regular recourse to violent coercion.

Therefore the state as a repressive institution based on secular force is not coterminous with civilization in the classic, primary developments. But it should be emphasized again that even if such force were present in some cases, it would be *controlled* violence, not just plain violence or disorder which can burst out at any stage of social development in the relative absence or weakness of government. We must emphasize that a good government in this sense is not necessarily or evidently a repressive body, since a responsible control of violence equals peace. The ideal government would *abolish* violence.

Furthermore, controls of any sort could be so effective as preventers of crime, feud, and violence as to become invisible to the archaeological investigator. It may be suspected, for example, that both positive and negative reinforcement by supernatural means was not only characteristic of the early civilizations, but sufficiently effective largely by itself. Just as much joy or terror can be promulgated by these means as any other—perhaps more when people are such true believers as they seem to have been in our historical examples of prestate chiefdoms.

But we have been speaking of internal affairs so far. Violence in external polity is another matter. All kinds of societies may use it at times and eschew it as others, but it can be put to political uses at some higher stages of political development that were impossible in simpler times. In particular, military means may become associated with new forms of political dominance of some societies over others, especially if there is some degree of regional differentiation in resources and technological specialization, all connected by administrated exchange and redistribution. The hierarchical government of the dominated societies then may be fitted into an organization that becomes a truly complicated pyramid of central organization.

This bureaucracy, now more like that of an empire than a simple local primitive homogeneous ethnic unit, may quite quickly acquire the specialized appurtenances usually attributed to the archaic civilizations: writing and mathematical notations with associated tax and census scribes, great specialized art, metallurgy, elaborate ceremonial religion, and grand public monuments and other works. They are the final benefits of a form of centralized and expanding political organization that began in the simple attempts of a big-man to perpetuate his social dominance by services to his fellows.

This is not to say that the developing governmental apparatus was uninfluenced by external adaptive circumstances, for of course it was, and those have constituted a considerable part of our discussion. But it has not been sufficiently understood that the development of civilization was so orthogenetic and so self-contained. Rather than the mere resultant of causes, this centralized bureaucracy was itself the creator of many new aspects of culture, in religion, art, literature, economics, technology, and warfare. This does not mean that there was something inexorable about the evolution of the institutionalized power of authority through its stages. Quite the contrary; it required just the right balance of several conditions and circumstances, like the growth of a rare and delicate new plant. But also like a plant, important determinants of the direction of its growth lay within itself.

Epilogue

The Fall of Civilizations

All things are subject to decay and change. When a state, having passed with safety through many and great dangers, arrives at the highest degree of power, and possesses an entire and undisputed sovereignty, it is manifest that the long continuance of prosperity must give birth to costly and luxurious manners, and that the minds of men will be heated with ambitious contests, and become too eager and aspiring in the pursuit of dignities.

So WROTE POLYBIUS in the second century before Christ. So far as I know this is the earliest explanation of the rise and decline of civilizations, so tantalizing and worrisome a speculation to all who would claim a general understanding of history. The question of the origin and rise of civilizations is for many no more interesting and important than its obverse, the apparent inevitability of their decline and fall.

We have mentioned, but not discussed, the demise of the six primary civilizations covered in this book. But since "rise" and "fall" are closely related in the sense that they are linked behaviors —success and failure—of only one institution, a government, we may now find it of interest to view the fall of civilizations from the same perspective used in the investigation of their rise.

First, let it be said that we are talking very generally about some kind of failure of bureaucratic governance. All of the specific historical happenings that signaled the decline of the civilizations —being overrun by barbarians, abandoning the home capital (or its ceremonial centers), being defeated in battle by a new rival state, civil war—all have one thing in common, the failure of the government to fulfill its primary mission of maintenance, of saving the society from external and internal threats to its integrity.

It has been tempting for many philosophers of history to see cycles of rise and fall in terms of changes in the personal attributes of the citizenry or of its rulers, as did Polybius. In its simplest form this thesis says that the people (or rulers) got fat and complacent as a consequence of success. Some would have it the other way, that success gives rulers too much imperial ambition or confidence, and thus leads them to overextend their capabilities. It should not be doubted that both of these are frequent personal consequences of personal successes. And the successes of a government do create the appearance of numerous personal successes. I do not know, however, how much influence such alterations in the characteristics of a government's personnel contribute to the success or weakness of the structure. It is perhaps as likely that leaders will "look good" during successful epochs of a government's history and "look bad" or "complacent" at other times. Therefore, as arbitrarily as we did in the preceding chapters, we may drop the "great men" and now the "weak men" and all other reductionist psychological or moral explanations. This is simply because we have no techniques for appraising their value, inasmuch as such attributes are only inferred from the behavior of the government itself.

Similarly, the commonplace explanations of rise and fall by means of such verbal devices as "growth and decay," "youth and senescence," "metabolic and catabolic processes," "challenge and response," "withdrawal and return," "changing views of man's destiny," and "internal contradictions" must be eschewed as the merest of tautologies.

It is also tempting to assume that there is in the nature of any specific form of government a critical population size, or scope of governance, beyond which its particular integrative institutions cannot cope. This may well be so—it *seems* sensible—but, again, since we do not really know, and there is no way to find out, the danger is in using it merely as a device.[1]

Similarly, it may well be that a successful polity, well adapted and "coherent" over a long period of time, becomes brittle or inflexible and thus cannot resist well, or easily readapt to, changing circumstances.[2] This may be particularly so of theocracies, which depend so on religion, especially ceremony and ritual, and on a highly traditionalized set of rules and policies in governance.

1. One is here reminded of Gibbons's famous epitomizations of Rome's fall: "Prosperity ripened the principle of decay" and "the stupendous fabric yielded to the pressure of its own weight" (1952, p. 621).

2. Kent Flannery says (1972, p. 423): "Enough centralization, promotion, and linearization may move the state toward hypercoherence and instability. Finally, hypercoherence can lead to collapse and devolution."

The sheer passage of time is an important factor in the creation of complex theocratic ideologies—traditions must be "old." And to appear old they cannot have changed noticeably.

But the most important implication of this obvious characteristic of theocracies is that a point of equilibrium seems to be in the very nature of the adaptation of cultural systems to environments. And it is true that theocracies are more likely than others to sanctify what other kinds of bureaucracies simply "routinize." Thus a normal bureaucratic stance against innovation becomes increasingly unyielding with time as it acquires the patina of religious tradition. But this factor, however likely, does not yet explain a society's fall, but only its failure to keep on rising.

There is another aspect to successful adaptation that is now relevant: its radiating, expanding movement. Along the route toward specialization, and to the eventual stasis of success, the developing culture tends to spread outward, and to increase its contacts with other societies. Adaptation, in other words, typically involves a reciprocating adjustment to newly encountered cultures as well as to new features of the natural environment. The expanding society in a certain sense feeds not only on the land but on other peoples that it can dominate, exploit, subsume, or ally with in symbiosis. But whatever the relationship, it is always a two-way process even if unbalanced—the dominated, formerly simpler, societies develop complementariness, if not similarity.

But since success in adaptation eventually bespeaks conservatism, successful dominant societies become less able to adapt to any new or different circumstances. This is so well known as to need no argumentation of further exemplification here. But an emphasis may be necessary: that it is the successful, the dominant, society of an environment that so strikingly demonstrates this; meanwhile, the dominated societies are more able and more likely to experiment in further efforts to strengthen themselves to change their status. Newer, less committed to conventional solutions, they have greater potential for experimentation and change. On the other hand, the successfully evolving center eventually suffers from what Thorstein Veblen called "the penalty of taking the lead"; while the hinterland benefits, in Leon Trotsky's phrase, from the "privilege of backwardness" that results from being able to borrow the latest techniques from the advanced societies, thus skipping over earlier developmental stages. With all other things constant, therefore, some of the newly civilized societies of the frontier have an increasing evolutionary potential that the original center steadily loses in the very act of successfully dominating its own local environment.

"Other things" are not constant in actual history, of course, so that to cite the significance of the complicated relationship of evolutionary advance to environmental adaptation does not specify exactly which one of the new societies will come to surpass its predecessor, or when or in what manner it may dramatize its new power. Each of our six classical cases of civilizational "rise" had a somewhat different kind of "fall." But all, I think, are in an important sense examples of the way in which potential for further advance decreases in proportion to adaptive success and maturity. This argues that the earlier classical governments were eventually bypassed, and therefore that their demise was caused by a weakness that was relative to others' new strength.[3]

China • Of all the works discussed in our present volume, Owen Lattimore's *Inner Asian Frontiers of China* (1940) contains the fullest and most convincing specific description of the complex interplay of adaptation between kinds of cultures in relation to kinds of geographical environments and then in relation to each other. It will be useful, therefore, to illustrate our theory first with his case study of China.

The competitive relations of extensive versus intensive land use and the greater feasibility of mobile warfare in the former and defensive urbanism in the latter is a beautiful instance of evolutionary adaptive flux. This was one kind of frontier relationship in the north, and it resulted in a kind of near-equilibrium as each pole successfully specialized. But to the south of the Great Bend of the Yellow River the spread of early Chinese

3. I have discussed this discontinuity of evolutionary progress in general and with many specific illustrations in various articles lately brought together in *Cultural Evolutionism* (1971). Interesting developments of these ideas may be found in Wertheim (1974), who also notes the independent coinage by a Dutch historian, Jan Romein, of the "hypothesis of the retarding lead," so reminiscent of Veblen's observation.

civilization was freer and more flowing, with the polity continuing with its moving frontier a trend of development that it had already begun, intensifying and diversifying as required. Lattimore contrasted the two frontiers as static and *ex*clusive to the north and dynamic and *in*clusive to the south.

Paradoxically (but naturally enough from our present point of the new civilization, but the open frontier of the south led to north led to creative political and military solutions on the part of the new civilization, but the open frontier of the south led to easy dominance in that direction. But that is precisely what led to new civilizational developments in the newly dominated areas, ending in the demise of the Shang-Chou cultural amalgamation first achieved at the Great Bend. The most striking illustration of the relation of dominance to evolution is seen in the spread of the northern culture southward to the Yangtse River Valley. Here began the basic differentiation into the classic cultural (and eventually imperial) rivalry of north and south. But long before the rise of the full southern civilization, the northern had begun an irregular leapfrogging advance that we may term, for short, the local discontinuity of progress.

Lattimore sums up the early classical situation as follows (1940, pp. 366–67):

> Comparison of the Yangtse valley field of history as a whole with that of the Yellow River as a whole, and of the alternating ascendencies of different geographical regions and political states within the Yellow River field of history, shows that the history of the last millennium B.C. cannot adequately be described by assuming a single line of development. There must have been a number of parallel lines of development. Some of these were of major and some of minor importance, and some were of later origin than others. No one line, however, abruptly destroyed or succeeded another. Although the Chou "dynasty" destroyed and succeeded the Shang "dynasty," *the age of the Shang decline can also be described as the age in which the Chou were growing to strength* [italics added]. Even more clearly, the rise of the Ch'i in the east and later of Chin in the north did not mean the decline of Ch'in in the west. . . . Even less did the growing importance of the Yangtse region and the state of Ch'u signify weakness or decay among the Yellow River states.

Mesopotamia • Turning briefly to Mesopotamia, we find that a cyclical rise and fall and a local discontinuity of successive advances was so characteristic of the history of the wider Near Eastern scene in archaic times that many of the cyclical theories were born out of contemplation of it. In Sumer, the birthplace of the first civilizations, the several independent city-states clashed with each other and were also preyed upon at times by barbarians. But all were bypassed by Sargon of Akkad, who finally united them under his imperial leadership. "At that time, Akkad constituted a zone of transition between the high civilization of the south and the barbarism of outlying regions. Thus the Akkadians were in a favorable position to unit barbarian prowess with civilized technique to form a powerful military force; and in fact, Sargon was only one of the earliest of a long line of lords marcher who created empires by successfully exploiting a similarly strategic position on the frontier between civilization and barbarism" (McNeill 1963, p. 46.)

The eclipse of the theocratic Sumerian city-states by Sargon's newer kind of imperial polity had its later counterpart in the Gutian penetration from the wilder northeast. This new empire lasted about a century until overthrown by the Third Dynasty of Ur, which in turn ruled for about one hundred years (ca. 2050–1950 B.C.). This dynasty surpassed the others not only in military but in administrative strength and in a significant cultural enrichment, especially in sculpture and literature. But rise again seemed to require fall as the previously less-civilized Elamites and Amorites (the famous Hammurabi was an Amoritic king) overthrew Ur, later to be overthrown themselves by the barbarian Kassītes. By this time (the sixteenth century B.C.) large movements of formerly uncivilized peoples had brought an end to the great classic epoch in Crete, in Egypt, and in India, making a "significant breakpoint in the history of ancient civilization" (McNeill 1963, p. 51).

Egypt • In contrast to Mesopotamia, Egypt was remarkably protected by desert and sea for a long time. This kind of nearly complete geographical circumscription no doubt provided great political support for the regime during the very long peaceful period of the Old Kingdom. But this was also a kind of straitjacket, preventing the movements and new relationships of societies that not only create dangers and problems but also stimulate new advances in culture. The long period of peace was not, therefore, an exception to the present supposition about the evolutionary potentiality of new adaptive circumstances; the culture became remarkably adapted and stabilized because of its unique, protected environment, and thus became thoroughly ritualized and traditionalized in all respects. The Old Kingdom did eventually break up after nearly a thousand years of orderly theocratic rule.[4] But, as McNeill says (1963, p. 79): "The wonder is not that insubordination occurred but that it was so long delayed." The long delay could only have been due to the absence of nearby effective rival societies during all that time.

Indus River Valley • The widespread Indus civilization is of particular interest because its closest linkage was to Mesopotamia through intermediate societies (possibly common cultural ancestors) in Iran. Yet the closest structural and political resemblance is to Egypt, and this must have been due to the similar absence of competitor and predatory neighbors for such a long time (probably because of severe geographic circumscription). In the huge area occupied by this civilization, a remarkable uniformity even in local decorative styles prevailed. As McNeill put it (1963, p. 85): "Precocious political unification, analogous to that of Egypt, alone explains such uniformity."

According to interpretations made of the sanskritic Rig Veda (a classic case of "rewritten history"), invading "Aryans" eventually destroyed the Indus civilization. This should be doubted (Malik 1968; McNeill 1963, p. 89), for the observable results can be comprehended in terms of replacement or alteration of a religious system only, rather than destruction of the civilization. However that may be, for the present purpose the significant feature that the Indus culture shared with Egypt was a long-standing peaceful rule by theocratic government. This was due no doubt in both cases to their precocity and the dominance they consequently exerted over their neighbors, as well as to the long absence

4. It may be surmised, though it cannot be well proven, that the internal breakup of the government and the eventual weakness that permitted the Hittite invasions was related to the disruption of external trade routes in the developing adjacent areas of North Africa and the Fertile Crescent.

of an active dangerous frontier where new advances would be likely to be formed to successfully compete in later times.

Mesoamerica • In the New World, the fall of the first great city-state and empire of Mesoamerica, Teotihuacán, was the most striking one. Unknown assailants burned the huge capital city, and by about 600 A.D. the influence of Teotihuacán over other areas in Mesoamerica ceased. Nomadic invaders are popularly supposed to have accomplished the defeat of Teotihuacán, but since these "Chichimecs" were not cavalry it would seem that they could not have been a formidable enough military force to do other than harass and possibly plunder an already collapsing polity (or simply occupy it).

But this we do know: There were strong cultural continuities between Teotihuacán and the powerful empire of the Toltecs (based apparently at Tula) that succeeded, as well as nearby Cholula, and the later Aztecs and neighbors at Lake Texcoco. The appearance of successive empires, related, but in new geographic areas, is dramatically illustrative of the leapfrogging career that cultural evolution so typically takes under competitive conditions. The significance of this for the fall of Teotihuacán is that a related polity became stronger and dominated its hinterland. That the city itself was sacked, burned, and then occupied by some kind of intrusive peoples only signifies that the broad supportive hinterland and redistributional structure of Teotihuacán had already failed in some significant degree to compete with its rivals, the newer, broadly based regional imperiums such as Tula and Cholula.

Only three great unifying empires arose to dominate both highlands and lowlands (Coe 1962, p. 134). These were, in turn, Teotihuacán, the Toltec, and the Aztec, and all were from the central highlands. Their influence on the lowlands was apparently at long range, indirect, and primarily in terms of trade, except for the late Toltec invasion of the Maya lands in Yucatán. The Maya of the lowland Petén had important subservient trade relations with Teotihuacán via the imperial outpost city of Kaminaljuyu, but after the decline of the influence of Teotihuacán, the classic Petén region revived, presumably to dominate trade relations again. Conversely, the reemergence of central Mexico (Toltec dominance) at the close of the late Classic period hastened the Maya collapse as its complex redistributional system was disrupted.[5] This explanation accords well with decline of the power and economic function of the elite Mayan centers, with no evident military defeat or destruction. So here again, we see how the new can leap over the old in evolutionary potentiality and exert its dominance over a huge area.

Peru • As for Peru, the discontinuity of cultural developments was so notable that Steward called the post-classic stage "the era of cyclical conquests." The parallels with Mesoamerica are striking. The chiefdoms of Chavín in the Formative and Classic periods were much like the Mexican Olmec in structure and influence (though not in detail), and both were surpassed—in Peru by the long civilizational phase on the North Coast, and in Mexico by Oaxaca and the Petén Maya. These in turn were surpassed by the dominant military empires of the highlands: in Mexico Teotihuacán, followed by the Toltecs and then the Aztecs; in Peru, the parallel of rise and fall was almost exact, with Huari and Tiahuanaco followed by Chimu and then the Inca.

Adaptation and Evolutionary Potential

It may be well to begin these final paragraphs by repeating a salient but seemingly paradoxical feature of the evolutionary process: that there are both positive *and* negative aspects of adaptation to environment. And it is important to emphasize that "adaptation to environment" concerns relations with other societies as well as with geographical features. The positive potential of adaptation is that problems posed by the environment require the selection from among various possibilities those solutions that are more likely to result in survival; when this and growth are both achieved, the process has positive effects. But such successful adaptation has its obverse side—its self-limiting, unprogressive, conservative aspects—since as it succeeds it also stabilizes itself

5. In a new volume devoted to the Maya collapse (Culbert 1973), Willey and Shimkin argue as above (pp. 459–60). Chapter 16 by Webb in the same volume details the central Mexican domination of the long-distance trade. That the Maya were particularly dependent on such trade is described convincingly by Rathje (1972).

toward equilibrium with its environment.

These characteristics of adaptation are found in any successful biological population, but all the more so when it is a human society adapting by means of that special mechanism, a centralized bureaucracy, for such an organization can better direct itself, and can purposively solve adaptive problems more expeditiously, than can the simple elements in a biological selection-survival equation. Newly adapting societies can thus grow and spread into neighboring environments at a faster pace. But also, because of their bureaucratic nature, their very success bespeaks subsequent greater stabilization, an increasing inability to change in response to new environmental conditions. More adaptation equals less adaptability. And, to reemphasize, a bureaucracy that is also theocratic must become even more strikingly rigid in time, depending as it does so heavily on tradition, ceremony, ritual, and other such time-bound exigencies of priestcraft.

A second proposition that seems both logically as well as factually unassailable, is that as the precocious governments extended their influence over other societies they also transformed them in various ways (by conquering and incorporating them, allying with them, exchanging goods with them, providing successful models for their emulation, and so on). And eventually, then, some newly civilized area ruled by a less committed, less cumbersome government rose to dominance in turn by successfully initiating some bureaucratic methods, weapons, tactics, or whatever, that the original government was too complexly structured, too involuted, to adopt.

Thus the new evolutionary potential of the less-adapted society causes the apparent local discontinuity of evolutionary advance. This marks not exactly the decline and fall of the older culture, but simply that there is this obvious "penalty in taking the lead," so that the leader is bypassed and superceded by a later, more effective challenger.

The consequences of the earlier civilizations being surpassed in dominance powers over a wide region by later ones can leave various distinctive kinds of historical-archaeological records. But such great differences in the archaeological visible "falls" of civilizations would seem to have been only particular final manifestations of the very usual general process of the local discontinuity of advance. The most obvious signs of loss of dominance are military defeats resulting in destroyed or occupied capitals. The least obvious are simply stagnant or declining political economies such as the classic Indus, Egyptian, and Mayan centers. The relative decline of influence that results in loss of trade routes to rival centers would seem to be the best special explanation of these. But in all cases, the virtue of our present perspective on adaptation and its relationship to evolutionary potential is that it removes the focus from internally caused rises and falls, suggesting the usual cyclical tautologies and Toynbeean mysticisms, toward outside environmental factors that are real, true-to-life events that can be found in recorded history and investigated archaeologically.

The causes of the rise of a civilization lay in its solution of problems posed by the outside environment by means created inside itself—i.e., inside its bureaucracy. The explanation of its decline, however, lies within its environmental sphere but outside itself. This situation is caused by the rise of new and superior competitors. The "seeds of their own destruction" were not the internal causes of the downfall of the classic civilizations. The precocious developing society broadcasts its seeds, so to speak, outside its own area, and some of them root and grow vigorously in new soil, sometimes becoming stronger than the parent stock, finally to dominate both their environments.

The many theories of cultural evolution reviewed in this book never took enough account of a culture's interactions with its environment. And even most of the modern environmentalists (or "cultural ecologists," like Julian Steward), in combating this tendency, confined their attention too much to the geographic environment, never enough to reciprocal, intersocietal adaptations. So too with the theories of decline and fall, of devolution; there was never enough account taken of the wide competitive field in which these processes occur.

New evolutionary advances tend to take place in some continuity, due to the influence, the residual effect, of the already established advances; but they are also discontinuous in that they tend to take place after the movement of these advances to newer areas. Some one of the newly influenced societies then will be enabled to establish its own wide area of precocious dominance, thus to intrude on the older society's sphere of influence, and to disrupt it if not actually be required to defeat its armies in battle. The first classic civilizations, therefore, did not fall; they were pushed.

Caveat Lector

I want to emphasize that these general statements about evolutionary potentiality and discontinuity are not offered as *the* cause of the rise and fall of civilization—neither of the six classical cases under review, nor of any other (including the modern United States).

The likelihood of discontinuity in evolutionary advance, the bypassing potentiality of some newer, less adapted and less stabilized society, has been emphasized in this book because it has been so usually overlooked. And since all of the classical societies, and their later successful replacements, were in turn bypassed as part of an apparent very general process, it would seem that such a very general proposition could relevantly be broached. But this "law of evolutionary potential" is only a simple idea about the inverse relationship between two and only two things, success in adaptation and potentiality for further advance. In this statement of it, all other factors are considered as constants.

But of course numerous other factors are ultimately involved in the actual history of the rise and fall of a civilization. Disease, fire, flood, drought, earthquakes, overpopulation, soil depletion—who knows what else?—may have been involved in the various falls of any of these societies. And any such immediate causes may well become very convincingly proved in particular cases in years soon to come. But such findings would have no bearing on the general relevance of the adaptation/potentiality factor in evolution. That is, the presumed omnipresence of this factor does not at all preclude the presence of others. In each case it is but one among many: Its greatest significance lies in its generality; the others are all specific.

Because the generalization is so broad some readers may be tempted to apply it still further to include modern history, or to predict our own future. I have tried this elsewhere (1971), but cannot say with what success. But certainly it can be argued, for example, that the United States is so committed to the fossil fuels as the basic source of industrial energy that some less committed region might find it easier to begin industrialization with solar heating instead of coal, hydrogen fuel instead of gasoline, and so on. Or, to put it more immediately, would it not be a long-term advantage for some country like China to bypass our automobile age (the age of private gasoline-powered vehicles)? In a sense, all the law of evolutionary potential is saying is: Yes, it would and it is possible. Because the United States is so adapted to the automobile, its passage to a newer kind of mass transit would be much more difficult than some area that is not so committed. This inverse relationship between adaptation and potentiality is probably "true," and such an eventuality as the "fall," the bypassing of the United States by some other region, is probable—*other factors being constant.*

Other factors are not constant. As the most salient instance, the present dominance of the Western industrialized nations may be so great, the economic gap between "have" and "have-not" nations so wide (and the gap will become always wider as these latter fail to contain their population growth), that the have-nots are required to make short-run solutions and to adapt themselves as specialized subordinated parts of the Western industrial enterprise, most usually as suppliers of raw materials. In the recent past this was the colonial or imperial phase of industrial evolution; now it is a rather more voluntaristic, or free-market, kind of decision, but at any rate few unindustrialized countries have been large and strong enough to evade Western dominance, to pursue their own independent evolutionary course, in order to exercise the logical option of doing such a sensible thing as purposely bypassing the age of the gasoline-powered automobile.

Obviously the nation with the best opportunity for such a longer-term solution to the problem of future industrialization is China. It is not only large and powerful enough to remain independent (at least this seems true so far), but also the apparent relative scarcity of the fossil fuels in China may require that the automobile age be bypassed. And not only have China's size, history, political revolution, and geography, as well as favorable events in her recent history (such as Japan's loss of Manchuria in World War II) conspired to prepare her for a possible "great leap forward," but also there seems to be a conscious awareness of the potentiality that lies in China's relative isolation and lack of industrialization. At least Mao Tse-tung has said so in his typically picturesque language:

Apart from other characteristics, our people of over 600 million souls is characterized by poverty and by a vacuity which is like that of a sheet of blank paper. This may seem to be a bad thing, whereas in reality it is a good one. . . . Nothing is written on a sheet of paper which is still blank, but it lends itself admirably to receive the latest and most beautiful words and the latest and most beautiful pictures [quoted in Bettelheim 1959, p. 458].

Mao's remarks belong with Trotsky's and Veblen's in our collection of apt statements about the factor of evolutionary potential, or evolutionary discontinuity, or whatever it may be called. But does Mao's evident awareness of its significance mean that China's leaders will indeed purposely take advantage of this possibility that "history" (evolution) is, in a sense, "on her side"? Nobody could know the answer to this at the present writing. Her disagreements with the U.S.S.R. and the recent internal squabbling (like the cryptic "Cultural Revolutions") may to an important extent turn on the issues of long-term versus short-term economic plans, economic (and thus political and diplomatic) relations with the industrialized West, and perhaps even on the decision whether to allow off-shore oil explorations. All of these and countless other important questions are closely related to the great problem of how to judge the significance or strength in a specific history of the general factor of evolutionary potential—and this, to repeat, is not simply an easy application of a formula.

The universe is involved in the fall of a sparrow. The "other factors" that were held constant in order to talk about evolutionary potential and discontinuity must in fact be infinite in number. But they cannot be equal in significance. The single factor of evolutionary potential as inversely related to successful adaptation, though only one among many, and certainly never alone a sufficient predictor of particular historical events, seems demonstrably of considerable general importance in evolutionary theory.

Appendices / References / Index

Appendix 1

Literature on Egalitarian Societies

Because the peoples mentioned in chapter 3 did not constitute a representative sample, it may be desirable to list a sample of literature on egalitarian societies world-wide. The list is in some measure an attempt at representativeness, but we cannot achieve a good sample of egalitarian societies simply because such a sample has not been described. Our sample, like any ethnological sample, has to be of books, not peoples. Even in considering one continent, such as Australia, a sample can include only a few good descriptive monographs—and we have no idea how representative these few well-described cultures are of the hundreds that actually made up aboriginal Australia.[1]

The *Eskimos* are represented quite fully by several authoritative books. Kaj Birket-Smith, one of the greatest authorities on the Arctic, published in 1959 a general study on the Eskimos. Peter Freuchen's (1961) work contains some highly personalized anecdotes about this Danish explorer's many years in Greenland. Diamond Jenness (1959) recounts his adventures among the Copper Eskimos between the years 1913 and 1918.

1. A volume reporting a symposium on current research on hunting-gathering societies should be useful in addition to the following monographs. See Lee and DeVore (1968).

Knut Rasmussen (1927) presents a general account of Eskimo culture based on his extensive travels. Vilhjalmur Stefansson (1919), an American explorer of the Canadian Arctic, wrote for the general public. Edward Weyer (1932) has written a detailed comparative study and general summing up of Eskimo culture.

Most of the extensive forests of *aboriginal Canada* south of the Eskimos' area was inhabited by Indian hunters who were quite distinct in culture from the Eskimos. Diamond Jenness (1932), a modern authority on the Canadian Indians, has written a very general descriptive survey. A short monograph by Eleanor Leacock, "The Montagnais 'Hunting Territory' and the Fur Trade" (n.d.), uses modern ethnological materials to supplement early historical documents to show how the European fur trade altered the social and economic organization of the Algonkian Indains in Canada. Her bibliography is an excellent guide to earlier studies by Frank Speck and others.

June Helm MacNeish's "Leadership among the Northeastern Athabascans" (1956) is a particularly useful discussion of the nature of political organization both under aboriginal conditions and after the fur trade had become established. A missionary who spent much of his life among the Athabascans (*Dené*) in western Canada, Father A. G. Morice, became a recognized ethnological authority on this widespread language group with the publication of "The Great Dené Race" (1906–10).

Julian H. Steward (1938) has written the standard monograph on the *Shoshonean hunters and gatherers* of the Western desert. See also Steward's interpretative book, *Theory of Culture Change* (1955), particularly chapters 6, 7, and 8.

The Ona and Yahgan *Indians of Tierra del Fuego* are described best in their aboriginal state by E. Lucas Bridges (1949) in reminiscing about his childhood in Tierra del Fuego at his father's mission. John M. Cooper's "The Yahgan" (in J. H. Steward 1946*b*) is a summary of the scattered literature on the Yahgan.

Father Martin Gusinde (1931) provides the basic ethnological account of the Fuegians. Volume 1 is about the Ona; volume 2, covering the Yahgan, has been translated into English for the Human Relations Area Files.

Paul Schebesta (1933) has given a standard ethnological account of the *Pygmies of the African Congo*. Colin Turnbull's (1961) account, though written by an anthropologist, is not in the standardized ethnological form. Much as Thomas did in *The Harmless People* (see below), Turnbull personalizes his description of the culture with anecdotes about particular individuals.

D. F. Bleek (1928) has written a standard ethnological report on one of the best known of the *African Bushman* groups, the Naron. A basic source on Bushmen, Bergdama, and Hottentots, compiled from earlier writings about them, was published by Isaac Shapera (1930). Elizabeth Marshall Thomas (1959) has prepared a well-written, anecdotal account of her experiences among Bushmen as a member of a recent scientific expedition.

The *Australian aborigines* are presented in a general authoritative account by the foremost Australian ethnologist, A. P. Elkin (1954). M. J. Meggitt's (1962) well-conceived monograph is the first full-length study of a central Australian group since early in the century.

W. L. Warner's (1937) intensive study of the Murngin in northeastern Arnhem Land furnishes a good contrast to studies of the desert-living Arunta, for the Murngin live in a rainier, tropical, coastal region.

The field work for Baldwin Spencer and F. J. Gillen's (1927) anthropological classic was done around the turn of the century, before the culture of the Arunta of the Central Desert was seriously disturbed. The book is particularly famous for its depiction of Arunta religion. Spencer and Gillen also wrote a more general work (1899), as did Spencer alone (1914).

The hunting-gathering Pygmies of the *Malay Peninsula* are described by Paul Schebesta (n.d.), a well-known specialist on Pygmies and primitive religion. W. W. Skeat and C. O. Blagden (1906) have published an important general source on the peoples of Malaya.

E. H. Man (1882) has published probably the most important source on the *Andaman Islanders*. Man was for many years an officer of the Penal Settlement at Fort Blair and for four of these years was in charge of the Andamanese Homes, a mission and hospital for the natives.

The standard professional ethnographic account of the Andaman Islanders, supplementing Man's work, is by A. R. Radcliffe-Brown (1948). It is in some ways more sophisticated, but Man had the advantages of a longer stay, fuller comprehension of the language, and the fact that at the time of his residence aboriginal culture was more complete and the population not nearly so depleted.

Horticultural tribes are often in the upper level of segmental society. Good examples are found among *Indians of the northeastern United States*—Algonkian and Iroquoian speakers, mostly. The *Indians of the Great Plains* were an ephemeral adaptation of a nearly unique kind, paralleled most closely by the mounted Indians of Argentina. The *Indians of the American Southwest* were of two distinct cultures, the sedentary Pueblos and the somewhat nomadic Navajo and Apache. The literature is too voluminous to cite specifically here:

consult Murdock's bibliography (1953), Wissler (1931), Underhill (1953), and Farb (1968).

Horticultural *Indians of the tropical forest of South America* are summarized in Steward (1948).

In *Africa,* the Nuer part-pastoralists have been described well by Evans-Pritchard (1940), as have the Tiv by Bohannon (1957). For summaries of African cultures and with wide bibliographical coverage, see Murdock (1959) and Middleton and Tait (1958).

Appendix 2

Literature on Chiefdoms

POLYNESIA is the best-known well-researched culture area of chiefdoms. The following works are recommended: *General:* Oliver (1951), Sahlins (1958), Williamson (1924); *Hawaii:* Malo (1903); *Tikopia:* Firth (1936, 1939); *New Zealand:* Firth (1929).

For Melanesia, there are good comparative materials on both low-level chiefdoms and incipient big-man systems. For a *New Guinea* society, see Pospisil (1958); for the *Solomon Islands,* Oliver (1949); the *Trobriands,* Malinowski (1932, 1961); *Fiji,* Sahlins (1962).

The so-called circum-Caribbean societies of Central America, the Greater Antilles, and coastal northern South America were mostly chiefdoms. They are described in some variety in vol. 4 of Steward's *Handbook of South American Indians* (1948).

Many of the Indians of the southeastern United States were chiefdoms. Like the societies of the circum-Caribbean noted above, they were destroyed at an early date in the colonial period, and have been reconstructed from historical archives. Swanton (1946) has made a convenient summary of them.

The chiefdoms of the *northwest coast of North America* have been summarized by Drucker (1955), and a typical example, the *Nootka Indians,* described in depth ethnologically and from historical data by the same author (1951).

Africa had a tremendous number of chiefdoms in early colonial times, but the great increase in the slave trade and warfare caused the collapse of many, while others became full-fledged states. Some of those latter were discussed in chapters 5, 6, and 7 as former chiefdoms. A handy collection of articles contrasting egalitarian ("acephalous") African societies with centralized authority systems (some of which are chiefdoms) is by Fortes and Evans-Pritchard (1940). Stevenson (1968) provides an excellent critical review of the same material. Linton (1933) described an apparent transition from egalitarian to hierarchical society in *Madagascar*. The *Plateau Tonga* and their neighbors are interestingly described by Colson and Gluckman (1951).

Asian nomadic pastoralists are sometimes organized in chiefdom form (Krader 1955), particularly when closely engaged in plunder or war.

References

Adams, Robert McC.

1955 "Developmental Stages in Ancient Mesopotamia." In *Irrigation Civilizations: A Comparative Study*. Washington, D.C.: Pan American Union.

1960 "Early Civilizations, Subsistence, and Environment." In Carl H. Kraeling and Robert M. Adams (eds.), *City Invincible: A Symposium on Urbanization and Cultural Development in the Ancient Near East*. Chicago: University of Chicago Press.

1962 "Agriculture and Urban Life in Early Southwestern Iran." *Science* 136:109–22.

1965 *Land Behind Baghdad: A History of Settlement on the Diyala Plains*. Chicago: University of Chicago Press.

1966 *The Evolution of Urban Society: Early Mesopotamia and Prehispanic Mexico*. Chicago: Aldine.

1968 "Urban Revolution: Introduction." In the *International Encyclopedia of the Social Sciences*. New York: Macmillan and Free Press.

1972 "Patterns of Urbanization in Early Southern Mesopotamia." In Peter J. Ucko, Ruth Tringham, and G. W. Dimbleby (eds.), *Man, Settlement and Urbanism*, pp. 735–49. London: Duckworth.

Allchin, Bridget, and Raymond Allchin

1968 *The Birth of Indian Civilization*. Hammondsworth, Middlesex, England: Penguin Books.

Almond, Gabriel A., and James S. Coleman (eds.)

1960 *The Politics of Developing Areas*. Princeton: Princeton University Press.

Andreski, Stanislav

1972 *Social Sciences as Sorcery*. London: Andre Deutsch.

Arendt, Hannah

1961 *Between Past and Future*. New York: Viking Press.

Armillas, Pedro

1951 "Tecnología, Formaciones Socio-Económicas y Religión en Mesoamérica." In Sol Tax (ed.), *The Civilizations of Ancient America: Selected Papers of the 29th International Congress of Americanists*, pp. 19–30. Chicago: University of Chicago Press.

1964 "Condiciones Ambientales y Movimientos de Pueblos en la Frontera Septentrional de Mesoamérica." In *Homenaje a Fernando Marqués-Miranda*. Madrid and Seville: Prensa de Universidades de Madrid y Sevilla.

1968 "Urban Revolution: The Concept of Civilization." In the *International Encyclopaedia of the Social Sciences*. New York: Macmillan and Free Press.

Bagehot, Walter

1872 *Physics and Politics: Thoughts on the Application of the Principles of "Natural Selection" and "Inheritance" to Political Society*. Reprint ed., 1956. Boston: Beacon Press.

Barnett, Homer G.

1949 *Palauan Society*. Eugene: University of Oregon Press.

Barton, R. F.

1949 *The Kalingas: Their Institutions and Custom Laws*. Chicago: University of Chicago Press.

Bartram, William

1854 *Observations on the Creek and Cherokee Indians*. Transactions of the American Ethnological Society, vol. 3, pp. 11–81.

1928 *Travels of William Bartram*. Reprint ed., 1955. New York: Dover Publications.

Bascom, William

1969 *The Yoruba of Southwestern Nigeria*. New York: Holt, Rinehart and Winston.

Beattie, John

1958 *Nyoro Kinship, Marriage and Affinity*. London: Oxford University Press.

1960 *Bunyoro: An African Kingdom*. New York: Holt, Rinehart and Winston.

1971 *The Nyoro State*. Oxford: Clarendon Press.

Bennett, Wendell C.

1948 *A Reappraisal of Peruvian Archaeology*. American Antiquity Memoir, vol. 13, no. 4, part 2.

Bennett, Wendell C., and Junius B. Bird

1949 *Andean Culture History*. Revised ed., 1964. New York: Natural History Press.

Bernal, Ignacio

1965 "Archaeological Synthesis of Oaxaca." *Handbook of Middle American Indians*, vol. 3, pp. 788–831. Austin: University of Texas Press.

1967 "Teotihuacán ¿Capital de Imperio?" *Revista Mexicana de Estudios Antropológicos* 20(1):95–110.

Bettelheim, Charles
1959 "China's Economic Growth." *Monthly Review* 10(11): 429–58.

Birket-Smith, Kaj
1959 *The Eskimos.* London: Methuen.

Blanton, Richard E.
1973 *The Valley of Oaxaca Settlement Pattern Project: 1971 and 1972 Field Seasons.* A Project Report to the National Science Foundation.

Bleek, D. F.
1928 *The Naron, a Bushman Tribe of the Central Kalahari.* Cambridge: Cambridge University Press.

Bloch, Marc
1932 "Feudalism, European." In the *Encyclopaedia of the Social Sciences.* New York: Macmillan.
1939–1940 *Feudal Society.* Trans. from the French by L. A. Manyon. Reprint ed., 1961. Chicago: University of Chicago Press.

Bodde, Derk
1956 *Feudalism in China.* In Rushton Coulborn (ed.), *Feudalism in History.* Hamden, Conn.: Archon Press.

Bohannan, Paul
1957 *Justice and Judgment among the Tiv.* London: Oxford University Press.
1958 "Extra-Processual Events in Tiv Political Institutions." *American Anthropologist* 60(1):1–12.
1963 *Social Anthropology.* New York: Holt, Rinehart and Winston.
1967 *Law and Warfare: Studies in the Anthropology of Conflict.* Garden City, N.Y.: Natural History Press.

Bohannan, Paul, and Philip Curtin
1964 *Africa and Africans.* Reprint ed., 1971. Garden City, N.Y.: Natural History Press.

Borah, Woodrow, and Sherburne F. Cook
1963 "The Aboriginal Population of Central Mexico on the Eve of the Spanish Conquest." *Ibero-Americana* 45(6):22–44.

Boserup, Ester
1965 *The Conditions of Agricultural Growth.* Chicago: Aldine.

Bradley, Harold Whitman
1942 *The American Frontier in Hawaii: The Pioneers, 1789–1843.* Stanford: Stanford University Press.

Braidwood, Robert J., and Gordon K. Willey (eds.)
1962 *Courses Toward Urban Life.* Chicago: Aldine.

Bridges, E. Lucas
1949 *Uttermost Part of the Earth.* New York: E. P. Dutton.

Bronson, Bennet
1966 "Roots and the Subsistence of the Ancient Maya." *Southwestern Journal of Anthropology* 22(1):251–79.

Bryant, A. T.
1919 *Olden Times in Zululand and Natal: Containing Earlier Political History of the Eastern-Nguni Clans.* London: Longmans, Green.

Buck, Peter H. (Te Rangi Hiroa)
1938 *An Introduction to Polynesian Anthropology.* Bernice P. Bishop Museum [Honolulu] Bulletin no. 187.

Butzer, Karl W.
1971 "Agricultural Origins in the Near East as a Geographical Problem." In Stuart Struever (ed.), *Prehistoric Agriculture,* pp. 209–35. Garden City, N.Y.: Natural History Press.

Carneiro, Robert L.
1961 "Slash and Burn Cultivation Among the Kuikuru and its Implications for Cultural Development in the Amazon Basin." In Johannes Wilbert (ed.), *The Evolution of Horticultural Systems in Native South America: Causes and Consequences.* Caracas: Sociedad de Ciencias Naturales La Salle.
1967 "On the Relationship between Size of Population and Complexity of Social Organization." *Southwestern Journal of Anthropology* 23(3):234–43.
1970 "A Theory of the Origin of the State." *Science* 169(3947): 733–38.

Chagnon, Napoleon A.
1970 "The Culture-Ecology of Shifting (Pioneering) Cultivation among the Yanomamo Indians." In *Proceedings, 8th International Congress of Anthropological and Ethnological Sciences, 1968,* vol. 3, pp. 249–55. Tokyo and Kyoto.

Chang Kwang-chi
1963 *The Archaeology of Ancient China.* 2nd ed., 1968. New Haven: Yale University Press.

Cheng Te-K'un
1960 *Archaeology in China.* Toronto: University of Toronto Press.

Childe, V. Gordon
1936 *Man Makes Himself.* Paperback ed., 1951. New York: New American Library, Mentor Books.
1942 *What Happened in History.* Paperback ed., 1946. New York: Penguin Books.
1950 "The Urban Revolution." *Town Planning Review* 21(1): 3–17.
1952 "The Birth of Civilization." *Past and Present,* no. 2, pp. 1–10. Reprinted in Fried 1959, pp. 412–21.

Clark, Grahame
1969 *World Prehistory: A New Outline.* 2nd ed. Cambridge: Cambridge University Press.

Cocks, Edmond
1974 "The Servitude Theory of Population." *American Scholar* 43(3):472–80.

Coe, Michael D.
1962 *Mexico.* New York: Praeger.

Collier, Donald
1955 "Development of Civilization on the Coast of Peru." In *Irrigation Civilizations: A Comparative Study.* Social Science Monographs, no. 1, pp. 19–27. Washington, D.C.: Pan American Union.
1961 "Agriculture and Civilization on the Coast of Peru." In Johannes Wilbert (ed.), *The Evolution of Horticultural Systems in Native South America: Causes and Consequences,* pp. 101–109. Caracas: Sociedad de Ciencias Naturales La Salle.

1962 *The Central Andes.* In R. J. Braidwood and G. R. Willey (eds.), *Courses Toward Urban Life,* pp. 165–76. Chicago: Aldine.

Colson, Elizabeth, and Max Gluckman (eds.)
1951 *Seven Tribes of British Central Africa.* London: Oxford University Press.

Cooper, John M.
1946 "The Yahgan." In J. H. Steward (ed.), *Handbook of South American Indians,* vol. 1. Smithsonian Institution Bureau of American Ethnology Bulletin, no. 143.

Coulborn, Rushton (ed.)
1956 *Feudalism in History.* Princeton: Princeton University Press.

Covarrubias, Miguel
1946 *Mexico South: The Isthmus of Tehuantepec.* London: Cassell.

Cowgill, George
ms. "On Causes and Consequences of Ancient and Modern Population Changes."

Creel, Herrlee G.
1954 *The Birth of China: A Study of the Formative Period of Chinese Civilization.* New York: Reynal and Hitchcock.
1970 *The Origins of Statecraft in China.* Vol. 1. *The Western Chou Empire.* Chicago: University of Chicago Press.

Culbert, T. Patrick (ed.)
1973 *The Classic Maya Collapse.* Albuquerque: University of New Mexico Press.

Daniel, Glyn
1970 *The First Civilizations: The Archaeology of Their Origins.* New York: Thomas Y. Crowell.

Davenport, William
1969 "The 'Hawaiian Cultural Revolution': Some Political and Economic Considerations." *American Anthropologist* 71(1):1–20.

Davidson, Basil
1959 *The Lost Cities of Africa.* Boston: Little, Brown.
1961 *The African Slave Trade: Precolonial History 1450–1850.* Boston: Little, Brown.

Davis, Kingsley
1949 *Human Society.* New York: Macmillan.

Diamond, Stanley
1951 *Dahomey: A Proto State in West Africa.* Ann Arbor, Mich.: University Microfilms No. 2808.
1971 "The Rule of Law versus the Order of Custom." *Social Research* 38(1):42–72.

Díaz del Castillo, Bernal
1953 *The Discovery and Conquest of Mexico.* Mexico: Ediciones Tolteca.

Dobb, Maurice
1946 *Studies in the Development of Capitalism.* New York: International Publishers.

Drewitt, B.
1966 "Planeación en la Antiqua Ciudad de Teotihuacán." In *Teotihuacán: Onceava Mesa Redonda.* Mexico: Sociedad Mexicana de Antropología.

Driver, Harold
1961 *Indians of North America.* Chicago: University of Chicago Press.
Drucker, Philip
1951 *The Northern and Central Nootkan Tribes.* Smithsonian Institution Bureau of American Ethnology Bulletin, no. 144.
1955 *Indians of the Northwest Coast.* New York: McGraw-Hill.
Dumond, D. E.
1965 "Population Growth and Cultural Change." *Southwestern Journal of Anthropology* 21(4):302–24.
1972 "Demographic Aspects of the Classic Period in Puebla-Tlaxcala." *Southwestern Journal of Anthropology* 28(2):101–30.
Durkheim, Emile
1933 *The Division of Labor in Society.* Glencoe, Ill.: Free Press.
Eisenstadt, S. N.
1963 *The Political Systems of Empires.* New York: Free Press of Glencoe.
Elkin, A. P.
1954 *The Australian Aborigines: How to Understand Them.* Sydney: Angus and Robertson.
Ellis, William
1853 *Polynesian Researches.* 4 vol. London: Henry G. Bohn.
Engels, Frederick (Friedrich)
1891 *The Origin of the Family, Private Property, and the State.* Reprint ed., 1972. Ed. and with an introduction by E. B. Leacock. New York: International Publishers.
Erasmus, Charles J.
1965 "Monument Building: Some Field Experiments." *Southwestern Journal of Anthropology* 21(4):277–301.
Evans-Pritchard, E. E.
1940 *The Nuer.* Oxford: Oxford University Press.
Fage, J. D.
1955 *An Introduction to the History of West Africa.* Cambridge: Cambridge University Press.
Fairservis, Walter A., Jr.
1959 *The Origins of Oriental Civilization.* New York: New American Library.
Fallers, L. (ed.)
1964 *The King's Men.* London: Oxford University Press.
Farb, Peter
1968 *Man's Rise to Civilization as Shown by the Indians of North America from Primeval Times to the Coming of the Industrial State.* New York: E. P. Dutton.
Ferguson, Adam
1767 *An Essay on the History of Civil Society.* Reprint ed., 1966. Duncan Forbes (ed.). Chicago: Aldine.
Firth, Raymond
1929 *Primitive Economics of the New Zealand Maori.* London: Routledge.
1936 *We, the Tikopia.* New York: American Book Co.
1939 *Primitive Polynesian Economy.* London: Routledge.

Flannery, Kent V.
1968 "The Olmec and the Valley of Oaxaca: A Model for Interregional Interaction in Formative Times." In E. P. Benson (ed.), *Dumbarton Oaks Conference on the Olmecs.* Washington, D.C.: Dumbarton Oaks Research Library and Collections, Trustees of Harvard University.
1971 "Origins and Ecological Effects of Early Domestication in Iran and the Near East." In Stuart Struever (ed.), *Prehistoric Agriculture,* pp. 50–79. Garden City, N.Y.: Natural History Press.
1972 "The Cultural Evolution of Civilizations." *Annual Review of Ecology and Systematics* 3:399–426.

Flannery, Kent V., and Michael D. Coe
1966 "Social and Economic Systems in Formative Mesoamerica." In Sally R. Binford and Lewis R. Binford (eds.), *New Perspectives in Archaeology,* pp. 267–83. Chicago: Aldine.

Flannery, Kent V., Anne V. T. Kirkby, Michael J. Kirkby, and Aubrey W. Williams, Jr.
1971 "Farming Systems and Political Growth in Ancient Oaxaca." In Stuart Struever (ed.), *Prehistoric Agriculture,* pp. 157–78. Garden City, N.Y.: Natural History Press.

Ford, James A.
1969 *A Comparison of Formative Cultures in the Americas: Diffusion or the Psychic Unity of Man.* Smithsonian Contributions to Anthropology, vol. 2. Washington, D.C.: Smithsonian Institution Press.

Forde, Daryll
1950 *Yoruba-Speaking Peoples of Southwestern Nigeria.* London: International Publishers Service.

Forde, D. C., and P. M. Kaberry (eds.)
1967 *Western African Kingdoms in the Nineteenth Century.* London: Oxford University Press.

Fortes, M., and E. E. Evans-Pritchard (eds.)
1940 *African Political Systems.* London: Oxford University Press.

Frankfort, Henri
1948 *Kingship and the Gods.* Chicago: University of Chicago Press.
n.d. *The Birth of Civilization in the Near East.* Garden City, N.Y.: Doubleday, Anchor Books.

Freuchen, Peter
1961 *Book of the Eskimos.* New York: World Publishing Co.

Fried, Morton H.
1959 *Readings in Anthropology.* 2 vols. New York: Thomas Y. Crowell.
1967 *The Evolution of Political Society.* New York: Random House.
1968 "State." In the *International Encyclopedia of the Social Sciences.* New York: Macmillan and Free Press.

Furnas, J. C.
1947 *Anatomy of Paradise.* New York: William Sloane Associates.

Fynn, Henry
1845 *From Posthumous of Mr. Henry Fynn, 1750 to 1824.* Mr. John Bird (compiler). In *The Annals of Natal, 1495 to 1845,* vol. I. Cape Town: T. Maskew Miller.

Gay, Peter
1969 *The Enlightenment: An Interpretation.* Vol. 2. *The Science of Freedom.* New York: Alfred A. Knopf.
Gearing, Fred
1962 *Priests and Warriors.* American Anthropological Association Memoir, no. 93.
Geertz, Clifford
1963 *Agricultural Involution: The Process of Ecological Change in Indonesia.* Berkeley: University of California Press.
Gibbon, Edward
1952 *The Portable Gibbon: The Decline and Fall of the Roman Empire.* Ed. and with an introduction by Dero A. Sanders. New York: Viking Press.
Gibson, J. Y.
1911 *The Story of the Zulus.* London: Longmans.
Gifford, Edward W.
1929 *Tongan Society.* Bernice P. Bishop Museum [Honolulu] Bulletin, no. 61.
Gilbert, William H., Jr.
1937 "Eastern Cherokee Social Organization." In Fred Eggan (ed.), *Social Anthropology of North American Tribes,* pp. 285–340. Chicago: University of Chicago Press.
Ginsberg, Morris
1921 *The Psychology of Society.* London: Methuen.
Gluckman, Max
1940 *The Kingdom of the Zulu in South Africa.* In M. Fortes and E. E. Evans-Pritchard (eds.), *African Political Systems.* London: Oxford University Press.
1958 *Analysis of a Social Situation in Modern Zululand.* Rhodes-Livingstone Papers, no. 28. Manchester: Manchester University Press.
1960 "The Rise of a Zulu Empire." *Scientific American* 202(4): 157–68.
1963 *Order and Rebellion in Tribal Africa.* New York: Free Press.
1965 *Politics, Law and Ritual in Tribal Society.* Chicago: Aldine.
Goldman, Irving
1970 *Ancient Polynesian Society.* Chicago: University of Chicago Press.
Goldschmidt, Walter
1959 *Man's Way.* New York: Henry Holt.
1966 *Comparative Functionalism.* Berkeley and Los Angeles: University of California Press.
Goody, Jack
1971 *Technology, Tradition and the State in Africa.* London: Oxford University Press.
Gusinde, Martin
1931 *Die Feuerland Indianer.* 2 vols. Mödling bei Wien: Verlag der Internationalen Zeitschrift "Anthropos."
Harner, Michael
1970 "Population Pressure and the Social Evolution of Agriculturalists." *Southwestern Journal of Anthropology* 26(1): 67–86.

Hart, C. W. M., and Arnold R. Pilling
1960 *The Tiwi of North Australia.* New York: Holt, Rinehart and Winston.
Hartland, E. Sidney
1924 *Primitive Law.* London: Methuen.
Haviland, William A.
1969 "A New Population Estimate for Tikal, Guatemala." *American Antiquity* 34(4):429–33.
Henry, Teuira
1928 *Ancient Tahiti.* Honolulu: Bernice P. Bishop Museum Bulletin no. 48.
Hickerson, Harold
1960 "The Feast of the Dead Among the Seventeenth Century Algonkians of the Upper Great Lakes." *American Anthropologist* 62(1):81–107.
1962 *The Southwestern Chippewa: An Ethnohistorical Study.* American Anthropological Association Memoir, no. 92.
Hobbes, Thomas
1651 *Leviathan: Or, the Matter, Forme and Power of a Commonwealth, Ecclesiasticall and Civil.* Reprint ed., 1946. Ed. and with an introduction by Michael Oakeshott. Oxford: Clarendon.
Hobsbawm, E. J.
1964 *The Age of Revolution: 1789–1848.* New York: New American Library, Mentor Books.
Hocart, A. M.
1936 *Kings and Councillors.* Reprint ed., 1970. Chicago: University of Chicago Press.
Hoebel, E. Adamson
1954 *The Law of Primitive Man.* Cambridge, Mass.: Harvard University Press.
Hogbin, H. Ian
1934 *Law and Order in Polynesia: A Study of Primitive Legal Institutions.* London: Christophers.
1959 *The People of the Twilight.* Chicago: University of Chicago Press.
Hole, Frank, Kent V. Flannery, and James A. Neely
1971 "Prehistory and Human Ecology of the Deh Lurian Plain." In Stuart Struever (ed.), *Prehistoric Agriculture,* pp. 252–312. Garden City, N.Y.: Natural History Press.
Ibn Kaldun
1377 *The Muqaddimah: An Introduction to History.* 3 vols. Reprint ed., 1958. New York: Pantheon.
Isaac, Barry L.
ms. "Resource Scarcity, Competition, and Cooperation in Cultural Evolution." (Department of Anthropology, University of Cincinnati.)
Isaacs, N.
1836 *Travels and Adventures in Eastern Africa, Descriptive of the Zoolus, Their Manners, Customs, etc. etc. with A Sketch of Natal.* 2 vols. London: Edward Churton.

Jacobsen, Thorkild
1943 "Primitive Democracy in Ancient Mesopotamia." *Journal of Near Eastern Studies* 2(3):159–72.

Jenness, Diamond
1932 *Indians of Canada.* National Museum of Canada [Ottawa] Bulletin, no. 65.

Jouvenal, Bertrand de
1957 *Sovereignty, an Inquiry into the Political Good.* Chicago: University of Chicago Press.

Kaplan, David
1963 "Man, Monuments and Political Systems." *Southwestern Journal of Anthropology* 19(4):397–410.

Kidder, Alfred, II
1956 "Settlement Patterns—Peru." In Gordon R. Willey (ed.), *Prehistoric Settlement Patterns in the New World,* pp. 148–55. Viking Fund Publications in Anthropology, no. 23.

Kirchhoff, Paul
1959 "The Principles of Clanship in Human Society." In Morton H. Fried (ed.), *Readings in Anthropology,* vol. 2, pp. 259–70. New York: Crowell.

Kosok, Paul
1965 *Man, Land and Water in Peru,* New York: University of Long Island Press.

Kottack, Conrad P.
1972 "Ecological Variables in the Origin and Evolution of African States: The Buganda Example." *Comparative Studies in Society and History* 14(3):351–80.

Krader, Lawrence
1955 "Ecology of Central Asian Pastoralism." *Southwestern Journal of Anthropology* 11(4):301–26.

Kraeling, Carl H., and Robert McC. Adams (eds.)
1960 *City Invincible.* Chicago: University of Chicago Press.

Kramer, Samuel Noah
1956 *History Begins at Sumer.* Paperback ed., 1959. Garden City, N.Y.: Doubleday, Anchor Books.
1963 *The Sumerians.* Chicago: University of Chicago Press.

Kroeber, A. L.
1948 *Anthropology.* New York: Harcourt, Brace.

Kuper, H.
1947 *An African Aristocracy: Rank among the Swazi.* London: Oxford University Press.

Lamberg-Karlovsky, C. C., and Martha Lamberg-Karlovsky
1971 "An Early City in Iran." In *Biology and Culture in Modern Perspective: Readings from the Scientific American,* pp. 214–24. San Francisco: W. H. Freeman.

Landtman, Gunnar
1938 *The Origin of the Inequality of the Social Classes.* Chicago: University of Chicago Press.

Lanning, Edward P.
1967 *Peru Before the Incas.* Englewood Cliffs, N.J.: Prentice-Hall.

Larco Hoyle, Rafael
1948 *Cronología Arqueológica del Norte del Peru.* Trujillo, Peru: Hacienda Chiclín.

Lathrap, Donald W.
1966 "Relationships between Mesoamerica and the Andean Areas." In *Handbook of Middle American Indians,* vol. 4, pp. 265–75. Austin: University of Texas Press.

Lattimore, Owen
1940 *Inner Asian Frontiers of China.* Paperback ed., 1962. Boston: Beacon Press.
1962 "The Frontier in History." In *Studies in Frontier History: Collected Papers 1928–1958,* pp. 469–91. London: Oxford University Press.

Leach, E. R.
1954 *Political Systems of Highland Burma.* Paperback ed., 1964. Boston: Beacon Press.

Leacock, Eleanor
n.d. "The Montagnais 'Hunting Territory' and the Fur Trade." American Anthropological Association Memoir, no. 78.

Lee, Richard B., and Irven DeVore (eds.)
1968 *Man the Hunter.* Chicago: Aldine.

Lenin, Vladimir
1961 *State and Revolution.* In Arthur P. Mendel (ed.), *Essential Works of Marxism,* pp. 103–98. New York: Bantam Books.

Lenski, Gerhard
1966 *Power and Privilege: A Theory of Social Stratification.* New York: McGraw-Hill.

Li Chi
1957 *The Beginnings of Chinese Civilization.* Seattle: University of Washington Press.

Linton, Ralph
1933 *The Tanala, a Hill Tribe of Madagascar.* Field Museum of Natural History [Chicago] Anthropological Series, no. 22.
1936 *The Study of Man.* New York: D. Appleton-Century.

Lloyd, Peter C.
1965 "The Political Structure of African Kingdoms." In Michael Banton (ed.), *Political Systems and the Distribution of Power.* A.S.A. Monographs no. 2, pp. 63–112. London: Tavistock.

Lorenzo, José L. (ed.)
1968 *Materials para la Arqueología de Teotihuacán.* Instituto Nacional de Antropología e Hístoria [Mexico, D.F.] Serie Investigaciones, no. 17.

Lowie, Robert
1920 *Primitive Society.* New York: Boni and Liveright.
1927 *The Origin of the State.* New York: Harcourt, Brace and World.

Lundsgaarde, Henry P.
1970 "Law and Politics on Nonouti Island." In Thomas G. Harding and Ben J. Wallace (eds.), *Cultures of the Pacific,* pp. 242–64. New York: Free Press.

MacNeill, William H.
1963 *The Rise of the West.* Chicago: University of Chicago Press.

MacNeish, June Helm
1956 "Leadership among the Northeastern Athabascans." *Anthropologica* 2(1):131–64.

MacNeish, Richard S.
1964 "Ancient Mesoamerican Civilization." *Science* 143(3606): 531–37.

Mair, Lucy P.
1962 *Primitive Government.* Harmondsworth: Penguin Books.

Maine, Sir Henry S.
1861 *Ancient Law.* Reprint ed., 1931. London: Oxford University Press.

Malik, S. C.
1968 *Indian Civilization: The Formative Period.* Simla: Indian Institute of Advanced Study.

Malinowski, Bronislaw
1926 *Crime and Custom in Savage Society.* London: Routledge.
1932 *Argonauts of the Western Pacific.* London: Routledge.
1934 Introduction to H. Ian Hogbin, *Law and Order in Polynesia.* London: Christophers.
1942 "A New Instrument for the Interpretation of Law—Especially Primitive." *Yale Law Journal* 51:1237–54.

Malo, David
1903 *Hawaiian Antiquities.* Honolulu: Hawaiian Gazette.

Man, E. H.
1882 "On the Aboriginal Inhabitants of the Andaman Islands." *Journal of the Anthropological Institute* [London], vol. 12.

Mannheim, Karl
1936 *Ideology and Utopia.* New York: Harcourt, Brace and World.

Maquet, J. J.
1960 "The Problem of Tutsi Domination." In Simon and Phoebe Ottenberg (eds.), *Cultures and Societies of Africa,* pp. 312–17. New York: Random House.

Mariner, William
1827 *An Account of the Tongan Islands in the South Pacific Ocean.* 2 vols. Edinburgh: Constable Press.

Marx, Karl
1906 *Capital: A Critique of Political Economy.* New York: Modern Library.
1965 *Pre-Capitalist Economic Formations.* Trans. by Jack Cohen, ed. and with an introduction by E. J. Hobsbawm. New York: International Publishers.

Meggitt, M. J.
1962 *Desert People.* Sydney: Angus and Robertson.

Mendel, Arthur P. (ed.)
1961 *Essential Works of Marxism.* New York: Bantam Books.

Middleton, John, and David Tait
1958 *Tribes without Rulers: Studies in African Segmentary Systems.* London: Routledge and Kegan Paul.

Millon, Rene
1964 "The Teotihuacán Mapping Project." *American Antiquity* 29(3):345–52.
1966 "Extensión y Población de la Ciudad de Teotihuacán en sus Diferentes Períodos." In *Teotihuacán: Onceava Mesa Redonda.* Mexico, D. F.: Sociedad Mexicano de Antropología.
1967 "Teotihuacán." *Scientific American* 216(6):38–48.
1968 "Urban Revolution: The New World." In the *International Encyclopaedia of the Social Sciences.* 2nd ed. New York: Macmillan and Free Press.

Mills, C. Wright
1956 *The Power Elite.* Fair Lawn, N.J.: Oxford University Press.

Montesquieu, Charles Louis de Secondat
1748 *"The Spirit of the Laws" by Baron de Montesquieu.* Reprint ed., 1949. Trans. by Thomas Nugent, with an introduction by Franz Neumann. New York: Hafner.

Morgan, Lewis H.
1877 *Ancient Society.* Reprint ed., 1964. Ed. and with an introduction by Leslie A. White. Cambridge, Mass.: Harvard University Press, Belknap Press.

Morice, Father A. G.
1906 "The Great Dené Race." *Anthropos,* vols. 1, 2, 4, 5.
1907
1909
1910

Murdock, George P.
1953 *Ethnographic Bibliography of North America.* New Haven, Conn.: Human Relations Area Files.
1959 *Africa: Its Peoples and their Culture History.* New York: McGraw-Hill.

Nadel, S. F.
1942 *A Black Byzantium.* London: Oxford University Press.

Netting, Robert McC.
1972 "Sacred Power and Centralization: Aspects of Political Adaptation in Africa." In Brian Spooner (ed.), *Population Growth: Anthropological Implications.* Cambridge, Mass.: MIT Press.

Oberg, Kalervo
1940 "The Kingdom of Ankole in Uganda." In M. Fortes and E. E. Evans-Pritchard (eds.), *African Political Systems,* pp. 121–62. London: Oxford University Press.
1955 "Types of Social Structure Among the Lowland Tribes of South and Central America." *American Anthropologist* 57(3): 472–87.

Oliver, Douglas L.
1949 *Studies in the Anthropology of Bougainville, Solomon Islands.* Peabody Museum Papers [Cambridge, Mass.] vol. 29.
1951 *The Pacific Islands.* Cambridge, Mass.: Harvard University Press.
1955 *A Solomon Island Society.* Cambridge, Mass.: Harvard University Press.

Oppenheim, A. Leo
1964 *Ancient Mesopotamia: Portrait of a Dead Civilization.* Chicago: University of Chicago Press.

Oppenheimer, Franz
1914 *The State: Its History and Development Viewed Sociologically.* Reprint ed., 1926. New York: Vanguard Press.

Otterbein, K. F.
1964 "The Evolution of Zulu Warfare." *Kansas Journal of Sociology* 1(1):27–35.

Palerm, Angel
1955 "The Agricultural Bases of Urban Civilization in Mesoamerica." In *Irrigation Civilizations: A Comparative Study.* Washington, D.C.: Pan American Union.

Parsons, Jeffrey R.
1968*a* "An Estimate of Size and Population for Middle Horizon Tiahuanaco, Bolivia." *American Antiquity* 33(2):243–45.
1968*b* "Teotihuacán, Mexico, and its Impact on Regional Demography." *Science* 162:872–77.
1969 "Patrones de Asentamiento Prehispánico en la Región Texcocana." Boletín, Instituto Nacional de Antropología e Historia [Mexico, D.F.], no. 35:31–37.
1970 "An Archaeological Evaluation of the Codice Xolotl." *American Antiquity* 35(4):431–40.
1971 *Prehispanic Settlement Patterns in the Texcoxo Region, Mexico.* University of Michigan Museum of Anthropology Memoir, no. 3.

Parsons, Talcott
1951 *The Social System.* New York: Free Press of Glencoe.

Patterson, Thomas C.
1973 *America's Past: A New World Archaeology.* Glenview, Ill.: Scott, Foresman.

Piddocke, Stuart
1965 "The Potlatch System of the Southern Kwakiutl: A New Perspective." *Southwestern Journal of Anthropology* 21(3): 244–64.

Piggott, Stuart
1950 *Prehistoric India.* New York: Penguin Books.

Piggott, Stuart (ed.)
1961 *The Dawn of Civilization.* New York: McGraw-Hill.

Polanyi, Karl, Conrad M. Arensberg, and Harry W. Pearson (eds.)
1957 *Trade and Market in the Early Empires.* Glencoe, Ill.: Free Press.

Pospisil, Leopold
1958 *Kapauku Papuans and their Law.* Yale University Publications in Anthropology, no. 54. New Haven: Yale University Press.
1968 "Law and Order." In James Clifton (ed.), *Introduction to Cultural Anthropology.* Boston: Houghton Mifflin Co.
1971 *Anthropology of Law: A Comparative Theory.* New York: Harper and Row.
1972 "The Ethnology of Law." *McCaleb Modules in Anthropology,* module 12. Reading, Mass.: Addison-Wesley.

Price, Barbara
1971 "Prehispanic Irrigation Agriculture in Nuclear America." *Latin American Research Review* 6(3):3–60.

Puleston, D., and D. Calendar
1967 "Defensive Earthworks at Tikal." *Expedition,* no. 9, pp. 40–48.

Radcliffe-Brown, A. R.
1940 Preface to M. Fortes and E. E. Evans-Pritchard (eds.), *African Political Systems.* London: Oxford University Press.
1948 *The Andaman Islanders.* Glencoe, Ill.: Free Press.

Raikes, R. L.
1964 "The End of the Ancient Cities of the Indus." *American Anthropologist* 66(1):284–89.

Rasmussen, Knut
1927 *Across Arctic America.* London and New York: Putnam and Sons.

Rathje, William L.
1972 "Praise the Gods and Pass the Metates: A Hypothesis of the Development of Lowland Rainforest Civilizations in Mesoamerica." In Mark P. Leone (ed.), *Contemporary Archaeology.* Carbondale and Edwardsville: Southern Illinois University Press.

Rattray, Robert S.
1923 *Ashanti.* London: Oxford University Press.
1929 *Ashanti Law and Constitution.* London: Oxford University Press.

Read, K. E.
1959 "Leadership and Consensus in a New Guinea Society." *American Anthropologist* 61(3):425–36.

Redfield, Robert
1964 "Primitive Law." *University of Cincinnati Law Review* 33(1):1–22. Reprinted in Paul Bohannan (ed.), 1967, *Law and Warfare: Studies in the Anthropology of Conflict.* Garden City, N.Y.: Natural History Press.

Ribeiro, Darcy
1968 *The Civilizational Process.* Trans. and with a foreword by Betty J. Meggers. Washington, D.C.: Smithsonian Institution Press.

Richards, Audrey (ed.)
1960 *East African Chiefs.* London: Faber & Faber.

Ritter, E. A.
1955 *Shaka Zulu: The Rise of the Zulu Empire.* London: Longmans, Green.

Rivers, W. H. R.
1924 *Social Organization.* London: Routledge.

Roscoe, Rev. J.
1911 *The Baganda.* London: The Macmillan Company.
1923 *The Bakitara or Banyoro.* Cambridge: Cambridge University Press.

Ross, Alexander
1956 *The Fur Hunters of the Far West.* Norman: University of Oklahoma Press.

Rousseau, Jean-Jacques

1762 *The Social Contract.* Reprint ed., 1966. Introduction by Charles Frankel. New York: Hafner.

Sahlins, Marshall D.

1958 *Social Stratification in Polynesia.* Seattle: University of Washington Press.

1962 *Moala: Culture and Nature on a Fijian Island.* Ann Arbor: University of Michigan Press.

1963 "Poor Man, Rich Man, Big-Man, Chief: Political Types in Melanesia and Polynesia." *Comparative Studies in Society and History* 5(3):285–303.

1968 *Tribesmen.* Englewood Cliffs, N.J.: Prentice-Hall.

Saint-Simon, Comte Henri de

1952 *Selected Writings.* Trans. and ed. by F. M. H. Markham. Oxford: Blackwell.

Sanders, William T.

1956 "The Central Mexican Symbiotic Region." In G. R. Willey (ed.), *Prehistoric Settlement Patterns in the New World,* pp. 30–45. New York: Viking Fund Publications in Anthropology.

1962 "Cultural Ecology of Nuclear Mesoamerica." *American Anthropologist* 64(1):34–43.

1972 "Population, Agricultural History, and Societal Evolution in Mesoamerica." In Brian Spooner (ed.), *Population Growth: Anthropological Implications.* Cambridge, Mass.: MIT Press.

Sanders, William T., and Joseph Marino

1970 *New World Prehistory: Archaeology of the American Indian.* Englewood Cliffs, N.J.: Prentice-Hall.

Sanders, William T., and Barbara J. Price

1968 *Mesoamerica: The Evolution of a Civilization.* New York: Random House.

Schaedel, Richard P.

1951 "Major Ceremonial and Population Centers in Northern Peru." In Sol Tax (ed.), *The Civilizations of Ancient America: Selected Papers of the XXIXth International Congress of Americanists,* pp. 232–43. Chicago: University of Chicago Press.

1966*a* "Incipient Urbanization and Secularization in Tiahuanacoid Peru." *American Antiquity* 31(3):338–44.

1966*b* "Urban Growth and Ekistics on the Peruvian Coast." Paper read at 36th International Congress of Americanists, Seville.

1969 "On the Definition of Civilization, Urban, City and Town in Prehistoric America." Paper read at 37th International Congress of Americanists, Buenos Aires.

1971 "The City and the Origin of the State in America." Paper read at 38th International Congress of Americanists, Lima.

ms. "The Commonality in Processual Trends in the Urbanization Process: Urbanization and the Redistributive Function in the Central Andes."

Schebesta, Paul
1933 *Among Congo Pygmies.* London: Hutchinson and Co.
n.d. *Among the Forest Dwarfs of Malaya.* London: Hutchinson and Co.

Seagle, William
1946 *The History of Law.* New York: Tudor Publishing Co.

Service, Elman R.
1962 *Primitive Social Organization: An Evolutionary Perspective.* 2nd ed., 1971. New York: Random House.
1966 *The Hunters.* Englewood Cliffs, N.J.: Prentice-Hall.
1969 "Models for the Methodology of Mouthtalk." *Southwestern Journal of Anthropology* 25(1):68–80.
1971 *Cultural Evolutionism: Theory in Practice.* New York: Holt, Rinehart and Winston.

Shapera, Isaac
1930 *The Khoisan Peoples of South Africa.* London: Routledge.
1957 "Malinowski's Theories of Law." In R. Firth (ed.), *Man and Culture: An Evaluation of the Work of Malinowski.* London: Routledge & Kegan Paul.

Sharp, R. L.
1958 "People Without Politics." In Verne E. Ray (ed.), *Systems of Political Control and Bureaucracy in Human Societies.* Seattle: University of Washington Press.

Siegel, Bernard J. (ed.)
1959 *Biennial Review of Anthropology.* Stanford: Stanford University Press.

Simpson, S. P., and J. Stone
1948 *Cases and Readings on Law and Society.* Vol. 1. *Law and Society in Evolution.* St. Paul, Minn.: West Publishing Company.

Skeat, W. W., and C. O. Blagden
1906 *Pagan Races of the Malay Peninsula.* 2 vols. London: The Macmillan Company.

Skinner, B. F.
1971 *Beyond Freedom and Dignity.* Paperback ed., 1972. New York: Bantam, Vintage Books.

Smith, Adam
1776 *An Inquiry into the Nature and Causes of the Wealth of Nations.* Reprint ed., 1937. New York: Random House.

Southhall, Adrian W.
1956 *Alur Society: A Study in Processes and Types of Dominations.* Cambridge: Heffer.

Southwold, M.
1961 *Bureaucracy and Chieftainship in Buganda.* East African Studies, no. 14. London: Kegan Paul, Trench, Trubner.

Spence, M.
1968 "The Obsidian Industry of Teotihuacán." *American Antiquity* 32(4):507–14.

Spencer, Baldwin
1914 *The Native Tribes of the Northern Territory of Australia.* London: The Macmillan Company.

Spencer, Baldwin, and F. J. Gillen
1899 *The Northern Tribes of Central Australia.* London: The Macmillan Company.
1927 *The Arunta.* 2 vols. London: The Macmillan Company.
Spencer, Herbert
1967 *The Evolution of Society.* Ed. and with an introduction by Robert Carneiro. Chicago: University of Chicago Press.
Stefansson, Vilhjalmur
1919 *My Life with the Eskimos.* New York: Macmillan.
Stevenson, Robert F.
1968 *Population and Political Systems in Tropical Africa.* New York: Columbia University Press.
Steward, Julian H.
1938 *Basin-Pleateau Aboriginal Socio-political Groups.* Smithsonian Institution Bureau of American Ethnology Bulletin, no. 120.
Steward, Julian H. (ed.)
1946*a* *The Marginal Tribes.* Handbook of South American Indians, vol. 1. Smithsonian Institution Bureau of American Ethnology Bulletin, no. 143.
1964*b* *The Andean Civilizations.* Handbook of South American Indians, vol. 2. Smithsonian Institution Bureau of American Ethnology Bulletin, no. 143.
1948*a* *The Tropical Forest Tribes.* Handbook of South American Indians, vol. 3. Smithsonian Institution Bureau of American Ethnology Bulletin, no. 143.
1948*b* *The Circum-Caribbean Tribes.* Handbook of South American Indians, vol. 4. Smithsonian Institution Bureau of American Ethnology Bulletin, no. 143.
1949 "Cultural Causality and Law: A Trial Formulation of the Development of Early Civilizations." *American Anthropologist* 51(1):1–27.
1955 *Theory of Culture Change.* Urbana: University of Illinois Press. Also available in paper ed. (1972).
Steward, Julian H., and Louis C. Faron
1959 *Native Peoples of South America.* New York: McGraw-Hill.
Stocking, George W., Jr.
1968 *Race, Culture and Evolution.* New York: Free Press.
Strong, William Duncan
1951 "Cutural Resemblances in Nuclear America: Parallelism or Diffusion?" In Sol Tax (ed.), *The Civilizations of Ancient America: Selected Papers of the XXIX International Congress of Americanists,* pp. 271–79. Chicago: University of Chicago Press.
Strong, William Duncan, and Clifford Evans
1952 *Cultural Stratigraphy in the Viru Valley.* New York: Columbia University Press.
Struever, Stuart (ed.)
1971 *Prehistoric Agriculture.* Garden City, N.Y.: Natural History Press.
Suttles, Wayne
1960 "Affinal Ties, Subsistence, and Prestige Among the Coast Salish." *American Anthropologist* 62(2):296–305.

1968 "Coping with Abundance: Subsistence on the Northwest Coast." In Richard B. Lee and Irven DeVore (eds.), *Man the Hunter,* pp. 56–68. Chicago: Aldine.

Swanton, John R.
1946 *The Indians of the Southeastern United States.* Smithsonian Institution Bureau of American Ethnology Bulletin, no. 137.

Swartz, Marc J., Victor W. Turner, and Arthur Tuden
1966 *Political Anthropology.* Chicago: Aldine.

Thomas, Elizabeth Marshall
1959 *The Harmless People.* New York: Alfred A. Knopf.

Thompson, J. Eric S.
1954 *The Rise and Fall of Maya Civilization.* Norman: University of Oklahoma Press.

Thomson, Basil
1894 *The Diversions of a Prime Minister.* Reprint ed., 1968. London: Dawsons of Pall Mall.

Thwaites, Ruben Gold (ed.)
1896–1901 *The Jesuit Relations and Allied Documents.* 73 vols. Cleveland: Burrows Brothers Co.

Treistman, Judith M.
1972 *The Prehistory of China: An Archeological Exploration.* Garden City, N.Y.: Natural History Press.

Trigger, Bruce
1972 "Determinants of Urban Growth in Pre-Industrial Societies." In Peter J. Ucko, Ruth Tringham, and G. W. Dimbleby (eds.), *Man, Settlement and Urbanism,* pp. 575–99. London: Duckworth.

Turnbull, Colin
1961 *The Forest People.* New York: Simon and Schuster.

Tylor, Edward B.
1888 "On a Method of Investigating the Development of Institutions: Applied to the Laws of Marriage and Descent." *Journal of the Anthropological Institute* (18):245–69.

Underhill, Ruth
1953 *Red Man's America.* Chicago: University of Chicago Press.

Vaillant, George
1944 *Aztecs of Mexico.* Garden City, N.Y.: Doubleday, Doran.

Vansina, Jan
1962 "A Comparison of African Kingdoms." *Africa* 32(14):324–34.
1966 *Kingdoms of the Savanna.* Madison: University of Wisconsin Press.

Vasilev, L. S., and I. A. Stucheoskii
1967 "Three Models for the Origin and Evolution of Precapitalist Societies." *Soviet Review* 8(3):26–39.

Vayda, Andrew P.
1967 "Pomo Trade Feasts." In George Dalton (ed.), *Tribal and Peasant Economies.* Garden City, N.Y.: Natural History Press.

Vico, Giovanni Battista
1744 *The New Science of Giambattista Vico.* Reprint ed., 1968. Ed. and with an introduction by M. F. Fish and T. G. Bergins. Ithaca, N.Y.: Cornell University Press.

Vinogradoff, Paul
1920– 1922 *Outlines of Historical Jurisprudence.* 2 vols. Oxford: Oxford University Press.

Wagley, Charles
1940 "The Effects of Depopulation upon Social Organizations as Illustrated by the Tapirapé Indians." *Transactions of the New York Academy of Science* 3(12):12–16.

Walter, Eugene V.
1969 *Terror and Resistance: A Study of Political Violence.* New York: Oxford University Press.

Warner, W. L.
1937 *A Black Civilization.* New York: Harper and Brothers.

Weaver, Muriel Porter
1972 *The Aztecs, Maya, and their Predecessors.* New York: Seminar Press.

Webb, Malcolm C.
1964 "The Post-Classic Decline of the Peten Maya." Ph.D. dissertation, University of Michigan.
1965 "The Abolition of the Taboo System in Hawaii." *Journal of the Polynesian Society* 74(1):21–39.
1968 "Carneiro's Hypothesis of Limited Land Resources and the Origins of the State: A Latin Americanist's Approach to an Old Problem." *South Eastern Latin Americanist* 12(3):1–8.

Weber, Max
1946 *From Max Weber: Essays in Sociology.* Trans. and ed. by H. H. Gerth and C. Wright Mills. New York: Oxford University Press.
1947 *The Theory of Social and Economic Organization.* 2nd ed. Trans. by A. M. Henderson and Talcott Parsons; ed. with an introduction by Talcott Parsons. Glencoe, Ill.: Free Press.

Wertheim, W. F.
1974 *Evolution and Revolution.* Middlesex, England: Penguin Books.

Weyer, Edward M.
1932 *The Eskimos: Their Environment and Folkways.* New Haven, Conn.: Yale University Press.

Wheatley, Paul
1971 *The Pivot of the Four Quarters: A Preliminary Inquiry into the Origins and Character of the Ancient Chinese City.* Chicago: Aldine.

Wheeler, R. E. M.
1953 *The Cambridge History of India.* Supplementary volume. *The Indus Civilization.* Cambridge: Cambridge University Press.

White, Leslie A.
1959 *The Evolution of Culture.* New York: McGraw-Hill.

Willey, Gordon R.
1948 "A Functional Analysis of 'Horizon Styles'" In Wendell C. Bennett, *A Reappraisal of Peruvian Archaeology.* Memoirs of The Society for American Archaeology, no. 4, pp. 8–19.
1951 "The Chavín Problem: A Review and Critique." *Southwestern Journal of Anthropology* 7(2):103–44.

1955 "The Interrelated Rise of the Native Cultures of Middle and South America." In *New Interpretations of Aboriginal American Culture History,* pp. 28–45. 75th Anniversary Volume of the Anthropological Society of Washington, D.C.

1962 "The Early Great Styles and the Rise of the Pre-Columbian Civilizations." *American Anthropologist* 64(1):1–15.

1971 *An Introduction to American Archaeology.* Vol. 2. *South America.* Englewood Cliffs, N.J.: Prentice-Hall.

Williamson, R. W.

1924 *The Social and Political Systems of Central Polynesia.* 3 vols. Cambridge: Cambridge University Press.

Wilson, Edmund

1940 *To the Finland Station.* Reprint ed., 1955. Garden City, N.Y.: Doubleday, Anchor Books.

Wilson, John A.

1951 *The Burden of Egypt.* Chicago: University of Chicago Press.

Wissler, Clark

1931 *The American Indian.* London: Oxford University Press.

Wittfogel, Karl A.

1957 *Oriental Despotism: A Comparative Study of Total Power.* New Haven, Conn.: Yale University Press.

Wolf, Eric R.

1959 *Sons of the Shaking Earth.* Chicago: University of Chicago Press.

Woodbury, Richard B.

1961 "A Reappraisal of Hohokam Irrigation." *American Anthropologist* 63(3):550–60.

Woodward, Grace S.

1963 *The Cherokees.* Norman: University of Oklahoma Press.

Woolley, Sir Leonard

1963 *The Beginnings of Civilization.* New York: New American Library.

Index